MANCHEST
MEDIEVAL
LITERATURE
AND CULTURE

RIDDLES AT WORK IN THE EARLY MEDIEVAL TRADITION

Manchester University Press

Manchester Medieval Literature and Culture publishes monographs and essay collections comprising new research informed by current critical methodologies on the literary cultures of the Middle Ages. We are interested in all periods, from the early Middle Ages through to the late, and we include post-medieval engagements with and representations of the medieval period (or 'medievalism'). 'Literature' is taken in a broad sense, to include the many different medieval genres: imaginative, historical, political, scientific, religious. While we welcome contributions on the diverse cultures of medieval Britain and are happy to receive submissions on Anglo-Norman, Anglo-Latin and Celtic writings, we are also open to work on the Middle Ages in Europe more widely, and beyond.

Titles Available in the Series

18. *Aspects of knowledge: Preserving and reinventing traditions of learning in the Middle Ages*
    Marilina Cesario and Hugh Magennis (eds)
19. *Visions and ruins: Cultural memory and the untimely Middle Ages*
    Joshua Davies
20. *Participatory reading in late-medieval England*
    Heather Blatt
21. *Affective medievalism: Love, abjection and discontent*
    Thomas A. Prendergast and Stephanie Trigg
22. *The politics of Middle English parables: Fiction, theology, and social practice*
    Mary Raschko
23. *Performing women: Gender, self, and representation in late-medieval Metz*
    Susannah Crowder
24. *Contemporary Chaucer across the centuries*
    Helen M. Hickey, Anne McKendry and Melissa Raine (eds)
25. *Borrowed objects and the art of poetry:* Spolia *in Old English verse*
    Denis Ferhatović
26. *Rebel angels: Space and sovereignty in Anglo-Saxon England*
    Jill Fitzgerald
27. *A landscape of words: Ireland, Britain and the poetics of space, 700–1250*
    Amy Mulligan
28. *Household knowledges in late-medieval England and France*
    Glenn D. Burger and Rory G. Critten (eds)
29. *Practising shame: Female honour in later medieval England*
    Mary C. Flannery
30. *Dating Beowulf: Studies in intimacy*
    Daniel C. Remein and Erica Weaver (eds)
31. *Enacting the Bible in medieval and early modern drama*
    Eva von Contzen and Chanita Goodblatt (eds)
32. *Riddles at work in the early medieval tradition: Words, ideas, interactions*
    Megan Cavell and Jennifer Neville (eds)

Riddles at work in the early medieval tradition

Words, ideas, interactions

Edited by
MEGAN CAVELL AND JENNIFER NEVILLE

Manchester University Press

Published by Manchester University Press
Oxford Road, Manchester M13 9PL

www.manchesteruniversitypress.co.uk

British Library Cataloguing-in-Publication Data

A catalogue record for this book is available from the British Library

ISBN 978 1 5261 3371 7 hardback
ISBN 978 1 5261 7876 3 paperback

First published 2020

Typeset by
Servis Filmsetting Ltd, Stockport, Cheshire

Contents

Figures and tables

Figures

Tables

Contributors

Rafał Borysławski is an Associate Professor in the Institute of English Cultures and Literatures, University of Silesia, Poland. His research focuses chiefly on Old English culture and literature as well as on the questions of medieval culture associated with the field of socio-cultural history. He has published a book on the idea of enigmaticity in Old English literature and numerous papers discussing Old English philosophical and cultural outlooks, Middle English romances and *fabliaux*, and medieval visual culture.

Francesca Brooks is a Teaching Fellow in Old and Middle English at University College London. She recently completed her AHRC- and LAHP-funded doctoral thesis in English Literature at King's College London, and she is currently working on her first monograph, *Poet of the Medieval Modern: Reading the Anglo-Saxon Library with David Jones*, based on this research.

Peter Buchanan is an Assistant Professor in English at New Mexico Highlands University, where he teaches courses on medieval literature, linguistics, and literary theory. His research is broadly concerned with issues of adaptation and translation in the multilingual literature of the early medieval period. Additionally, he enjoys reading and studying avant-garde responses to medieval literature in the twentieth and twenty-first centuries.

Megan Cavell is a Birmingham Fellow and lecturer at the University of Birmingham. She works on a wide range of topics in medieval studies, from Old and early Middle English and Latin languages and literature to gender, material culture, and animal studies. Her first monograph, *Weaving Words and Binding Bodies: The Poetics of Human Experience in Old English Literature*, was published by the University of Toronto Press in 2016, and she is currently working on a second project about predators in medieval literature.

Corinne Dale gained her PhD from Royal Holloway, University of London in 2015, having completed a thesis on ecocritical and ecotheological readings of the *Exeter Book* riddles. In 2017, she published her book *The Natural World in the Exeter Book Riddles*. Her latest research applies the field of ecofeminism to Old English literature. She currently holds honorary research associate status at King's College London.

Pirkko A. Koppinen is a research student in the fields of heritage and material culture studies in the Department of Creative and Cultural Industries at the Kingston School of Art. Her previous PhD at Royal Holloway, University of London, was on the semiotics of Old English poetry. She is the author of 'Breaking the mould: solving the Old English Riddle 12 as *wudu* "wood"'. She has also translated the Old English poem *Judith* and the beginning of *Beowulf* into Finnish (forthcoming).

Britt Mize is Associate Professor and Associate Department Head in English at Texas A&M University. In addition to Old English language and poetics, he works on Middle English drama and has current projects on modern adaptations of *Beowulf*.

Neville Mogford is a research student based in the Department of English at Royal Holloway, University of London, working under the supervision of Jennifer Neville. His thesis focuses on the relationship between the poetry of early medieval England and the various conceptions of time expressed in early medieval scientific texts, calendars, and cultural and religious practices.

Jennifer Neville is a Reader in Anglo-Saxon Literature at Royal Holloway, University of London. She is the author of *Representations of the Natural World in Old English Poetry*, Cambridge Studies in Anglo-Saxon England (Cambridge University Press, 1999), as well as articles on seasons, law codes, monsters, plants, national identity, travel, the Assumption of the Virgin, out-of-body experiences, horses, Tolkien, and, especially, riddles. She is currently working on a monograph on the Old English riddles of the *Exeter Book*.

Miller Wolf Oberman is the author of *The Unstill Ones* (Princeton University Press, 2017). His translation of selections from the 'Old English rune poem' won Poetry Magazine's John Frederick Nims Memorial Prize for Translation in 2013. Miller's poems and translations have appeared in *Poetry*, *Tin House*, *London Review of Books*, and *The Nation*. He teaches writing at The New School and lives in Brooklyn, New York.

Karin Olsen is Senior Lecturer in English Language and Literature of the Middle Ages at the University of Groningen. Her research interests include the literature of early northwest Europe and conceptual poetics. She is the author of *Conceptualizing the Enemy in Early Northwest Europe: Metaphors of Conflict and Alterity in Anglo-Saxon, Old Norse, and Early Irish Poetry* (Brepols, 2016) and co-editor of three volumes of the Germania Latina series (Peeters, 2001–9). Her current research focuses on concepts of alterity in Old English poetry.

James Paz is a Lecturer in Early Medieval English Literature at the University of Manchester. He is the author of *Nonhuman Voices in Anglo-Saxon Literature and Material Culture* (Manchester University Press, 2017) and the co-editor of *Medieval Science Fiction* (Boydell & Brewer, 2016). He has published articles on texts and topics such as *Beowulf*, the *Dialogues of Solomon and Saturn*, the Old English charms, and Eilmer the 'flying monk' of Malmesbury.

Sharon E. Rhodes studies Old English literature and translation theory. She received her PhD from the University of Rochester in 2017 and is currently working on her monograph, *Turning the Tide: Four Old English Translations of the Flood Story*. She is also a practising literary translator working in both Old English and modern Danish.

Mercedes Salvador-Bello is Associate Professor of English at the Universidad de Sevilla. Her main research interests include early medieval English and insular Latin literature with a particular focus on the *Exeter Book*, the Old English riddles, and Latin *enigmata*. She is the author of *Isidorean Perceptions of Order: The Exeter Book Riddles and Medieval Latin Enigmata* (West Virginia University Press, 2015), which was awarded the ISAS Best First Monograph on an Anglo-Saxon Topic.

Robert Stanton is Associate Professor of English at Boston College. He specialises in the early medieval period, and is the author of *The Culture of Translation in Anglo-Saxon England* (Boydell & Brewer, 2002), as well as numerous articles on translation, saints' lives, medieval mystics, and animal studies. He is currently at work on a book entitled *Holy Signs and Fruitful Toil: Signification and Animal Voice in Anglo-Saxon England*.

Victoria Symons completed her PhD and taught Old and Middle English literature at University College London before joining the university access charity, The Brilliant Club, as a programme officer. Her research has focused on ideas of writing and communication in and about early medieval England, from runes and riddles to video games.

Jonathan Wilcox is Professor of English and Collegiate Fellow at the University of Iowa, where he specialises in medieval literature and culture. He has published widely on Old English literature, particularly on homilies, manuscripts, and emotions and gestures. He is currently struggling with the idea of humour.

Acknowledgements

This volume is the result of several years' worth of co-organised sessions at the International Medieval Congress in Leeds. We are indebted to the Congress team and to all of our speakers—those represented in this volume and those not—for allowing us time and space to discuss the early medieval riddle tradition in depth and with such welcoming enthusiasm. We would especially like to thank Victoria Symons for her assistance at the early stages of this volume's planning, and for co-writing the Introduction with us.

The team at Manchester University Press have been extremely helpful throughout the publication process, and we would like to thank Meredith Carroll and this series' editors and reviewers for their valuable feedback and suggestions.

Finally, we would like to acknowledge the support of our families as we worked toward the completion of this volume. Megan would like to dedicate it to James and the Seacaves (what a band name that would be!), especially to Buttons and to little Aoife—who did not even exist at the start of this volume's life. Jennifer would like to thank Carlos (again) for staying and waiting, and Caitlin and Sophie for their patience with a mother who kept shutting herself in the study: *leoð is asungen.* All errors should be attributed to Romeo, who has stepped on the keyboard and blocked the view of the monitor far too many times.

Megan Cavell and Jennifer Neville

Abbreviations

ASE	*Anglo-Saxon England*
ASPR	Anglo-Saxon Poetic Records
B-T	Bosworth and Toller's *Anglo-Saxon Dictionary*
CCSL	Corpus Christianorum Series Latina
DOE	*Dictionary of Old English: A to I Online* (Cameron, *et al.*)
DOEC	*Dictionary of Old English Corpus on the World Wide Web* (Healey, *et al.*)
ES	*English Studies*
EETS	Early English Text Society
JEGP	*Journal of English and Germanic Philology*
MÆ	*Medium Ævum*
MP	*Modern Philology*
MGH	Monumenta Germaniae Historica
N&Q	*Notes & Queries*
OED	*Oxford English Dictionary*
PL	Patrologia Latina
PQ	*Philological Quarterly*
PMLA	*Publications of the Modern Language Association of America*
RES	*Review of English Studies*

Exeter Book riddle titles

For explanation, see the General Introduction that follows this list. For a full discussion of these titles, see Jennifer Neville, 'A Modest Proposal: Titles for the *Exeter Book Riddles*', *MÆ* 88 (2019), 116–23.

Riddle title	Title translation	ASPR riddle no.
Þrymful Þunie	'Glorious I Thunder'	1
Under Yþa Geþræc	'Under the Force of Waves'	2
Min Frea Fæste Genearwað	'My Lord Constrains Me Tightly'	3
Þrymful Þeow	'Glorious Servant'	1–3 as one riddle
Garsecges Grund	'Ocean's Bottom'	2–3 as one riddle
Þragbysig	'Periodically Busy (?)'	4
Anhaga	'Lone Dweller'	5
Ic Cwice Bærne	'I Burn the Living'	6
Ferende Gæst	'A Travelling Spirit'	7
Eald Æfensceop	'Old Evening Poet'	8
Mec Deadne Ofgeafun	'They Gave Me up for Dead'	9
Neb Wæs Min on Nearwe	'My Nose was in Confinement'	10
Hasofag	'Grey (?)'	11
Fotum Ic Fere	'I Travel on Foot'	12
X Gebroþor ond Sweostor	'Ten Brothers and Sisters'	13
Wæpenwiga	'Weapon-Warrior'	14
Hals Hwit ond Heafod Fealo	'White Neck and Fallow Head'	15
Wiþ Wæge Winnan	'Fight against a Wave'	16
Mundbora	'Protector'	17
Wide Wombe	'Large Womb'	18
Heafodbeorht	'Bright-headed'	19
Wæpnum Awyrged	'Cursed among Weapons'	20
Neol ic Fere	'I Go Down'	21

Riddle title	Title translation	ASPR riddle no.
Fridhengestas	'Peace-horses (?)'	22
Agof	'Wob' ('bow' misspelled backwards)	23
Siex Stafas Sweotule Becnaþ	'Six Letters Clearly Show'	24
Staþol min is Steapheah	'My Foundation is Steep and High'	25
Nama Min is Mære	'My Name is Famous'	26
Bindere ond Swingere	'Binder and Scourger'	27
Dream bið in Innan	'Joy is Inside'	28
Lyftfæt Leohtlic	'Bright Air-Vessel'	29
Legbysig	'Occupied with Flame'	30a
Ligbysig	'Occupied with Flame'	30b
Feþegeorn	'Eager to Go'	31
Grindan wið Greote	'Grind Against Grit'	32
Gryrelic Hleahtor	'Terrible Laughter'	33
Seo þæt Feoh Fedeð	'The One who Feeds Cattle'	34
Hyhtlic Gewæd	'Hopeful Garment'	35
Monn Wiif Hors	'Man, Woman, Horse'	36
Siex Heafdu	'Six Heads'	36.1–7
For Flodwegas	'Travel the Flood-ways'	36.8–13
Womb wæs on Hindan	'Womb was Behind'	37
Geoguðmyrþe Grædig	'Greedy for Youth-Mirth'	38
Earmost Ealra Wihta	'Most Wretched of All Creatures'	39
Ymbhwyrft	'Circle of the Earth'	40
Ymbhwyrft Edniwu	'Circle Renewed'	40–41 as one riddle
Moddor Monigra Cynna	'Mother of Many Races'	41
Heanmode Twa	'Two Low-Minded Ones'	42
Giest in Geardum	'Guest in the Enclosures'	43
Wrætlic Hongað	'A Wonder Hangs'	44
Banleas	'Boneless'	45
Wer Sæt æt Wine	'A Man Sat at Wine'	46
Moððe	'Moth'	47
Hring butan Tungan	'Ring without a Tongue'	48
Eardfæst	'Earth-fast'	49
Torht Wiga	'Bright Warrior'	50
Wuhte Feower	'Four Creatures'	51
Ræpingas	'Captives'	52
Beam Hlifian	'Tree Towers Up'	53
In Wincsele	'In a Corner'	54
Wulfheafedtreo	'Wolf-head Tree'	55
Holt Hweorfende	'Turning Wood'	56

Riddle title	Title translation	ASPR riddle no.
Sanges Roþe	'Abounding in Song'	57
Anfetu	'One-footed'	58
Hring Gylden	'Golden Ring'	59
Be Sonde Muðlease	'Mouthless by Sand'	60
Heafod Sticade	'A Head Stuck In'	61
Hingonges Strong	'Strong in Going Out'	62
Glæd mid Golde	'Shining with Gold'	63
Wynn ond Is	'Joy and Ice'	64
Cwico wæs Ic	'I was Alive'	65
Mare Þonne Middangeard	'Bigger than the Earth'	66
Wordgaldor	'Word-Spell'	67
Wiht on Weg Feran	'A Creature Went Away'	68
Wundor Wearð on Wege	'A Wonder Happened on the Way'	69
Wæter Wearð to Bane	'Water Turned to Bone'	68–9 as one riddle
Orþoncum Geworht	'Made with Skill'	70
Singeð Þurh Sidan	'Sings through its Sides'	70a
Heah ond Hleotorht	'Tall and Beautiful'	70b
Reade Bewæfed	'Clothed in Red'	71
Mearcþaþas Walas Træd	'I Trod the Welsh Boundary-Paths'	72
Brægnloca	'Brain-Locker'	73
Feaxhar Cwene	'Grey-Haired Queen'	74
Swift on Swaþe	'Swift on a Track'	75
Swift ond Sittende	'Swift and Sitting'	75–6 as one riddle
Ides Sittende Ane	'Woman Sitting Alone'	76
Ides Feþeleas	'Footless Woman'	76–77 as one riddle
Feþeleas	'Footless'	77
Orþonc Yþum Bewrigene	'Cunning Thing Covered with Waves'	78
Æþelinges Æht ond Willa	'Noble's Possession and Desire'	79
Æþelinges Eaxlgestealla	'Noble's Shoulder-Companion'	79–80 as one riddle
Fyrdrinces Gefara	'Warrior's Companion'	80
Byledbreost	'Puff-breasted'	81
Greate Swilgeð	'Swallows Grit'	82
Frod Wæs Min Fromcynn	'My Ancestry was Old'	83
Modor Monigra	'Mother of Many'	84
Nis Min Sele Swige	'My Hall is not Silent'	85
XII Hund Heafda	'Twelve Hundred Heads'	86

Riddle title	Title translation	ASPR riddle no.
Beorcade Wancode	'Barked, Wavered'	87
Broþorleas	'Brother-less'	88
Se Wiht Wombe Hæfde	'The Creature had a Womb'	89
Lupus	'Wolf'	90
Heafod Homere Geþuren	'Head Forged by a Hammer'	91
Brunra Beot	'Boast of Brown Ones'	92
Gingra Broþor Mec Adraf	'Younger Brother Drove Me Out'	93
Hyrre þonne Heafon	'Higher than Heaven'	94
Ic Swaþe Hwilum Mine Bemiþe	'I Sometimes Hide my Track'	95

Note on language

Up until very recently, we would have said 'Anglo-Saxon England', as the term usefully covers the literature written in both Anglo-Latin and Old English. At the end of this book's gestation, however, the authors and editors together agreed to dispense with the term 'Anglo-Saxon' because of its historical associations with racism. We are conscious that we have not yet developed an elegant and precise terminology to replace it. In general, therefore, this book uses 'early medieval England' as the location of the literature, art, culture, and history that arose in what is now England between 600 and 1100 CE.

General Introduction

Megan Cavell, Jennifer Neville, and Victoria Symons

The riddling tradition of early medieval England was a vibrant one: numerically speaking, riddles outnumber all other types of poetry that survive from this period. The earliest extant collection of riddles composed in England is Aldhelm's *Enigmata*: a round hundred of mostly brief poems wrought in Aldhelm's characteristic, alliterative-flavoured Latin verse on topics ranging from the celestial to the mythical, from the exotic to the emphatically prosaic. Aldhelm begins his collection with a verse preface that serves as a literary manifesto, laying out both his debt to literary tradition and his own literary ambitions. This preface is valuable on a number of counts. It is rare to have such a mission statement attached to any early medieval literary collection. No comparable reading context or textual framework exists for the Old English riddles of the *Exeter Book*, for example. But it also tells us something about how these riddles work. Aldhelm sings the praises not only of the Christian God, but also of his prophet Moses, Job the soldier, and the psalmist David, alongside references to Castalian nymphs and the peaks of Parnassus. This wide-ranging naming serves a purpose beyond the elevation of famous music-makers: the first and last letter of each line of the preface support a double-acrostic naming Aldhelm as the author of the riddle collection that follows.

This stylistic conceit strikes a particular balance between the communal and the individual that informs the *Enigmata* as a whole. The communal mingling of past poets comes together in the preface to support the individual name of the present author, while the individual author simultaneously stakes his claim as the sole progenitor of the multitudinous compositions that follow: *Aldhelmvs cecinit millenis versibvs odas* ('Aldhelm has sung songs in a thousand verses').[1] Each individual riddle has its own individual solution, and is spoken in the first person with its own individual voice. But these individual voices are, themselves, parts of something greater. Jumping from leeches to unicorns, from the sun and the moon to pregnant pigs, we come at last to the final riddle, *Creatura* ('Creation'), which draws together the preceding cacophony of individual voices into a unified celebration of communal diversity.

It is this interplay between the individual and the communal that, we suggest, lies at the heart of the early medieval riddling tradition. It also speaks to the present popularity of these poems, among both academics and the wider public.[2] The riddles of early medieval England, and particularly the vernacular riddles of the *Exeter Book*, have enjoyed a surge of critical interest in the past twenty years. No longer nugatory, marginal amusements, they now feature in discussions of gender, literacy, runic encoding, slavery, agriculture, metre, among many other mainstream threads of criticism. Seen through such a variety of lenses, it is not surprising to find individual riddles provoking a multitude of different readings. Similarly, the potential of these texts has been better recognised in part because we now perceive that they participate in larger traditions: they are no longer an odd selection of ill-defined, short texts but rather the tip of at least two mighty icebergs: early medieval riddling and the broader riddling tradition explored most fully in folklore studies.

Despite having secured their place in a wide field for investigation, however, we still mostly turn to the *Exeter Book* riddles to hunt for new solutions. And who can blame us? Faced with texts like the one that most scholars know as Riddle 42, how could any reader refrain?

Ic seah wyhte wrætlice twa
undearnungav ute plegan
hæmedlæces; hwitloc anfeng
wlance under wædum, gif þæs weorces speow,
fæmne fyllo. Ic on flette mæg
þurh runstafas rincum secgan,
þam þe bec witan, bega ætsomne
naman þara wihta. þær sceal Nyd wesan
twega oþer ond se torhta Æsc
an an linan, Acas twegen,
Hægelas swa some. Hwylc þæs hordgates
cægan cræfte þa clamne onleac
þe þa rædellan wið rynemenn
hygefæste heold heortan bewrigene
orþoncbendum? Nu is undyrne

werum æt wine hu þa wihte mid us,
heanmode twa, hatne sindon.[3]

[I saw two amazing creatures—they were playing openly outside in the sport of sex. If the work was successful, the woman, proud and bright-haired, received her fill under her garments. Through rune-letters I can say the names of both creatures together to those men in the hall who know books. There must be two **Needs** and the bright **Ash**—one on the line—two **Oaks** and just as many **Hails**. Who can unlock the bar of the hoard-gate with the power of the key? The heart of the riddle was hidden by cunning bonds, proof against the ingenuity of men who know secrets, but now for men at wine it is obvious how those two low-minded creatures are named among us.]

A text like this demands a response. It is impossible simply to read passively to its end. We want to be those ingenious men—and women—who know books, runes, and secrets. We want to assemble the pieces to come up with an answer. We want to know how to interpret this blatant, non-judgemental reference to sex within a monastic context. That is, *anfeng / … gif þæs weorces speow, / fæmne fyllo* ('if the work succeeded, the woman received her fill') (2b–5a). This statement is, of course, a rather blunt description of the copulation of a cock and hen, but we can also take it as a summary of how the riddles of the early medieval tradition work: if the text succeeds, we will receive our fill—not simply a solution, but much, much more.

For example, the approach that this poem takes to riddling overlaps with Aldhelm's prefatory poem in striking ways. Both engage in letter games, whether acrostics or jumbled runes, and therefore invite multiple interpretations by reminding us that there is, literally, more than one way to read a text. Both also figure riddling as a kind of gift or precious item; Aldhelm entreats God to grant him the gift of poetic prowess, while the solution to the *Exeter Book* riddle is a treasure protected by keys and cunning bonds. The same relationship between the communal and the individual that stands at the heart of Aldhelm's poem is also explored by the Old English riddle, although in a very different way, and with a very different image in its sights. From the *ic* of the opening line to the *us* of the penultimate one, this riddle is all about different ways of uniting individuals. The sex being enjoyed by the cock and the hen is one sort of union, of course, but so too is the 'unlocking' of the hoard-gates that conceal the riddle's solution. To solve a riddle is, after all, to get into the mind of the person who poses it. And how do we solve this riddle? By uniting its jumbled mess of runic letters into one coherent solution.

Modern scholars have been engaging in this game of uniting apparently disparate clues for over a century. In 1857, Heinrich Leo 'solved' *Wulf and Eadwacer*.[4] He answered the ambiguities of this little poem with the name 'Cynewulf', and proposed that some—perhaps all—of the riddles that follow it in the manuscript were written by the poet whose name appears in runes at the end of *Christ II*, *Juliana*, *Elene*, and *The Fates of the Apostles*. Today, the riddles are not considered to be the work of a single author, let alone a named one, and *Wulf and Eadwacer* is generally grouped with the *Exeter Book* elegies. Leo's argument does, however, remind us of one crucial consideration when it comes to these poems: there is more than one way to solve a riddle.

The fact that the Old English riddles' demands for solutions are offset by our inability to confirm our hypotheses with absolute certainty has in many ways shaped scholarly interactions with these texts. The *Exeter Book* riddles began to appear in print in the early decades of the nineteenth century, although the first edition solely devoted to the riddles themselves would not emerge until 1910.[5] In this early scholarship the quest for solutions—singular and definitive—looms large.[6] Franz Dietrich, Moritz Trautmann, and Frederick Tupper, Jr, among many others, proposed extensive sets of solutions, frequently differing from one another, and often changing their own minds in subsequent publications.[7] Many of these early solutions are still accepted today, others have been refined over the years, and some have been thrown out entirely.[8]

At the same time, the Anglo-Latin riddles had scarcely entered the scholarly consciousness. With the exception of the editorial work of Ernst Dümmler in the late nineteenth century,[9] Tupper's early twentieth-century edition of the *enigmata* attributed to Bede,[10] and Rudolph Ehwald's edition of Aldhelm's riddles—as part of his edition of Aldhelm's entire corpus[11]—in the second decade of the twentieth century, it would not be until 1968 that multiple collections of Latin riddles were edited and translated *en masse*.[12] The forthcoming Dumbarton Oaks edition and translation of the entire early medieval English and Latin riddle tradition, alongside analogues from Ireland, Iceland, the continent, and further afield, is poised to make these texts significantly more accessible.[13] Indeed, scholarly engagement with the Latin riddles is finally on the rise. Unlike the Old English riddles of the *Exeter Book*, the more numerous and diverse Anglo-Latin and comparative tradition has received less attention, perhaps in part because the game of solution-hunting is not an overt goal of all these texts. Many Latin riddles circulate in manuscripts that include their solutions, though whether these solutions are always singular or 'correct' is another matter.[14]

Numbering and naming

While hunting for solutions dominated early approaches, as it still does today, another question also defined the infancy of early medieval riddle scholarship: that of definition. What, exactly, is a riddle? For Leo, the *Exeter Book* riddle collection began with *Wulf and Eadwacer*, while other early scholars pushed the sequence back further still to include *Deor*, or even *Soul and Body I*.[15] Even within the currently recognised boundaries of the corpus, the questions of where individual riddles start and end, how many we have, and how many we have lost, continue to be debated. When George Philip Krapp and Elliott Van Kirk Dobbie arranged the riddles for their ASPR edition of the *Exeter Book*, their count came to ninety-five. This numbering is still widely used today, although their individual editorial choices are far from universally accepted. Craig Williamson's influential 1977 edition, on the other hand, begins by presenting Krapp and Dobbie's Riddles 1–3 as a single poem, with the knock-on effect that every subsequent riddle is numbered differently from the ASPR sequence.[16] Bernard J. Muir, the most recent editor of the entire manuscript, re-numbers the riddles once more, replacing Williamson's ninety-one with a new count of ninety-four,[17] while Andy Orchard questions this count with his edition's ninety-one *Exeter Book* riddles.[18] Just as there are no solutions to the riddles themselves, there seems to be no solution to the problem of how we number them.

The editors of this volume have, for some time, been interested in this problem. The issue of numerical consistency is just the tip of the iceberg. The very act of numbering the riddles emphasises a homogeneity that we do not believe the *Exeter Book* riddles possess: we would like to see them approached not just as a generic entity, but also as individual poems in their own right. Furthermore, numbering these poems makes it difficult to remember which riddle is which, providing a barrier to engagement for those uninitiated into the study of this collection. Titling the poems by their solutions is not, however, a less controversial option, since many of these riddles defy scholarly consensus. Is there a better way to approach the naming of the *Exeter Book* riddles? We believe that there is, and this volume provides an ideal opportunity to test out a new system. As discussed in Neville's recent note, this system draws key words from individual riddles, with 'unique nouns, adjectives, or noun phrases that directly describe the riddle-subject and aim to be an answer from within the text to the question "What am I?" or "What is it?"'.[19] Titles that stem from the texts in question provide highly appropriate alternatives to increasingly complex and competing numbering systems. A full list of the titles adopted here, in both Old and Modern English, can be found on the pages preceding this Introduction; from this point onward, the *Exeter Book* riddles will be referred to by these titles, accompanied by their ASPR numbering in brackets.

Although numbering the Anglo-Latin riddles has proven far less problematic, the extent to which these self-proclaimed *enigmata* should be held separately from the Old English riddles—as more serious pedagogical tools or exercises, rather than playful explorations of an occasionally bawdy world—also perplexed early investigators of this genre. This question of differences within the genre has now been attenuated by a scholarly trend away from an emphasis on the uniqueness of Old English poetry and toward an appreciation of the multilingual nature of early medieval English literary culture. Thus, alongside issues of solutions, editing, and generic cohesion, recent scholarship has favoured a focus on *how* we read the riddles. For many, context is key. Dieter Bitterli, for example, advocates for reading the *Exeter Book* riddles in the context of Anglo-Latin collections, arguing that they form 'a vigorous, common tradition of Old English and Anglo-Latin enigmatography'.[20] The common thematic thread that links these collections is, Mercedes Salvador-Bello argues, the encyclopaedising tradition of Isidore of Seville.[21] In a structural analysis of extant early medieval riddle collections, Salvador-Bello argues that the organisational principles underlying Isidore's eminently popular *Etymologiae* inform the selection and grouping of poems across the Old English and Anglo-Latin collections. Yet there are other riddles, too, and other contexts for interpretation. Patrick J. Murphy thus argues for the relevance of popular and folkloric conundrums to the *Exeter Book* group.[22] Murphy also lays out a theoretical context for reading the riddles: a riddle's description (what Murphy terms its 'proposition') can at times relate both to its ultimate solution and to an underlying set of metaphors (its 'focus'), which are extended and coherent in their own right.[23]

Language is key to this coherence, and thus John D. Niles draws our attention to another kind of context—a linguistic one.[24] A linguistic context means, first and foremost, answering the riddles in their own language, whether that be Old English or Latin.[25] But Niles also emphasises playfulness, prioritising an approach to the riddles as a match of wits between riddling authors and adventurous readers.[26] Niles is not, of course, the first critic to emphasise language and play as vital elements in the riddles. Fred C. Robinson's 'Artful Ambiguities in the Old English "Book-Moth" Riddle', a seminal study of a single poem, also reminds us of the central role of linguistic play in riddling texts.[27] Insightful studies, both of individual poems and of the collection as a whole, celebrate the plethora of puns, wordplay, euphemism, and humour that characterises this tradition. These are, after all, poems designed to make us look at the world afresh. And, as Jennifer Neville demonstrates, the humour of incongruous description can pave the way for radical statements about the order of the world and the categories—artificial and restrictive as they are—that we attempt to impose on it.[28]

When it comes to categorisation, the riddles once again pose a challenge to scholars. It is important to note that the riddle genre is not a rigid one but rather one that shares characteristics with many other early medieval literary types: elegiac, heroic, didactic, hagiographic, and devotional, to name just a few. Given this tendency for genre-blending and -borrowing, it would be negligent to approach the ninety-five or so Old English riddles and the several hundred Anglo-Latin *enigmata* simply as one uniform entity: these are riddles, but not *only* riddles. As complex pieces of poetry, they should be read as the separate but intersecting texts that they are. Each riddle, after all, deserves scrutiny in its own right, and scrutiny—for at least some of these texts—is precisely what that this volume aims to provide.

This brief overview only hints at the multifarious nature of the scholarship devoted to the early medieval riddles. Indeed, plurality defines the field as much as it defines the material. The variety that characterises this scholarship reveals something important about the texts themselves: they invite multiple, varying, and sometimes contradictory readings. Consequently, this volume presents sixteen chapters that consider the riddles from different angles. This number of chapters, of course, could never cover every current approach, but this volume aims to represent more than the sum of its contents. The variety included here may be taken as an illustrative corner of the vast, colourful quilt-work that is the wider field of early medieval riddle studies. And so, our volume aims to present a microcosm of riddle scholarship to date, embodying both traditional and experimental approaches to this complex genre. It represents, then, a casebook or sampler of scholarly interpretations. In bringing together chapters that offer philological, theoretical, and comparative approaches to early medieval riddling, this volume will help modern readers—both riddling debutant(e)s and old fans—to navigate a complex and growing field. Together, the chapters here ask what has been done, what can be done, and what are the future directions of riddle scholarship.

What is in Part I: Words

This volume is divided into three parts. Part I represents what might be called philological approaches to early medieval riddles—interpretations rooted in close readings of the texts—for, above all, the riddles work by making us question what their words really mean. Hence, Jennifer Neville's 'Sorting out the rings: astronomical tropes in *Þragbysig* (R.4)' analyses *Þragbysig*, arguing that previous interpretations have failed to identify tropes that are key to solving it. Neville investigates its potential astronomical contexts, positing a new solution: *sunna* ('sun'). In the process, the chapter clearly lays out a riddle-solving methodology—identifying what to focus on when approaching these texts—in a way that will undoubtedly prove fruitful to other would-be solvers of ambiguous riddles. Ambiguity can be put to marvellous effect, as Sharon E. Rhodes demonstrates in '*Wundor* and *wrætlic*: the anatomy of wonder in the sex riddles'. This chapter probes several sex riddles from the *Exeter Book*—*Womb wæs on Hindan* (R.37), *Wrætlic Hongað* (R.44), *Banleas* (R.45), and *In Wincsele* (R.54)—arguing that these texts' focus on wonder highlights the value of mundane topics that are all too frequently dismissed as low-status or obscene. Rhodes' reading teases out hidden meanings in the words of each text, while simultaneously putting them in conversation with thing theory and emphasising the way *objects* in these riddles are transformed into *things*.

Like things, animals also emerge from their place in the background of early medieval England to take centre stage in the riddles, as we see in Megan Cavell's 'Domesticating the devil: the early medieval contexts of Aldhelm's cat riddle'. This chapter explores the historical and comparative contexts of Aldhelm's *Enigma 65*,

Muriceps ('mouse-catcher'). Cavell's close reading of this largely neglected poem identifies an ambivalence toward the early medieval cat, who straddles the roles of domestic guardian and diabolical sinner. Fascinating insights into cat/human relations can be gleaned from the limited textual evidence of the early medieval world, as cats travelled down their complex pathway to domestication. At times, the textual evidence is crying out to be heard, as Francesca Brooks explores in 'The crafting of sound in the riddles of the *Exeter Book*'. This chapter draws a parallel between materially crafted artefacts and aurally crafted language in three *Exeter Book* riddles: *Be Sonde Muðlease* (R.60), *Nama Min is Mære* (R.26), and *Feþegeorn* (R.31). Highlighting the materiality of the spoken and written word, Brooks argues that these riddles' shared interest in craft and sound are evidence of a self-conscious exploration of poetic acoustic structures, and the metaphors that link craft and sound in these texts continue to resonate in contemporary idioms for sound and language. This examination of the aural qualities of the riddles is taken in a different direction in Robert Stanton's 'Sound, voice, and articulation in the *Exeter Book* riddles', which analyses connections between sound, noise, and voice, placing these concepts within their classical and early medieval philosophical and grammatical contexts. Stanton explores the enigmatic focus on sound's performative effects, arguing that these effects function through those principles essential to riddles: incongruity and the blurring of categories. This chapter concludes by connecting the masterful acoustic effects found in the Old English riddles back to the Latin enigmatic tradition and calling for further work on the subtle relationships between the two languages at play in the early medieval riddling tradition.

What is in Part II: Ideas

While reading carefully may lead to elegant solutions, such solutions are not the end of the story or the end of the riddling game. The riddles work by presenting common things in uncommon ways, with the result that we think about objects, relationships, and experiences anew, and this new thinking can be facilitated through engagements with literary theory. This section begins with Karin Olsen's 'Warriors and their battle gear: conceptual blending in *Anhaga* (R.5) and *Wæpnum Awyrged* (R.20)', which draws on cognitive theory to discuss the mental labour that underlies the identification and evaluation of riddle solutions. After mapping out the process of conceptual blending, Olsen analyses *Anhaga* (R.5) and *Wæpnum Awyrged* (R.20), demonstrating how clues replace a blend's narrative context and allow would-be solvers to narrow down possible referents. In so doing, Olsen makes the case for the multiplicity of solutions stemming from the diversity of ways in which we think and process information. Riddles not only provide ideal case studies for assessing how ambiguous references are processed into clues; they also speak to their audience's reaction to said ambiguity. Jonathan Wilcox's 'Humour and the *Exeter Book* riddles: incongruity in *Feþegeorn* (R.31)' explores how humour works, both in a theoretical context and in relation to *Feþegeorn*. Wilcox outlines three types of humour theory—incongruity, superiority, and release theories—and argues that both humour in general and riddles in specific share an investment in appropriate incongruity, ambiguity, and release. Having established his theoretical foundations, Wilcox unpicks a riddle case study in forensic detail, laying bare its inner workings and providing a method for other humour-theory practitioners to follow. And yet, riddles can also have a darker side, as Rafał Borysławski emphasises in 'Memory and transformative fear in the *Exeter Book* riddles'. This chapter explores riddling fear, engaging with psychological and philosophical approaches and putting the different levels within which fear operates (structural, narrative, affective) into conversation with medieval Christian thought. Borysławski focuses especially on *XII Hund Heafda* (R.86), *Gryrelic Hleahtor* (R.33), and *Nama Min is Mære* (R.26), arguing that fear in these (and other) riddles is transformative; the experience of fear is a reminder of and therapy for the human condition. These short, apparently trivial texts thus can be seen to intersect with important philosophical, moral, and theological issues.

Riddles have also been known to push at boundaries in tremendously non-trivial ways. Hence, Peter Buchanan's 'Monstrous healing: Aldhelm's leech riddle' addresses Aldhelm's *Enigma 43, Sanguisuga*, arguing that the leech riddle queers dichotomies and unsettles hierarchies through its dual focus on monstrous body and healing touch. Drawing on Mel Y. Chen's work on animacy as well as recent scholarship in the fields of animal studies and new materialism, Buchanan emphasises the importance of recognising the animal body, alongside the poetic resonances and lexical play at work in the poem. In combining theoretical and philological methodologies so effectively, this chapter provides a model for future work in Anglo-Latin riddling. Integrated methodologies are also at play in Corinne Dale's '*Freolic, sellic*: an ecofeminist reading of *Modor Monigra* (R.84)', which applies ecocritical theory to this riddle, alongside *Feþegeorn* (R.31) and *Earmost Ealra Wihta* (R.39). Dale demonstrates biblical echoes of the powerfully feminised concept of Wisdom in the gendering of *Modor Monigra*'s solution, 'water', arguing that gender and the natural world may be read together and within the context of oppressive, hegemonic structures. In urging a reassessment of assumptions about grammatical gender and solutions, furthermore, this chapter will undoubtedly lead to discussion of other riddles that employ gender in a meaningful way. Similarly committed to riddle ecologies is James Paz, in 'Mind, mood, and meteorology in *Þrymful Þeow* (R.1–3)'. This chapter engages with ecologically-invested new materialist theories, especially Timothy Morton's concept of the 'hyperobject', in order to analyse nonhuman agency and ontology in *Þrymful Þeow*. Paz argues that the confined state of the wind within this riddle resembles the turbulence of the human mind in other early medieval English texts, a resemblance that troubles boundaries between the internal self and the external world. Paz thus makes a convincing case for the immediate relevance of premodern riddling to contemporary ecological crises.

What is in Part III: Interactions

Although we rightly begin our reading of the early medieval riddles by focusing close attention on their words and ideas, these texts also work by leading us to make connections with other fields, other languages, other times, and other places. Part III begins with an emphasis on cultural connections, in Mercedes Salvador-Bello's 'The nursemaid, the mother, and the prostitute: tracing an insular riddle topos on both sides of the English Channel'. This chapter explores the complexity of the early medieval riddling tradition, arguing conclusively for a two-way cultural transfer between England and the continent. Salvador-Bello's case study is the personification of Wisdom as a breastfeeding nursemaid, whose movement and adaptation (into mother and prostitute) she traces through a wide range of insular and continental contexts. In giving equal weighting to the riddle tradition's life beyond the shores of early medieval England, Salvador-Bello provides an important reminder to scholars working in this global world. Bridging the same insular/continental divide, while at the same time emphasising interdisciplinary connections, is Neville Mogford's 'The moon and stars in the Bern and Eusebius riddles'. This chapter maps out the interaction between riddles, astronomy, and computus in the Bern and Eusebian collections. Mogford argues that the understanding of complex computistical calculations is essential to the understanding of individual riddles' metaphors and motifs, such as those surrounding familial relations. In so doing, he draws together two types of intellectual work that are rarely discussed alongside each other. Drawing connections between the part and the whole, Britt Mize's 'Enigmatic knowing and the *Vercelli Book*' refocuses our attention on the Old English tendency to riddle—to solicit intellectual labour and contemplation—which Mize dubs 'conditional revelation'. The process is not restricted to riddles, and this chapter explores it in relation to wisdom literature generally and the *Vercelli Book* in particular, emphasising the collection's aim to inspire spiritual improvement through contemplation. In so doing, Mize identifies rhetorical techniques and motivations that speak to the broader context of the intellectual work at play in early medieval England.

Intellectual work is everywhere inflected by personal experience, as the final two chapters in this volume highlight. Pirkko A. Koppinen, in 'The materiality of fire in *Legbysig* and *Ligbysig* (R.30a and b) and an unexpected new solution', explores fire in two related riddles from the *Exeter Book* and their wider poetic context, and in relation to materiality as a cultural process. After outlining previous solutions to these riddles, Koppinen draws on her own experience of fire as essential to life growing up in Finland in order to propose a new solution: *Ora* ('ore'). Her reminder that our sensory experiences interact with and shape our thinking—something that struck home for Koppinen when translating Old English riddles into her native tongue—invites a new approach to the riddles that looks both forward and back. That the translation process is such a powerful way into these texts is, finally, the topic of Miller Wolf Oberman's '*Dyre cræft*: new translations of Exeter riddle fragments *Modor Monigra* (R.84), *Se Wiht Wombe Hæfde* (R.89), and *Brunra Beot* (R.92), accompanied by notes on process'. In this chapter, Oberman offers reflections on the poetic translation process—informed by Walter Benjamin and Gayatri Chakravorty Spivak—that focus especially on handling damaged riddles in a way that respects their fragmentary nature. His translation of *Se Wiht Wombe Hæfde* maps out the process with a view to its stages, and Oberman then provides new poetic versions of this and two other fragmentary riddles. In highlighting the opportunities afforded by creative translation, this chapter speaks to the vitality of thousand-year-old verses that continue to inspire.

At the end of the volume, Cavell and Neville attempt to synthesise the multifarious contributions made by our authors—to delineate how the riddles have worked on and in this community of individuals. The range covered by the chapters in this collection is very wide. Yet we are conscious that the riddles continue to work, and so we look forward to the new solutions, new approaches, and new ideas that will arise in future, perhaps in part as a response to the work presented here.

Notes

1 Fr. Glorie, ed., *Collectiones Aenigmatum Merovingicae Aetatis*, CCSL, 133–133A (Turnhout: Brepols, 1968), 133, pp. 377–81. Unless otherwise stated, all translations in this volume are those of the chapters' authors.

2 Translations of the *Exeter Book* riddles that speak to non-specialist and non-academic audiences include Greg Delanty, Seamus Heaney and Michael Matto, eds, *The Word Exchange: Anglo-Saxon Poems in Translation* (New York: Norton, 2010); Kevin Crossley-Holland, trans., *The Exeter Book Riddles*, rev. edn (London: Enitharmon, 2008); Craig Williamson, trans., *A Feast of Creatures: Anglo-Saxon Riddle-Songs* (Philadelphia: University of Pennsylvania Press, 1982); and Megan Cavell, with Matthias Ammon and Victoria Symons, *The Riddle Ages: Old English Riddles, Translations and Commentaries*, theriddleages.wordpress.com. Popular knowledge of the early medieval riddle tradition can also be attributed to its influence on J. R. R. Tolkien's *The Hobbit* and *The Lord of the Rings*; see Adam Roberts, *The Riddles of the Hobbit* (New York: Palgrave, 2013).

3 George Philip Krapp and Elliott Van Kirk Dobbie, eds, *The Exeter Book*, ASPR, 3 (New York: Columbia University Press, 1936), pp. 203–4. Translation by Jennifer Neville. Unless otherwise noted, all Old English poetry cited in this volume is taken from ASPR, with the exception of *Beowulf*, which is cited from R. D. Fulk, Robert E. Bjork, and John D. Niles, eds, *Klaeber's Beowulf and the Fight at Finnsburg*, 4th edn (Toronto: University of Toronto Press, 2008).

4 Heinrich Leo, *Commentatio quae de se ipso Cynevulfus, sive Cenewulfus, sive Coenevulfus poeta Anglo-Saxonicus tradiderit* (Halle: Hendel, 1857).

5 Frederick Tupper Jr, ed., *The Riddles of the Exeter Book* (Boston: Ginn, 1910).

6 For a bibliography of the field up to 1992, see Russell G. Poole, *Old English Wisdom Poetry*, Annotated Bibliographies of Old and Middle English Literature, 5 (Cambridge: D. S. Brewer, 1998), pp. 244–32.

7 See Poole, *Wisdom Poetry*, p. 248.

8 Catalogues of proposed solutions are given in Bernard J. Muir, ed., *The Exeter Anthology of Old English Poetry: An Edition of Exeter Dean and Chapter MS 3501*, 2nd edn, 2 vols (Exeter: University of Exeter Press, 2000); Donald K. Fry, 'Exeter Book Riddle Solutions', *Old English Newsletter*, 15.1 (1981), 22–33; Craig Williamson, ed., *The Old English Riddles of the Exeter Book* (Chapel Hill: University of North Carolina Press, 1977).

9 [Lorsch Riddles], Ernst Dümmler, ed., 'Lörscher Rätsel', *Zeitschrift für deutsches Altertum*, 22 (1878), 258–63; [Lorsch Riddles], Ernst Dümmler, ed., 'Aenigmata anglica', MGH, *Poetae Latini Aevi Carolini*, 1 (Berlin: Weidmann, 1881), pp. 20–3, and Ernst Dümmler, ed., 'Aenigmata Bonifatii', MGH, *Poetae Latini Aevi Carolini* 1 (Berlin: Weidmann, 1881), pp. 1–15.

10 Frederick Tupper, Jr, 'Riddles of the Bede Tradition: the *Flores* of pseudo-Bede', *Modern Philology*, 2 (1905), 561–72.

11 Aldhelm, *Aldhelmi Opera*, ed. Rudolf Ehwald, MGH, Auctores Antiquissimi, 15 (Berlin: Weidmann, 1919).

12 Glorie, *Collectiones Aenigmatum*.

13 Andy Orchard, ed. and trans., *The Anglo-Saxon Riddle Tradition*, Dumbarton Oaks Medieval Library (Cambridge, MA: Harvard University Press, forthcoming).

14 Andy Orchard, 'Enigma Variations: the Anglo-Saxon Riddle-Tradition', in *Latin Learning and English Lore: Studies in Anglo-Saxon Literature for Michael Lapidge*, 2 vols, ed. Katherine O'Brien O'Keeffe and Andy Orchard (Toronto: University of Toronto Press, 2005), pp. 284–304, at p. 285.

15 James E. Anderson, '*Deor*, *Wulf and Eadwacer* and *The Soul's Address*: How and Where the Old English Exeter Book Riddles Begin', in *The Old English Elegies: New Essays in Criticism and Research*, ed. Martin Green (Rutherford: Associated University Presses, 1983), pp. 204–30.

16 Williamson, *Old English Riddles*.

17 Muir, *Exeter Anthology*.

18 Orchard, *Anglo-Saxon Riddle Tradition*.

19 Jennifer Neville, 'A Modest Proposal: Titles for the *Exeter Book Riddles*', *MÆ* 88 (2019), 116–23.

20 Dieter Bitterli, *Say What I Am Called: The Old English Riddles of the Exeter Book and the Anglo-Latin Riddle Tradition* (Toronto: University of Toronto Press, 2009), p. 4.

21 Mercedes Salvador-Bello, *Isidorean Perceptions of Order: The Exeter Book Riddles and Medieval Latin Enigmata* (Morgantown: West Virginia University Press, 2015).

22 Patrick J. Murphy, *Unriddling the Exeter Riddles* (University Park: Penn State University Press, 2011), pp. 17–18.

23 Murphy, *Unriddling the Exeter Riddles*, pp. 18–19.

24 John D. Niles, *Old English Enigmatic Poems and the Play of the Texts* (Turnhout: Brepols, 2006), pp. 6–7.
25 Niles, *Old English Enigmatic Poems*, pp. 101–3.
26 Niles, *Old English Enigmatic Poems*, p. 4.
27 Fred C. Robinson, 'Artful Ambiguities in the Old English "Book-Moth" Riddle', in *Anglo-Saxon Poetry: Essays in Appreciation: for John C. McGalliard*, ed. Lewis E. Nicholson and Dolores Warwick Frese (Notre Dame: University of Notre Dame Press, 1975), pp. 355–62.
28 Jennifer Neville, 'The Unexpected Treasure of the "Implement Trope": Hierarchical Relationships in the Old English Riddles', *RES*, 62.256 (2011), 505–19.

Part I

Words

Introduction to Part I

Megan Cavell and Jennifer Neville

There is a long history of philological approaches to Old English language and literature. These approaches, rooted in the words of texts and what they can tell us about their moment in history, derive from the historical and comparative analysis of Germanic languages as a group. Working from words outward—to text, genre, language as a whole, and sometimes even wider language family—is rewarding because the gradual amassing of evidence as the frame of reference expands is orderly, methodical, systematic. It should not, however, be mistaken as the only, or the correct, way to approach a text. Ultimately, philological approaches rely on the interpretation of words, and there are many ways to interpret both words and the texts in which they survive. These interpretations all rely, to greater or lesser extent, on good close reading—the bread and butter of all the methodologies at work in this book (and in our field). Hence, not all of the chapters in this section are philological in a strict sense. Rather, this section includes chapters that explore words as words, and sound, and language. This exploration may manifest through a focus on solutions, register, allusion, and poetic craft, with authors' analyses stretching out to touch the sciences and/or critical theory, before returning to the words that stand at the core of the chapters.

Studying the riddles has always meant grappling with words and their polysemy, and with translation as an act of interpretation. As Jonathan Wilcox puts it: 'Riddles with their multiple possibilities become ideal microcosms for the interpretative act of reading all Old English poetry. As a result, riddles richly reward close reading'.[1] Riddles—whether in Old English, Latin or another language altogether—play with words and their meanings in the same way that all good poetry does, but nowhere else are the interpretative stakes higher. Misinterpret a word in a riddle and the prospect of solving it becomes more remote. Likewise—for modern interpreters—translate a word in one way or another and the proposed solution can be skewed towards or away from a particular reading.

Solutions themselves require a word or phrase, sometimes a specific one (or in a specific language) and sometimes a more general one. Riddles can and do call for particular words when providing clues and demanding solutions, but they also withhold certainty when they travel without a solution, with a solution that does not fit, or with a range of possible solutions, some of which fit better than others. This is why solving riddles is only a part of a process, which invites reading and re-reading, interpretation and re-interpretation. We hope that the chapters in this section will provoke re-interpretations in their own right, as we all engage in the act of scholarly discussion. Riddling is, after all, always a conversation.

Note

1 Jonathan Wilcox, '"Tell Me What I Am": The Old English Riddles', in *Readings in Medieval Texts: Interpreting Old and Middle English Literature*, ed. David Johnson and Elaine Treharne (Oxford: Oxford University Press, 2005), pp. 46–59, at p. 58.

1

Sorting out the rings: astronomical tropes in *Þragbysig* (R.4)

Jennifer Neville

Þragbysig has proven itself to be one of the most productive members of the *Exeter Book* riddle collection, inspiring modern readers, at least, to propose a very large number of solutions, including (in roughly chronological order) bell, millstone, necromancy, flail, lock, handmill, pen, phallus, bucket, guard-dog, devil, plough-team, sword, and city gate.[1] Yet it is the range of *types* of solutions rather than the number of solutions that is most remarkable, for *Þragbysig*'s previous solutions include the inanimate and the animate; the homely and the exotic; the physical, the abstract, and the spiritual; and, of course, the plausible and the implausible. That is, modern readers have tried their best but failed to come up with a response that is not flawed in some way—one that does not provoke other readers to try yet again. Such a plethora of failed attempts may indicate that there is something wrong with the text itself.[2] Conversely, it may indicate that modern readers of the text have missed something important. In this chapter, I propose that what we may have missed is the learned perspective on the physical world of early medieval England.

Given the excellence of the past scholarship that has failed to answer *Þragbysig*'s challenge, I am conscious that I have set myself a potentially impossible task in trying to propose yet another solution. I am also conscious that this attempt may seem to contradict my contention elsewhere that solutions are not an adequate response to the riddles of the *Exeter Book*.[3] Like others before me, however, I have been seduced by *Þragbysig*'s intractability into playing the riddle game. My opening move is to pinpoint the places where previous solutions have failed so as to identify the ambiguous language and the riddling tropes that need to be addressed by a solution. I then investigate some of the learned, astronomical discourses that, I suggest, may be concealed by *Þragbysig*'s metaphorical surface. Finally, I propose a solution that is not disqualified by the text's combination of language, tropes, and discourses. This solution, like others before it, may fail to convince future readers, but I hope that my attempt will provide some insight into how this riddle works.

Manuscript and scholarly context

Þragbysig appears near the beginning of the *Exeter Book*'s collection of riddles, immediately after the long opening sequence of meditations on the power of the natural world demonstrated by storms on land and sea. Unlike that opening sequence, which scholars have interpreted as one, two, or three separate texts,[4] there is no ambiguity surrounding *Þragbysig*'s boundaries: the scribe clearly marks its opening with the usual style of large capital and its closing with the usual end punctuation.[5] In addition, in comparison with the grandeur, religious significance, and length of the opening sequence, *Þragbysig* appears to offer a radical change in topic and scale:

> Ic sceal þragbysig þegne minum,
> hringum hæfted, hyran georne,
> min bed brecan, breahtme cyþan
> þæt me halswriþan hlaford sealde.
> Oft mec slæpwerigne secg oðþe meowle
> gretan eode; ic him gromheortum
> winterceald oncweþe. Wearm lim
> gebundenne bæg hwilum bersteð;
> se þeah biþ on þonce þegne minum,
> medwisum men, me þæt sylfe,
> þær wiht wite, ond wordum min
> on sped mæge spel gesecgan.

> [Periodically labouring, confined in rings, I must eagerly obey my servant, break my bed, and announce loudly that the lord gave me a neck-collar. Often a man or woman went to greet me, sleepy and weary, and I, winter-cold, reply to those grim-hearted ones. Sometimes a warm limb bursts through the bound ring; that, however, is agreeable to my servant, a foolish man, and to myself—if I were to know anything, and could tell my story successfully in words.]

What is happening here? Dietrich and many others see the ringing of a bell: when greeted 'periodically'—that is, at appointed hours—by its grumpy servant (the bell-ringer), the bell 'answers' by making its distinctive and pleasant sound, even though, as an inanimate object, it is not able to tell its own story. This solution accounts for the speaking and answering aspects of the text very well, but in my view it does not adequately explain what the multiple rings are, what it means for a bell to 'break its bed', who or what the neck-ring-giving lord (as opposed to the bell-ringing thegn) is, what the warm limb is doing when the ring bursts, and why the thegn (as opposed to the inanimate riddle-subject) is said to be foolish.

There are similar problems with millstone, pen, flail, and bucket. Although a bucket does offer images that may illuminate the multiple rings mentioned in the text (2a, 4a, 7a), millstones, pens, and flails do not possess obvious rings. All four of these solutions rely upon the implement trope to explain the relationship between a user and his or her tools,[6] but none of them addresses the complications caused by the presence of both a *þegn* ('servant') (1b, 9b) and a *hlaford* ('lord') (4b) alongside the speaker in the text. Similarly, despite Doane's convincing efforts to explain the process of breaking ice on the surface of a well, I remain puzzled by the warm limb and the insistence that the bucket's servant, the human being attempting to draw water in the morning, is foolish.

A more recently proposed solution, 'plough-team', initially seems promising. The speaker is the ox, who complains when dragged out of his warm stall in the early morning and bound with a round collar to a wheeled plough. The thegn is the goad-boy, who is not very bright, and so, like the ox, is happy when the plough breaks down; the lord is the ploughman. This solution admirably accounts for the text's multiple rings and actors, but it, too, has a sticking point, for Cochran interprets *lim* in line 7 as 'lime, earth' instead of 'limb' and imagines this mud sticking to the plough and breaking its wheel. Although it is possible that mud could cause a wheel to break, it is odd that is *wearm* ('warm') (7b). My search of the *DOEC* reveals no reference to earth being warm at any time, and the earth would certainly not be warm at ploughing time, in January. Therefore, although I accept Cochran's point that, grammatically and metrically, the text could be referring to 'lime' here, logically I do not think that it can be. I am also not convinced that a lack of intelligence is the constituting characteristic of a goad-boy.[7]

I find fault in these readings not to heap scorn on them but rather to understand what *Þragbysig*'s key points are. Having scrutinised previous solutions, I believe that any solution for *Þragbysig* needs to address the relationship between the first-person subject, the thegn whom it serves or follows, and the lord who gives it a neck-collar. Such a solution also needs to explain the identity and multiplicity of the rings, the breaking of the bed, the *wearm lim*, the idea of speaking and answering, and the foolishness of the thegn.

Ambiguous diction

As *Þragbysig* is a riddle, it is not surprising that these things that we most need to understand map very tidily onto the ambiguous language in the text. This ambiguity begins in the first line, with the term *þragbysig* itself. Although I have translated it above as 'periodically busy', the word is a *hapax legomena* whose meaning is not certain. *Bysig* may mean 'busy' or 'afflicted'. Either meaning points to activity, but of what kind? Affixing *þrag* to *bysig* unhelpfully reveals that the riddle-subject is 'busy or afflicted at one time', 'at some times', or 'at all times'.[8] Thus we know that the object does something (or has something done to it) once, sometimes, or always. That is, we know nothing at all; as with many riddles, we cannot begin to interpret this word until after we have read the rest of the text. In the following line we may initially be relieved to find some apparently physical objects, but the rings bring their own problems, since the relationship between the *hringum* ('rings') (2a) by which the creature is bound, the *halswriþan* ('neck-collar') (4a) given by the lord, and the *gebundenne bæg* ('bound ring') (8a) that bursts is not at all clear. Do these words refer to the same things, or are there two or three different types of rings? In addition, as I have already noted, the identity of the *wearm lim* ('warm limb [or lime]') (7b) is frustratingly opaque, and thus it is hardly surprising that we cannot construe what it means for such a thing to break a *bed* ('bed') (3a). Unlike *þragbysig*, *hring* ('ring') (2a), *bed* ('bed') (3a), *halswriþan* ('neck-ring, collar') (4a), and *bæg* ('ring, collar, crown') (8a) are ordinary, well-known words; like *þragbysig*, however, their referents are frustratingly unclear. Identifying a context for *þragbysig*, the rings, the bed, and the limb should determine the solution of the riddle.

There is also another word that, although not seen as problematic in the past, contains ambiguity that warrants some consideration: *breahtme* (3b). Despite the spacing in the manuscript, which presents the word as *breaht me*, editors take this as a single word, an adverb, which specifies the manner in which the riddle-subject announces that the lord gave it a neck-collar. Most readers have taken it as a word referring to sound, and so the bell or ox or bucket replies 'noisily'. This is reasonable: according to the *DOE*, *breahtm* (also spelled *bearhtm* or *byrhtm*) means 'loud noise' in twenty-seven of its occurrences, across both poetry and glosses.[9] For example, when Holofernes' men march off to collect Judith, they can be seen to step forth *bearhtme* ('noisily') (*Judith* 39b), equipped as they are with jingling mail-shirts and weapons. However, the word may also refer to time, and so Holofernes' men may obey his orders 'instantly' rather than 'noisily'.[10] Elsewhere, *bearhtm* means 'moment, instant' in nine of its occurrences.[11] Among these are five references to the *bryhtm* ('twinkling') of an eye; there are also two occurrences of *bearhtm-hwæt* ('swift as the twinkling of an eye, momentary'). These latter instances suggest that the word might also convey connotations of light, perhaps because of the similarity of some of its spellings to variations of *beorht* ('bright'). Indeed, there is one case in which light seems to be the most likely meaning for the word: in Hrothgar's advice to the young hero, Beowulf, he warns that life endures only a short time before *eagena bearhtm / forsiteð ond forsworceð* ('the light of the eyes fails and darkens') (*Beowulf* 1766b–7a). Here, too, *bearhtm* maintains a clear connection with the idea of time; it is possible that the word connotes combinations of its meanings. Overall, then, only context can determine whether *breahtm* refers to sound, time, or light, or a combination of those ideas. In *Þragbysig*, however, the context is (at least initially) unknown, so its subject may reply 'noisily', 'instantly', or 'brightly'. The possibility that this riddle-subject might be characterised by time or light rather than noise is the starting point for my consideration of astronomy as a defining context for the riddle.

Riddling tropes

Before I turn to astronomy, however, I would like to consider one other important component of the game that this text plays with its readers. In addition to the ambiguous language discussed above, *Þragbysig* employs known riddling tropes. By 'trope' I mean both 'a particular manner or mode' and a 'turning' of a word or phrase's meaning away from its literal sense.[12] I have already mentioned one such trope: the implement trope, in which the interaction between a human user and a tool is represented as the relationship between a lord and a thegn. This is a fairly common trope in the *Exeter Book* riddle collection, appearing in thirteen of the approximately ninety-five riddles still remaining in the *Exeter Book*.[13] The presence of the implement trope in *Þragbysig* is thus a potentially important clue, for it provides a context that limits the number of meanings allowed by its ambiguous language. That is, the implement trope may direct us toward the tangible, domestic solutions that are, in fact, most popular among modern riddle-solvers. However, *Þragbysig* turns the trope one more time: while other riddles may play with the hierarchy between a tool and a user, sometimes even having lords serve their servants,[14] here we have a riddle-subject that has both a lord (a user?) and a thegn (a tool?). Even an experienced riddle-solver, who has successfully unravelled the relationships in those other riddles, is unlikely to find that by recognising the implement trope they unveil *Þragbysig*'s solution. Indeed, the apparent presence of the trope may be a red herring, a false trail.

A second recognisable trope in *Þragbysig* is imprisonment.[15] Imprisonment is mentioned twice in the text: the subject claims that it is *hringum hæfted* ('confined in—or with, or by—rings') (2a) and that a *gebundenne bæg* ('bound ring') (8a) sometimes breaks. To interpret these phrases, we can look at the method or mode of discussing imprisonment in a number of other *Exeter Book* riddles. Often, the binding refers to an aspect of construction, as, for example, it does for the *beona hyf* ('beehive') of *Mundbora* (R.17), the *sulh* ('plough') of *Neol ic Fere* (R.21), or the *boga* ('bow') of *Agof* (R.23).[16] Sometimes the imprisonment is literal, as, for example, it is for the Welsh male slaves tied by leather bonds in *Fotum Ic Fere* (R.12) or the *cipe* ('onion') boxed by the churl's daughter in *Staþol min is Steapheah* (R.25).[17] Sometimes the imprisonment is both literal and metaphorical, as it is for the *sweord* ('sword') of *Wæpnum Awyrged* (R.20), which is both confined within a scabbard and bound by its loyalty to its lord, and for the *wind* ('wind') in *Min Frea Fæste Genearwað* (R.3), which is both confined beneath the earth and restrained by its lord's command. The key thing to note here is that the trope of imprisonment can indicate rather different things. In *Þragbysig*, therefore, references to imprisonment could suggest that the riddle-subject is manufactured, literally imprisoned, or held in place by a sense of loyalty transferred via anthropomorphism from the human social world. That is, once again, recognising the trope does not reduce its ambiguity.

A third trope potentially shared by *Þragbysig* and other members of the *Exeter Book* collection is the method or mode of representing an inanimate object as a person with limited intelligence or abilities. Once again, this trope is common enough. For example, in *Wæpnum Awyrged* (R.20), the *sweord* ('sword') fails to answer the woman's verbal attack because it is *dol* ('foolish') in its trappings (32a); in *Torht Wiga* (R.50), the *lig* ('fire') is born from *dumbum* *twam* ('two dumb ones') (2b), steel and flint; in *Eardfæst* (R.49), the riddle-object—usually taken to be an *ofen* ('oven') or *boc-fodder* ('bookcase')—is *deafne, dumban* ('deaf and dumb') (2a); and in *Anfotu* (R.58), the **rad rod* ('well-sweep') cannot walk, ride, fly, drink, or eat. A riddle-solver might therefore interpret the *med-wisum men* ('foolish man') (10a) not as a literal reference to a dull-witted goad-boy, bell-ringer, or water-bearer but rather as meiosis (understatement) for a non-sentient, inanimate object. In addition, the riddle-subject later asserts that it is pleased *þær wiht wite* ('if [it] were to know anything') (11a); if this puzzling statement means that the riddle-subject does *not* know anything and therefore cannot feel pleasure, this line may support the assumption that the subject of *Þragbysig*, too, is an inanimate object. Yet, as I have already mentioned, most modern solvers assume that the stupid servant is the animate, *human* user of an inanimate object. This is not impossible: *Fotum Ic Fere* (R.12) refers to a human being, a Welsh serving girl, as being *dol* ('foolish') (9a). However, whereas the complex intertwining of race, gender, and class in *Fotum Ic Fere* provides a context for such an insult to her intelligence,[18] in *Þragbysig* an accusation of stupidity seems unmotivated unless an inanimate object is intended. The point here is that *Þragbysig* seems to use the familiar trope of the limited inanimate object, but that trope, far from restricting or defining the text's meaning, renders it ambiguous.

Although there may well be hints of other tropes in this brief text, the final trope that I would like to consider is the method or mode used in the riddles to describe writing as paradoxical speech. For example, in *Hring butan Tungan* (R.48), a riddle about an inscribed *husel-disc* ('paten'),[19] we hear *endean / torhtne butan tungan* ('a bright ring speaking without a tongue') (1b–2a); in *Hring Gylden* (R.59), the inscribed chalice *word æfter cwæð* ('spoke a word back') to those gazing upon it and *hælend nemde / tillfremmendra* ('named the healer of those who do good') (5b, 6b–7a); and in *Be Sonde Muðlease* (R.60) the reed (used as either a writing implement or the material upon which a text is inscribed) *muðleas sprecan* ('speaks mouthless') (9b) to those sitting on the mead-bench. In *Þragbysig* we have a subject that 'announces' (3b) what its lord has done and 'replies' (7a) to those who greet it. There is no reference to silence here, but, as noted above, the text's last lines seem to cast doubt on the riddle-subject's ability to tell its own story in words, for the use of the subjunctive and *þær* mark the conclusion of the riddle as a clause of rejected conditions.[20] That is, the riddling speaker says, 'This *would* be agreeable to me, *if* I were able to know anything and say my story successfully in words' (10b–12)—with the implication that this actually means: 'because I am insentient, I am not able to know or say anything, and so this situation is neither agreeable nor disagreeable to me'. Although it has been solved as a writing implement before,[21] I do not think that this hint of paradoxical speech indicates that *Þragbysig* is a riddle about literacy. Indeed, the paradox here probably belongs to the trope of the inanimate object discussed above, rather than the trope of speech. Once again, however, the point is that a good riddle-solver, one who has successfully answered riddles from the *Exeter Book* or the Anglo-Latin riddling tradition before, will find in *Þragbysig* tropes that she has seen before, but those tropes prove to be unreliable guides to a solution. Indeed, a significant part of the game played by *Þragbysig* seems to be the thwarting of the tropes that it contains. To solve this riddle, we need to do something different with these tropes. We need to look farther afield.

Looking farther afield

It is unsurprising that many of the solutions—flail, handmill, bucket, plough-team—previously presented for *Þragbysig* have come from agricultural contexts, since many of the *Exeter Book* riddles seem to work best when answered with specific, physical objects. However, 'many' is not the same as 'all'. *Giest in Geardum* (R.43) is almost universally interpreted as a spiritual allegory of *gæst ond lic-hama* ('soul and body'), for example, and *Ymbhwyrft* (R.40), *Mare þonne Middangeard* (R.66), and (probably) *Hyrre þonne Heafon* (R.94) attempt to convey the immensity of the created world (*Creatura*) as a whole.[22] It is plausible, therefore, that we might find a context for the riddle-subject of *Þragbysig* by looking beyond the domestic and agricultural worlds.

For the rest of this chapter I shall attempt to read this short text through a different frame of reference: astronomy. I have chosen astronomy, as opposed to architecture, geometry, medicine, or another learned discipline, for two reasons. The first is *breahtme*, with its hint that we should be thinking about light or time as opposed to noise. The second is the rings, the *hringum* (2a), *halswriþan* (4a), and *gebundenne bæg* (8a). Rings do appear in other riddles in the *Exeter Book*, including two that I have already mentioned—*Hring butan Tungan* (R.48) and *Hring Gylden* (R.59)—but most modern critics do not consider these rings to be the kind that one might wear on their fingers.[23] Indeed, the 'rings' in these two texts seem to indicate a line traced around the object's exterior shape. That is, if these two riddles have been solved correctly as *husel-disc* 'paten' and *calic* 'chalice', what we learn from them is that a *hring* may, in fact, be a circle.[24]

For early medieval thinkers, the sky was scored with circles. Twelfth-century illustrations accompanying Macrobius' *Commentarii in Somnium Scipionis* and Isidore's *De natura rerum*, for example, present the earth enclosed in the circular orbits of the zodiac and the seven planets.[25] Although these illustrations post-date the *Exeter Book*, the ideas presented by the image are much older and can be found widely in the texts that were the main source for the discipline of Astronomy in early medieval England. For example, Macrobius' fifth-century *Commentarii in Somnium Scipionis* describes the spheres, lines, cycles, and subdivisions into which the heavens are divided;[26] in Martianus Capella's fifth-century *De nuptiis Philologiae et Mercurii*, Geometry holds a model of the universe adorned with its complex pattern of circles, zones, and constellations;[27] and Isidore's great seventh-century encyclopaedia, the *Etymologiae*, has two chapters on the circles of heaven.[28] Perhaps most importantly, we can observe the idea of a sky marked with circles in the influential and widely distributed works of the Venerable Bede.[29] The familiar image of the earth surrounded by circles appears in a diagram accompanying the text of his early eighth-century *De natura rerum*,[30] for example, and chapter 34 of his *De temporum ratione* is replete with circles.[31]

If *Þragbysig*'s repeated references to rings do indicate that we should be turning our eyes to a sky imagined as being inscribed with circles, what is its subject? It could be the sun—the sun as seen through the eyes of a student of Isidore, Boethius, and Bede. As I have already noted, to be convincing any solution must explain the following: the relationship between subject, thegn, and lord; the identity and multiplicity of the rings; the breaking of the bed; the warm limb; the ideas of speaking and answering; and the foolishness of the thegn. I shall address each of these, along with the key instances of ambiguous language, in turn.

Subject—thegn—lord

The three-way relationship that is so puzzling in the context of implements like buckets and bells makes good sense in the context of astronomy. The speaker is the sun, its thegn or servant is

Mercury, and its lord is God. Macrobius, Martianus Capella, and Bede all note the proximity of Mercury to the sun;[32] in the language of the riddle, at dawn the sun closely follows—or *hyran georne* ('precisely obeys') (2b)—its attendant as it climbs into the sky. The same could, of course, be said of Venus, the more famous Morning (or Evening) Star. We might assume that Venus, the quintessentially female goddess of love, is ruled out by the reference later in the riddle to the *medwisum men* ('foolish man') (10a), but the riddles play complicated games with grammatical gender,[33] and, in fact, the Old English *Metres of Boethius* present Venus, in just this kind of context, with masculine pronouns: God *genedest þone / þæt he þære sunnan sið bewitige* ('impels him [Venus] so that he guides the sun's journey') (*Metre 4*, 15–16). However, the foolishness of this 'man' suggests some additional reasons for choosing Mercury rather than Venus, which I shall address later in this discussion, and so I shall persist with Mercury even though initially Venus suits the context equally well. In the meantime, it is useful to note that imagining this trio of sun, Mercury, and God allows the ambiguous term, *þragbysig*, to come into focus. Rather than referring to a singular event or a continuous state, in this context we can see the word as referring to the reliable return of the sun each day: to be *þragbysig* is to be 'periodically busy'.

Imprisonment

The illustration accompanying Bede's scientific text *De natura rerum* presents the earth surrounded by the rings traced by the circling planets; the sun, which occupies the fourth ring from the earth, is encircled and locked in by rings on both sides. This image of the universe thus provides a useful way to think about the riddle-subject of *Þragbysig,* which is *hringum hæfted* ('locked in rings') (2a): rather than being a reference to a method of manufacturing, the phrase indicates a literal, if abstract, imprisonment. Although it is possible that the *halswriþan* two lines later is just another way of referring to these same encircling rings, I believe that this different terminology refers to a different kind of imprisonment. The *Metres of Boethius* supply an image that speaks specifically of it. In *Metre 13*, Wisdom tells us:

> Hafað swa geheaðorad heofona wealdend,
> utan befangen ealla gesceafta,
> geræped mid his racentan, þæt hi aredian ne magon
> þæt hi hi æfre him of aslepen. (6–9)

[The ruler of heaven has shut in [and] surrounded from the outside all creations—he has fettered [them] with his chain so that they cannot find a way by which they might ever escape from him.]

This passage reiterates what had been stressed earlier, in *Metre 11*, in which the poet refers repeatedly to God's *bridle* ('bridle') and *gewealdleðer* ('controlling leathers'),[34] and this context allows us to think about *Þragbysig*'s *halswriþan* in a more focused way. It is not simply another 'ring' but rather the control and order imposed on the heavenly spheres by God. Once again, reading *Þragbysig* in the context of astronomy allows the ambiguous language of the text to fall into place, for thinking about the sun and its periodic arrival suggests that the connotations of *breahtme* (3b) that pertain to time and even, perhaps, to light are most appropriate here. In fact, the idea of light might lead us to another image for the *halswriþan* in Bede's *De temporum ratione*:

Undique gyrum caeli rotundissium per lineam zodiaci circuli, quasi per zonam quondam amplissimae spherae circumdatam distincti ordines gemmarum xii sese invicem contingentium obsident.[35]

[[The twelve signs of the zodiac] surround the circuit of the sky, most round on every side, with the line of the zodiacal circle, as if [they were] separate rows of twelve gems, one after another, placed on a belt around the largest of spheres.]

A gem-studded belt might indeed be a *halswriþan*. The ability of the astronomical context to flesh out and make specific the ambiguous language of this text is its greatest strength. However, a riddle's solution must not only illuminate one instance of ambiguous language in the text; it must match up comfortably with *all* its language. As previous attempts to solve *Þragbysig* have shown, this is a serious challenge.

Winter-cold

In my reading, *Þragbysig* presents a scenario in which men and women get up grumpily to greet the sun, which, following Mercury, brightly (*breahtme*) comes to meet them at dawn. If, like me, you are not a morning person, it may seem completely natural for a man or woman to be *gromheort* ('grim-hearted') early in the morning, but it is less natural to think of the sun as *winterceald* ('winter-cold'). However, in a recent article Chad Schrock investigates the Old English stereotype of the miserable time of dawn and notes that 'not once does *Beowulf* associate dawn or morning with a warming effect'; 'morning always brings light, but in these northern climes, it may not be able to accompany that light with heat'.[36] On a cold winter day, then, the early morning sun may indeed be *winterceald*. Its lack of heat may account for the sour mood of those rising at dawn.

Sleep-weary

It would seem logical that it would be the grumpy men and women greeting the winter sun who would be 'sleep-weary', but in fact the singular, accusative ending on the adjective (*slæpwerigne*) indicates that it is the riddle-subject who is weary from sleep—or, as is usually assumed, from lack of sleep. Although the sun seems to rise fresh and new every morning, some people in early medieval England were aware that, in fact, the sun also labours through the night. In the prose dialogue, *Adrian and Ritheus*, the location of the sun during nocturnal hours is stated to be:

> on þrim stowum; ærest on þæs hwales innoðe þe is cweden Leuiathan and on oðre tid heo scynð on helle and þa ðridda tid heo scynð on þam ealond þæt is Glið nemned, and þar restað haligra manna saula oð domesdæig.[37]
>
> [in three places: first in the belly of the whale that is named Leviathan, and in the second time it shines in hell, and in the third time it shines on the island that is named Glith, and there the souls of holy people rest until Judgement Day.]

The idea that the task allotted to the sun is demanding and potentially tiring is also hinted at in section 56 of the *Prose Solomon and Saturn*:

> Hwi scyneð heo swa reade on morgene. Ic þe secge, for ðon hyre twynað hwæðer heo mæg þe ne mæg þisne myddaneard eondscynan swa hyre beboden ys.[38]
>
> [Why does [the sun] shine so red in the morning? I tell you, [it is] because it is doubtful to her that she will be able to shine throughout this world as is commanded to her.]

These brief references provide some explanation for why the sun might be seen as weary as it rises in the morning.

Breaking the bed

In contemporary English it is not unusual to speak of the sun breaking over the horizon, but generally no bed is involved. There is a reference in the Bible, however, that may bring the rest of the language of this phrase into focus. In the Old English version of Psalm 19.4–5 we hear: *Seo sunne arist swiðe ær on morgen up, swa swa brydguma of his brydbure*[39] ('The sun arises very early in the morning, just like a bridegroom from his wedding bower]. This is an image which strongly suggests, even if it does not explicitly mention, a bed. The image of the light of the sun breaking through its resting place may also underlie the puzzling reference to the bursting of the 'warm limb'.

The warm limb

The use of 'limb' to refer to 'the edge of the disk of a heavenly body, especially of the sun and moon' is tempting in this context, but this meaning of the word dates back only to 1676,[40] and so the early medieval poet probably had something else in mind. I think that the 'limb' breaking through the bound rings refers to rays—what Isidore calls a 'crest' or 'mane':

> Hic proprie et 'iubar' dicitur eo quod iubas lucis effundat, sed et splendor solis ac lunae et stellarum 'iubar' vocatur, quod in modum iubae radii ipsorum extendantur.[41]
>
> [[Venus] is properly called 'brightness', because it pours out a mane of light, but the splendour of the sun, moon, and stars is also called 'radiance', because their rays are extended in the manner of a mane.]

The *wearm lim* ('warm limb') bursting through the *gebundenne bæg* ('bound ring') is thus a learned reference combined with personal observation: it is an image created by superimposing the idea of a sky marked with invisible circles upon an actual dazzling dawn. Unless the time between the initial arrival of the sun and the shining of the rays brings a slight increase in temperature, however, it is still puzzling that the ray bursting from the *winterceald* sun should be *wearm* ('warm') (7).

The foolish man

There is, however, a very good explanation for the *medwisum men* ('the foolish [or: only somewhat wise] man') (10a) who serves as the sun's thegn. As previously mentioned, the reference to a 'man' here undermines the otherwise natural assumption that the sun's attendant would be the planet named after the female goddess, Venus. The foolishness, however, is important, for it makes the connection with Mercury as opposed to Venus specifically meaningful. The pagan god, Mercury, was very widely associated with wisdom. For example, Isidore, in his overview of the pagan gods, links Mercury to speech, trickery, persuasion, interpretation, knowledge, and intelligence.[42] Byrhtferth notes that *Hig wende, ure yldran, þæt hig hæfdon gast of þære sunnan and lichaman of þam monan and andgyt of Mercurio* ('our ancestors believed that the spirit came from the sun and the body from the moon and understanding from Mercury').[43] The *Prose Solomon and Saturn* and *Adrian and Ritheus* both identify 'Mercury the Giant' as the one who first wrote letters, the 'deity appropriately associated with travelling and wit'.[44] At the same time, of course, Christian writers are scathing about the wisdom and power of pagan gods. The *medwisum men* ('the only somewhat wise man') (10a) is thus an ironic reference to Mercury, the god who supposedly gave writing to the Egyptians. The planet shining in the sky that bears his name is similarly deficient in wisdom.

Wisdom and writing return us once again to the final two and a half lines of the riddle and the idea of speaking and answering. Although the sun might demonstrate its subservience to the order of God by its regular rising and setting,[45] and although it might 'greet' those who get up at dawn, the sun is not a sentient creature that can tell its own story. More importantly, like other heavenly bodies, the sun also cannot 'tell' in another way. That is, these final lines, with their clause of rejected conditions, refer to the use of the heavenly bodies for foretelling the future—another thing that good Christians are not supposed to do. Isidore, for example, pours scorn on predictions based on astrology,[46] and Byrhtferth rejects the *ealdra witan ungewitt* ('foolishness of old philosophers') who rely on such wisdom[47]—although he still includes the astrological signs in his wonderful diagram.[48] At the end of *Þragbysig*, then, the sun, although endowed with a voice by prosopopoeia, correctly denies that it and its attendant know anything.

Conclusion

Any solution for *Þragbysig* must bring the text's ambiguous language into focus; explain the relationship between subject, thegn, and lord; identify the rings; explain the breaking of the bed and the action of the warm limb; attend to the ideas of speaking and answering; and justify the foolishness of the thegn. The text's frustratingly artful use of riddling tropes has defied scholarly efforts for generations, but in the context of the learned discipline of astronomy, with its attendant idea of divine order, these words and tropes become meaningful in a new way. Thus, we may see here the sun, imprisoned by the *halswriþan* of its loyal subservience to God and encircled by the trails of planetary orbits (*hringum*)—an image familiar from diagrams accompanying the works of Bede. Despite the nightly labours that leave it *slæpwerig*, the sun brightly (*breahtme*) departs from its rising point (*bed*) at its appointed time (*þragbysig*), attended by its *þegn*, the planet Mercury. Its radiance (*wearm lim*) bursts across the imagined lines scoring the sky (*gebundenne bæg*), but the *winterceald* sun brings no heat to those who greet it (*gromheort*). If the sun and Mercury were deities with the power to foretell the future as gullible pagans used to believe, they would be pleased with themselves for this action, but *Þragbysig*'s speaker knows better: Mercury, despite its long-standing association with wisdom and intelligence, is foolish (*medwis*). Neither sun nor planet is able to tell its own story—except here, where the anthropomorphism of the riddle form ironically allows the *sunna* ('sun') to tell us that it cannot speak, and also in the next text but one in the manuscript, for in *Ic Cwice Bærne* (R.6) we hear the sun's voice again. If this reading is correct, *Þragbysig* turns out to be not such a radical change in the cosmological scale established by the opening sequence of storm riddles after all. Instead, it is a continuation of the *Exeter Book* collection's musing on the *rerum … enigmata* ('mysteries of things'), starting, as Aldhelm did, from the top.[49]

Notes

1 The *belle* 'bell' solution, which has received the most support, was first proposed by Franz Dietrich, 'Die Rätsel des Exeterbuchs: Würdigung, Lösung und Herstellung', *Zeitschrift für deutsches Altertum*, 11 (1859), 448–90, at p. 461. A significant number of scholars have preferred, however, Dietrich's second solution, *cweorn-stan* 'millstone'; see 'Die

Räthsel des Exeterbuch: Verfasser, Weitere Losungen', *Zeitschrift für Deutsches Altertum und Deutsche Literatur*, 7 (1865), 232–52, at p. 239. For *licwiglung* 'necromancy', see Henry Bradley, 'Two Riddles of the Exeter Book', *Modern Language Review*, 6 (1911), 433–40, at pp. 435–6. For *þerscel* 'flail', see Moritz Trautmann, ed., *Die altenglischen rätsel* (Heidelberg: Carl Winter, 1915), pp. 68–9; this solution has also received more recent support in Hans Pinsker and Waltraud Ziegler, eds, *Die altenglischen Ratsel des Exeterbuchs: Text mit deutscher Ubersetzung und Kommentar* (Heidelberg: Carl Winter, 1985), pp. 153–5. For *loc* 'lock', see Ferdinand Holthausen, 'Zu altenglischen denkmälern', *Englische Studien*, 51 (1917), 180–8. For **hand-mylen* 'handmill', see Ferdinand Holthausen, 'Zu altenglischen Dichtungen', *Anglia*, 44 (1920), 345–56; Erika von Erhardt-Siebold, 'Old English Riddle No. 4: Handmill', *PMLA*, 61 (1946), 620–3. For *feðer* or *penna* 'pen', see Laurence K. Shook, 'Riddles Relating to the Anglo-Saxon Scriptorium', in *Essays in Honour of Anton Charles Pegis*, ed. J. Reginald O'Donnell (Toronto: Pontifical Institute of Mediaeval Studies, 1974), pp. 215–36, at pp. 227–8. For 'phallus', see Gregory K. Jember, 'An Interpretive Translation of the Exeter Riddles', unpublished PhD thesis (University of Denver, 1975), p. 72. For *wæter stoppa* 'bucket', see Ann Harleman Stewart, 'The Solution to Old English Riddle 4', *Studies in Philology*, 78 (1981), 52–61; this solution has been further developed by A. N. Doane, 'Three Old English Implement Riddles: Reconsiderations of Numbers 4, 49, and 73', *MP*, 84 (1987), 243–57, at pp. 245–9; John D. Niles, *Old English Enigmatic Poems and the Play of the Texts* (Turnhout: Brepols, 2006), p. 144. For *weard-hund* 'guard-dog', see Ray Brown, 'The Exeter Book's Riddle 2: A Better Solution', *English Language Notes*, 29 (1991), 1–4. For *deofol* 'devil', see Melanie Heyworth, 'The Devil's in the Detail: A New Solution to Exeter Book Riddle 4', *Neophilologus*, 91 (2007), 175–96. For *sulh-team* 'plough-team', see Shannon Ferri Cochran, 'The Plough's the Thing: A New Solution to Old English Riddle 4 of the Exeter Book', *JEGP*, 108 (2009), 301–9. For *sweord* 'sword', see Corinne Dale, 'A New Solution to Exeter Book Riddle 4', *N&Q*, 64 (2017), 1–3. For 'city gate', see Andrew Breeze, 'Exeter Book Riddles 4 and 43: City Gate and Guardian Angel', *Devon and Cornwall Notes and Queries* (forthcoming).

2 For an outline of the metrical and grammatical problems in lines 7–8, for example, see Craig Williamson, ed., *The Old English Riddles of the Exeter Book* (Chapel Hill: University of North Carolina Press, 1977), pp. 144–5.

3 Jennifer Neville, 'The Unexpected Treasure of the Implement Trope: Hierarchical Relationships in the Old English Riddles', *RES*, 62.256 (2011), 505–19.

4 For a strong argument for a single, long riddle and an overview of previous editorial practices, see Williamson, *Old English Riddles*,

pp. 127–33. Many subsequent scholars have supported Williamson's view. See, for example, Michael Lapidge, 'Stoic Cosmology and the Source of the First Old English Riddle', *Anglia*, 112 (1994), 1–25 and the discussion by Paz (Chapter 11) in this volume.

5 These markers of text boundaries can easily be viewed in a facsimile of the manuscript. See Raymond W. Chambers, Max Förster, and Robin Flower, eds, *The Exeter Book of Old English Poetry* (London: Percy Lund, 1933); Bernard J. Muir, ed., *The Exeter Anthology of Old English Poetry: The Exeter DVD*, with software by Nick Kennedy (Exeter: Exeter University Press, 2006).

6 For the implement trope, see Doane, 'Three Old English Implement Riddles', p. 243; Neville, 'Unexpected Treasure', pp. 506–8; and further discussion below.

7 Three further solutions, Heyworth's devil, Dale's sword, and Breeze's city-gate, are worth considering and have different strengths and weaknesses, but there is not space to address them here.

8 See the range of possibilities offered for the adverbial use of *þrag* in B-T.

9 *DOE*, *s.v. bearhtm*. Cf. also B-T *s.v. bearhtm*.

10 *DOE*, *s.v. bearhtme*.

11 Cf. the nine occurrences of *beorht-hwil* 'moment, instant' listed in the *DOE*.

12 *OED*, *s.v.* trope.

13 See Neville, 'Unexpected Treasure', pp. 506–7.

14 See discussion in Neville, 'Unexpected Treasure'.

15 Cf. Jerry Denno, 'Oppression and Voice in Anglo-Saxon Riddle Poems', *CEA Critic*, 70.1 (2007), 35–47.

16 Cf. discussion of 'structural binding' in Megan Cavell, *Weaving Words and Binding Bodies: The Poetics of Human Experience in Old English Literature* (Toronto: University of Toronto Press, 2016), pp. 68–91.

17 Cf. discussion of slavery and servitude in Cavell, *Weaving Words*, pp. 157–91.

18 See John W. Tanke, '*Wonfeax Wale*: Ideology and Figuration in the Sexual Riddles of the Exeter Book', in *Class and Gender in Early English Literature: Intersections*, ed. Britton J. Harwood and Gillian R. Overing (Bloomington: Indiana University Press, 1994), pp. 21–42.

19 Megan Cavell, 'Powerful Patens in the Anglo-Saxon Medical Tradition and Exeter Book Riddle 48', *Neophilologus*, 101 (2017), 129–38.

20 See Bruce Mitchell and Fred C. Robinson, eds, *A Guide to Old English*, 8th edn (Oxford: Blackwell, 2012), p. 97 for Clauses of Condition, type 3: unfulfilled or rejected or imaginary conditions (§179).

21 See discussion in Shook, 'Riddles Relating to the Anglo-Saxon Scriptorium'.

22 For a full examination of the Creation riddle, see Erin Sebo, *In Enigmate: The History of a Riddle, 450–1500* (Dublin: Four Courts Press, 2018).

23 The exception is Elisabeth Okasha, who does solve these two texts as finger rings. See 'Old English *Hring* in Riddles 48 and 59', *MÆ*, 62 (1993), 61–9.

24 For an overview of the eleven shades of meaning that may be attributed to *hring*, see Okasha, 'Old English *Hring*', p. 64.

25 Copenhagen, Det Kongelige Bibliotek, ms. NKS 218 4°, fol. 25r; the digitised image is available online: http://www.kb.dk/permalink/2006/manus/33/eng/25+recto/ (accessed 1 February 2019). Oxford, Bodleian Library, St John's MS 17, fol. 37v; the digitised image is available online: https://digital.bodleian.ox.ac.uk/inquire/p/b9508b65-b35c-4176-a9d3-e4069d55246e (accessed 1 February 2019).

26 Ambrosius Theodosius Macrobius, *Opera Volume 2: Commentarii in Somnium Scipionis*, ed. Jacob Willis (Leipzig: Teubner, 1963), 1.15, pp. 61–4; William Harris Stahl, trans., *Macrobius: Commentary on the Dream of Scipio* (New York: Columbia University Press, 1952), pp. 148–52.

27 Martianus Capella, *Martianus Capella*, ed. James Willis (Leipzig: Teubner, 1983), 6.583, p. 205; William Harris Stahl, Richard Johnson, and E. L. Burge, trans., *Martianus Capella and the Seven Liberal Arts, Vol II. The Marriage of Philology and Mercury* (New York: Columbia University Press, 1977), p. 219.

28 Isidore of Seville, *Etymologiarum sive Originum Libri XX*, ed. W. M. Lindsay, 2 vols (Oxford: Clarendon, 1911), I, 3.44–5, p. 152; Stephen A. Barney, W. J. Lewis, J. A. Beach, and Oliver Berghof, trans., *The Etymologies of Isidore of Seville* (Cambridge: Cambridge University Press, 2006), p. 101.

29 Bede's two main works on time survive in 333 manuscripts. See Faith Wallis, trans., *Bede: The Reckoning of Time* (Liverpool: Liverpool University Press, 1999), p. lxxvi.

30 Bodleian MS Canon. Misc. 560, fol. 23r. The digitised image is available online: https://digital.bodleian.ox.ac.uk/inquire/p/3c55d54c-8080-480b-a6f2-2f7000985796 (accessed 12 April 2019).

31 Bede, *Beda Venerabilis. De temporum ratione liber*, ed. Charles W. Jones, CCSL, 123B (Turnhout: Brepols, 1977), 34.1–75, pp. 244–6 (hereafter *DTR*). For translation see Wallis, *Bede*, pp. 96–9.

32 Macrobius 1.17, p. 67; for translation, see Stahl, *Commentary*, p. 155. Martianus Capella 1.8, p. 5; for translation, see Stahl, *Marriage*, p. 8. Bede, *DTR*, 8.46–8, p. 197; for translation, see Wallis, *Bede*, p. 34.

33 For discussion of the games that riddles might play with grammatical gender, see Elena Afros, 'Linguistic Ambiguities in Some Exeter Book Riddles', *N&Q*, n.s. 52 (2005), 431–7; Niles, *Old English Enigmatic Poems*, pp. 36–7; see also the discussions of grammatical gender in

Chapters 3, 7, and 10 (by Cavell, Wilcox, and Dale) in this volume. 'Sun' itself, although more commonly feminine, can also be a masculine noun.

34 See Metres 11.23a, 24a, 28a, 29a, 75a, 76a, and 79a.

35 *DTR* 16.23–5, p. 213.

36 Chad Schrock, 'Light without Heat: *Beowulf*'s Epistemological Morning', *ES*, 97.1 (2016), 1–14, at p. 3, n. 11, and at p. 12. Note also the earlier discussion of this topic in Elizabeth Deering Hanscom, 'The Feeling for Nature in Old English Poetry', *JEGP*, 5 (1903–5), 439–63.

37 James E. Cross and Thomas D. Hill, eds, *The Prose Solomon and Saturn and Adrian and Ritheus* (Toronto: University of Toronto Press, 1982), p. 36. *Gliþ* is probably a scribal error for *gliw* 'joy'.

38 Cross and Hill, *Prose Solomon*, p. 34.

39 Patrick P. O'Neill, ed., *King Alfred's Old English Prose Translation of the First Fifty Psalms* (Cambridge, MA: Medieval Academy of America, 2001), p. 120. The Old English translation of the psalm is numbered 18, and this passage comes in verse 6.

40 *OED*, *s.v.* 'limb'.

41 Isidore, *Etymologiarum* I, 3.71.18, p. 161; for translation see Barney, *et al.*, *Etymologies*, p. 105.

42 Isidore, *Etymologiarum* I, 8.11.45–9, p. 334; for translation see Barney, *et al.*, *Etymologies*, p. 186.

43 Peter S. Baker and Michael Lapidge, eds and trans, *Byrhtferth's Enchiridion*, EETS ss, 15 (Oxford: Oxford University Press, 1995), 2.3.221–5, p. 118.

44 Daniel Anlezark, ed., *The Old English Dialogues of Solomon and Saturn* (Cambridge: D. S. Brewer, 2009), p. 13.

45 Cf. Psalm 19.1–4, in which the heavens silently tell of God's power.

46 Isidore, *Etymologiarum* I, 3.71.37–9, p. 164; for translation see Barney, *et al.*, *Etymologies*, p. 106.

47 Byrhtferth, *Enchiridion* 2.3.224, p. 118.

48 The diagram is reproduced in Baker and Lapidge, *Byrhtferth's Enchiridion*. A facsimile of the manuscript (Oxford, Bodleian Library, St John's MS 17, fol. 7v) is available online: https://digital.bodleian.ox.ac.uk/inquire/p/688e1e71-6e0e-4153-8d94-1f9c34058c86 (accessed 12 April 2019).

49 Aldhelm's verse preface to his *Enigmata* (7–8), in Rudolf Ehwald, ed., *Aldhelmi Opera*, MGH, Auctores Antiquissimi, 15 (Berlin: Weidmann, 1919), pp. 97–9.

2

Wundor and *wrætlic*: the anatomy of wonder in the sex riddles

Sharon E. Rhodes

Riddles alter their audiences' perceptions of familiar objects and phenomena through precisely true yet entirely foreign descriptions. The novel perspective of such descriptions—such as the voice of an inanimate object or a speaker looking down on something that most speakers look up at—disguises the object of description. We can accuse riddles of a topsy-turvy inversion of high and low subject matter or of falsely raising the low to the level of the high through so-called inappropriate diction. However, we can also read riddles as meditations, albeit often humorous ones. These short poems force readers to meditate on the wonders of the natural and constructed worlds, such as in the shortest Exeter riddle, *Wundor Wearð on Wege* (R.69), which reads simply *Wundor wearð on wege—wæter wearð to bane* ('There was a wonder on the road—water became bone'). Patrick J. Murphy maintains that this riddle cannot be solved with certainty but concedes that the answer 'must involve ice'.[1] However, Murphy also points out that scholars resist simple solutions and instead reach for 'dramatic answers to match the outlandish descriptions' of the riddles. Thus, while 'the current favourite solution' to *Wundor Wearð on Wege* is 'iceberg', Murphy prefers the 'simple icicle'. The dramatic changes in properties that water undergoes in the phase shift from liquid to solid are, however common, wondrous. Other simple answers, too, are wondrous and, in turn, highlight the wondrous power of language to obscure and reveal simultaneously, or, as Murphy says, '[t]his sense of the miraculous in the mundane is at the heart of the Old English riddling tradition'.[2] This interpretation of the essence of the riddle genre holds not only for the more serious riddles but also for the humorous sex riddles: *Womb wæs on Hindan* (R.37), *Wrætlic Hongað* (R.44), *Banleas* (R.45), and *In Wincsele* (R.54). Each of these riddles can be solved in at least two ways—by a polite answer and an obscene one—forcing the audience to take note of the wonders implied by both readings, even as they may laugh and blush at the implicit comparison. Although scholarly reactions to these riddles have ranged from intense disapproval to religious allegorical readings, the *double entendre* riddles—in each of their answers—focus our attention on the foundations of society that English literary discourse so often ignores, whether the ins and outs of sexual intercourse or the hard, manual labour that goes into the production of bread and butter.

Before we turn to the riddles themselves, we might stop to wonder about wonder itself and the cultural work that it does. In his essay 'Resonance and Wonder', Stephen Greenblatt defines the phenomenon of wonder as something that causes us literally to stop in our tracks by 'evok[ing] an exalted attention.'[3] In the same essay Greenblatt goes on to discuss the role of wonder in the work of the poet. No doubt the poems we cherish most cultivate a sense of wonder. However, the Old English riddles stand out by cultivating a sense of wonder, in many cases, in what is not preconceived as wonderful. Rather than painting a wondrous linguistic portrait of a battlefield or a saint-wrought miracle, riddles cultivate wonder in, as Murphy says, the everyday, the mundane, or even the disdained. Caroline Walker Bynum picked up on this issue of mundanity in her 1997 American Historical Association Presidential Address, 'Wonder.' In this instance, Bynum uses the concept of wonder and a study of the wonders and marvels of the Middle Ages to help us resist the presentist habit of 'flattening the past'.[4] That is, since past cultures, like present ones, comprise complex and disparate human experiences, modern scholarship must avoid thinking of the past in monolithic terms. Working from the French wall slogan that she translates as 'Every view of things that is not strange [i.e. bizarre or foreign] is false', Bynum argues that when we assume that we understand something rather than wondering at it, we inhibit our ability to fully understand it. In other words, by assuming coherent logic we undermine the value, and forget the inescapability, of the unexplained and illogical. Indeed, Bynum finds that, in texts from the later Middle Ages, 'marvelling and astonishment as reactions seem to be triggered most frequently and violently by what Bernard of Clairvaux called *admirabiles mixturae*: events or phenomena in which ontological and moral boundaries are crossed, confused, erased'.[5] Riddles give three-dimensional clarity not to a particular time or place, but to the everyday that overexposure and lack of status flattens in spite of its utility, centrality, and true wondrousness. The Old English riddles illustrate the *wundor* inherent in situations or objects that society generally fails to appreciate or even notice: pens, the way bookworms consume words without digesting them, or, as I discuss below, the generative nature of certain repetitive motions.

These unappreciated objects and phenomena gain wondrousness in the riddles through their reification, as explained by thing theory.[6] As Benjamin C. Tilghman, among others, has observed, the shift in perspective that riddles inspire and require makes them a rich subject for the application of thing theory, which posits that objects become things when broken.[7] Once they become things—that is, once they are literally reified—objects become entities with their own existences beyond human utility. Bill Brown in his foundational essay 'Thing Theory' explains that

> [w]e begin to confront the thingness of objects when they stop working for us: when the drill breaks, when the car stalls, when the windows get filthy, when their flow within the circuits of production, consumption and exhibition, has been arrested, however momentarily. The story of objects asserting themselves as things, then, is the story of a changed relation to the human subject and thus the story of how the thing really names less an object than a particular subject-object relation.[8]

In this parlance, the Exeter riddles become a literary means of breaking objects—a category which can, depending on the view of the speaker and the cultural system in play, include people, animals, ideas, acts, and the inanimate material objects of the built and natural world—into things. The difference in the riddles is that the objects themselves are not physically broken into things. Rather, it is the description of the objects that is broken, through a consummate violation of Grice's Maxim, which allows the audience to let go of the solutions' objectness and instead perceive the thingness of the solutions described in the riddles.[9] *Womb wæs on Hindan*, *Wrætlic Hongað*, *Banleas*, and *In Wincsele*, solved respectively (and decorously) as 'bellows', 'key', 'bread dough', and 'butter churn', verbally break their decorous answers into things, while at the same time forcing us to reconsider our preconceptions of their obscene answers. These riddles are particularly ripe for this analysis for two reasons. Firstly, although human sexuality is integral to human life, civilisation demands a certain degree of sexual restraint codified in different ways according to time and place. The constraints surrounding sexuality lend the topic and the act shades of shame. These sex riddles, however, humorously and innocently remove us from these constraints without challenging the nature and system of those constraints.[10] Consequently, they allow us to appreciate a serious aspect of human activity without breaking social mores. Secondly, because these riddles are *double entendres*, they emphasise the genuinely wondrous nature of their alternative and less blush-inducing answers whose generative effects are highlighted by their resemblance to their 'obscene' counterparts.

Jennifer Neville argues that the sexual riddles contain 'radical ideas pertaining to hierarchical relationships', pointing not only to the evidence within the Exeter riddles but also to Ælfric's *Catholic Homilies*.[11] For instance, in 'Feria III de Dominica Oratione', Ælfric points out that 'the powerful man who sits on his high seat will quickly be lacking his feast if his servants abandon their work'.[12] *Womb wæs on Hindan*, *Wrætlic Hongað*, *Banleas*, and *In Wincsele* not only re-evaluate hierarchical relationships; they also force us to meditate on the foundations of civilisation and re-evaluate the value of labour. Indeed, these *things*—bellows, keys, butter, and bread, for instance—are important, and they require effort and skill to produce. Most importantly, without these *things* we would be diminished in very real ways: for example, much as we are diminished by stalled cars or calculators that break in the middle of an important exam, our lives in general are made easier by the presence of cars and calculators. While the principles of modern capitalism—and perhaps human nature—encourage us to view objects as objects, discrete yet interchangeable entities, riddles ask us to wonder at their solutions as things, unique and valuable in their singularity and their roles in human life. These things are found in corners or under clothing, and are operated by boys, low-status men, and women. Yet without them the swords, feasts, and treasures of other riddles and Old English literature more generally would be impossible. By insistently resisting the reader's expectations of what merits poetic description, the riddles create space in which to appreciate the mundane and see past simple ubiquity to these things', and their makers', deep and foundational worth to society as a whole.

Womb wæs on Hindan presents us with a so-called creature (*wiht*, 1a) that possesses recognisable anatomical features such as a *womb* ('belly') (1b), an *eage* ('eye') (4b), and a *bosme* ('bosom') (7a). But it also features a clearly human operator in the form of a *þegn*. The obscene answer paints an image of a man engaging in a presumably procreative sex act. The polite answer is a bellows, which, as the riddle illustrates, possesses important animate and generative qualities in parallel to the obscene answer. Like the other *double entendre* riddles I discuss, *Womb wæs on Hindan* is told from the point of view of an outside observer:

> Ic þa wihte geseah; womb wæs on hindan
> þriþum aþrunten. þegn folgade,
> mægenrofa man, ond micel hæfde
> gefered þæt hit felde, fleah þurh his eage.
> Ne swylteð he symle, þonne syllan sceal
> innað þam oþrum, ac him eft cymeð
> bot in bosme, blæd biþ aræred;
> he sunu wyrceð, bið him sylfa fæder.

> [I saw that creature; his belly was behind violently swollen. A servant followed, a man of strength, and the great one brought forth what filled it; it flew through his eye. He does not die continually, when he must give a second belly-full, but it comes again for him an offering in [his] bosom, breath/glory is erected he creates sons, he is the father of himself.]

It is difficult to think of bellows when told that the riddle-object *micel hæfde / gefered þæt hit feld, fleah þurh his eage* ('the great one brought forth what filled it; it flew through his eye') (3b–4). Any reading of the term *eage* in this case relies on the dead metaphor of *eye* to indicate a small round hole as in the *eye of a needle*. This recognisable dead metaphor allows us easily to dismiss any answer that would suggest the visual organ in vertebrate animals. However, once we move on from literal eyes, the number of possible answers only grows. We might argue that the sense given in line 2—*þegn folgade* ('a servant followed')—invalidates the idea that the answer involves a human penis, but this ignores the many ways in which the sexual organs are socially constructed as things rather than as parts of the human self. And of course, if what flew through this eye was semen it would have the potential to make new men, themselves the possessors of penises, as well as women. *Womb wæs on Hindan* is a wonder of self-perpetuation. The gender specificity of *he*, *sunu*, and *fæder* also creates space for the argument that the riddle is referencing some masculine noun, such as *brand* ('fire, flame'), which is also self-perpetuating, rather than referencing human sexual activity.

Of course, this decorous reading is no less mysterious if we allow ourselves to wonder. The process of pumping bellows to create alternating vacuum states within and to fuel a fire with the resulting forced air is a wondrous perpetual cycle, both in the labour required and the effect on the fire's temperature. Moreover, the fires produced by bellows grow, counterintuitively, hotter with increased air, even though, in the wrong context, forcefully blown air can extinguish flames. In light of the clue that the solution does not die a permanent death but is revived to give *innað þam oþrum* ('a second belly-full') (6a), we may return to interpreting this riddle in sexual terms where *la petite mort* becomes as integral to life as oxygen is to fire. The effort involved in operating this thing is succeeded by further effort, death by life: *eft cymeð / bot in bosme* ('again comes a remedy in his breast') (6b–7a). As Murphy explains, '[t]he convention of Old English riddling is to animate inanimate objects of all kinds—to imagine the stoic endurance of a shield or the graceful flight of a feather pen—but in sex riddles this translates into a sense of anatomical autonomy as the implied sex organ works its own will'.[13] In other words, at least in this line, the wonder is not the source of the object or its work so much as its seeming inevitability. The cycles of sexual reproduction and fire production are almost self-perpetuating. They occur without the aid of human cognition, but not without human effort. While Murphy argues that such analogies 'deflate the puffed-up *blæd* ("glory" or "wind") of sexual pride and emphasise the ridiculous, awkward, and even slavish position of men and women who serve their own implements',[14] they do so by raising up such implements as a source of wonder in their thingness.

Finally, to see the wonder of the bellows, we need to recall the general wonder of a smithy—the context of bellows. This uncomplicated machine, and the simple and laborious repetitive action of the *þegn*, is literally what makes the cutting edge, that is the swords, knives, and axes, of early medieval technology, possible. The swords and treasures of elite culture depend upon this strange *wiht* ('creature') and the boy that fills its belly over and over with air. We may chuckle at the obscene answer and struggle for the polite one, but ultimately this is a succinct poem on the modes of production. By illustrating the effort taken to create and sustain a fire hot enough for metal working, *Womb wæs on Hindan* allows the audience to wonder at the tool, the bellows, and the servant working them rather than simply admiring the products. Both this lower-class human and the bellows he works are integral to the expected objects of poetic description—such as swords—but it is only through the inverted rhetoric of the riddle that we can properly marvel at the things and people working behind the scenes.

Arguably the most explicit of the obscene riddles, *Wrætlic Hongað* was called by Paull Franklin Baum 'an inferior piece, meant only for its impropriety'.[15] Yet this text, like the other sexual riddles, creates space within which to marvel at the mundane, polite answer as well as to appreciate the workings of human sexuality. *Wrætlic Hongað* explicitly describes its answer as *wrætlic* ('wondrous' or 'curious'). Unlike *Womb wæs on Hindan*, *Wrætlic Hongað* dwells on the location of the answer and suggests a degree of secrecy; yet, ultimately, like *Womb wæs on Hindan*, it forces us to think about technology and interdependency:

Wrætlic hongað bi weres þeo,
frean under sceate. Foran is þyrel.
Bið stiþ ond heard, stede hafað godne;
þonne se esne his agen hrægl
ofer cneo hefeð, wile þæt cuþe hol
mid his hangellan heafde gretan
þæt he efenlang ær oft gefylde.

[A wonder hangs by a man's thigh, under its lord's garment. In front is the opening. It is stiff and hard, it has a good place; when the man raises his own clothing over his knee, he wishes to greet that familiar hole with the head of his hanging-thing which he often filled, equally long, before.]

Despite the location of the solution in relation to the man, the hanging-thing by the *weres þeo* in this text need not be a penis. Thus, both the speaker and audience of the riddle are safe from the necessity of wondering at such a loaded piece of human anatomy.

As mentioned above, the sex riddles refuse the concept of impropriety by freely transgressing the usual constraints concerning sex without ever violating the taboo against explicit discussion of sexuality. Simultaneously, they draw parallels between what we openly talk about—such as keys—and what we do not. Baum's evaluation of *Wrætlic Hongað* fails to appreciate the technological marvel of keys as much as it fails to appreciate the marvel of sex. Admittedly, the opening lines are eyebrow-raising: *wrætlic hongað bi weres þeo / frean under sceate* ('a marvellous thing hangs by a man's thigh / under its lord's garment') (1–2). Yet, in a time and place when archaeologists have reason to believe that people really did wear long hard implements, including keys, on their belts,[16] the decorous answer is still a source of wonder: keys are impressive feats of engineering that, in the presence of the right lock, can change the state of a vessel from open to closed and back again. While a common key is not ordinarily seen as wondrous or *wrætlic*, the riddle allows us to see this object anew by rendering it as a thing. Every key—although superficially similar to every other key—is in fact a unique object with a special relationship to both an individual human being and to other objects. Moreover, the obscene ambiguity here points to the tendency for people to attribute phallic power to their tools. Or tool-like power to phalluses. Yet, because this particular tool seems to have been more often associated with women than with men, the expectation of masculine-gendered power is unmet.[17] Christine Fell, and others since her, convincingly argued that the term *locbore*, used in the laws of Æðelberht, refers not to long hair, as Bosworth and Toller define it,[18] but to responsibility for locks and, by extension, keys.[19] Fell, among others, cites II Cnut to point out the association between women, keys, and responsibility: if a woman is accused of complicity in a crime, *butan hit under þaes wifes caeglocan gebroht waere, si heo claene* ('unless it has been brought under the woman's key-lock, she is clear').[20] Citing the same law, Meaney explains the significance of keys for women and asserts that

> [t]he item perhaps most intimately connected with the life of the housewife is the key ... it was a woman's duty to keep the keys of her store-room, her chest and her cupboard: if her husband brought stolen goods home to the cottage she could not forbid it; but unless they were found under her lock and key she could not be accused as an accessory.[21]

Thus, even as the obscene solution is decisively masculine, the polite answer of *cæg* ('key') is both a feminine noun and a symbol of feminine power.

Stolen or otherwise, keys and their locks are associated with secrecy and the known/unknown. Moreover, the concealment implied by the use of cloth heightens our wonder at the wonder described in *Wrætlic Hongað*, which exists *under sceate* ('under the [man's] garment') until the man *his agen hrægl / ofer cneo hafeð* ('raises his own clothing over his knee) (4–5). The cloth is lifted, but what is underneath is an open secret, something universally known and politely ignored despite being a status symbol. It is perhaps ironic that the polite answer, 'key', was a status symbol for early medieval English women. The refusal of explicit reference both conceals and reveals. The riddle then taunts us with its intimation that the hole which the *hangellan heafde* ('head of his hanging-thing') (6) greets is *cuþe* ('known, familiar') (5b).

A hole—by definition an absence of matter rather than a material presence—is difficult to appreciate fully, particularly from the outside. Yet this one is familiar, if only to the answer that enters it. And *cuþe* ('known'), is another specifically unspecific term—sometimes made less vague in the phrase 'carnal knowing'—which refuses to name what we know it signifies, in at least one context. Moreover, it is the *cuþe hol* that allows us to solve the riddle—both ways—and without which the *hangellan* thing is meaningless. This hole is as much a part of the meditation as that which fills it, but its importance must be highlighted through circumlocutions. Keys are paired objects, or, in the terms of thing theory, keys are objects that become things in the absence of their mates: keys require a counterpart in order to serve their purpose in human life, like plugs and sockets, and genitalia.[22] Keys require the equally complex engineering feat of locks in order to serve any purpose. Lockless, a key is a useless piece of metal.

In her discussion of the marvel of sex in *Wrætlic Hongað*, Mercedes Salvador-Bello argues that this text uses 'a sensual image ... to offer ideas related to learning, spiritual life, and salvation', but that this functions via 'the allegorical interpretation of erotic imagery in the Song of Songs'.[23] The latter, of course, abounds with directions to wonder, such as verse 1.14, which says: *ecce tu pulchra es amica mea ecce tu pulchra oculi tui columbarum* ('Behold you are beautiful, my lover, behold you are beautiful [with] your doves' eyes').[24] Like the substantive adjective with which *Wrætlic Hongað* begins (*wrætlic*), *ecce* ('behold') suggests wonder at both the literal and allegorical levels. Moreover, as suggested above, *Wrætlic Hongað* is not only about keys; it is also about locks.[25] Given Salvador-Bello's allegorical reading of the 'key and lock' trope, we might surmise a mutually dependent relationship between Christ and humanity. However, leaving this allegory aside momentarily, we can stop and wonder at keys and locks which require a complex society working cooperatively to bring together raw materials and specialised tools and training. Moreover, we can marvel at the complexity of gendered power dynamics, the interdependency of the solution and the 'familiar hole', and the subtle control exerted by the generally female keeper of keys even within a patriarchal society.

A third wonder riddle, *Banleas*, adds a corner, *wincle*, to the secrecy provided only by cloth in *Wrætlic Hongað*, where the answer is hidden *under sceate*. Further, as in *Womb wæs on Hindan*, we are presented with a mixture of anatomical features and animated actions over the course of the riddle. However, despite the added privacy of the corner—which can be read as either the corner of a room or the corner of a male crotch—the answer to *Banleas* seems to be a similarly open secret. Finally, *Banleas* stands out because of the human player's female gender and the subsequent revaluation of female work:

> Ic on wincle gefrægn weaxan nathwæt,
> þindan ond þunian, þecene hebban;
> on þæt banlease bryd grapode,
> hygewlonc hondum, hrægle þeahte
> þridende þing þeodnes dohtor.

> [I learned of something growing in a corner, swelling and standing, lifting its cover; a bride held that boneless thing; proud with her hands she covered with clothing the swelling thing, this ruler's daughter.]

This open secret—whether bread dough or penis—is a source of wonder to the speaker of the riddle who begins the description with the first-person singular form of *gefrignan* ('to hear', 'to learn of'). *Gefrignan* is a story-telling verb common to many Old English narratives from *Beowulf* to *Widsith*, as well to an array of riddles. This word, however, functions in the Exeter riddles quite differently from the way it does in the other poems. In many texts *gefrignan* announces the sharing of knowledge, which moves from speaker to audience. In the first-person plural form found in the opening of *Beowulf*, for example, it is a means of announcing that the story to come is a retelling of previously told stories known to all, the rehearsal of which unifies a culture and cements the collective identification thereof. In the riddles, however, *gefrægn* introduces what the speaker knows and the audience does not. More precisely, *gefrægn* points to something obvious to the audience, but which is so novel or differently experienced by the narrator that communication is foiled by the speaker's misdirected description. The terms of the description disguise rather than disclose because, while the audience has learned to overlook bread dough as much as it has erections, the speaker is seemingly enthralled by the growth taking place in this corner.

The emphasis placed on mystery in *Banleas* goes beyond the division between speaker/audience and knowing/unknowing implied by *gefrægn*. The very setting, *on wincle* ('in a corner') is a covert one. *Wincle* establishes a stage of secrecy, but a special type of secrecy. The occupants of corners—animate or otherwise—are common knowledge. Yet their marginalisation prevents their being fully seen and thus their being fully understood. The phrase *weaxan nathwæt* ('something growing') also suggests a mystery. The type and rate of growth is unspecified, and *nathwæt* is the opposite of specificity. *Nathwæt*, particularly, deserves more attention. Defined as 'something unknown' by Bosworth and Toller, *nathwæt* functions as one of those nonspecific terms we often use specifically for genitalia.[26] Matti Rissanen traces the use of *nathwæt*, which he finds only four times in the Old English corpus and exclusively in the Exeter riddles; notably, in three of those four instances *nathwæt* can be interpreted as, in his words, 'the sexual organ'.[27] Similarly, the modern, if somewhat rare, word 'whatnot' is defined by the *OED* as 'a euphemism for something the speaker does not wish to name'.[28] It is likely that this sort of word existed long before 1964, but, as with all things that 'a speaker does not wish to name', recorded instances are rare. In any case, the phenomenon is multilingual. Chaucer's Wife of Bath refers to 'thynges smale' when discussing the differences between men and women.[29] And J. N. Adams, in his volume *The Latin Sexual Vocabulary*, states that the Latin *res* ('thing') 'is used both of sexual intercourse ... and of the sexual organs of either sex'.[30] In short, lack of specificity suggests a sexual interpretation: decorum demands that we avoid naming genitalia directly. Then again, perhaps the speaker really does not know what he or she describes, and speaker and audience are united in their unknowledge of this wondrous *nathwæt*. Does anyone know what this 'something' or 'whatnot' that stands up *banlease* ('boneless') is, and what role the *bryd* ('bride') plays?

The clue encoded in *bryd*—a 'bride, woman about to be married or newly-married; wife; woman'[31]—in *Banleas* adds to the wonder of the poem and points to the identification of the *nathwæt*. Like its Modern English descendant 'bride', *bryd* encodes sexual associations by way of its connection to the nuptial bed and marital consummation. While general usage of the OE term and modern equivalent do not necessarily place sexual connotations at the forefront, the association with both nuptials specifically and biological sex more generally hovers in the background, even in religious contexts. This can be seen, for example, in the metaphor cited in *DOE* under definition 2b: *his gelaðung... is gecweden Cristes bryd and clæne mæden* ('his congregation is called Christ's bride and a clean maiden'). In this example, the premarital state of virginity, the bride's presumed condition on the eve of the wedding, is emphasised and contrasted with the sexual activity of married women in the earthly, lay realm. Although any reference to gender could encode such an idea by the nature of gender specifications, *bryd* and 'bride' are more closely linked to the sexual aspect of marriage as opposed to the political and public aspects of 'wife'. However, although brides—publicly and privately—are not limited to sexual activity, the associations of the term tease us with this mention of someone who is expected to have sex. The *double entendre* of *Banleas* not only amuses with its description of what a bride does when something rises, but also forces us to reconsider the roles of women and the quotidian mysteries of domesticity. The addition of details describing a woman's hands and a rising cloth in a corner could very well be answered by an erect penis.

However, as we search for the obscene answer, we re-wonder at bread dough. We may know that yeast consumes sugar and produces carbon dioxide resulting in bubbles that, in aggregate, cause bread dough to rise in the absence of bones—*banlease*—or other solid structural supports. And we may know that a complex series of physiological processes serve to fill a penis with blood until it becomes erect despite lacking the calcified material of which true bones consist. However, these everyday happenings, erections and rising bread dough, are still things of wonder when viewed anew because these phenomena occur whether we understand the scientific principles behind them or not. The obscene answer gives us a new way to look at the polite one, because the riddle articulates universal knowledge that normal discourse ignores or suppresses and thereby brings the quotidian back into the realm of the marvellous. The wonders of bread dough and so-called women's work are largely unexamined and consequently unappreciated.[32] Our staple foods—and still more their production—are difficult to portray as special because of their utility and ubiquity. Yet ubiquity underlies importance as much as it disguises it. That is, while we may be awed by intricate pastries or elaborately decorated cakes, such delicacies are hardly the staff of life.[33] Nevertheless, the more common, foundational foods and their creators often go unnoticed and unappreciated. Rather than being highlighted by rarity, the miracle of daily bread is here highlighted by riddling which allows us to see the wonder in what is mundane.

Finally, as in *Banleas*, the action of *In Wincsele* takes place in a corner, where the human actor lifts clothing in order to expose something stiff. And, as in the other riddles, the amusement is a path toward reconsidering both the depiction of labour and the product of that labour:

Hyse cwom gangan, þær he hie wisse
stondan in wincsele, stop feorran to,
hror hægstealdmon, hof his agen
hrægl hondum up, hrand under gyrdels
hyre stondendre stiþes nathwæt,
worhte his willan; wagedan buta.
þegn onnette, wæs þragum nyt
tillic esne, teorode hwæþre
æt stunda gehwam strong ær þon hio,
werig þæs weorces. Hyre weaxan ongon
under gyrdelse þæt oft gode men
ferðþum freogað ond mid feo bicgað.

[A young man came where he knew her to be standing in a corner of the room. He stepped there from afar, the brave young-man/virgin; he lifted his own clothing up with his hands, he thrust under the girdle of her, the standing one, a stiff whatnot. He worked his will; both shook. The thegn hastened; he was useful at times, a fit labourer; nevertheless he tired each time, previously stronger than she, weary of that work. There began to grow in her, under her girdle, what often good people embrace in spirit and buy with money.]

As in *Wrætlic Hongað*, the lifting of *hrægl*, unambiguously referring to a man's clothing, points us in the direction of the obscene interpretation. In the same way, a sort of intimate clothing is suggested for the answer, the feminine entity; this *hie* has a *gyrdels* ('girdle') under which the man is able to thrust his *nathwæt stithes* ('stiff whatnot'). The refusal to say something more explicit than *nathwæt* again suggests that this 'something' cannot be politely specified, ironically making the meaning appear unmistakable—or does it? All the while the trick of the riddle is to lead us to mistake one thing for this theoretically unmistakable and unspecifiable something. However, unlike *Banleas*, wherein the *nathwæt* itself grows, here something *hyre weaxan ongon / under gyrdelse* ('began to grow in her under her girdle') in reaction to the motion of the *stiþes nathwæt*.

The product of this thrusting is the first real suggestion of the decorous answer; it is something that is loved and bought: *þæt oft gode men / ferðþum freogað on mid feo bicgað* ('what often good people embrace in spirit and buy with money') (11–12). The process of churning cream into butter can in the right socioeconomic conditions be big business and, like the bread of *Banleas*, butter has a special place in northern Europe. Not only was it an important and prized food, it was a key ingredient in many medicines.[34] Felix

Grendon notes that '[i]f disease be contracted indoors, charm AA 13 is to be sung over water; if outdoors, the same charm must be recited over butter'.[35] The product of the obscene answer is far more nebulous: it could be new life, love, or pleasure, all of which are cherished and, in a way, bought. Whatever the result, *In Wincsele* demands that we compare the labour of butter-making to the labour of love. Although the *OED* cites this definition only since the 18th-century, the modern phrase 'bread and butter'—referring to something common, yet precious—highlights the importance of butter and the act of churning, as well as, by analogy, the importance of sex and its varied products. However, like the sex act denigrated by Christianity, churning butter was not a glorified task. Initially, the labour of the man and the semi-heroic description thereof is amusing, yet the value of the product testifies to the validity of the implied heroism and thereby reorients the audience to wonder at the effort involved in both tasks.

In conclusion, I argue that *Womb wæs on Hindan*, *Wrætlic Hongað*, *Banleas*, and *In Wincsele* share far more than their *double entendres*. Three take place in secret, in corners, or under cloth. They describe that which cannot be fully described in terms like *nathwæt*. They animate the inanimate. And they highlight the value of laborious tasks relegated to the lower classes and to women. While some of the Exeter riddles 'describe the elegant transformation of raw materials into crafted books, swords, inkhorns, and ships', the *double entendre* riddles call attention to that which is rarely celebrated yet which provides the foundation of society.[36] While thing theory posits that objects become things when broken and thereby assert 'a changed relation to the human subject,' the riddles discussed above accomplish a literary breaking of objects into things.[37] By utterly violating Grice's Maxim they reposition the audience such that the relationship between thing and human subject can be revisited. In so doing, the bellows are able to stand, momentarily, next to the sword they help produce; the key and its wielder are re-envisioned as a source of power which, although loosed from gender, nonetheless highlights the two parts of the whole and their interdependency; bread dough and the skill of the one who can make it rise are brought to the fore; and the churn and its product are shown in the heroic light befitting the centrality of butter in both food and medicine. By thus breaking our perspective through *double entendre* and misdirection, *Womb wæs on Hindan*, *Wrætlic Hongað*, *Banleas*, and *In Wincsele* short-circuit our inclination to avoid taking note of what we see every day—what we either disregard or regard only pejoratively. For ordinary discourse to succeed, we must ignore such ambiguities and uncomfortable correlations. However, ambiguity is functional in literary discourse, which here serves to elevate what systemic structures fail or refuse to value. As Greenblatt writes, wonder is an arresting quality. All riddles ask us to stop in our tracks and think deeply. The riddles explored above force us to stop and wonder at that which we cannot name—whether from politeness or from obliviousness—and see the wondrous in the everyday.

Notes

1 Patrick J. Murphy, *Unriddling the Exeter Riddles* (University Park: Pennsylvania State University Press, 2011), p. 7.
2 Murphy, *Unriddling the Exeter Riddles*, p. 7.
3 Stephen Greenblatt, 'Resonance and Wonder', in *Exhibiting Cultures: The Poetics and Politics of Museum Display*, ed. Ivan Karp and Steven Lavine (Washington: Smithsonian Institution Press, 1991), pp. 42–56, at p. 42.
4 Caroline Walker Bynum, 'Wonder', *American Historical Review*, 102.1 (1997), 1–26, at p. 1.
5 Bynum, 'Wonder', p. 21.
6 For further exploration of thing theory, see also Paz, Chapter 11 in this volume.
7 Benjamin C. Tilghman, 'On the Enigmatic Nature of Things in Anglo-Saxon Art', *Different Visions: A Journal of New Perspectives on Medieval Art*, 4 (2014), n.pag., http://differentvisions.org/on-the-enigmatic-nature-of-things-in-anglo-saxon-art (accessed 20 January 2019).
8 Bill Brown, 'Thing Theory', *Critical Inquiry*, 28.1 (2001), 1–22, at p. 4.
9 Grice's Maxim is also known as Grice's 'cooperative principle'. For more on this, see Robert B. Kaplan, ed., *The Oxford Handbook of Applied Linguistics* (Oxford: Oxford University Press, 2010), at p. 233.
10 Jennifer Neville, 'The Unexpected Treasure of the "Implement Trope": Hierarchical Relationships in the Old English Riddles', *RES*, 62.256 (2011), 505–19, at p. 506. See also Mercedes Salvador-Bello, 'The Key to the Body: Unlocking Riddles 42–46', in *Naked Before God: Uncovering the Body in Anglo-Saxon England*, ed. Benjamin C. Withers and Jonathan Wilcox (Morgantown: West Virginia University Press, 2003), pp. 60–96; Bogislav von Lindheim, 'Traces of Colloquial Speech in OE', *Anglia*, 70 (1951), 22–44, especially 26.
11 Neville, 'Unexpected Treasure', 506.

12 As cited by Neville; Ælfric of Eynsham, *Ælfric's Catholic Homilies: The First Series*, ed. Peter Clemoes, EETS ss, 17 (Oxford: Oxford University Press, 1997), p. 333.
13 Murphy, *Unriddling the Exeter Riddles*, p. 218.
14 Murphy, *Unriddling the Exeter Riddles*, p. 218.
15 Paull F. Baum, ed. and trans., *Anglo Saxon Riddles of the Exeter Book* (Durham, NC: Duke University Press, 1963), pp. 57–8.
16 Gale R. Owen-Crocker, *Dress in Anglo-Saxon England* (Woodbridge: Boydell, 2010), pp. 65–71. Other implements were worn at the waist as well, including knives, latch-lifters, tweezers, and cosmetic brushes.
17 Christine Fell, Cecily Clark, and Elizabeth Williams, *Women in Anglo-Saxon England and the Impact of 1066* (London: British Museum Publications, 1984), pp. 59–60. See also Owen-Crocker, *Dress*, pp. 65–71.
18 B-T defines *locbore* as 'one wearing long hair, a free woman'.
19 Christine Fell, 'A "friwif locbore" Revisited', *ASE*, 13 (1984), 157–65, at p. 161.
20 Fell, 'friwif locbore', p. 162. See also Carole Hough, 'Women and the Law in Seventh-century England', *Nottingham Medieval Studies*, 51 (2007), 207–30; Anne L. Klinck, 'Anglo-Saxon Women and the Law', *Journal of Medieval History*, 8 (1982), 107–21.
21 Audrey L. Meaney, *Anglo-Saxon Amulets and Curing Stones*, BAR, British Series, 96 (Oxford: Oxford University Press, 1981), p. 178.
22 Of course, genitalia serve purposes in other contexts, but for the purposes of procreation they are paired opposites.
23 Salvador-Bello, 'Key to the Body', 79–81. Salvador-Bello also finds parallel imagery in other Old English texts in which 'Jesus is characterized as the guardian of the key' that can open the lock of the soul (at p. 79).
24 Bonifatius Fischer, *et al.*, eds, *Biblia Sacra Iuxta Vulgatam Versionem* (Stuttgart: Deutsche Bibelgesellschaft, 1994).
25 Salvador-Bello points out multiple instances in which the idea of 'key and lock' are used allegorically: 'Key to the Body', 80.
26 B-T, *s.v. nathwæt.*
27 Matti Rissanen, 'Nathwæt in the Exeter Book Riddles', *American Notes and Queries*, 24.7–8 (1986), 116–20, at p. 119.
28 The earliest cited instance in the *OED* of 'whatnot' dates from 1964.
29 Geoffrey Chaucer, 'The Wife of Bath's Prologue', in *The Riverside Chaucer*, ed. Larry D. Benson, 3rd edn (Boston: Houghton Mifflin 1987), p. 106, l. 121.
30 James Noel Adams, *The Latin Sexual Vocabulary* (Baltimore: Johns Hopkins University Press, 1982), p. 62.
31 *DOE*, *s.v. bryd.*
32 Here the gender of the person interacting with the bread dough is explicitly feminine as indicated by the use of the term *bryd*. However,

Fell notes that 'Old English has both masculine and feminine nouns for bakers, *bæcere* and *bæcestre*, both presumably in fairly common use'. *Women in Anglo-Saxon England*, p. 49. Fell adds, moreover, that, since 'pressures of time and weather would mean that men and women shared generally in many tasks as they needed to be done, it is improbable that jobs were rigidly allocated according to sex'.

33 Interestingly, the Eucharist literally dresses bread up in special cloth and mystery. However, this occurs without any reference to the production of the bread.

34 M. L. Cameron finds that butter is the fourth most prescribed substance in *Leechbook III* after water, milk, and ale. See 'Anglo-Saxon Medicine and Magic', *ASE*, 17 (1988), 191–215, at p. 196.

35 Felix Grendon, 'The Anglo-Saxon Charms', *Journal of American Folklore*, 22.84 (1909), 105–237, at pp. 118–19.

36 Murphy, *Unriddling the Exeter Riddles*, p. 22.

37 Brown, 'Thing Theory', p. 4.

3
Domesticating the devil: the early medieval contexts of Aldhelm's cat riddle

Megan Cavell

> 'But I am a cat, and no cat anywhere ever gave anyone a straight answer'.[1]

Infamous for an ambivalence that riles some and charms others, the domestic cat's relationship with humans is now the subject of extensive zooarchaeological study. Exploring the complex role of cats in early medieval England, Kristopher Poole has recently demonstrated that—though present in mid- to late-Saxon human communities—these animals were generally left to their own devices.[2] Cats hunted small and unwanted animals, scavenged rubbish and nurtured their young largely without human interference. There are, naturally, exceptions, like the cats exploited for their fur in a number of late Saxon towns, and the cat from mid- to late-Saxon Bishopstone whose diet implies that he or she may have been kept as a favoured pet.[3] And yet, whether we can refer to these creatures as truly domesticated is the subject of debate.

Poole's analysis goes some way toward explaining the sparse linguistic evidence for cats in Old English: the term *cat(te)* does not appear in a single narrative text, but is limited to penitentials, glosses, charters and place-names.[4] There is, however, one fascinating Anglo-Latin poetic riddle that explores the role of this animal in vivid detail: Aldhelm's *Enigma 65*, *Muriceps* ('mouse-catcher)'. After placing Aldhelm's cat in her wider historical and comparative contexts, I provide a close reading of this unique riddle—an exciting case study, given the limited depictions of cats that survive from the early medieval period. I argue that the semi-domesticated nature of early medieval English cats is evident in Aldhelm's poem, which employs imagery of the mouser's role as a domestic guardian alongside hunting techniques that echo biblical depictions of Satan and sinners. As both a welcome cohabiter and diabolical presence in the human household, Aldhelm's feline subject provides previously unrecognised insights into early medieval cat–human relationships.

The domestication of the cat

Domestication is a complex and multi-staged process that can follow a variety of pathways, involving the intention and direction of humans to varying degrees.[5] The zooarchaeological consensus is that cats followed the commensal pathway, which:

> does not begin with intentional action on the part of people to bring wild animals (juvenile or otherwise) into their camps. Instead, as people manipulated their immediate surroundings, different populations of wild animals would have been attracted to elements of the human niche, including human food waste and/or smaller animals that were also attracted to the refuse. Those animals most capable of taking advantage of the resources associated with human camps would have been the tamer, less aggressive individuals with shorter fight or flight distances.[6]

That domestication is a long process involving genetic change through natural selection has been obscured by the prominence of the human-directed pathway in recent years.[7] In addition to horses, donkeys and camels (all brought by humans into their niche thousands of years ago because of their usefulness in transportation), the majority of animals now domesticated—from small pets to aquatic species—were actively cultivated and often selectively bred over the past several hundred years.[8] And yet, it remains the case that 'people could not begin intentionally domesticating animals until they had procured them through entirely unintentional means.'[9] We are surrounded by these unintentionally domesticated, commensal animals in our daily lives—including not only cats, but also dogs, rats, mice, crows, and urban foxes[10]—although our categories of 'domestic' and 'wild' conceal the commonalities between species that exploit the same niche to take up significant roles in our lives.[11]

Cats are an important part of this picture. While the precise timeline of their domestication is difficult to pin down, it is thought that modern domestic cats derive from the North African wildcat, *Felis silvestris lybica*, which was already associating with people in the Levant around 10,000 years ago.[12] It is possible that, despite tamed wildcats abounding in the Mediterranean and Middle East, full domestication did not occur until the heyday of Ancient Egypt.[13] The matter is a complex one, as James A. Serpell notes: 'it could be argued that the cat was only fully domesticated during the last 200 or so years, although it is probably more accurate to view [*Felis silvestris catus*] as a subspecies that has drifted unpredictably in and out of various states of domestication, semi-domestication and feralness depending on the particular ecological and cultural conditions prevailing at different times and locations.'[14] A unique and crucial element in the cat's domestication is the continued interbreeding with local wildcats, which introduced genetic diversity and led to a hybridisation that could make offspring more difficult to socialise with humans.[15]

When it comes to northern Europe, there is some debate about whether the Romans were responsible for introducing domestic cats, or whether they arrived earlier—in the Iron Age or even the Neolithic.[16] Either way, it was likely in Roman Britain that domestic cats got a proper foothold; their presence at this time is firmly established by the remains found in third/fourth-century assemblages.[17] The most famous Roman British feline find in the current archaeological record is the group of clay tiles from Silchester that are marked by small paw-prints.[18] However, the Silchester find is by no means unique: similar prints have since been discovered on tiles excavated from Gloucester and Lincoln.[19] Whether these prints belong to domestic cats or wildcats is not entirely clear, though their close proximity to human settlements may suggest the former. Either way, domestic cats are found in widespread, though still relatively small, numbers throughout Europe and Asia by the tenth century.[20]

Ultimately, the process of cat domestication developed according to the following model: 'an uninvited dinner guest ... became a tolerated lodger, and then a member of the family.'[21] The period with which this chapter is concerned may be placed only part-way through this model's progression. Domestic cats in early medieval England are for the most part tolerated lodgers, existing in the background of everyday life and playing a very small role in the literature that survives today.

Early medieval cats in context

That cats existed mainly in the background is nowhere more evident than at the level of language. The Old English word *cat(te)* occurs only eight times in the extant corpus, generally in glosses of the Latin terms *cattus*, *feles*, *muriceps*, *murilegus* and *musio*.[22] The only extended references are found in penitentials, which proscribe eating food touched by cats, dogs, mice, and unclean animals.[23] Additionally, forms of *cat(te)* survive in place-names, with secondary elements referring to hills (*-beorg*, *-dene*, *-hlinc*), bodies of water (*-ege*, *-mere*, *-broc*, *-flot*), boundaries (*-gemæra*) and stones (*-stan*).[24] A related compound, *cathol* ('cat-hole', i.e. den) occurs only three times in the extant written record, exclusively in charter bounds, where it likely relates to wildcats.[25] In vernacular contexts, then, the existence of cats is shadowy at best.

More cats appear in Latin than Old English, although even there the picture is far from full. Both the classical and biblical traditions provided limited material for Anglo-Latin writers to draw on. The only biblical precedent occurs in the deuterocanonical Baruch 6:21, where the leaping of birds and cats upon the bodies and heads of idols is given as evidence of their falseness. Though still underrepresented when compared with other domestic animals, there are more references to cats in classical natural histories. Aristotle's *History of Animals* is famous for its loaded description of these animals' mating behaviour: 'Cats are different: they do not copulate hindways, but the male stands erect and the female places herself under him. Female cats are naturally lecherous, and lure the males on to sexual intercourse, during which time they caterwaul.'[26] However, Aristotle's work was not widely known in western Europe before the twelfth century,[27] and Pliny the Elder's adaptation of this section in his *Naturalis Historia* removes the majority of it—including the moralising statement about female cats' lechery—and mentions only the position of the cats during mating.[28] With only passing references to cats in life and their medicinal uses after death, Pliny the Elder's work does not provide a key source of influence for later feline depictions.

Isidore of Seville, on the other hand, whose influence in the Middle Ages was substantial, does include an interesting description of a particular type of cat in his early seventh-century *Etymologiae*:

> Musio appellatus, quod muribus infestus sit. Hunc vulgus cattum a captura vocant. Alii dicunt, quod cattat, id est videt. Nam tanto acute cernit ut fulgore luminis noctis tenebras superet. Vnde a Graeco venit catus, id est ingeniosus, ἀπὸ τοῦ καίεσθαι.[29]
>
> [The mouser is so called because it is dangerous to mice. The common people name the cat after 'catching'. Others say [it has its name] because *cattat*, that is, 'it sees'. For it can see so acutely that it overcomes the darkness of night with the brightness of its eyes.

Hence, *catus* comes from Greek, that is, 'ingenious', from καίεσθαι (i.e. to be kindled).]

The link between the name for cats and their mousey prey, as well as their predatory behaviour and keen eyesight, are key to the discussion below of Aldhelm's *Enigma 65*.

It is mousers like these that we see in the comparative literature and art of early medieval Europe.[30] Hence, the value of cats in the tenth-century Welsh *Laws of Hywel Dda* is partly tied to their skill at catching mice.[31] Likewise, the Book of Kells' Latin gospels (Ireland, c. 800) include several depictions of cats alongside mice—including mice attempting to eat the Eucharist.[32] On the continent, stories circulate about monks with cat companions from the ninth century onward; one hermit, who dotes on his cat so much that he is blinded to spiritual visions, rectifies the situation by casting the cat out of his dwelling and commanding it to go and catch mice.[33] More famous, however, is the affable relationship between scholar and cat in the ninth-century Old Irish poem *Pangur Bán*, surviving from (and likely written on) the continent and preserved in the St Paul Codex (monastery of St Paul, Carinthia, Austria).[34] It is worth dwelling briefly on Pangur, since Susan Crane has recently discussed the cat's cohabitation with the scholar in relation to domestication.[35] Stanzas 4–6 read:

Gnáth, hūaraib, ar gressaib gal
glenaid luch inna línsam;
os mé, du-fuit im lín chéin
dliged ndoraid cu ndronchéill.

Fūaichaidsem fri frega fál
a rosc, a nglése comlán;
fūachimm chēin fri fēgi fis
mu rosc rēil, cesu imdis.

Fāelidsem cu ndēne dul
hi nglen luch inna gērchrub;
hi tucu cheist ndoraid ndil
os mē chene am fāelid.[36]

[It is usual at times that because of bold attacks, / a mouse sticks in his net; / and as for me, there falls into my own net / a difficult rule with robust meaning. // He hones against an inner-wall hedge / his eye, the full bright one; / I myself hone against clarity of knowledge / my clear eye, though of little consequence. // He is joyful when with swift motion / a mouse sticks in his sharp claw; / when I understand a difficult, prized question / I too am joyful.[37]]

The references to catching mice in stanzas 4 and 6, and the description of the cat's bright eye in stanza 5 echo Isidore's generic mouser, though *Pangur Bán* itself is an intensely personal poem. In fact, Gregory Toner argues that the cat's name, Pangur, which is Welsh for 'fuller' (i.e. a wool-cleanser), is an indication of this personal tone: 'for if the cat were a mere device or conceit, we might not expect it to bear what appears to be a genuine and idiosyncratic name.'[38]

Nor is the cat's name the poem's only idiosyncrasy. The metaphor of the net in stanza 4 is especially interesting, given that there is no precedent in early natural histories or Isidore. Hildegard L. C. Tristram argues that we should read this image in relation to the New Testament's references to Christ's disciples as fishers of men.[39] Toner, on the other hand, points out that the poem contains no pastoral elements, focusing instead on the sheltered existence of the scholar and cat.[40] The net should, thus, not be read in terms of fishing, but in terms of hunting; nets were, after all, used to hunt land animals like deer.[41] Crane likewise notes that the net may align Pangur with hunting, but prefers to read the stanza as anthropomorphising the cat as a 'net-wielding gladiator', arguing that any mock-heroic potential in such a grand association is shared equally between cat and scholar.[42] The hunting interpretation is perhaps better supported by the term *lín*, which refers primarily to nets used for fishing or hunting, with figurative uses especially linking it to either diabolic and sinful nets or the protective covering of Christianity.[43]

These contradictory associations—of both distinctly negative and positive nets—in the Christian tradition speak to the varying interpretations of another cat from the early medieval world. A hundred years or so before *Pangur Bán* and the images from the Book of Kells, an intricately interlaced cat stalked the borders of the Lindisfarne Gospels.[44] Composed in the early eighth century by Eadfrith, the Bishop of Lindisfarne, this manuscript is the earliest evidence for an interest in cats from early medieval England.[45] It is not clear whether the cat on fol. 139r (who is hunting some unsuspecting birds, to add to those already inside her or his stomach) is depicted in this manuscript for humorous effect, as a symbol of the diabolic ensnarement of unwary sinners, or simply because these animals were commonly observed around the scriptorium.[46] The fact that the prey here are birds, rather than the mice who were so potentially destructive in monastic settlements and workplaces, injects some moral ambiguity.[47]

Indeed, cats would become firmly associated with evil and witchcraft in later medieval and early modern Europe. Douglas Gray maps these associations in British literature from the twelfth-century reference to heretical orgies and cat-/Satan-worship in Walter Map's *De nugis curialium* to the thirteenth-century *cat of helle* in the *Ancrene Wisse* and the devil-sinner/cat–mouse comparison in the fourteenth- and fifteenth-century *Ayenbite of Inwyt* and *Castle of Perseverance*.[48] Rainer Kampling, however, argues that there is a distinct shift in attitudes toward cats in the theological landscape of twelfth-century Europe, noting that the association between cats and poisonous creatures in Hildegard of Bingen's *Physica* is the earliest overt example of feline demonisation.[49] This demonisation gained authority in 1233 when Gregory IX's papal letter, *Vox in Rama*, linked cats to heresy and the devil.[50]

Even so, cats continued to be associated with monastic environments; that they were the only animals permitted to the anchoress in *Ancrene Wisse* speaks to their functional role as mousers.[51] For Gray, cats are ambiguous and productive metaphors because, unlike other domestic animals, they belong between day and night … and between tame and wild.[52] Serpell picks up on this liminality to argue that it is the partial domestication of cats that leads to their denunciation in the later Middle Ages:

> the cat is one of the few domestic species that does not need to be caged, fenced in, or tethered in order to maintain its association with people. Cats, however, tend to display a degree of independence that is uncharacteristic of dogs, and which inclines them to wander at will, and indulge in noisy sexual forays, particularly during the hours of darkness. In other words, cats lead a sort of double life—half domestic, half wild; part culture, part nature—and it was perhaps this failure to conform to human (and especially male) standards of proper conduct that led to their subsequent harassment.[53]

The independence that cats display may also speak to their scapegoating in a world of highly-structured religious hierarchies. In refusing to obey, cats rejected the divinely-sanctioned exceptionalism that placed the governance of all other animals under human control, demonstrating, in the words of Katharine Rogers, 'their antagonism to man and God. It therefore seemed likely that the cat's secret nocturnal world was presided over by the Prince of Darkness.'[54] This association between cats and the devil could have been further bolstered by an earlier link between cats and pagan gods/goddesses and fertility cults—from the Egyptian Bast to the

Scandinavian Freyja.[55] Deep-seated prejudices relating to paganism, gender and sexuality, taken together with their night-time predation, independence, and semi-domesticated nature merged into a toxic cocktail of associations that led to the Othering of cats across the high/late medieval and early modern periods. Whether any trace of this negativity can be detected in early medieval England comes down essentially to one text.

Aldhelm's cat

Neglected in most discussions of medieval cats to date is Aldhelm's seventh-century riddle about an unnamed and nonspecific—though gendered—*muriceps* ('mouse-catcher'). *Enigma 65* reads:

> Fida satis custos conseruans peruigil aedes
> Noctibus in furuis caecas lustrabo latebras
> Atris haud perdens oculorum lumen in antris.
> Furibus inuisis, uastant qui farris aceruos,
> Insidiis tacite dispono scandala mortis.[56]
> Et uaga uenatrix rimabor lustra ferarum,
> Nec uolo cum canibus turmas agitare fugaces,
> Qui mihi latrantes crudelia bella ciebunt.
> Gens exosa mihi tradebat nomen habendum.[57]

> [Trustworthy enough, I am a watchful warden guarding the hall; in dark nights I wander its shady nooks, not losing the light of my eyes even in black caves. I silently with snares arrange deadly traps for detested/unseen thieves, who lay waste to stores of grain. A roving huntress, I will search beasts' dens, but I am not willing to chase fleeing hordes with hounds, who, barking at me, incite bitter battles. The hateful race gave me the name I have.]

While the solution given in the first manuscript recension of Aldhelm's *Enigmata* is *Muriceps*, it should be noted that the second recension includes several options and glosses: *De Catto vel Muricipe vel Pilace* 'on a cat or mouse-catcher or cat'.[58] Changes to the titles were likely made to facilitate the inclusion of the *enigmata* in the *Epistola ad Acircium*, a metrical treatise that Aldhelm sent to Aldfrith, king of Northumbria.[59] Given that the final line of *Enigma 65* contains a linguistic puzzle, however, Aldhelm's initial solution of *muriceps* is most useful for solving the riddle: the word *muriceps* means 'mouse-catcher', from the noun *mus* (gen. *muris*) and the perfect tense root of the verb *capere* (*cep*-). The final clue, then, demands a name for the cat that is derived from its much-hated victims.[60]

Karen Jolly and Andy Orchard suggest that the solution might just as easily have been Isidore's *musio*,[61] whose description of the mouser also emphasised the creature's bright eyes penetrating the darkness. This is an apt observation of a feline adaptation that makes nocturnal hunting easier: 'With large eyes and flexible pupils that can dilate from small slits or dots in bright sunshine to circles that seem to fill their eye sockets, they can see in near darkness where the light is only one sixth as bright as humans require, without losing the capacity to protect their retinas from the full light of midday.'[62] The light-reflecting surface of cats' eyes would be striking to anyone who stumbled across them in the darkness—no doubt a likely encounter, given that the riddle's action unfolds in the *aedes* ('hall'), which could signify either a house or monastery.

In a mock-heroic fashion, the quotidian setting also clashes with the rhetorically-heightened depiction of the *uaga uenatrix* ('roving huntress'). A more famous *uenatrix* can be found in the form of Camilla—the warrior and servant of Diana—in Virgil's *Aeneid*, whose influence upon this riddle is fairly extensive.[63] The use of *uenatrix* here throws into sharp relief the fact that this mouser is female, a decision that may be explained with reference to the grammatical gender of the original solution, *muriceps*. This medieval Latin term is fairly obscure,[64] and could potentially be one of Aldhelm's neologisms, perhaps through analogy with *auceps* ('bird-catcher'), which—like *muriceps*—has a kenning-like quality to it.[65] If *muriceps* is a neologism, the decision to include additional solutions that are more immediately familiar in versions of or glosses in the *Epistola ad Acircium* makes a great deal of sense. Regardless, while all the additional solutions listed above are masculine, we know that *muriceps* is feminine because Tatwine refers to it as such in his *Ars grammatica*.[66] Personifications that stem from grammatical gender—common in classical and medieval Latin texts—could provide riddle-solvers with a tidy clue.[67] Although Corinne Dale's chapter in this volume argues against assuming that the feminisation of all riddle-subjects rests solely on grammatical gender, with such a blatant emphasis on the etymology of the solution at the end of this particular poem, viewing the cat's gender as further linguistic play is fitting here.

Such play can also be detected in an earlier reference to the hatefulness of mice, in line 4's punning use of *inuisum* (both 'detested' and 'unseen'). Given that the cat's eyes are so much more adept at night, it is likely that it is only for humans that these mice are unseen, though dislike of this pest may have united both poet and cat.[68] After all, these unwanted creatures are not just rodents, but also *fures* ('thieves') who spoil the grain stores of the human inhabitants of the hall. This cat's hunting is clearly encouraged, and—like Pangur above—she excels at it. Unlike the cat in the Old Irish poem, however, this cat is imagined on her own terms and not in relation to any specific human companion. Apart from references to the hall and its grain stores, human life is not visible in this riddle.

Another animal's appearance does, however, hint at human presence: the *canes* ('hounds') who rile the riddle-cat so much are clearly hunting dogs. In fact, Emily Thornbury notes that a hunter's refusal to work alongside dogs in this period 'must have seemed absurd enough to make lines 6–8 something of a paradox',[69] though I disagree with her suggestion that the cat fears these dogs; there is no fear to be seen in this cat's portrayal, only unwillingness. The reference to *crudelia bella* ('bitter battles') demonstrates just how long humans have identified the antagonistic relations between cats and dogs. The domestication of cats has over time led to individuals able to tolerate closer proximity to humans and other animals, but it would be foolish to expect even now that the close proximity of predators and competitors should never result in territorial defensiveness.

In addition to the riddle-cat's defensiveness, it is also interesting to note the differences in how she and the dogs are depicted—the latter are a plural unit, while the former is a solitary individual. These divergent hunting strategies speak to the broader dynamics of human relations with both types of animal:

> Because the cat was defined as a rodent killer, and because it hunts on its own, it was and still is seen as more predatory than the dog. Hounds and terriers were bred for killing prey and are still enthusiastic about chasing small animals, but they are rarely presented as ruthless and bloodthirsty. The fact that the cat hunts for itself rather than for human gratification supports the prevailing idea that it selfishly pursues its own interests, in contrast to the dog, who serves and supports man.[70]

Aldhelm's cat is, however, certainly seen to be supporting humans as a *custos conseruans* ('warden guarding') the hall and protecting grain stores. Yet, some doubt is injected into her dedication to service by the opening of the poem: *fida satis* ('trustworthy enough'). Juster draws a link between this phrase and both Virgil's

Aeneid and Claudian's *De raptu Proserpinae*.[71] In the first passage, Androgeos—the Greek soldier who confuses Aeneas's band of Trojans for allies—realises the trouble he is in when no reply given to him is *fida satis*.[72] In the second text, Ceres does not believe her home to be *fida satis* to protect her daughter Proserpina from danger.[73] The emphasis in both these texts—in which *fida satis* is negated—is on the discomfort that arises from sharing space with those whose trust is questionable. While Aldhelm may well have found inspiration in these sources, his riddle does not include negation. The legendary and mythical characters may not be trustworthy, but this cat appears to be ... or at least she is trustworthy *enough*. Perhaps *satis* appears for metrical reasons; perhaps it is litotic; perhaps it implies the cat is nothing more or less than satisfactory. Whichever reading we adopt, the presence of *satis* qualifying *fida* imbues the opening lines with an ambiguity that is essential to the play of the riddle.

Equally ambiguous is the description of the cat's hunting methods, when she silently arranges *scandala* ('traps'). *Scandalum*, indicating variously 'that which causes one to stumble', a 'stumbling-block', 'inducement to sin', 'temptation' or 'cause of offence',[74] is found frequently in the Latin Vulgate, where it is especially associated with idolatry, the Jewish faith, hypocrisy, the sinful, and Satan.[75] A remarkable parallel to *Enigma 65* is found in Psalm 139:6: *absconderunt superbi laqueum mihi, et funes extenderunt in laqueum; juxta iter scandalum posuerunt mihi* ('The proud have hidden a net for me. And they have stretched out cords for a snare: they have laid for me a stumbling-block by the wayside').[76] This psalm provides a vivid and corporeal depiction of the ability of sinful people to trap the unwary. Likewise, a parallel occurs in Christ's words to Peter when the latter opposes the former's willingness to undergo suffering and crucifixion in Matthew 16:23: *Vade post me Satana, scandalum es mihi: quia non sapis ea quae Dei sunt, sed ea quae hominum* ('Go behind me, Satan, thou art a scandal unto me: because thou savourest not the things that are of God, but the things that are of men'). Satan is invoked as the originator of temptation and entrapment, influencing Peter's refusal to accept God's plan.

And yet, despite the negativity associated with the majority of biblical *scandala*, positive contexts occasionally occur. Ecclesiasticus 32:19, for example, imagines God's law as a stumbling-block for the deceitful: *Qui quaerit legem replebitur ab ea, et qui insidiose agit scandalizabitur in ea* ('He that seeketh the law, shall be filled with it:

and he that dealeth deceitfully, shall meet with a stumbling-block therein'). This is an ambiguous passage, however, since God's law is not inherently a stumbling-block, but one that arises from the deceitful intentions of sinners. Interestingly, the adverbial *insidiose* is related to the nominal (pl.) *insidiae*, which we find alongside the *scandala* of *Enigma 65*. Not unlike *scandalum*, *insidiae* can point to 'an ambush', 'artifice', 'crafty device', 'plot' or 'snare'.[77] Psalm 9's description of the sinner waiting *in insidiis* ('in ambush') to trap the poor is, therefore, compellingly relevant to this riddle:

> 29. Sedet in insidiis cum divitibus in occultis, ut interficiat innocentem. / 30. Oculi ejus in pauperem respiciunt; insidiatur in abscondito, quasi leo in spelunca sua. Insidiatur ut rapiat pauperem; rapere pauperem dum attrahit eum. / 31. In laqueo suo humiliabit eum; inclinabit se, et cadet cum dominatus fuerit pauperum.

> [He sitteth in ambush with the rich in private places, that he may kill the innocent. / His eyes are upon the poor man: He lieth in wait in secret like a lion in his den. He lieth in ambush that he may catch the poor man: to catch the poor, whilst he draweth him to him. / In his net he will bring him down, he will crouch and fall, when he shall have power over the poor.]

In addition to the secret ambush, this psalm also includes a *laqueus* ('net'), an emphasis on eyes (*oculi*), and of course a felid—though in this case a large and undomesticated one, whom Aldhelm may not have identified as a type of cat.

Kampling's reading of *Enigma 65*—which he mobilises in support of his argument that the demonisation of cats begins no earlier than the eleventh/twelfth centuries—does not take note of these possible biblical echoes. He is one of the only critics to include Aldhelm's poem in a wider analysis of medieval cat/human relations (albeit in passing) and he asserts that the poet has only words of praise for the cat.[78] This is, perhaps, an overstatement. Certainly, the poem contains positive elements, but its use of imagery of ensnarement and its lukewarm reference to the cat's trustworthiness together highlight the creature's ambiguity.

Conclusion

As Rogers notes in her cultural history of cat/human relations: 'Because modern cat lovers take for granted that cats have unique and special qualities, they sometimes overenthusiastically project this attitude back through history.'[79] Such a cautionary statement is especially relevant when it comes to the early medieval period, whose sparse documentation makes each surviving feline depiction key to understanding the history of this animal's pathway to domestication.

Informed by the field of critical animal studies, Susan Crane has already begun pushing back against the imposition of modern human–animal relations on the past, discussing *Pangur Bán*'s scholar and cat as cohabiters rather than owner and pet. My chapter aims to bring Aldhelm's *Enigma 65* into this discussion, by providing a close reading of a complex poem with well-documented classical borrowings and potential biblical references. In arguing that Aldhelm's riddle provides neither a thoroughly positive nor exhaustively negative portrayal of a mouser who is both a domestic guardian and a snare-laying sinner, I propose that this poem also gestures toward the semi-domesticated status zooarchaeologists have posited for cats in this period. That dogs were further along the commensal pathway is, likewise, suggested by the riddle's use of these animals as a stand-in for human-directed hunting methods: the unwillingness of Aldhelm's cat to participate in such behaviour serves to further highlight her liminal position in early medieval English society.

The archaeological record makes it clear that individual cats participated in this society in a variety of ways, and were the recipients of both good and bad treatment by humans—ranging from deliberate sharing of high-status foods to exploitation for fur.[80] The reality for most cats, however, must have been life in the background, as largely unmediated hunters and scavengers within the human niche. Aldhelm's *Enigma 65* provides an intriguing, seventh-century snapshot of such an existence, which has to date been largely neglected. As the foregoing discussion has made clear, this early medieval riddle deserves greater recognition and should be placed alongside the canonical cats of *Pangur Bán*, the Lindisfarne Gospels and beyond. Together, these texts and images shed light on a creature who would continue down the pathway of domestication, though a period of intensive persecution, to become one of the most common domestic animals prowling the homes and streets of the modern world.

Notes

1 Peter S. Beagle, *The Last Unicorn* (London: Ballantine, 1971), p. 167.

2 Kristopher Poole, 'The Contextual Cat: Human-Animal Relations and Social Meaning in Anglo-Saxon England', *Journal of Archaeological Method and Theory*, 22 (2015), 857–82.
3 Poole, 'Contextual Cat', pp. 868 and 873–4.
4 *DOE*, *s.v. cat, catte* and *cathol*. See also Karen Louise Jolly, 'A Cat's Eye View: Vermin in Anglo-Saxon England', in *The Daily Lives of the Anglo-Saxons*, ed. Carole Biggam, Carole Hough, and Daria Izdebska (Tempe, AZ: ACMRS, 2017), pp. 105–28, at pp. 112–17.
5 Greger Larson and Dorian Q. Fuller, 'The Evolution of Animal Domestication', *Annual Review of Ecology, Evolution, and Systematics*, 45 (2014), 115–36, at p. 117.
6 Larson and Fuller, 'Evolution', p. 117.
7 Larson and Fuller, 'Evolution', p. 127.
8 Larson and Fuller, 'Evolution', p. 120.
9 Larson and Fuller, 'Evolution', p. 127.
10 Terry O'Connor, 'Making Themselves at Home: The Archaeology of Commensal Vertebrates', in *Anthropological Approaches to Zooarchaeology: Colonialism, Complexity and Animal Transformations*, ed. Douglas V. Campana, Pamela Crabtree, S. D. deFrance, Justin Lev-Tov and A. M. Choyke (Oxford: Oxbow, 2010), pp. 270–4, at p. 271.
11 O'Connor, 'Making Themselves at Home', p. 271.
12 James A. Serpell, 'Domestication and History of the Cat', in *The Domestic Cat: The Biology of its Behaviour*, ed. D. C. Turner and P. Bateson (Cambridge: Cambridge University Press, 3rd edn, 2014), pp. 83–100, at pp. 84–5 and 86–7.
13 Serpell, 'Domestication', p. 88.
14 Serpell, 'Domestication', p. 86.
15 On hybridisation, see John Bradshaw, *Cat Sense: The Feline Enigma Revealed* (London: Penguin, 2013), pp. 28–33.
16 Bradshaw, *Cat Sense*, pp. 60–1 and 93; Andrew C. Kitchener and Terry O'Connor, 'Wildcats, Domestic and Feral Cats', in *Extinctions and Invasions: The Social History of British Fauna*, ed. Terry O'Connor and Naomi J. Sykes (Oxford: Windgather, 2010), pp. 83–94, at p. 90; Poole, 'Contextual Cat', p. 865.
17 Bradshaw, *Cat Sense*, pp. 91–2.
18 Serpell, 'Domestication', p. 93; Katharine M. Rogers, *The Cat and the Human Imagination: Feline Images from Bast to Garfield* (Ann Arbor: University of Michigan Press, 1998), p. 18.
19 Jason Daley, 'Cat Left a Pawprint in a 2,000-Year-Old Roman Roof Tile', *Smithsonian.com*, 2 June 2017, www.smithsonianmag.com/smart-news/cat-left-pawprint-2000-year-old-roman-roof-tile-180963556/ (accessed 13 December 2017).
20 Serpell, 'Domestication', p. 93.
21 Kitchener and O'Connor, 'Wildcats', p. 89.
22 *DOE*, *s.v. cat, catte*.

23 *DOE*, s.v. *cat, catte.* For a discussion of cats in medieval Latin penitentials, see Rainer Kampling, 'Vom Streicheln und Nutzen der Katze: Die Wahrnehmung der Katze bei christlichen Autoren von der Spätantike bis zum. 12. Jahrhundert', in *Eine seltsame Gefährtin: Katzen, Religion, Theologie und Theologen*, ed. Rainer Kampling (Frankfurt am Main: Peter Lang, 2007), pp. 95–119, at pp. 108–10; and Jolly, 'Cat's Eye View', pp. 115–16.

24 *DOE, s.v. cat, catte.*

25 *DOE, s.v. cathol.*

26 Aristotle, *History of Animals, Volume II: Books 4–6*, trans. A. L. Peck, Loeb Classical Library, 438 (Cambridge, MA: Harvard University Press, 1970), pp. 102–5, bk 5, ch. 2.

27 For an introduction to the medieval reception of Aristotle's work, see C. H. Lohr, 'The Medieval Interpretation of Aristotle', in *The Cambridge History of Later Medieval Philosophy: From the Rediscovery of Aristotle to the Disintegration of Scholasticism, 1100–1600*, ed. Norman Kretzmann, Anthony Kenny, Jan Pinborg, and Eleonore Stump (Cambridge: Cambridge University Press, 1982), pp. 80–98. Only excerpts of Aristotle's *Categoriae* and *De interpretatione*, translated into Latin by Boethius, survive from early medieval England. See Helmut Gneuss and Michael Lapidge, *Anglo-Saxon Manuscripts: A Bibliographical Handlist of Manuscripts and Manuscript Fragments Written or Owned in England up to 1100* (Toronto: University of Toronto Press, 2014), pp. 167 (no. 200.5) and 211–12 (no. 269.1).

28 Pliny the Elder, *Natural History, Volume III: Books 8–11*, trans. H. Rackham, Loeb Classical Library, 353 (Cambridge, MA: Harvard University Press, 1940), pp. 402–3, bk 10, ch. 174.

29 Isidore of Seville, *Etymologiarum sive originum libri XX*, ed. W. M. Lindsay, 2 vols (Oxford: Clarendon, 1911), II, 12.2.38, lines 19–23. Unless otherwise stated, all Latin translations are my own.

30 On cats and rodents, see Jolly, 'A Cat's Eye View', pp. 109–27.

31 Poole, 'Contextual Cat', p. 871; Rogers, *Cat and the Human Imagination*, p. 19. Cf. the complex legal material concerning Irish cats edited by Kevin Murray, 'Catshlechta and Other Medieval Legal Material Relating to Cats', *Celtica*, 25 (2007), 143–59.

32 Dublin, Trinity College, MS 58, fols 34r and 48r, available at http://digitalcollections.tcd.ie/home/index.php?DRIS_ID=MS58_003v (accessed 6 February 2019).

33 Kampling, 'Vom Streicheln', pp. 113–17. A cat also thwarts its human companions' spiritual aspirations by catching and sharing too many fish in a late Old/early Middle Irish story edited by Elizabeth Boyle, 'Three Junior Clerics and their Kitten (from the Book of Leinster)', *Bloga (fragments)*, 6 March 2017, available at https://blogafragments.wordpress.com/2016/03/06/three-junior-clerics-and-their-kitten-from-the-book-of-leinster/ (accessed 6 February 2019).

34 Gregory Toner, '*Messe ocus Pangur Bán*: Structure and Cosmology', *Cambrian Medieval Celtic Studies*, 57 (2009), 1–22, at pp. 1–2.

35 Susan Crane, *Animal Encounters: Contacts and Concepts in Medieval Britain* (Philadelphia: University of Pennsylvania Press, 2013), pp. 12–23. On the peaceful coexistence of the two, see also Toner, '*Messe ocus Pangur Bán*', p. 8.

36 Gerard Murphy, ed., *Early Irish Lyrics, Eighth to Twelfth Century* (Oxford: Clarendon, 1956), p. 1.

37 Toner, 'Messe ocus Pangur Bán', 3–4.

38 Toner, 'Messe ocus Pangur Bán', 9.

39 Hildegard L. C. Tristram, 'Die irischen Gedichte im Reichenauer Schulheft', in *Studia Celtica et Indogermanica. Festschrift für Wolfgang Meid zum 70. Geburtstag*, ed. Peter Anreiter and Erzsébat Jerem (Budapest: Archaeolingua, 1999), pp. 503–29, at p. 509; discussed in Toner, '*Messe ocus Pangur Bán*', p. 10.

40 Toner, 'Messe ocus Pangur Bán', p. 10.

41 Toner, 'Messe ocus Pangur Bán', p. 11.

42 Crane, *Animal Encounters*, p. 17.

43 E. G. Quin, *et al.*, eds, *Dictionary of the Irish Language Based Mainly on Old and Middle Irish Materials* (Dublin: Royal Irish Academy, 1983), Digital edition: Gregory Toner, ed., *Electronic Dictionary of the Irish Language* (*eDIL*), www.dil.ie/, *s.v.* 2 *lín*, sense III, (a), (b) and (c) (accessed 4 January 2018).

44 London, British Library, Cotton MS Nero D IV, fol. 139r, available at www.bl.uk/manuscripts/Viewer.aspx?ref=cotton_ms_nero_d_iv_f139r (accessed 6 February 2018). Cf. the interlaced cat and birds in the late eighth/early ninth-century Stowe Missal (MS D.II.3, fol. 121r), which may have been inspired by the scene in the Lindisfarne Gospels. See George F. Warner, ed., *The Stowe Missal, MS. D II 3 in the Library of the Royal Irish Academy, Dublin*, 2 vols (London: Henry Bradshaw Society, 1906), I, facsimile; and Michelle P. Brown, *The Lindisfarne Gospels: Society, Spirituality and the Scribe* (London: British Library, 2003), pp. 215 and 224.

45 On the context of the manuscript's composition, see Brown, *Lindisfarne Gospels*, pp. 104–10; Janet Backhouse, *The Lindisfarne Gospels* (Oxford: Phaidon, 1981), p. 12.

46 See George Henderson, *From Durrow to Kells: The Insular Gospel-books, 650–800* (London: Thames & Hudson, 1987), p. 108; Brown, *Lindisfarne Gospels*, p. 341; and Janet Backhouse, *The Lindisfarne Gospels: A Masterpiece of Book Painting* (London: British Library, 1995), pp. 23–4.

47 For a comparative context, note also the tenth-century Irish cross in Louth, which features carved cats at its base, including one catching a bird. Rogers, *Cat and the Human Imagination*, p. 19.

48 Douglas Gray, 'Notes on Some Medieval, Mystical and Moral Cats', in *Langland, the Mystics and the Medieval English Religious Tradition*, ed. Helen Philipps (Cambridge: Brewer, 1990), pp. 185–202, at p. 188. Further high to late medieval examples—including some more positive images—are given in Kathleen Walker-Meikle, *Medieval Pets* (Woodbridge: Boydell, 2012), pp. 10–13.
49 Kampling, 'Vom Streicheln', pp. 112 and 117.
50 Kampling, 'Vom Streicheln', pp. 96 and 117.
51 Gray, 'Notes on Some Medieval ... Cats', p. 191. The passage reads: *ne schulen habbe na beast bute cat ane.* Robert Hasenfrantz, ed., *Ancrene Wisse*, TEAMS Middle English Texts (Kalamazoo: Medieval Institute Publications, 2000), part 8, lines 76–7, http://d.lib.rochester.edu/teams/text/hasenfrantz-ancrene-wisse-part-eight (accessed 5 February 2019).
52 Gray, 'Notes on Some Medieval ... Cats', p. 190.
53 Serpell, 'Domestication', p. 98.
54 Rogers, *Cat and the Human Imagination*, p. 47.
55 Serpell, 'Domestication', p. 94; and Kitchener and O'Connor, 'Wildcats', p. 93.
56 This line is repeated word-for-word at the opening of pseudo-Symphosius' *Enigma 2*, *Pilax* ('cat'), immediately following Symphosius's *Enigma 25*, *Mus* ('mouse') in two tenth-/eleventh-century English manuscripts. See Andy Orchard, ed. and trans., *The Anglo-Saxon Riddle Tradition*, Dumbarton Oaks Medieval Library (Cambridge, MA: Harvard University Press, forthcoming).
57 Fr. Glorie, ed., *Collectiones Aenigmatum Merovingicae Aetatis*, CCSL, 133–133A (Turnhout: Brepols, 1968), 133, p. 467.
58 Orchard, *Anglo-Saxon Riddle Tradition*.
59 Orchard, *Anglo-Saxon Riddle Tradition*.
60 The potentially racist connotations in line 9's *gens exosa* ('hateful race)' should not be overlooked. A. M. Juster suggests that an allegorical interpretation may have linked this phrase to the Jews; see *Saint Aldhelm's Riddles* (Toronto: University of Toronto Press, 2015), p. 129. Later in the eleventh century, Embrico of Mainz uses it to disparage Muslims; see Embricon de Mayence, *La vie de Mahomet*, ed. Guy Cambier, Collection Latomus, 52 (Brussels: Latomus, 1962), p. 56, line 191.
61 Jolly, 'A Cat's Eye View', p. 116; Orchard, *Anglo-Saxon Riddle Tradition*.
62 Katharine M. Rogers, *Cat* (London: Reaktion, 2006), pp. 12–13.
63 Virgil, *Aeneid: Books 7–12, Appendix Vergiliana*, trans. H. Rushton Fairclough, rev. G. P. Goold, Loeb Classical Library, 64 (Cambridge, MA: Harvard University Press, 1918), p. 290, bk 11, line 780. For a line-by-line analysis of Virgil's influence on *Enigma 65*, see Glorie, *Collectiones Aenigmatum*, 133, p. 467; and for further classical echoes, see Juster, *Saint Aldhelm's Riddles*, pp. 128–9.

64 See Thomas Lindner, *Lateinische Komposita: Ein Glossar vornehmlich zum Wortschatz der Dichtersprache* (Innsbruck: Institut für Sprachwissenschaft der Universität Innsbruck, 1996), p. 121.

65 I am grateful to Robert Gallagher for this suggestion. On Aldhelm's fondness for esoteric vocabulary and his influence on later writers, see Michael Lapidge, 'The Hermeneutic Style in Tenth-Century Anglo-Latin Literature', *ASE*, 4 (1975), 67–111, at pp. 67 and 73–6; Aldhelm, *Aldhelm: The Poetic Works*, trans. Michael Lapidge and James Rosier (Cambridge: D.S. Brewer, 2009), pp. 1–4.

66 Tatwine, *Tatuini Opera Omnia: Ars Tatuini*, ed. Maria de Marco, CCSL, 133 (Turnhout: Brepols, 1968), p. 40, bk I, no. 114, line 1272. Note that, while *feles* is feminine, too, it is not given as a solution to this riddle.

67 Clare A. Lees and Gillian R. Overing discuss and problematise the relationship between grammatical and 'natural' gender in *Double Agents: Women and Clerical Culture in Anglo-Saxon England* (Philadelphia: University of Pennsylvania Press, 2001), pp. 204–16. See also the discussions of grammatical gender by Wilcox, Dale, and Salvador-Bello, Chapters 7, 10, and 12 in this volume.

68 For the negative view of mice in (later) medieval literature, see Lisa J. Kiser, 'Resident Aliens: The Literary Ecology of Medieval Mice', in *Truth and Tales: Cultural Mobility and Medieval Media*, ed. Fiona Somerset and Nicholas Watson (Columbus: Ohio State University Press, 2015), pp. 152–67.

69 Emily V. Thornbury, 'Aldhelm's Cat', *Arcade: Literature, Humanities, and the World*, Stanford University blogs, 19 April 2010, http://arcade.stanford.edu/blogs/aldhelms-cat (accessed 12 January 2018).

70 Rogers, *Cat*, p. 28.

71 Juster, *Saint Aldhelm's Riddles*, p. 128. For a comprehensive list of Aldhelm's citations of both these texts, see Michael Lapidge, *The Anglo-Saxon Library* (Oxford: Oxford University Press, 2006), pp. 180 and 188–90.

72 Virgil, *Eclogues, Georgics, Aeneid: Books 1–6*, trans. H. Rushton Fairclough, rev. G. P. Goold, Loeb Classical Library, 63 (Cambridge, MA: Harvard University Press, 1916), p. 340, bk 2, line 377.

73 Claudian, *On Stilicho's Consulship 2–3, Panegyric on the Sixth Consulship of Honorius, The Gothic War, Shorter Poems, Rape of Proserpina*, trans. M. Platnauer, Loeb Classical Library, 136 (Cambridge, MA: Harvard University Press, 1922), p. 354, bk 3, line 118.

74 Charlton T. Lewis and Charles Short, eds, *A Latin Dictionary, Founded on Andrews' Edition of Freund's Latin Dictionary* (Oxford: Clarendon, 1879), *s.v. scandalum*.

75 References to this noun and the related verb *scandalizare* are found in: Exodus 10:7, 23:33; 1 Kings (1 Samuel) 18:21; Psalms 48:14, 49:20, 68:23, 105:36, 118:165, 139:6; Proverbs 22:25; Ecclesiasticus 1:37,

7:6, 9:5, 27:26, 32:19, 32:25; Ezechiel 7:19, 14:3–4, 14:7; Malachias 2:8; 1 Machabees 5:4; Matthew 5:29–30; 13:21, 16:23, 17:26, 18:6–9, 26:31; Mark 9:41–6; Luke 17:2; John 6:62; Epistle of Saint Paul to the Romans 11:9, 14:13; 1st Epistle of Saint Paul to the Corinthians 1:23, 8:13; Epistle of Saint Paul to the Galatians 5:11; 1st Epistle of Saint John 2:10; Apocalypse of Saint John (Revelation) 2:14.

76 All Vulgate quotations and translations are from *The Holy Bible: Douay-Rheims Version* (Baltimore: John Murphy, 1899), http://drbo.org (accessed 16 January 2018).

77 Lewis and Short, *Latin Dictionary*, *s.v. insidiae*.

78 Kampling, 'Vom Streicheln', pp. 107–8.

79 Rogers, *Cat and the Human Imagination*, p. 5.

80 Poole, 'Contextual Cat', pp. 868 and 873–4.

4
The crafting of sound in the riddles of the *Exeter Book*

Francesca Brooks

In her 2001 study on *Graffiti and the Writing Arts of Early Modern England*, Juliet Fleming argues that '[t]o contemplate a song of pearl, or a "poysee" "made of letters of fine gold" [...] is to be unable to distinguish between a poem, a jewel, an acoustical structure and a feat of embroidery'.[1] This chapter explores a shared interest in the Old English riddles of the *Exeter Book* in materially crafted artefacts and aurally crafted riddle poems. More specifically, this chapter explores a group of the *Exeter Book* riddles that share a semantic and metaphorical interest in craft and sound: these riddles are both highly self-conscious acoustical structures and representations (often the voices) of finely wrought material structures. Although the Old English *cræft* encompasses a wide range of meanings related to 'skill', 'power', and 'ability',[2] 'craft', as I have chosen to define it, does not include mental or cognitive skills (although such skills are nevertheless relevant to my discussion here) but is confined to the works of craftsmen such as smiths, carpenters or weavers, and any of the processes associated with these crafts. 'Craft' also includes any kind of artificial adornment with precious metals, jewels and fabrics. Sound, on the other hand, has here been interpreted more broadly, encompassing all noise, both linguistic and non-linguistic, but with a particular attentiveness to the anthropomorphising features of linguistic sound: breath, voice and speech.

The riddles that I have identified as sharing an interest in both material craft and sound include *Ferende Gæst* (R.7), *Wæpenwiga* (R.14), *Wæpnum Awyrged* (R.20), *Nama Min is Mære* (R.26), *Dream bið in Innan* (R.28), *Feþegeorn* (R.31), *Grindan wið Greote* (R.32), *Hyhtlic Gewæd* (R.35), *Be Sonde Muðlease* (R.60), *Wordgaldor* (R.67) and *Orþoncum Geworht* (R.70). In these texts, craft and sound interact in a number of different ways, figuring the relationship between the aural and the material. Most of the riddles' subjects are worked objects, with the exception of *Ferende*

Gæst, which is a swan with all the embellishments of an acoustic, crafted artefact. In *Nama Min is Mære*, *Be Sonde Muðlease* and *Wordgaldor*, we are presented with writing implements and books, yet these scribal riddles nevertheless remind us of the successive stages of craft involved in shaping them into tools and containers for language, demonstrating how sound is worked into bound and enclosed texts in the early medieval English imagination.

In all of these riddles, worked objects speak, ring, and resound, and the material processes that transform raw materials into crafted artefacts are often represented as euphonious and aurally resonant in their own right. Weaving shuttles hum and rattle (*Hyhtlic Gewæd*), the gold-plated boards of a gospel book sing (*Nama Min is Mære*), horns embellished with twisted wires clamour with war cries (*Wæpenwiga*), jewelled instruments play with words (*Feþegeorn*), and the sharpened point of a pen might even communicate across the mead-bench (*Be Sonde Muðlease*). The two acts—material and linguistic crafting—share a significant semantic overlap and a common hoard of vocabulary. Language is often treated as a material substance that must be crafted into shape, while the crafting of objects involves many of the cognitive and perceptual skills (rather than purely technical and physical) that are necessary in the decoding of poetic language.

In this chapter, I explore the relationship between craft and sound in three representative texts: *Be Sonde Muðlease*, *Nama Min is Mære*, and *Feþegeorn*. In each of these riddles human technologies are celebrated as both finely wrought material things and articulate vessels for human language. Although much criticism of the *Exeter Book* riddles, and of Old English literature more generally, has focused on how these texts record a new interest in the materiality of written texts and, more particularly, in how writing might encode the essential orality of speech, I want to suggest that in the imaginative world of the *Exeter Book* the material qualities of sound and language are not confined to written speech or seen as a sensory effect that is limited to writing technologies.[3] Linguistic and non-linguistic sounds need not be fixed to the page in ink or inscribed upon the surface of an early medieval speaking-object to be perceived in material terms or indeed in terms of acts of material craft. A shared semantic and metaphorical interest in material craft and sound across *Be Sonde Muðlease*, *Nama Min is Mære*, and *Feþegeorn* suggests a richer perception of the relationship between craftsman and poet, and materiality and aurality, than our modern understanding might accommodate. In the *Exeter Book* riddles, it may not in fact matter whether the enigmatic subject contemplated, to quote Juliet Fleming again, is a 'poem, a jewel, an acoustical structure, or a feat of embroidery'.

Since Laurence K. Shook's essay, 'Riddles Relating to the Anglo-Saxon Scriptorium', editors and critics of the riddles have focused their attention on a slowly expanding corpus of riddles that take as their subject and inspiration the early medieval scriptoria, scribal practice, and literary traditions.[4] Analysis of the scribal riddles tends to focus on their engagement with the tangible materials of literate culture. Dieter Bitterli, for example, quotes Robert DiNapoli's discussion of the 'almost obsessive physicality' at work in *Nama Min is Mære* in his reassessment of the riddles that take as their focus 'the materiality of writing and book-making'.[5] Most recently, Peter Ramey has argued for the ways in which ideas of writing in the *Exeter Book* riddles offer us a 'distinctly Anglo-Saxon vernacular concept of writing ... one that perceives writing technology, through the lens of an oral poetics, as a material form of speech'.[6] I want to begin by thinking about a potential scribal riddle that is less concerned with the form (whether aural or material) of speech and more interested in how an act of human craft transforms a silent reed into a sound-and-language-producing artefact.

Debate surrounding *Be Sonde Muðlease* has often focused on whether the subject is the sound-producing reed pipe, the reed pen with its written language, or even a rune staff incised with obscure letters.[7] Its potential source, Symphosius's second Latin riddle, is solved as reed pipe or reed pen.[8] The Latin riddle plays with the etymology of its solution, *calamus*, which comes, Isidore claims, from *calere* ('rousing') and means a 'pouring forth' of voices.[9] Although the etymological play of the Latin does not appear to translate into the Old English, the ability of the subject of *Be Sonde Muðlease* to *abeodan bealdlice* ('boldly announce') (16a) *ærendspræce* ('a spoken message') (15b) certainly seems to resonate with Symphosius's earlier verbal play in creating a subject that is a messenger of the tongue. John D. Niles suggests a solution for *Be Sonde Muðlease* in the Old English neuter noun *hreod* ('a reed', 'a writing instrument'), which might also suggest the *hreod-pipere* ('player of a reed pipe'), and, as James Paz also concludes, the reeds of the riddle's opening are thus 'the source of both a flute and a pen'.[10] For the purposes of my discussion here, I will follow Niles and Paz in thinking of the subject of *Be Sonde Muðlease* as an artefact made from the *hreod*, whose final shape by the end of the riddle, with its focus on linguistic communication, is that of the reed pen.

Be Sonde Muðlease is interested in how physical tools and the skill involved in human craft facilitate verbal communication and the production of linguistic sounds. Despite the aural potentialities of the scene with which it begins, the first seven lines of the riddle are peculiarly silent:

Ic wæs be sonde, sæwealle neah,
æt merefaroþe, minum gewunade
frumstaþole fæst; fea ænig wæs
monna cynnes, þæt mine þær
on anæde eard beheolde,
ac mec uhtna gehwam yð sio brune
lagufæðme beleolc. (1–7a)

[I was by the sand, near the seawall, at the sea-swell; I dwelt fast-rooted in my dwelling place; few were those kinsmen that beheld my home in this wilderness. Daily with the dawn the dark waves enclosed me in their watery embrace.]

The setting of the first seven lines is characterised by the powerful flux of the natural world, isolated from the human. Although the riddle-subject remains *frumstaþole fæst* ('fast-rooted in [its] dwelling place') (2b–3), it is subject to the tidal shifts and forces of the sea as *uhtna gehwam yð sio brune / lagufæðme beleolc* ('daily with the dawn the dark waves enclosed [it] in their watery embrace') (6–7a). As with the *wineleas* ('friendless') subject of the *Exeter Book* elegy, *The Wanderer*, who has only the *fealwe wegas* ('fallow waves') (45) and *baþian brimfuglas* ('bathing wave-birds') (47) to greet him, the subject of the riddle is presented as existing in a kind of social exile here at the sea margin. Surprisingly, where we might expect to find the rush of the *merefaroþe* ('sea-swell') as it crashes against the seawall, or the wind rustling the reeds, we are left in an aural vacuum. This dwelling place is not only the *anæde* ('wilderness' or 'desert-like solitude'), a place removed from the social and communal setting of early medieval life, it is also a place of silence.

It is only in the second half of the riddle that we are launched into the euphony of linguistic sounds with the subject's movement into the crafted human world of the mead-hall:

Lyt ic wende
þæt ic ær oþþe sið æfre sceolde
ofer meodubence muðleas sprecan,
wordum wrixlan. Þæt is wundres dæl,
on sefan searolic þam þe swylc ne conn. (7b–11)

[Little did I think that sooner or later I should ever speak mouthless across the mead-bench, exchange words. That is a share of wonder, artful to the mind that does not know such things.]

The mead-hall is a site where words are exchanged (*wordum wrixlan*); the reed pen is presented here as a kind of poet or performer. *Wordum wrixlan* is an Old English collocation used to describe the work of poets who weave words (*wrixlan*: 'to change, vary, alter; to exchange, deal') from the poetic *wordhord* into new texts in the social economy of the word exchange, familiar from *Beowulf*'s Heorot.[11] Like several of the riddles' subjects, *Be Sonde Muðlease* speaks 'mouthless': the mechanism by which it can participate in the word exchange offers another enigma, appearing *searolic* ('ingenious, cunning, artful') to the mind that cannot unriddle it.[12] In its various compound occurrences, *searo*, meaning 'device, design; craft, artifice; that which is contrived with art', binds material, intellectual, and linguistic elements.[13] Its compounds range in meaning from the cunning of thought, to a finely crafted piece of armour, to prized hoards of stone, and to skill in fighting.[14] Here *searo* defines the mental and linguistic skills required to solve the riddle. However, the use of *searo* also suggests the act of cunning artifice that enabled the riddle's subject to produce its enigmatic sounding voice: in *Be Sonde Muðlease* this is an act of material craft.

The subject's movement from the solitude of the natural world to the centre of society is only made possible by an act of craft, which transforms the silent reed into a communicative tool with the power to engage in the word exchange. The enigma of the riddle is:

hu mec seaxes ord   ond seo swiþre hond,
eorles ingeþonc   ond ord somod,
þingum geþydan,   þæt ic wiþ þe sceolde
for unc anum twam   ærendspræce
abeodan bealdlice,   swa hit beorna ma
uncre wordcwidas   widdor ne mænden. (12–17)

[how the point of a knife and a strong hand, the inner-thought and the blade joined me into agreement, so that I should boldly announce to you a spoken message, for us two alone, so that no other can speak of our word-sayings.]

The riddle's subject is plunged into a world of linguistic sound and speech when shaped by one person's hand, their thought, and the point of their knife. Although the *ord* ('point of a weapon') is referred to twice (12a, 13b), the most important elements in this act of craft are the *swiþre hond* (12b), the physical craftiness of the human hand, and the *eorles ingeþonc* (13a), the inner thought and crafty intelligence of the maker. The maker bestows linguistic sentience on the crafted object through his or her own intellectual skill. The verb *geþydan* (14a) has social implications—meaning to 'join, unite, associate'—reflecting the process by which the subject is initiated into the human world of language through an act of craft.[15]

The act of crafting is a means of activating the reed pen's linguistic abilities, becoming not merely a vessel for human language but an active participant in the exchange of dialogue. The verbs *mænan* (17b) and *abeodan* (16a) both have multiple meanings, indicating the richness of linguistic exchange. While *abeodan* means to 'proclaim, make public, preach, announce', its usages suggest that it can be applied to specifically oral and written contexts through 'writing', the 'publication of an edict' or by means of 'voice' by 'shouting out'.[16] *Mænan* can mean 'to mean, to signify', 'to communicate, to utter', 'to express one's feelings', 'to commune with one's self, to consider', as well as 'to tell, say', and 'to speak a language'—offering a whole range of actions that include both linguistic and supra-linguistic modes of expression.[17] *Be Sonde Muðlease*'s mouthless speech is also communicated through the compounds *ærendspræce* (15b) and *wordcwidas* (17a). The 'verbal message' of *ærendspræce* is a compound of *ærend* ('a message') and *spræce* ('a talk, discourse'), while the *wordcwidas* ('speech, language') are a compound of *word* ('word') and *cwidas* ('sayings').[18] Although the subject's claim that its message is *for unc anum twam* ('for us two alone') (15a) perhaps implies a written message rather than a spoken one that might be overheard, the vocabulary used in *Be Sonde Muðlease* nevertheless asserts the primacy of the oral in the word exchange of the mead-hall. These compounds and the wider vocabulary for linguistic exchange display the word-craft of the riddler as much as they point towards the unlocking of further language. Both Bitterli and Niles have discussed the self-reflexive nature of *Be Sonde Muðlease* as a crafted riddle-song that also offers its own enigmatic and private message for the reader of the manuscript.[19] If *Be Sonde Muðlease* is a reflection on its own poetic craft, then it presents the craft of the text as a thing intimately bound to the craftsman who transformed the *hreod* from a work of nature to a work of human artifice.

I want to return now to the 'obsessive physicality', as Robert DiNapoli puts it, of another of the scribal riddles, *Nama Min is Mære*, in order to consider how the text might also speak to our auditory imagination in depicting acts of material craft. Solved as a gospel book or Bible, *Nama Min is Mære* speaks in the first person, recounting in detail the material processes of book production.[20] Rather than focusing on itself as a 'speaking-book' its interest is primarily in the visual and material elements of the written text's creation:

> Mec feonda sum feore besnyþede,
> woruldstrenga binom, wætte siþþan,
> dyfde on wætre, dyde eft þonan,
> sette on sunnan, þær ic swiþe beleas
> herum þam ic hæfde. Heard mec siþþan
> snað seaxses ecg, sindrum begrunden. (1–6)

> [A certain enemy deprived me of life, stole my world-strength, afterward soaked me, dunked me in water, then pulled me out again, set me in the sun. There I was swiftly stripped of the hairs I had. Afterwards the hard edge of a knife, ground clean, cut me.]

In these lines, the focus is on the tactile and visceral nature of the washed, dried, and scraped manuscript pages, which will later be filled with the inky tracks of script and enclosed in jewelled gold boards. *Nama Min is Mære*'s book, this artefact of the Word, is presented as a product of multiple material, rather than linguistic, processes: with its *gereno ond se reada telg* ('ornaments and red dye') (15), the book is a thing to behold and to touch (Bitterli remarks upon its 'hands-on detail') rather than to listen to.[21]

However, *Nama Min is Mære* also presents us with an auricular teaser that suggests that the material processes of book production do not elide the aural potential of the written word: even though this book is never read aloud here, we know that in the early medieval English imagination the writing might be made to speak. The teaser comes in the form of an encoded reference to song in the smith's role in the making of the book:

> Mec siþþan wrah
> hæleð hleobordum, hyde beþenede,
> gierede mec mid golde; forþon me gliwedon
> wrætlic weorc smiða. (11b–14a)

> [Afterwards they covered me with sheltering boards, stretched the concealing hide over me, then clothed me with gold. On me sang[22] the wonder-crafted work of smiths.]

With the text enclosed and protected within the boards of the book, sound plays instead on the wrought surface of the manuscript. The work of the smith is described as *wrætlic* ('wondrous, wonder-crafted'), a word that appears frequently throughout the Exeter riddling corpus and elsewhere to describe wrought artefacts and even linguistic structures that provoke and inspire feelings of awe and wonder.[23] As Peter Ramey has argued, *wrætlic* suggests a work of artifice, 'an object that has been *made* beautiful through the work of hands and a creative, shaping consciousness'.[24] Furthermore, as a descriptor, *wrætlic* is itself riddlic, representing, as Ramey proposes, 'the enigmatic encounter with a beautifully wrought creation'.[25] In the context of *Nama Min is Mære*, the *wrætlic* or enigmatic quality of the smith's work might be connected to the verb *gliwian*, a word that has continued to confound translators and editors.

The *DOE* lists several definitions for the verb *gliwian* including 'to play on a musical instrument', 'to sing, recite', along with a separate entry for the verb's occurrence in Riddle 26:

> *me gliwedon wrætlic weorc smiða*, the sense of which is uncertain but where the object (me) is a book or bible; *gliwedon* has been taken as a figurative extension of sense and translated 'on me played the splendid work of smiths', with *gliwian* as perhaps referring to the sound made by the metalwork on an ornamented book when it was moved about or opened; a sense 'to adorn', otherwise unattested, has been suggested.[26]

Many critics and translators of the riddle opt to translate *gliwedon* in material rather than aural terms: Bitterli, for example, chooses 'I am embellished with the wondrous work of smiths', while Kevin Crossley-Holland has 'I am enriched'.[27] Craig Williamson chooses a dual interpretation that emphasises both the aural and the visual effect of the smith's work with: 'The bright song / Of smiths glistens on me'.[28] However, we can read the verb's occurrence literally rather than figuratively here: the riddle reflects on the noisy process with which the smith encloses the gospel book in its gold covering.

In the 'singing' (or the 'playing', as of an instrument) of the smith's work there may also be an elliptical reference to the Macrobian account of Pythagoras' discovery of the rational principles of music when passing the noisy workshop of some blacksmiths.[29] Isidore references the episode in his *Etymologiae*, writing that *Graeci vero Pythagoram dicunt huius artis invenisse primordia ex malleorum sonitu et cordarum extensione percussa* ('the Greeks say that Pythagoras discovered the elements of [music] from the sound of hammers and taut strings').[30] While the riddle is primarily focused on the book's production, the singing of the smith's work hints at the life of the manuscript beyond its initial moment of production when its script will be brought to voice through song and speech. *Gliwian* implicates the work of the smith in the crafting of both the visual *and* the aural wonders of the gospel book and suggests here how the material crafting of the book cannot be disentangled from the verbal crafting of its contents. The craft of writing is momentarily indistinguishable from the craft of the smith, or from those other material processes that have contributed to the book's final form as a thing *halig* ('holy') (27a) and *niþum to nytte* ('useful to men') (29b).

As a final example, I want to move away from the scribal riddles to consider a closely related musical riddle. *Feþegeorn* offers us an ornate, 'song'-producing instrument that appears to have several dangling attachments, including a 'foot' through which it can be played. The riddle is generally solved as some kind of musical instrument, specifically a wind instrument: Frederick Tupper suggests 'bagpipe', while Niles proposes *blæstpipe* 'windpipe'.[31] Although *Feþegeorn* presents us with a thing that sings, it is also *wisum gewitlegad wrættum gefrætwed* ('wisely formed, adorned with works of art') (2) and a visual spectacle. In a confusion of the sensory categories the riddler declares, *Ic seah sellic þing singan on ræcede* ('I saw a strange thing sing in the hall') (3). The craft of song is closely aligned here with the craft of the instrument's maker. Despite the subject's primary role as a sound-producing artefact, there is also a curious focus on its material adornment, suggesting that its status as a materially crafted artefact is imaginatively bound up with the beautiful quality of the sound it produces.

Feþegeorn introduces its instrumental subject as an ambiguous *wiht* ('creature/thing') with animalistic features:

> Niþerweard wæs neb hyre,
> fet ond folme fugele gelice;
> no hwæþre fleogan mæg ne fela gongan.
> hwæþre feþegeorn. (6–9a)

> [Downward hangs her beak, with feet and hands in the likeness of a bird; yet she cannot fly or go forward at all, though longing for movement.]

The subject of *Feþegeorn* is a strange flightless bird with a beak, feet and hands. Perhaps drawing on the same aural associations invoked by the birds of the *Exeter Book* riddles more broadly, the description of the instrument's birdlike features keeps us focused on the visual spectacle of the instrument, its physical form, while hinting at its melodic capabilities. Encounters with birds in the riddles of the *Exeter Book* are almost always accompanied by accounts of the sounds of their varied songs or, indeed, in the case of *Ferende Gæst*'s swan, of their plumage.[32] In the *Etymologiae*, Isidore explains that *[a]vium nomina multa a sono vocis constat esse composita ... Varietas enim vocis eorum docuit homines quid nominarentur* ('many birds' names are evidently constructed from the sound of their calls ... the variety of their calls taught people what they might be called').[33] Thus the key to the enigma of a bird's identity can be seen to lie primarily in its characteristic song.[34]

It is precisely its birdlike form that enables the subject of *Feþegeorn* to produce sound and, ultimately, to access language:

Deor domes georn,   hio dumb wunað;
hwæþre hyre is on fote   fæger hleoþor,
wynlicu woðgiefu.   Wrætlic me þinceð,
hu seo wiht mæge   wordum lacan
þurh fot neoþan,   frætwed hyrstum.
Hafað hyre on halse,   þonne hio hord warað,
bær, beagum deall,   broþor sine,
mæg mid mægne.   Micel is to hycgenne
wisum woðboran,   hwæt sio wiht sie. (16–24)

[Brave, eager for glory, she remains dumb; yet in her foot she has a beautiful voice, a glorious gift for song. It is wondrous to me how this creature can play with words, through its foot below, adorned with jewels. Bare, proud with rings, a mighty kinswoman, she has on her neck, as she guards her hoard, her brothers. It is a great thing for wise speech-bearers to consider what this creature is.]

The riddle reflects on the musical craft of its instrumental subject and on the word-craft of the riddle itself: the subject's adornment with *hyrstum* ('jewels') and rings is matched by the verbal adornment of treasure vocabulary and the aural adornment of alliteration, assonance, and consonance. As Pauline E. Head has written: '[v]erbal and visual Anglo-Saxon texts share a predominance of ornamentation, an elaboration of structure, which indicates that their form is not subordinate to and separable from their meaning'.[35] It is through her foot that the subject gains access to her *fæger hleoþor* ('beautiful voice') and *giefu* ('gift') for song. The riddler claims that the subject's ability to *wordum lacan / þurh fot neoþan* ('play with words, through its foot below') is *wrætlic* ('wondrous'), but we are also reminded that this foot is part of the adorned artefact of the instrument—*frætwed hyrstum* ('adorned with jewels'). It is artifice rather than any natural phenomenon that gives this birdlike creature its gift for song: the instrument has been crafted for sound.

Like *Be Sonde Muðlease*, *Feþegeorn* offers a moment of reflection on the art of the riddle-song as well as on the art of the musical instrument. This is expressed both through the collocation *wordum lacan* ('play with words') (19b) and through the riddler's claim that *hio hord warað* ('she guards her hoard') (21b). The *hord* here seems to be related to the instrument's decorated nature: its jewelled foot and proudly displayed rings contribute to the material wealth that the instrument must protect. However, the *hord* also represents a more abstract treasure, suggesting the hollowed space within which the wind instrument gathers the music-producing breath that will become its song. This hoard of air is a treasury of linguistic possibility, invoking associations with the poetic *wordhord*. The riddle's classification as a wind instrument introduces human breath as a key element in acoustic production: as Isidore claims, wind instruments are *in sonum vocis animatur* ('animated with the sound of voice') when they are filled with breath.[36] The subject's *hord* gives the material of music and indeed of other vocal utterances (that is, animating breath) a peculiar sense of material form. Breath is a kind of resource that is stored and transformed by the instrument's physical form into an acoustic structure that is as beautiful as the jewelled instrument that produced it.

The association of the instrument's *hord* with the poetic *wordhord* is strengthened by the collocation *wordum lacan*. The collocation is unattested elsewhere in the Old English corpus but appears to have a similar meaning to the *wordum wrixlan* of *Be Sonde Muðlease* and of *Beowulf*, suggesting an artful playing with words.[37] In *wordum lacan*, we may also have an extension of the scribal motif of the flight path or track of birds as a visual metaphor for written letters or script, found in *Nama Min is Mære* and *Wuhte Feower* (R.51) and, as recently argued by Patrick J. Murphy, *Sanges Rope* (R.57).[38] The motif may play with broader ideas about the pursuit of knowledge through reading, as expressed in the Alfredian translation of *Boethius* and in the preface to the Old English *Pastoral Care*. In the preface to the *Pastoral Care*, Alfred laments that his people can no longer *æfterspyrigean* ('pursue, follow after') the *swæþ*—literally the 'tracks', but also the writings of their ancestors—because they cannot read Latin (11–18).[39] Similar language of tracking and pursuit, also found here in the riddles, is used in the fourth prose and metrum of Book 4 of the Old English *Boethius* too (8–15).[40]

The verb *lacan* also suggests 'to swing, wave about ... as a bird does in its flight': such an interpretation of *lacan* in the context of *Feþegeorn* would also be consonant with the instrument's desire for movement (*feþegeorn*), as the outpouring of music is associated with the flight of the bird through the sky.[41] Alongside *woð*, meaning 'a sound, cry, noise; of articulate or melodious sound: voice, song, speech', the *wordum lacan* in *Feþegeorn* blurs the distinction between wordless music and a word-crafted song, poem or speech.[42] In *Feþegeorn* we have a musical instrument rather than a scribal tool, and yet sound remains a material substance that can be crafted into acoustical structures, which rival the materially adorned artefacts that produced them.

Christian Metz and Georgia Gurrieri define the concept of the 'aural object' in order to readdress 'the conception of sound as an attribute, as a non-object, and therefore the tendency to neglect its own characteristics in favour of those of its corresponding "substance", which in this case is the visible object, which has emitted the sound'.[43] We can read the material and visual interests of the scribal *Nama Min is Mære* and *Be Sonde Muðlease*, and of the musical *Feþegeorn*, as a reflection of an 'obsessive materiality' provoked by writing technologies; however, we should also remain attentive to the overriding interests of these riddles in the aural objects, the sound effects, of these highly crafted artefacts. There is no reason to think that sound, and especially linguistic sound, whether fixed to the page, inscribed upon the surface of an early medieval speaking-object, or given life through the breath and voice of human, animal or musical instrument, should not be seen as a substance capable of being crafted into *wrætlic* acoustical structures. In our own contemporary idioms, we can *work* and *re-work* a sentence, *spin* a yarn, *twist* somebody else's words, *tangle* ourselves in a *web* of lies; and our own verbal dexterity might even allow us to *weave* our words into an elaborate story. Such idioms and metaphors, these *turns* of phrase, remind us of the extent to which we rely on material and technical craft vocabularies to express the immaterial shaping of language which takes place, ephemerally and intangibly, in our minds and with our ears before it might be committed materially to a written surface. Craft allows the reader or listener to get a material purchase on the slippery aural medium of word-sounds.

The Old English collocations *wordum wrixlan* and *wordum lacan* suggest that metaphors for crafting language in material terms are not a modern phenomenon. In these Old English texts, spoken language borrows from the material structures of wrought artefacts and the social structures of the gift economy, using the material to negotiate its own acoustics in the poetic realm. The riddles prove themselves to be a play of language and a celebration of the aural possibilities of this essentially human gift. The crafted nature of these acoustic and linguistic artefacts in the riddles of the *Exeter Book* remind us of the vernacular's essential orality, even when we find it recorded in the written word. I have argued that the acoustic element, interwoven with the language of material craft, can be read as evidence of riddlic self-reflexivity: a self-conscious exploration of how Old English can be worked into *wrætlic* acoustic structures in poetry. The riddles do not rely only on the voices of their poets for their meaning; their linguistic mechanisms presuppose the social and communal value of the text within the word exchange and leave space for the reader's own voice to resonate in response.

Notes

1 Juliet Fleming, *Graffiti and the Writing Arts of Early Modern England* (London: Reaktion, 2001), p. 10.
2 *DOE*, *s.v. cræft*.
3 See, for example, Katherine O'Brien O'Keeffe, *Visible Song: Transitional Literacy in Old English Verse* (Cambridge: Cambridge University Press, 1991); Carol Braun Pasternack, *The Textuality of Old English Poetry* (Cambridge: Cambridge University Press, 1995); Mary Hayes, 'The Talking Dead: Resounding Voices in Old English Riddles', *Exemplaria*, 20 (2008), 123–42.
4 Laurence K. Shook, 'Riddles Relating to the Anglo-Saxon Scriptorium', in *Essays in Honour of Anton Charles Pegis*, ed. J. Reginald O'Donnell (Toronto: Pontifical Institute of Mediaeval Studies, 1974), pp. 215–36. For more recent work on the scribal corpus, see Dieter Bitterli, *Say What I Am Called: The Old English Riddles of the Exeter Book and the Anglo-Latin Riddle Tradition* (Toronto: University of Toronto Press, 2009), pp. 135–50; Patrick J. Murphy, '*Bocstafas*: A Literal Reading of Exeter Book Riddle 57', *PQ*, 84 (2005), 139–60.
5 Bitterli, *Say What I am Called*, pp. 9 and 136. See also: Robert DiNapoli, 'In the Kingdom of the Blind, the One-Eyed Man is a Seller of Garlic: Depth Perception and the Poet's Perspective in the Exeter Book Riddles', *ES*, 81 (2010), 422–55, at p. 437.
6 Peter Ramey, 'Writing Speaks: Oral Poetics and Writing Technology in the Exeter Book Riddles', *PQ*, 92 (2013), 335–56, at p. 335.
7 Although speculation that *Be Sonde Muðlease* might be part of *The Husband's Message*, the poem that follows it in the *Exeter Book* manu-

script, led to the popularisation of 'rune-staff' as a solution, this idea is now largely discredited. See Craig Williamson's arguments for both rune-staff and reed-pen in *The Old English Riddles of the Exeter Book* (Chapel Hill: University of North Carolina Press, 1977), pp. 315–18. See also: Roy F. Leslie, 'The Integrity of Riddle 60', *JEGP*, 67 (1968), 451–7; Ian J. Kirby, 'The Exeter Book, *Riddle 60*', *N&Q*, 48 (2001), 219–20.

8 Williamson, *Old English Riddles*, p. 317.

9 *Calamus nomen est proprium arboris a calendo, id est fundendo voces vocatus* ('"Reed" is the particular name of a tree, and comes from "rousing", that is, from "pouring forth" voices'). Isidore of Seville, *Etymologiarum sive originum libri XX*, ed. W. M. Lindsay, 2 vols (Oxford, Clarendon, 1911), I, 3.21.5; *The Etymologies of Isidore of Seville*, trans. Stephen A. Barney, W. J. Lewis, J. A. Beach, and Oliver Berghof (Cambridge: Cambridge University Press, 2006), p. 97.

10 John D. Niles, *Old English Enigmatic Poems and the Play of the Texts* (Turnhout: Brepols, 2006), pp. 131–2; James Paz, *Nonhuman Voices in Anglo-Saxon Literature and Material Culture* (Manchester: Manchester University Press, 2017), p. 89. See also *DOE*, *s.v. hreod* and *hreod-pipere*.

11 See B-T, *s.v. wrixlan*. See also the occurrences of the collocation in *Beowulf*, lines 366 and 874.

12 See B-T, *s.v. searolic*.

13 See B-T, *s.v. searo*.

14 See *DOEC*, *s.v. searo*.

15 See B-T, *s.v. geþeodan*.

16 See *DOE*, *s.v. abeodan*.

17 See B-T, *s.v. mænen*.

18 See *DOE*, *s.v. ærend, cwiddas*; B-T, *s.v. spræce, word*.

19 Bitterli, *Say What I am Called*, p. 139; Niles, *Old English Enigmatic Poems*, p. 131. The essential self-reflexiveness of the riddles is well-established. Elaine Tuttle Hansen proposes that the subject of the collection as a whole is 'language', while Seth Lerer describes them as 'miniature essays in linguistic play'. Elaine Tuttle Hansen, *The Solomon Complex: Reading Wisdom in Old English Poetry* (Toronto: University of Toronto Press, 1988), pp. 127 and 142; Seth Lerer, *Literacy and Power in Anglo Saxon Literature* (Lincoln: University of Nebraska Press, 1991), p. 25.

20 See Niles, *Old English Enigmatic Poems*, pp. 117–19.

21 Bitterli, *Say What I am Called*, p. 174.

22 The translation of *gliwedon* is discussed below.

23 See B-T, *s.v. wrætlic*. See also the discussion by Rhodes in Chapter 2 of this volume.

24 Peter Ramey, 'The Riddle of Beauty: The Aesthetics of *Wrætlic* in Old English Verse', *MP*, 114 (2017), 457–81, at pp. 478 and 467.

25 Ramey, 'The Riddle of Beauty', p. 467.
26 *DOE*, *s.v. gliwian*, sense 4.
27 Bitterli, *Say What I am Called*, p. 176; Kevin Crossley-Holland, trans., *The Exeter Book Riddles*, rev. edn (London: Enitharmon, 2008), p. 29.
28 Craig Williamson, trans., *A Feast of Creatures: Anglo-Saxon Riddle Songs* (Philadelphia: University of Pennsylvania Press, 1982), p. 84.
29 See also Bruce Holsinger's discussion of the episode from Macrobius: *Music, Body, and Desire in Medieval Culture: Hildegard of Bingen to Chaucer* (Stanford: Stanford University Press, 2001), p. 8.
30 Isidore, *Etymologiarum*, ed. Lindsay, I, 3.16.1; *Etymologies*, trans. Barney, *et al.*, p. 95.
31 See Frederick Tupper, Jr, ed., *The Riddles of the Exeter Book* (Boston: Ginn, 1910), p. 143; Niles, *Old English Enigmatic Poems*, p. 108. See also Wilcox, Chapter 7 in this volume, for further discussion of this riddle.
32 See, for example, the magpie of *Siex Stafas Sweotule Becnaþ* (R.24), the songbird of *Eald Æfensceop* (R.8), and the swan of *Ferende Gæst* (R.7).
33 Isidore, *Etymologiarum*, ed. Lindsay, II, 12.7.9; *Etymologies*, trans. Barney, *et al.*, p. 264.
34 See also Eric Lacey's discussion of the importance of aurality in early medieval bird categorisation. Lacey finds that while many birds' names in Old English derive from their appearance, a far larger proportion come from the sounds they make. 'Birds and Words: Aurality, Semantics, and Species in Anglo-Saxon England', in *Sensory Perception in the Medieval West*, ed. Simon C. Thomson and Michael D. J. Bintley (Turnhout: Brepols, 2016), pp. 75–98.
35 Pauline E. Head, *Representations and Design: Tracing a Hermeneutics of Old English Poetry* (Albany: SUNY Press, 1997), p. 115. See also John Leyerle, 'The Interlace Structure of *Beowulf*', *University of Toronto Quarterly*, 37 (1967), 1–17.
36 Isidore, *Etymologiarum*, ed. Lindsay, I, 3.21.1; *Etymologies*, trans. Barney, *et al.*, p. 97.
37 See *DOEC*, *s.v. lacan*; B-T, *s.v. lacan.*
38 See Patrick J. Murphy, *Unriddling the Exeter Riddles* (University Park: Pennsylvania State University Press, 2011), pp. 79–108.
39 See Henry Sweet, ed., *King Alfred's West-Saxon Version of Gregory's Pastoral Care* (London: Trübner, 1871), p. 5.
40 See Malcolm R. Godden and Susan Irvine, ed. and trans., *The Old English Boethius with Verse Prologues and Epilogues Associated with King Alfred*, Dumbarton Oaks Medieval Library (Cambridge, MA: Harvard University Press, 2012), pp. 326–7.
41 See B-T, *s.v. lacan.*

42 See B-T, *s.v. woþ*. See also Elizabeth Eva Leach on the relationship between speech and song in medieval literature: *Sung Birds: Music, Nature, and Poetry in the Later Middle Ages* (Ithaca, NY: Cornell University Press, 2007), p. 26.
43 Christian Metz and Georgia Gurrieri, 'Aural Objects', *Yale French Studies*, 60 (1980), 24–32, at p. 30.

5
Sound, voice, and articulation in the Exeter Book riddles

Robert Stanton

The *Exeter Book* riddles present a symphony of acoustic effects, deploying a multitude of linguistic resources to reflect aesthetically on the metaphysical relationship, long examined by philosophers and grammarians, between sounds, speech, concepts, and subjects and objects both animate and inanimate.[1] This chapter discusses the different ways that sounds signify in these riddles, especially the sensory, cognitive, and culturally formed categories through which sound effects evoke the rhythms and textures of natural phenomena, technologically produced objects, and human and animal experience. Like all Old English poetry but especially vividly, the riddles pleasurably combine received fields of knowledge and familiar poetic forms with the surprising, sometimes unsettling aural effects produced by specific lines. I want to tease out some connections between the concepts of sound, noise, and voice as the early medieval English inherited them from the classical and early medieval philosophical and grammatical traditions, and the achievable performative effects of sound via the techniques of English enigmatic poetry. Ultimately, on a broader and more ambitious scale that I can only gesture towards, I want to follow the lead of Maurizio Bettini in the subtitle of his 2008 book *Voci* to ponder the possibilities of a 'sound anthropology' of early medieval England.[2]

Certain fundamental concepts of sound and voice going back to Aristotle reached early medieval England via the grammarians Priscian and Donatus, the encyclopaedist Isidore of Seville, and the early medieval scholar and writer Aldhelm, whose work on poetic theory and his own Latin riddle collection make him a vital bridge between classical language theory and the Old English poetic tradition. Aristotle, in his *De interpretatione*, notes that

> Ἔστι μὲν οὖν τὰ ἐν τῇ φωνῇ τῶν ἐν τῇ ψυχῇ παθημάτων σύμβολα, καὶ τὰ γραφόμενα τῶν ἐν τῇ φωνῇ … ὧν μέντοι ταῦτα σημεῖα πρώτων, ταὐτὰ

πᾶσι παθήματα τῆς ψυχῆς, καὶ ὧν ταῦτα ὁμοιώματα, πράγματα ἤδη ταὐτά … Ὄνομα μὲν οὖν ἐστὶ φωνὴ σημαντικὴ κατὰ συνθήκην ἄνευ χρόνου, ἧς μηδὲν μέρος ἐστὶ σημαντικὸν κεχωρισμένον … τὸ δὲ κατὰ συνθήκην, ὅτι φύσει τῶν ὀνομάτων οὐδέν ἐστιν, ἀλλ' ὅταν γένηται σύμβολον, ἐπεὶ δηλοῦσί γέ τι καὶ οἱ ἀγράμματοι ψόφοι, οἷον θηρίων, ὧν οὐδέν ἐστιν ὄνομα.[3]

[Now spoken sounds are symbols (σύμβολα) of affections in the soul, and written marks symbols of spoken sounds … But what these are in the first place (πρώτων) signs (σημεῖα) of—affections of the soul—are the same for all; and what these affections are likenesses (ὁμοιώματα) of—actual things—are also the same … A name is a spoken sound significant by convention, without time, none of whose parts is significant in separation … I say 'by convention' because no name is a name naturally but only when it has become a symbol. Even inarticulate noises (of beasts, for instance), do indeed reveal something, yet none of them is a name.]

Spoken sounds, then, are symbols of affections in the soul, but they are in the first place signs of those affections. Vocal sounds become symbols only when they are assigned meanings by convention. An animal, for example, cannot speak a noun because nouns signify only within a system of language that is a specifically human institution. Yet there is a high degree of continuity between the natural signification of the sign and the conventionalised signification of the symbol. As Lia Formigari has noted, in the *Poetics*, Aristotle

> derives the arts of language from the bodily arts of dance and rhythm and organizes them in a series according to the extent they employ bodily or musical rhythm. Similarly, in [Aristotle's] *Rhetorics*, prosody contributes to the production of meaning through opening and closing clauses of the sentence that serve to distinguish the syntactic and semantic units.[4]

Natural and conventional systems of signification thus exist on a continuum and in relation to one another.

This genetic derivation of persuasive language from natural sounds and rhythms plays out vividly in the context of orally-based poetry. Old English verse possessed a highly conventionalised form whose sound patterns—especially alliteration, assonance, and stress—gesture to natural systems, not only of human speech but also of noises produced by animals, human-made objects, and natural phenomena such as wind and rain. The opening riddle of the *Exeter Book* collection, *Þrymful Þunie* (R.1), which depicts a violent storm complete with wind, thunder and lightning, provides a stunning example, a *tour de force* of sound effects derived both from onomatopoeia and from metaphorical correspondences between the sounds and destructive power of wind and those of an army:

Hwylc is hæleþa þæs horsc ond þæs hygecræftig
þæt þæt mæge asecgan, hwa mec on sið wræce,
þonne ic astige strong, stundum reþe,
þrymful þunie, þragum wræce
fere geond foldan, folcsalo bærne,
ræced reafige? (1–6a)

[Who among people is so clever and wise that they can declare who drives me on my course, when I arise, strong, sometimes cruel, I who thunder mightily, often with vengeance move through the land, burning houses, ravaging halls?]

In this instance, the poet has virtuosically collapsed the categories of a natural sign, which signifies inferentially (that is, the sounds of wind and thunder are symptoms of the violent storm) and an intentional human symbol (that is, the sound of an army deliberately figures and forebodes its destructiveness, thus generating that essential martial quality, fear). *Þrymful Þunie* is a terrifying start to the collection, not only because of its vivid sound effects (*þrymful þunie* ['thunder mightily'] in 4a is the first of many examples) but because its solution highlights the shared helplessness of victims of natural violence (a storm) and human violence (the depredations of an army).

Such riddlic blurring of human and nonhuman sounds is not only a neat trick played by a riddling poet; it is also a function of systems of sound classification transmitted through late antique grammarians and then the seventh-century Aldhelm (d. 709/10), whose own Latin riddle collection heavily influenced later Anglo-Latin riddles as well as the *Exeter Book* riddles. The most clearly elaborated classification of sound signification was set out by the sixth-century grammarian Priscian in his *Institutiones Grammaticae*:

Vocis autem differentiae sunt quattuor: articulata, inarticulata, literata, illiterata. Articulata est, quae coartata, hoc est copulata cum aliquo sensu mentis eius, qui loquitur, profertur. Inarticulata est contraria, quae a nullo affectu proficiscitur mentis. Literata est, quae scribi potest, illiterata, quae scribi non potest. Inveniuntur igitur quaedam voces articulatae, quae possunt scribi et intellegi, ut: 'Arma virumque cano', quaedam, quae non possunt scribi, intelleguntur tamen, ut sibili hominum et gemitus: hae enim voces, quamvis sensum aliquem significent proferentis eas, scribi tamen non possunt. Aliae autem sunt, quae, quamvis scribantur, tamen inarticulatae dicuntur; cum nihil significent, ut 'coax', 'cra'. Aliae vero sunt inarticulatae et illiteratae, quae nec scribi possunt nec intellegi, ut crepitus, mugitus et similia.[5]

[But there are four types of sounds: articulate, inarticulate, writeable, not writeable. Articulate sound is that which is produced as something constrained, that is, joined with some meaning in the mind of the one who speaks. Inarticulate sound is the opposite, which proceeds from no affection of the mind. Writeable sound is that which can be written; not writeable sound is that which cannot be written. Thus, certain sounds are found to be articulate, which can be written and understood, such as 'I sing arms and the man'. Some, which cannot be written, are nonetheless understood, such as the whistlings or groanings of people; for these sounds, although they signify a certain meaning for the one making them, nonetheless cannot be written. There are still others which, even if they are written, are nonetheless said to be inarticulate, since they signify nothing, like 'coax', 'cra'. And others are inarticulate and not writeable, which can be neither written nor understood, such as creaking, mooing, and the like.]

Priscian's examples of inarticulate but written sounds include *coax* (the sound of frogs), and *cra* (the sound of crows). His examples of inarticulate, unwriteable sounds include *crepitus*, which has a wide semantic range, including rattling, creaking, clattering, clashing, and rustling; and *mugitus*, the mooing or lowing of cattle. As Umberto Eco and others have noted, there is a problem of internal coherence in this scheme: why are the sounds of frogs and crows transcribable in alphabetic letters, but the bellowing of oxen is not?[6] It is also worth noting that a number of writers differed from Priscian in extending the principle of articulation to nonhuman animals.[7] But for Priscian, *articulatio* is specifically and solely the principle of intelligibility of the human voice.

The early medieval English scholar and poet Aldhelm modifies Priscian's view and provides a crucial link in the philosophy of voice and articulation in his *De Pedum Regulis*, a treatise on metrical feet (composed 685–695). Just after beginning a discussion of one particular foot (the ionic minor) Aldhelm seemingly gets distracted by the sound of an ass braying, then follows a bizarre stream of consciousness through voice theory to a list of seventy-seven 'confused' noises, almost all of them made by animals:

M[agister]: Ionico minori huiuscemodi pauxillula sufficiant exempla ut sapientes, populares, seniores, furibundi, rubicundi, verecundi, moribundi, rudibundi id est rudentes et boantes; nam ruditus proprie asellorum est, ut poeta:

linguaque rudenti

Edidit humanas animal pecuale loquelas.

Et quia apta se vocis occasio praebuit, non modo propter structuram pedum et rationem metrorum, verum etiam ob differentiam vocum et discretionem sonorum non absurdum arbitror quadripedum et volucrum et reptilium voces cum generalitate pluralitatis et specialitate singularitatis subtiliter dirimere, siquidem vocis qualitatem quadripertitam, tam philosophorum quam grammaticorum auctoritas propalavit: articulatam, inarticulatam, litteratam, illitteratam, quamvis alii duas esse vocis species attestentur, hoc est articulatam et confusam; nam articulata hominum tantummodo dicta est, quod articulo scribenti comprehendi possit, confusa est, quae scribi non potest.
D[iscipulus]: Pande exempla vocis confusae de diversis rerum naturis congesta!
M[agister]: Haec sunt species vocis confusae, ut maiorum auctoritas tradidit. Nam apes ambizant vel bombizant, aquilae clangunt, anseres crinciunt vel trinsiunt ... [8]

[**Master:** For the ionic minor, let a very small number of examples of this sort suffice, as *sapientes* [wise ones], *populares* [popular], *furibundi* [furious], *rubicundi* [rosy], *verecundi* [modest], *moribundi* [mortal], *rudibundi* [braying], that is braying and bellowing; for braying is properly of asses, as the poet says, 'And with braying tongue, the brutish animal uttered human speech'. And since a fitting opportunity for voice presents itself, not only because of the structure of the feet and the explanation of the metres, but also because of the differentiation of the voices and the distinction of the sounds, I judge it not absurd to distinguish minutely the voices of quadrupeds and birds and reptiles with the generality of multiplicity and the particularity of individuality; indeed, the authority of both philosophers and grammarians has described the fourfold quality of voice: articulate, inarticulate, writeable, not writeable, although others claim that there are two types of voice, namely articulate and confused; for an articulate voice is said to be proper only to people, because it can be understood by a writing joint, and a confused voice is one that cannot be written.
Student: Reveal examples of confused voice assembled from the diverse natures of things!
Master: These are the types of confused voice, as the authority of the elders has passed down. For bees buzz, eagles cry, geese hiss or honk ...]

What is the connective tissue of Aldhelm's development here? To answer this, we need to grapple with another seemingly odd fact, namely that Aldhelm's two metrical treatises, *De Metris* and *De Pedum Regulis*, precede and follow, respectively, Aldhelm's Latin *Enigmata*, as parts of a larger textual unit known as the *Epistola ad Acircium*.

Michael Lapidge and Michael Herren observe that, although Aldhelm claims to be using the riddles as examples of the metrical principles under discussion, in fact they are largely unrelated to them.[9] Mercedes Salvador-Bello, however, has recently challenged this view, noting that in one important manuscript (Vatican City, Pal. Lat. 1753) the same textual order (metrical treatise/riddles/ metrical treatise) occurs for works by both Aldhelm and Boniface, suggesting 'the presence of these riddles as exercises to practice Latin metrics'; more broadly, she asserts that the manuscript context of many Latin riddles embeds them closely with grammatical, encyclopaedic, glossarial, and metrical study.[10] Carin Ruff further notes that the study of metrical principles was highly privileged in early medieval grammatical education, both because grammar was traditionally conceived of as a key to elucidating poetry and, crucially, because

> [t]he emphasis on the smallest phonological units of Latin and their representation (the letter and the syllable) in the teaching grammars of late antiquity meant that students were acquainted from the very beginning with the building-blocks of quantitative meter ... The foundational stages of grammar instruction were, therefore, literally 'elementary': they taught that language was composed of minimal, indivisible units that could be combined into larger units, which could in turn be combined into larger units, and so on.[11]

Aldhelm's pivot from discussing the ionic minor foot to focusing on *rudibundi* (the sound made by a braying ass) to the structural process of voice production thus begins to seem less random. That particular metrical foot is made up of a particular sequence of long and short syllables, but *rudibundi* is an even more specific example, since its combination of sounds is particular to one animal alone. The ensuing long list of animal noises exemplifies 'the differentiation of the voices and the distinction of the sounds', by insisting on both the uniqueness of each noise and its actual representation in human language, through unique combinations of sounds. Aldhelm thus finds it necessary 'to distinguish minutely the voices of quadrupeds and birds and reptiles with the generality of multiplicity [i.e., the general principle that each sound is unique] and the particularity of individuality [i.e., the specific instantiation of that principle in the unique articulation of each sound word]'. Aldhelm's next move is both logical and authoritative: he theorises the question of articulated sound by briefly outlining the two principal taxonomies relating articulation, intelligibility, and writing: Priscian's fourfold system and Donatus' twofold one, both of them known in early medieval England through a number of sources, including Isidore of Seville's widely read and influential *Etymologiae*.[12]

Aldhelm's various lists—his example words for each metrical foot and his long list of animal noises—provide a partial repertoire for would-be poets, each one an articulated representation of a unique noise. He hews to the conventional view that articulation is proper only to people, but blurs the distinction by presenting 'confused' animal noises that are nonetheless written in analysable units made up of articulated parts (like the long and short syllables of individual feet). Unlike Priscian, he does not insist that articulate sounds *per se* are uniquely joined to a meaning in a human mind. Instead, in an Isidorean etymological move, he melds the concepts of articulation and writing by claiming that articulate sound is proper to people because it can be encompassed by means of a writing joint (*articulo scribenti comprehendi possit*). *Articulo* presumably refers to the series of joints in the hand that are necessary to grasp a stylus, or perhaps to the conjunction of the fingers and the stylus together to produce a technology of writing.

By shifting to Donatus' simpler twofold scheme, in which articulate sound is writeable sound, and by identifying articulation with the bodily and technical aspects of writing, Aldhelm has perhaps unwittingly strayed into the territory of the alternative scheme of the third-century Greek philosopher Ammonius, who insisted that articulate sound is any sound divisible into distinct elements and hence liable to transcription into letters. For Ammonius, syllables are like limbs, and phonetic elements are like physical elements in a body; articulation is 'not a principle of intelligibility, but rather a principle of distinction'.[13] Thinking about articulation as a technical process animated by the principle of distinction and involving multiple parts of a body can help us understand Aldhelm's complex development here. Paradoxically, his claim that confused (i.e. animal) voices cannot be written is immediately followed by a list of seventy-seven sounds, almost all of them made by nonhuman animals, and expressed by a dazzling range of Latin verbs.

Aldhelm's invocation of the writing joint brings us immediately back to the *Exeter Book* collection, which contains one riddle (*Wuhte Feower*, R.51) with a widely agreed solution of 'pen and fingers':

Ic seah wrætlice wuhte feower
samed siþian; swearte wæran lastas,
swaþu swiþe blacu. Swift wæs on fore
fuglum framra; fleag on lyfte
deaf under yþe. Dreag unstille
winnende wiga, se him wægas tæcneþ
ofer fæted gold feower eallum.

[I saw four marvellous creatures travelling together; the tracks were dark, the traces very black. It was swift on its journey, bolder than birds; it flew in the air, dove under the wave. The fighting warrior worked restlessly, who marks out their path over plated gold, all four of them.]

Here, the four creatures are the pen and three fingers, guided by the scribe (the 'fighting warrior'). Once again, the articulation of the various parts enunciates a principle of distinction, with individual parts moving together, led by a warrior who enables and coordinates their activities. The complete organism is distinctly animal, flying in the air and diving into the liquid as birds do; significantly, there is no mention of intelligibility or any signifying practice: instead of humans paradoxically understanding this animal and its tracks, the principle of communication is understood only after the riddle is fully solved. Two Latin riddles also play on the idea of an organic body and its constituent members: Aldhelm's *Enigma 30*, *Elementum* presents a family, with a mother (the pen) and three brothers (the fingers), and Tatwine's *Enigma 6*, *Penna* describes his pen as *vincta tribus* ('held by three').[14] The *Exeter Book* pen/fingers riddle may refer either to a quill pen or a reed pen, hinting at aspects of both. As Craig Williamson notes, 'most of the Latin "pen" riddles are built upon the paradox of the birdlike creature that is caught and forced to travel the flat land', and Dieter Bitterli points out that the riddle's middle passage, with the creature flying and diving, 'may also be read as a flashback to the time when the quill was still part of a bird's plumage'.[15] Thus the motile function of feathers on a bird is transferred to the motion necessary to make a pen work, and the parts become a whole.

At the same time, the implicit, melancholy reference to a feather's origin aligns this riddle with the closely related *Be Sonde Muðlease* (R.60), generally solved as 'reed pen' or 'reed flute'.

Ic wæs be sonde sæwealle neah
æt merefaroþe minum gewunade
frumstaþole fæst. Fea ænig wæs
monna cynnes þæt mine þær
on anæde eard beheolde,
ac mec uhtna gehwam yð sio brune
lagufæðme beleolc. Lyt ic wende
þæt ic ær oþþe sið æfre sceolde
ofer meodubence muðleas sprecan,
wordum wrixlan. Þæt is wundres dæl,
on sefan searolic þam þe swylc ne conn,
hu mec seaxes ord ond seo swiþre hond,
eorles ingeþonc ond ord somod,
þingum geþydan, þæt ic wiþ þe sceolde
for unc anum twam ærendspræce
abeodan bealdlice, swa hit beorna ma,
uncre wordcwidas, widdor ne mænden.

[I was by the sand, near the seawall, I dwelt by the seashore, fixed in my first home. Few of the human kind saw my land, there in the wilderness. But every dawn the dark wave played with me in its watery embrace. Little did I expect that I would ever speak, early or late, mouthless over a mead-bench, exchange words. That is a deal of wonder, strange to the mind of one who knows no such things, how a knife's point and the right hand, a man's intention and the point together, pressed me for this purpose, to bring you a message just for us two, so that no more people would deliver our speeches any further.]

Jerry Denno has discussed this riddle as an instance of what he calls 'the discourse of servitude', noting that a number of riddles feature an inanimate object whose circumscribed subjectivity paradoxically 'achieves insight into its own limited, material, condition'.[16] A number of these objects 'tell of a prior place from which they were long since removed', describing their separation from a previous place of integrity; thus the reed pen reminisces about its *frumstaþole* (place of origin) by the seashore.[17] The reed riddle, of course, deploys the paradox of mouthless speech, *muðleas sprecan*, but the paradox is not a static existential condition: it is achieved through a violent manufacturing process involving uprooting the reed from its original place and cutting it with a sharp knife, a detail absent from Symphosius' reed-pen riddle (*Enigma 2*). The manufacture of useful objects is often described in terms of pain and trauma, including riddles about the transformation of ore into metal, an animal into vellum, an ox into leather, grain into alcohol, and antlers into inkhorns; Jonathan Wilcox has eloquently described the objects' narration of these processes as 'the lament for a movement from natural innocence to manufactured suffering'.[18]

This mechanical assemblage incorporates the articulated nature of the product: the riddle's 'deal of wonder' is 'how a knife's point and the right hand, a nobleman's thought and the point together, pressed me for this purpose'. The beautiful envelope structure in lines 12–13, *hu mec seaxes ord ond seo swiþre hond, / eorles ingeþonc ond ord somod*, requires careful interpretation: I take the first *ord* to be the knife point that opens the hole at the end of the reed, the right hand to be the writing hand (or, in a minor key, the hand that cuts the reed), the nobleman's thought to be the intended meaning of the writer (or, again in the minor key, the skill of the cutter), and the final *ord* to be either a repetition of the cutting technology or a reminder that the same knife could be used for erasures while writing, or perhaps a bit of both. The mouthless speech is articulate only because the writing system is articulated: it involves not only the joints of the hand and the hand grasping a pen, but also the manufacture of the pen, which in turn involves hands, knives, and the reed itself, which has been removed from its natural environment and used as a raw material. This riddler goes well beyond Aldhelm in insisting not only on the highly physical nature of articulation (the writing joint), but on the necessity of compatible component parts joined by a technological process, thereby merging the principle of intelligibility with the notion of distinction and compatible parts.[19]

Numerous other riddles deploy sound words (mostly verbs and nouns) that blur the distinction between articulate and inarticulate sound. Whether looking back to Priscian's fourfold classification of sounds as articulate, inarticulate, writeable, and not writeable, or Donatus' simpler distinction between articulate and confused, it is clear that the riddles, by their very nature, deploy the concept of sounds, noises, and voices as one element in a ludic zone of signification that deliberately blurs distinctions between speaking subject and represented object. Thus, the ship in *Grindan wið Greote* (R.32) moves while yelling (*giellende*, 4b), the bagpipe in *Feþegeorn* (R.31) and the harp in *Orþoncum Geworht* (R.70) sing (*singan*, 3b and 2a), the iceberg in *Gryrelic Hleahtor* (R.33) calls (*cleopian*, 2b), and the horn in *Wæpenwiga* (R.14) has a *stefn* (18a), a word for 'voice' that is used overwhelmingly for human speakers or singers.[20]

One group of riddles not only blurs the categories of articulated and rational speech, but does so in a way that raises ancient questions about reason, will, intention, and consciousness; these are the riddles comprising animal voices, fifteen and a half of the approximately ninety-five *Exeter Book* riddles, the half being the fish in *Nis Min Sele Swige* (R.85), Fish and River. The animal riddles raise large questions about the ethical dimensions of social and economic arrangement: to cite just one example, the status of animals as useable objects in the riddles and elsewhere can be enlivened by considering their relation to the so-called 'implement riddles', with their complex reorganisation of lord–servant and master–slave relationships, as Jennifer Neville, Edward B. Irving, Jr, Jerry Denno, and others have explored.[21]

All of the animal riddles deploy a fascinating array of sounds and noises, and their relationship to the encyclopaedic tradition and the mini-genre of animal noise catalogues, especially Aldhelm's *tour de force* version, needs much more exploration. To join the animal riddles to questions of voice and articulation, consider *Siex Stafas Sweotule Becnaþ* (R.24), whose narrator/solution is something that imitates animals. This impressive creature deploys some common verbs in a bravura repertoire of show-stopping impressions:

> Ic eom wunderlicu wiht, wræsne mine stefne:
> hwilum beorce swa hund, hwilum blæte swa gat,
> hwilum græde swa gos, hwilum gielle swa hafoc.
> Hwilum ic onhyrge þone haswan earn,
> guðfugles hleoþor; hwilum glidan reorde
> muþe gemæne, hwilum mæwes song,
> þær ic glado sitte. .ᚷ. (giefu) mec nemnað,
> swylce .ᚨ. (æsc) ond .ᚱ. (rad) ᚩ. (os) fullesteð,
> .ᚻ. (hægl) ond .ᛁ. (is) Nu ic haten eom
> swa þa siex stafas sweotule becnaþ.[22]
>
> [I am a wondrous creature—I vary my voice; sometimes I bark like a dog, sometimes I bleat like a goat, sometimes I cry like a goose, sometimes I shriek like a hawk. Sometimes I imitate the grey eagle, the sound of the war-bird; sometimes the kite's voice I speak with my mouth, sometimes the seagull's song, where I sit cheerful. *G* names me, also *Æ* and *R*. *O* helps, *H* and *I*. Now I am named as the six letters clearly signify.]

This riddle is unusual in providing two sets of clues, one auditory and one visual (the runes, when rearranged, spell out *higoræ*, the female form of a jay or magpie). The bird's mimicry is vividly reenacted in the aural effects of the poem, especially lines 2 and 3: in addition to the anaphora of *hwilum*, *beorce* and *blæte* alliterate, *blæde* and *græde* assonate, and all four verbs are heavily onomatopoeic. But these onomatopoeic verbs occupy complex semantic and semiotic positions. *Beorcan* can refer straightforwardly to the barking of dogs and foxes but can also designate imitative or figurative barking: in the *Old English Martyrology*, devils appear *swa beorcende fox* ('like a barking fox'); pagans or infidels are often said to bark like dogs; and Ælfric, in an exegesis of Isaiah 56:10—*canes muti non possunt latrare* ('mute dogs cannot bark')—enjoins the clergy to *beorcan and bodigan þam læwedum* ('bark and preach to the unlearned').[23] *Blætan* is usually just the sheep noise, but is transferred to swine in another Aldhelm gloss when it translates *grunnire* ('to grunt'), emphasising the stereotypically porcine grunting of pagans.

Like *beorcan*, *grædan* crosses species boundaries by means of metaphor: in the translation of Gregory the Great's *Pastoral Care*, a teacher must *grædan* ('cry' or 'crow') like a rooster in the night to awaken his hearers from spiritual sleep.[24] The metaphorical usages of *beorcan* and *grædan* situate them in the realm of articulate, salvific speech, even though they can at other times remain inarticulate, though still meaningful: in a saint's life, a man possessed by an evil spirit cries out (*grædan*) a noise rather than a word (*heu! heu!* in Latin and *walawa! walawa!* in Old English). *Giellan* (in this poem, the shrieking of a hawk) covers an even broader semantic range, straddling not only human and nonhuman animals, but also animate and inanimate noise-makers: it is used of birds, wolves, dogs, a flying spear, a resounding harp string, and, as we have seen, a ship scraping against pebbles.[25] Whereas the modern etymon 'yell' usually refers to humans, and very often to verbal speech (yelling intelligible words), Old English *gyllan* is used only once of humans: in the poem *Exodus*, Egyptians drowning in the Red Sea scream *gyllende gryre* ('with shrieking terror'); their unrighteousness and the depth of their terror produce an inarticulate, perhaps animalistic noise.[26]

Ultimately, the sound effects of the *Exeter Book* riddles function through the fundamental principles that make enigmatic texts work. A harp singing, an iceberg laughing, a ring speaking, a pen speaking mouthlessly, a cow's teats murmuring: all draw their mystery, and their solution, from incongruity and the blurring of categories. And the categories themselves run together in pleasant confusion before being (provisionally) resolved at the riddle's solution: people, inanimate objects, and the vexed middle cohort of noisy animals borrow one another's characteristics in a dizzying alternation of conjunction and disjunction. The beguiling onomatopoeia of the swan's feathers whistling and sounding (*swogað … ond swinsiað*, 7) in *Ferende Gæst* (R.7) gives way to the confusingly mimetic sonic repertoire of the jay in *Eald Æfensceop* (R.8). Can we trace a coherent theory, or theories, of voice in these riddles? And to what extent were the riddlers playing with the terms established by the philosophers and grammarians? Much work remains to be done, but it is clear that the Old English riddlers were working closely in a tradition with the Latin enigmatists, who both theorised and played with the concepts of voice and articulated sound. In a startling moment conjoining grammatical and metrical articulation with ludic poetic possibility, Aldhelm performs a surprising leap across Priscian's divide of writeable and non-writeable sounds: he introduces his riddles by pithily theorising the way voice can work in poetry, and then provides examples of 'confused' or 'inarticulate' animal voices that are nonetheless both articulable and writeable in poetic language. The *Exeter Book* riddles enact this paradox in virtuosic English verse.

Notes

1 For discussions of sensory effects in the riddles, see Francesca Brooks, 'Sight, Sound, and the Perception of the Anglo-Saxon Liturgy in Exeter Book Riddles 48 and 59', in *Sensory Perception in the Medieval West*, ed. Simon C. Thomson and Michael D. Bintley (Turnhout: Brepols, 2016), pp. 141–58; Dieter Bitterli, *Say What I Am Called: The Old English Riddles of the Exeter Book and the Anglo-Latin Riddle Tradition* (Toronto: University of Toronto Press, 2009), pp. 38–56. On the interplay of sound and silence in the riddles, see Jordan Zweck, 'Silence in the Exeter Book Riddles', *Exemplaria*, 28 (2016), 319–36.

2 Maurizio Bettini, *Voci: Antropologia Sonora del Mondo Antico* (Turin: Giulio Einaudi, 2008).

3 Aristotle, *De Interpretatione* 1–2, in J. L. Ackrill, ed. and trans., *Categories and De Interpretatione* (Oxford: Oxford University Press, 1975), pp. 49–50.

4 Lia Formigari, *A History of Language Philosophies* (Amsterdam: Benjamins, 2004), p. 25.

5 Priscian, *Prisciani Insititutiones Grammaticarum*, ed. Martin Hertz, 2 vols (Leipzig: Teubner, 1855), I.1–2, pp. 5–6. On Priscian's classification, see Valerie J. Allen, 'Broken Air', *Exemplaria*, 16 (2004), 305–22.

6 U. Eco, R. Lambertini, C. Marmo, and A. Tabarroni, 'On Animal Language in the Medieval Classification of Signs', in *On the Medieval*

Theory of Signs, ed. Umberto Eco and Costantino Marmo (Amsterdam and Philadelphia: Benjamins, 1989), p. 11.

7 Eco, *et al.*, 'On Animal Language', p. 25, n.1.

8 Aldhelm, *De Pedum Regulis*, in Rudolf Ehwald, ed., *Aldhelmi Opera*, MGH, Auctores Antiquissimi, 15 (Berlin: Weidmann, 1919), p. 179. On the dating of Aldhelm's life and this treatise, see Aldhelm, *Aldhelm: The Poetic Works*, trans. Michael Lapidge and James L. Rosier (Cambridge: D. S. Brewer, 2009), pp. 6 and 12. In the appendix to *The Poetic Works* (at pp. 212–19), Neil Wright provides a partial translation of *De Pedum Regulis* but does not include this passage. Further on lists of animal noises, see Robert Stanton, 'Bark Like a Man: Performance, Identity, and Boundary in Old English Animal Voice Catalogues', in *Animal Languages in the Middle Ages: Representations of Interspecies Communication*, ed. Alison Langdon (New York: Palgrave Macmillan, 2018), pp. 91–111.

9 Aldhelm, *Aldhelm: The Prose Works*, trans. Michael Lapidge and Michael Herren (Cambridge: D. S. Brewer, 2009), p. 13.

10 Mercedes Salvador-Bello, *Isidorean Perceptions of Order: The Exeter Book Riddles and Medieval Latin Enigmata* (Morgantown: West Virginia University Press, 2015), p. 83.

11 Carin Ruff, 'The Place of Metrics in Anglo-Saxon Latin Education: Aldhelm and Bede', *JEGP*, 104.2 (2005), 149–70, at p. 151.

12 Donatus, *Ars Grammatica*, ed. Heinrich Keil (Leipzig: Teubner, 1864), p. 367: *Omnis vox aut articulata est aut confusa. Articulata est quae litteris conprehendi potest; confusa quae scribe non potest* ('Every sound is either articulated or confused. Articulate sound is what can be comprehended in letters; confused sound is what cannot be written'). Isidore, *Etymologies* 1.15, in *Sancti Isidori Hispalensis Episcopi Opera Omnia*, ed. Jacques-Paul Migne, PL 82 (Paris: Garnier, 1850), coll. 9–728, at 89A–B: *Vox est aer ictus sensibilis auditu, quantum in ipso est. Omnis vox, aut est articulata, aut confusa. Articulata est hominum, confusa animalium. Articulata est quae scribi potest, confusa quae scribi non potest* ('Sound is struck air perceptible to the hearing, according to its strength. Every sound is either articulated or confused. Articulate sound is that of people, confused sound is that of animals. Articulate sound is what can be comprehended in letters; confused sound is what cannot be written').

13 Andrea Tabarroni, 'On Articulation and Animal Language in Ancient Linguistic Theory', in *Signs of Antiquity and Antiquity of Signs*, ed. Giovanni Manetti [=*Versus* 50/51] (1988), 103–21, at p. 105.

14 Fr. Glorie, ed., *Collectiones Aenigmatum Merovingicae Aetatis*, CCSL, 133–133A (Turnhout: Brepols, 1968), 133, pp. 413 and 173; see Craig Williamson, ed., *The Old English Riddles of the Exeter Book* (Chapel Hill: University of North Carolina Press, 1977), p. 293.

15 Williamson, *Old English Riddles*, p. 293; Bitterli, *Say What I Am Called*, p. 293.

16 Jerry Denno, 'Oppression and Voice in Anglo-Saxon Riddle Poems', *CEA Critic*, 70.1 (2007), 35–47, at p. 35.
17 Denno, 'Oppression and Voice', p. 43.
18 Jonathan Wilcox, 'New Solutions to Old English Riddles: Riddles 17 and 53', *PQ*, 69 (1990), 393–408, at p. 398. See also James Paz, *Nonhuman Voices in Anglo-Saxon Literature and Material Culture* (Manchester: Manchester University Press, 2017), pp. 88–92.
19 For further discussion of this riddle see Brooks, Chapter 4 in this volume.
20 See B-T, *s.v. stefn.* All citations are either to human or divine voices.
21 Jennifer Neville, 'The Unexpected Treasure of the "Implement Trope": Hierarchical Relationships in the Old English Riddles', *RES*, 62.256 (2011), 505–19; Edward B. Irving, Jr, 'Heroic Experience in the Old English Riddles', in *Old English Shorter Poems: Basic Readings*, ed. Katherine O'Brien O'Keeffe (New York: Garland, 1994), pp. 199–212; and Denno, 'Oppression and Voice'. See also Dale, Chapter 10 in this volume.
22 Williamson, *Old English Riddles*, p. 82.
23 Günter Kotzor, ed., *Das Altenglische Martyrologium* (Munich: Bayerischen Akademie der Wissenschaften, 1981), p. 236; Ælfric of Eynsham, *Die Hirtenbriefe Ælfrics*, ed. Bernard Fehr (Hamburg: Henri Grand, 1914; repr. Darmstadt: Wissenschaftliche Buchgesellschaft, 1966), p. 15; *DOE, s.v. beorcan, blætan.*
24 Henry Sweet, ed., *King Alfred's West-Saxon Version of Gregory's Pastoral Care* (London: Trübner, 1871), p. 459.
25 *DOE, s.v. gyllan 1. Gyllan* is used of birds in the poems *Solomon and Saturn*, *The Seafarer*, and this riddle; of wolves and dogs in *The Battle of Finnsburh* and a ninth-century gloss; of a flying spear in *Widsith* and a metrical charm; of a harp string in *The Riming Poem*; and of a ship on gravel in *Grindan wið Greote* (R.32).
26 *DOE, s.v. grædan, giellan.*

Part II
Ideas

Introduction to Part II

Megan Cavell and Jennifer Neville

The riddles challenge us with unheard of, unspeakable, unimaginable ideas. We do not need theory to reveal those ideas, but theoretical interventions from other fields of study have often proven productive in opening up the riddles' intellectual richness. It is safe to say that, as a field, the study of early medieval England has tended to resist engaging with the latest trending theories—or, at the least, has come late to the party. Even so, while the early study of Old English and Latin riddles necessarily focused on issues of editing and translating—including the numbering, structure, and genre of the riddles as a whole and as individual poems, damage to the texts and, of course, their solutions—these often-neglected texts have also elicited theoretically-engaged interpretations for a good half-century. Given their occasional but explicit references to sex, for example, the riddles are prime candidates for analysis that is informed by gender and sexuality studies, and their contents were examined in relation to the sexual revolution of the 1970s in that very decade.[1] Since then, the riddles' approach to gender, sexuality, class, and ethnicity has continued to prove how stimulating these texts can be when approached critically and with an eye to intersectionality.[2] After all, the subversive power dynamics underpinning the very functioning of the riddles reward readings that probe the experiences of marginalised groups.

The pleasurable discomfort that riddles impose on their audiences also provides opportunities for the scrutiny of our inner lives. They make us laugh; they make us anxious; they show us how we think about things; they make us think twice. In all these ways they reward the application of ideas derived from studies of emotions, cognition, and humour from other disciplines.

And yet, for all that the riddles lend insights into human lives, their focus most often is on the ostensibly nonhuman. Thus, the riddles provide excellent opportunities for critical readings that are engaged in the work of breaking down binaries and hierarchies between humans and the world around them. Many of the riddles describe objects or natural phenomena, and so are open to thing theory and new materialism where other types of text may resist. Furthermore, many of these objects are constructed through natural materials, and the riddles tell us of these materials' experience before they were co-opted for human use. The positioning of animals and natural phenomena as marginalised, first-person speakers demands critically-engaged interpretations that re-imagine ways of living alongside the world that we now threaten to destroy.

In this section, then, we present chapters that test ideas about humour, sentience, monstrosity, ecofeminism, hyperobjects, and conceptual blending. The application of these ideas helps us not only to understand the riddles better but also to see the uses and limitations of the ideas themselves.

Notes

1 See Edith Whitehurst Williams, 'What's So New about the Sexual Revolution?: Some Comments on Anglo-Saxon Attitudes toward Sexuality in Women Based on Four Exeter Book Riddles', *Texas Quarterly*, 18.2 (1975), 46–55.

2 John W. Tanke, '*Wonfeax Wale*: Ideology and Figuration in the Sexual Riddles of the Exeter Book', in *Class and Gender in Early English Literature: Intersections*, ed. Britton J. Harwood and Gillian R. Overing (Bloomington: Indiana University Press, 1994), pp. 21–42.

6

Warriors and their battle gear: conceptual blending in *Anhaga* (R.5) and *Wæpnum Awyrged* (R.20)

Karin Olsen

If we ask ourselves why the Exeter riddles have received considerable scholarly attention over the last century, we may come up with different answers, but one of these answers will certainly relate to the challenge in trying to find a solution. The Old English riddler provides us with many clues, some of which seem to be straightforward, others mysterious or even misleading, but in all cases we solve—or fail to solve—the riddle only after some mental effort. Paradoxes and obfuscation are typical features of the Exeter riddles, as Patrick J. Murphy has illustrated so convincingly.[1] Nor is there any guarantee that only one answer will be the reward of all the mental labour. Unless the solution is already provided together with the riddle, as is the case with *Agof* (R.23) and its solution 'bow',[2] different solvers may arrive at different, equally defensible answers, which may never have been in the riddler's mind. A notorious example of this diversity is *Þragbysig* (R.4), which has been solved as 'bell', 'handmill', 'millstone', 'bucket of water', 'flail', 'lock', 'necromancy', 'devil', 'phallus', '(watch) dog', and, most recently, as 'sun'.[3] It appears that the riddler's solution is irretrievable and that modern scholars try to fill the interpretative lacunae in diverse and often very creative ways. Since the solutions of the Exeter riddles are the outcome of the readers' interpretations of the clues, furthermore, they can be quite diverse in nature and number. In an extreme case like *Þragbysig*, the number of solutions remains undetermined, but even less contentious riddles often encourage more than one interpretation. In this chapter, I will focus on the cognitive process that underlies the creation, evaluation, and acceptance or rejection of riddle solutions. I have selected *Anhaga* (R.5) and *Wæpnum Awyrged* (R.20), both of which have at least one solution related to 'warfare', while also allowing various alternatives.

The mental process in question is the process of conceptual blending, also called conceptual integration. It entails the (partial) blending of mental spaces that are, according to Gilles Fauconnier and Mark Turner, 'small conceptual packets constructed as we think and talk for purposes of local understanding and action'.[4] Blending occurs in conceptual integration networks, which consist of at least two input spaces, a generic space that contains information shared by both input spaces, and a blended space. The networks, moreover, are divided into various types, including single-scope and double-scope networks and complex megablends. As Fauconnier and Turner point out, single-scope networks are the 'prototypes of highly conventional metaphors'.[5] This type of metaphor has two inputs, i.e. a framing input (source), which organises the blend, and a focus input (target) with its own frame. The metaphor 'digesting a book' is such a blend, consisting of the focus input (target) 'reading' and the framing input (source) 'eating': in the blend, reading is conceptualised in terms of the eating process.[6] A one-solution riddle can fall into the category of single-scope network, too, as long as the frame of the framing input (the 'wrong' solution) organises all parts of the riddle. However, most Exeter riddles, including *Anhaga* and *Wæpnum Awyrged*, evoke double-scope networks or complex megablends with multiple inputs. For clarity's sake, we explore first the workings of a relatively simple double-scope network, namely that of a two-element kenning, which is in fact the most rudimentary form of a riddle.[7] The integration network underlying the nominal compound *hildeleoma* ('battle-light'), which occurs only in *Beowulf*, will serve as an example.

The network consists of the blend *hildeleoma* which receives its elements from the two input spaces *hild* (1) and *leoma* (2). Both spaces have their own rudimentary frames, here 'conflict' and 'light' (in a more general sense), which correspond to Marie Nelson's 'referential frames' in a riddle.[8] But what is a battle-light? In order to construct the referent of the compound, we need to postulate meanings for the two inputs and identify possible relations between them, as well as between each input and the still-to-be determined referent in the blend: is the *hildeleoma* literally a light in battle (relation of space), something that shines in battle like a light (relation of space but with additional analogical or metonymic mappings between referent and input 2), or perhaps something that is bright and aggressive/destructive? The blend certainly allows all of these (and most probably more) options, which can only be rejected or confirmed on the basis of the compound's (immediate) context.

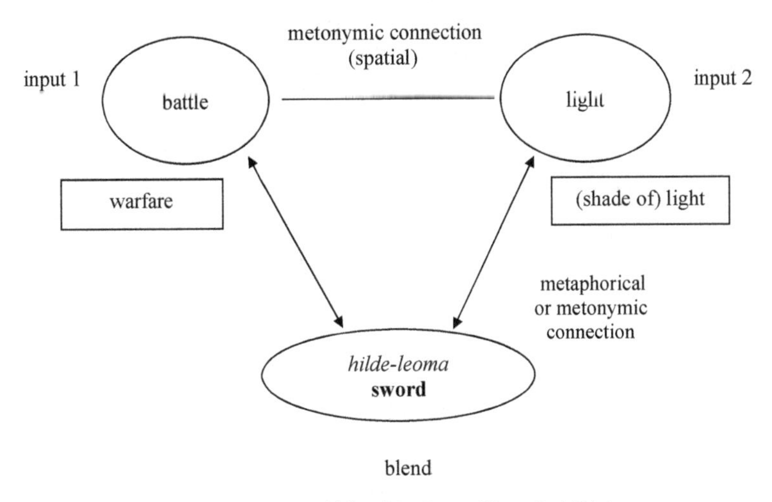

Figure 6.1 Inputs and blend in *Beowulf* 1143b: *hildeleoma*

In *Beowulf* 1143–4a, it is stated that Hunlafing put a *hildeleoma, billa selest* ('battle-light, best of swords') into Hengest's lap to rekindle hostilities between Danes and Frisians.[9] The appositive phrase *billa selest* ('best of swords') indicates that the referent of the kenning must be a flashing sword, and since the blend's structure emerges from both input spaces, it becomes part of a double-scope network (see Figure 6.1).[10] The connection between blend and input 1 (*hild*) is one of identity, while the second connection between blend and input 2 (*leoma*) allows at least two cognitive relations. If the sword is conceptualised as a light, the mapping is metaphorical, but if the flashing is seen as a quality of the sword, the mapping is metonymic (QUALITY OF OBJECT FOR OBJECT). In fact, the two mental processes are related. It is the flash of light emanating from the sword that makes the metaphorical relation possible via generalisation: the sword is identified by means of one particular characteristic, its gleam (rusty swords do not qualify in this case), which is generalised to allow the emergence of the metaphor *leoma*. Indeed, the kenning refers to more than one visual characteristic of the sword. Unlike its rusty counterpart, a gleaming sword suggests good maintenance and thus optimal functionality in battle. *Hildeleoma* reflects an ideal, not necessarily a reality.

It may be objected that the word formation of *hildeleoma* is conventional—compare *beaduleoma* ('battle-light': sword) (*Beowulf* 1523) and ON *gunnlogi* ('battle flame': sword)—and would also have been recognised by an early medieval audience without the addition

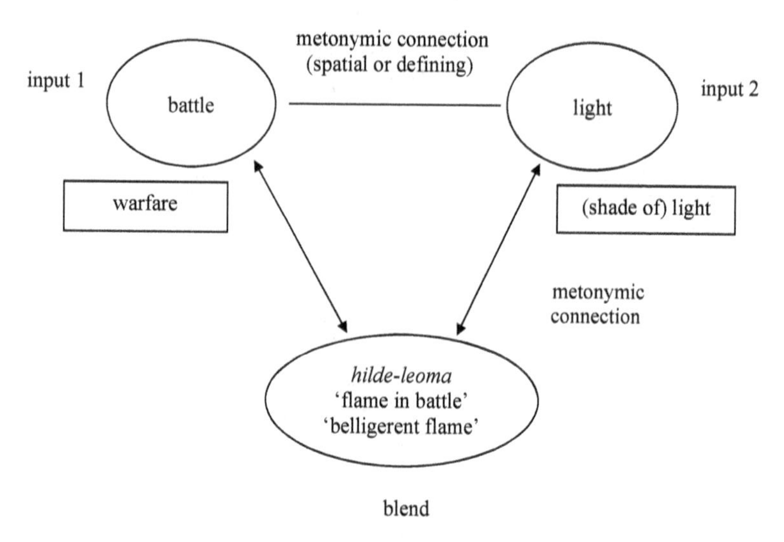

Figure 6.2 Inputs and blend in *Beowulf* 2583a: *hildeleoma*

of an appositive phrase. However, context can take precedence over convention. In *Beowulf* 2582–3a, *hildeleoma* also constitutes a double-scope network, but here the conceptualisation process is different (see Figure 6.2). The poet states that in response to Beowulf's attack on the dragon, the scaly creature threw out *wælfyr* (literally 'slaughter-fire') so that the *hildeleoman* spread widely. The context immediately excludes the solution 'sword', suggesting the serpent's bright flames as the referent instead.[11] The mappings between the two inputs are less clear. On the one hand, the *hildeleoman* could be conceptualised as the flames that the dragon spews in its hostile attack (*hild*) on Beowulf (spatial relation), or, on the other hand, they could be belligerent flames equally reflecting back on the dragon's hostile nature (defining relation). As in the case of the occurrence of *hildeleoma* in line 1143b, the kenning incorporates the structures of both input spaces, although in this case the metonymic relationship between flames and light is much more straightforward—light being a defining quality of fire—than that between a sword and light. In other words, whereas the referent 'sword' is closely tied to the frame of input 1 ('conflict'), the referent 'flame' has strong affinities with that of input 2 ('light').

Accordingly, it is the narrative context of the blend *hildeleoma* that determines the reduction of possible referents to one (i.e. sword or flames).[12] In a riddle, the narrative context is replaced by incongruent clues, which are components of the blend and which have been projected from two or more input spaces. Riddle-solving entails the construction and rejection of such input spaces with their organising frames until an input space is created that integrates all clues without any inconsistencies, thus providing the solution. Multiple solutions arise if different kinds of cultural knowledge are utilised in the process, or if the selection is only partial. A good example is provided by *Anhaga* (R.5), for which scholars have proposed various solutions, including 'shield', 'chopping board', and 'whetstone'. The first two options have found considerable support, though 'whetstone', proposed by William Sayers, is by no means less plausible.[13] In fact, in all three instances the audience have to take similar cognitive steps in order to arrive at any of the solutions, steps which are outlined in the following linear reading of the riddle.

The speaker of *Anhaga* begins:

> Ic eom anhaga, iserne wund
> bille gebennad, beaduweorca sæd,
> ecgum werig. Oft ic wig seo,
> frecne feohtan. (1–4a)

> [I am a lonely one, wounded with iron, wounded by the sword, sated by battle-works, weary of edges. I often see war, fierce battle.]

The first clue is provided by the speaker's identification of him-/itself as *anhaga*. Since the noun *anhaga* denotes a solitary person or, in two instances in the Old English poetic corpus, a solitary animal (the wolf in *Maxims II*, line 19a and the phoenix in *The Phoenix*, line 87a),[14] we can visualise a lonely, perhaps exiled warrior who has been wounded in many conflicts (input 1; see Figure 6.3). On the other hand, the conventional use of prosopopoeia in the Old English riddles suggests that the speaker of the riddle is most probably not a human being, let alone a warrior, for this option would make the riddle cease to be a riddle. As mentioned above, riddles are blends that have two or more input spaces. Depending on the complexity of the riddle, at least one of these inputs is both obvious and incorrect: whatever the *anhaga* turns out to be, the referent is not an exile like the Wanderer. At the same time, however, it is important to remember that the prioritisation of input spaces does not exclude their competitors, for blending entails the compression of inputs that are nevertheless held separate.[15] Regardless of whether these inputs turn out to be counterfactual, they are part of the integration process. To put it differently: we can choose among alternatives only if we are aware of them in the first place.

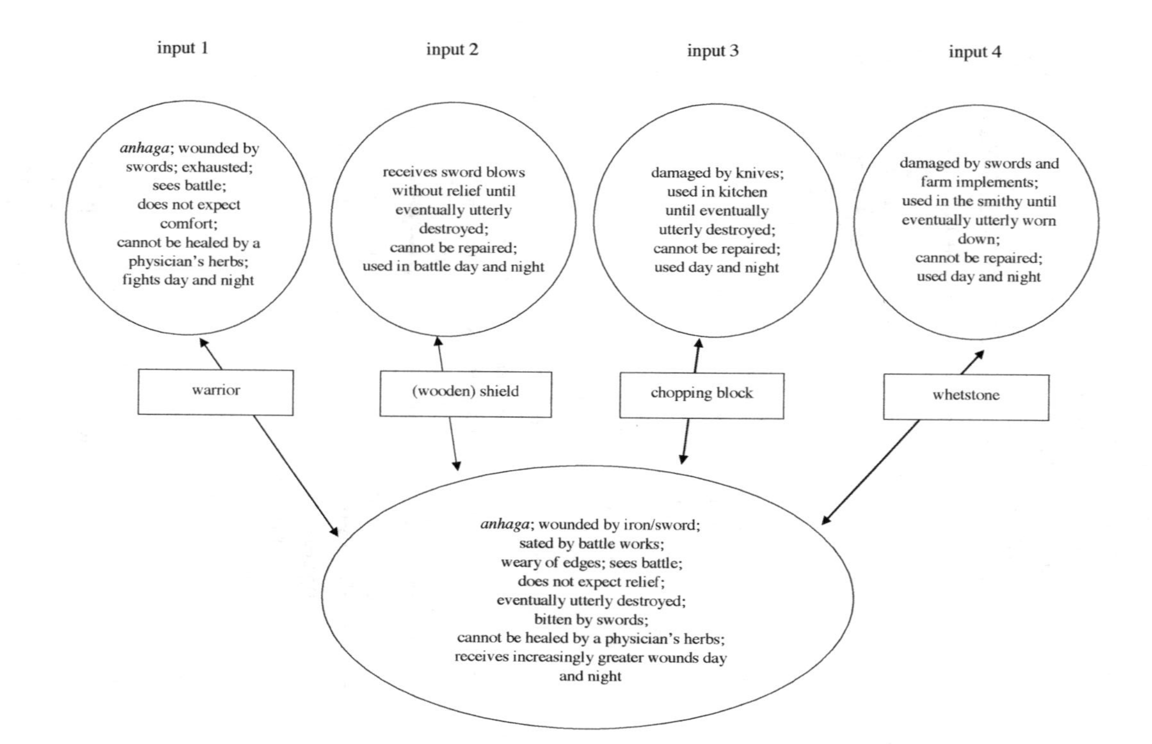

Figure 6.3 Inputs and blend in *Anhaga* (R.5): warrior, shield, chopping block, whetstone

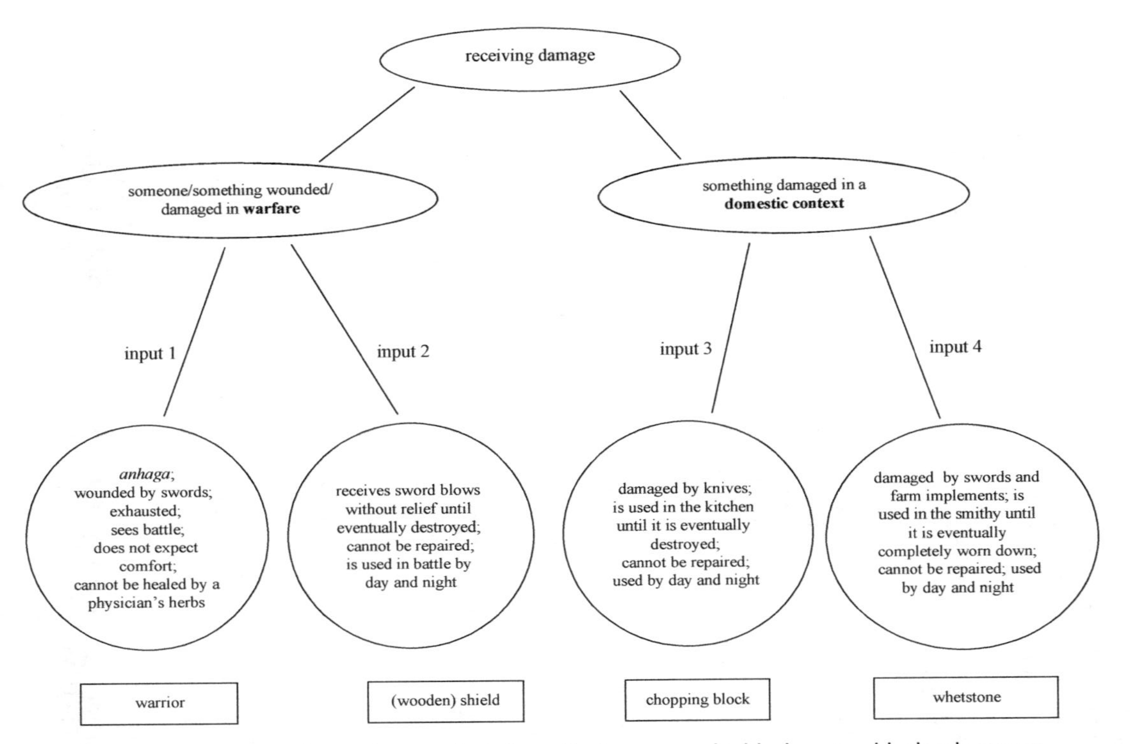

Figure 6.4 Inputs and generic space in *Anhaga* (R.5): warrior, shield, chopping block, whetstone

Since in *Anhaga* the speaker is not a human warrior, a second input space has to be constructed with both the help of the clues provided in the blend and the application of the aforementioned riddle conventions. This second space is most likely characterised by an inanimate nature and the quality of receiving sword blows entirely on its own (*an-*). All defensive armour has these characteristics, but the shield that the warrior holds before him to fend off the blows is the most likely candidate. The idea that the speaker is a wooden shield is strengthened by the notion that he/it is *utterly* destroyed after a (long) series of attacks:

Frofre ne wene,
þæt mec geoc cyme guðgewinnes,
ær ic mid ældum eal forwurde,
ac mec hnossiað homera lafe,
heardecg heoroscearp, hondweorc smiþa,
bitað in burgum; ic a bidan sceal
laþran gemotes. (4b–10a)

[I do not expect relief, that help in the turmoil of battle might come to me before I am utterly destroyed among men/by the flames; but the remnants of hammers beat me, hard-edged and very sharp [literally sword-sharp], the handiworks of smiths in the fortified towns bite me; I must always expect a very hostile meeting.]

In fact, the most decisive clue occurs in lines 10b–15:

Næfre læcecynn
on folcstede findan meahte,
þara þe mid wyrtum wunde gehælde,
ac me ecga dolg eacen weorðað
þurh deaðslege dagum ond nihtum.

[I could never find a race of physicians in the people-place who would heal [my] wounds with herbs, but the wounds from the edges [i.e. swords] increase by deadly blows day and night.]

How can any living organism receive ever-increasing untreatable injury, survive it, and be sent back to the battlefield? This is impossible. If the given clues are hooked up to the input 'shield', on the other hand, we arrive at a coherent interpretation with both metaphorical and metonymic relations between the two inputs: the shield is an indispensable piece of a warrior's armour (metonymy), which in the blend takes on some of the qualities of its owner (metaphor).

The riddle solution 'shield' also seems to be supported by the *s*-rune (*sigel*), which appears beneath the text in the manuscript and could stand for either OE *scyld* or Latin *scutum*. This, of course, does not mean that all clues are unambivalent. The observation that the speaker cannot be healed by herbs, though literally true, points back to the 'wrong solution' of input 1: warriors, not shields, are treated by physicians with herbal cures.[16] Furthermore, the described integration network that produces the solution 'shield' is only one option. As Figure 6.4 illustrates, the two constructed input spaces are determined by the generic space 'someone/something wounded/damaged in warfare', with 'warfare' supplying the required referential framework: warriors and shields are closely associated with the battlefield. Yet other frameworks are also possible. If the heroic diction is seen as parodic, for example, a far less prestigious referent and framework can be constructed. Such a framework could be 'household', with the referent being a board that receives ceaseless blows by knives and in this way is eventually destroyed. Scholars have suggested the solution 'cutting board, chopping block' (input 3), whose function in the kitchen is roughly analogous to that of the shield in battle. Within the 'household' framework, the conventional sword-kennings *homera laf* ('leavings of hammers') and *hondweorc smiþa* ('handiwork of smiths') obtain a new referent, i.e. knife. Other clues are also reassessed, like the strong emphasis on edges (Riedinger) or the medicinal herbs which transform into vegetables to be chopped on the board/block (Tigges).[17] The *s*-rune only reveals the cognitive steps that the (main) scribe of the *Exeter Book* undertook to arrive at a solution, which is after all only one option.[18]

Finally, Sayers's solution 'whetstone' (*s*-rune for *stan*) is related to both the household and the battlefield. Used to sharpen weapons, it also wears down, though over a substantially longer period of time than the shield.[19] And since whetstones are also used for the everyday sharpening of farm and household tools, the solution to the riddle simultaneously constitutes a response to 'the pompous, conventional epic style and its attempt at pathos and, like numerous other Old English riddles, brings us down to the no less interesting everyday'.[20]

If Sayers's alternative is just as convincing as the solution 'chopping block/cutting board', this is because the clues are interpreted differently. The emphasis on edges still exists but these edges are honed rather than used for cutting. Another example is the speaker's declaration: *oft ic seo wig* ('often I see battle') (3b). The statement may initially appear clear enough but actually contains considerable gaps (Wolfgang Iser's *Leerstellen*) that can be filled differently.[21] Is the seeing of battle a first- or second-hand experience for the speaker, and what kind of battle is he/it referring to? A shield is directly involved in the fighting, but a whetstone would only metonymically see the traces of battle on the swords to be honed. The important point to remember is that riddle-solving is a complex mental process that depends on the recipient's knowledge and imagination as much as on the existent text. Although we cannot know for certain which solution(s) the riddler had in mind, the very fact that the clues given in the riddle (and in the blend) have counterparts in the input spaces 'shield', 'chopping block/cutting board', and 'whetstone', make all three solutions viable alternatives.

The second riddle under investigation is *Wæpnum Awyrged* (R.20). This riddle has posed a particular challenge to scholars, as it falls into two distinct parts. At the beginning of the first part the speaker declares:

> Ic eom wunderlicu wiht, on gewin sceapen,
> frean minum leof, fægre gegyrwed.
> Byrne is min bleofag, swylce beorht seomað
> wir ymb þone wælgim þe me waldend geaf,
> se me widgalum wisað hwilum
> sylfum to sace. Þonne ic since wege
> þurh hlutterne dæg, hondweorc smiþa,
> gold ofer geardas. Oft ic gæstberend
> cwelle compwæpnum. Cyning mec gyrweð
> since ond seolfre ond mec on sele weorþað;
> ne wyrneð wordlofes, wisan mæneð
> mine for mengo, þær hy meodu drincað,
> healdeð mec on heaþore, hwilum læteð eft
> radwerigne on gerum sceacan,
> orlegfromne. Oft ic oþrum scod
> frecne æt his freonde; fah eom ic wide,
> wæpnum awyrged. (1–16a)

[I am a marvellous creature created for strife, dear to my lord, beautifully adorned. My byrnie is variegated; likewise a bright wire hangs around the slaughter gem which the ruler gave me, who at times guides my very self, in my wandering, to battle. Then I carry treasure through the bright day, handiwork of smiths, gold across the regions. Often I slay soul-bearers with battle-weapons. A king adorns me with treasure and silver and honours me in the hall, he does not withhold praise, relates my habits before the company, where they drink mead, holds me in restraint, at times again lets [me] travel-weary roam at large, valiant in battle. Often I injured another dangerously at the hand of his friend; I am hateful far and wide, cursed among weapons.]

The speaker claims to be a *wunderlicu wiht* ('marvellous creature') that was created for (or: in) strife, is dear to his lord, and is also beautifully adorned (2). The lord also decorates the *wiht*, leads him into battle, rewards him for his services in the hall, but also restrains him (13a). Both war and hall imagery seem to suggest that the *wiht* is a warrior (input 1), yet it is equally clear that this cannot be the solution. Indeed, although *wiht* usually denotes any creature in the Old English corpus, it refers to things or, somewhat less commonly, to animals in the Exeter riddles. Only in one riddle is the speaker a human being, namely a one-eyed seller of garlic (*XII Hund Heafda* (R.86)). Accordingly, a second input space is constructed right from the beginning, which is most probably an object associated with warfare and gift-giving. It is manufactured for strife (1b), has a variegated colour (3a), owns a bright jewel (3b–4a), is adorned with treasure and silver (10a), seems to be an instrument for killing friends (5b–16a), and is cursed among weapons (17a). A likely candidate, as many scholars have pointed out, is a warrior's sword.[22] According to this interpretation, the scabbard is conceptualised as the sword's byrnie (3a), and the *gim* mentioned in line 4a could be a jewel decorating the scabbard or sword pommel. But, again, other solutions based on different assessments of the clues have been suggested. Laurence Shook and Marie Nelson have argued for *heoruswealwe* ('sword-swallow': hawk), which would turn the input 'sword' into another misleading solution to the riddle.[23] Shook's assumption rests on his knowledge of hawking and other customs involving hawks, as well as on unconventional though not impossible interpretations, such as the rendering of *wælgim* ('death gem') as the hawk's talon or the identification of the abusive woman as a female hawk in the second part of the riddle.[24] A different approach is provided by Donald Kay, who discerns *double entendre* (sword/penis) throughout the riddle.[25] Kay's observations have evoked criticism mainly because lines 1–16a do not contain any overt sexual overtones and hence violate the usual practice of sustaining the sexual and non-sexual solution throughout the riddle.[26] Yet it might be too hasty to dismiss Kay's interpretation for this reason alone, since there is always the possibility that a particular riddle does not conform to riddle conventions.

Thus, the various interpretations are based on divergent assumptions, which in turn lead to the construction of different input spaces. The remainder of this chapter, however, focuses on the inputs 'warrior' and 'sword' in order to illustrate a blending mechanism different from that in *Anhaga*. This mechanism seems to be quite straightforward in the first sixteen-and-a-half lines, with metaphorical and metonymical connections between the two inputs that facilitate the conceptualisation of the sword as a warrior. Nevertheless, a couple of loose ends remain. It is not clear how a sword can kill men with 'battle-weapons' (8b–9a), while the phrase *hondweorc smiþa* allows two different renderings. Should

þonne ic sinc wege
þurh hlutterne dæg, hondweorc smiþa,
gold ofer geardas

in lines 6b to 8a be translated as 'then I carry treasure, the handiworks of smiths [swords], gold, through the bright day', or as 'then I, the handiwork of smiths, carry treasure, gold through the bright day'? Both inputs are highlighted by this syntactical ambiguity, and even though 'warrior' is not the solution for the very reasons given above, it remains a contender in the audience's mind. In the second half of the riddle, furthermore, input 1 receives increased emphasis:

Ic me wenan ne þearf
þæt me bearn wræce on bonan feore,
gif me gromra hwylc guþe genægeð;
ne weorþeð sio mægburg gemicledu
eaforan minum þe ic æfter woc,
nymþe ic hlafordleas hweorfan mote
from þam healdende þe me hringas geaf.
Me bið forð witod, gif ic frean hyre,
guþe fremme, swa ic gien dyde
minum þeodne on þonc, þæt ic þolian sceal
bearngestreona. Ic wiþ bryde ne mot
hæmed habban, ac me þæs hyhtplegan
geno wyrneð, se mec geara on
bende legde; forþon ic brucan sceal
on hagostealde hæleþa gestreona.
Oft ic wirum dol wife abelge,
wonie hyre willan; heo me wom spreceð,
floceð hyre folmum, firenaþ mec wordum,
ungod gæleð. Ic ne gyme þæs compes (17b–34)

* * *

> [I need not expect that a son would avenge me on the life of my slayer if some enemy attacks me in battle; nor will the family from which I was born be increased with my offspring unless I must turn lordless from the protector who gave me rings. Henceforth it is decreed for me, if I follow a lord to do battle for him, as I formerly did willingly for my lord, that I must forgo the procreation of children. I may not have intercourse with a bride, but he still denies me this joyous play, he who formerly laid bonds on me; therefore I must enjoy the treasure of men in bachelorhood. Often, foolish in my ornamental wires, I enrage a woman, diminish her desire; she abuses me verbally, strikes her hands together, chides me with words, yells evil. I do not care for that combat * * *]

The clues in this part of the blend do not easily conform to the input 'sword'. For example, how should we assess the observation that the speaker cannot have any children unless he turns from his lord (17b–23)? Hilda R. E. Davidson has argued that this detail corresponds to a used-up sword that is returned to the smithy and subsequently reforged there.[27] Davidson's solution is certainly possible but also shows how much a reader (in this case Davidson) uses her or his cultural insights and imagination when linking the blend to the postulated input space. In fact, the riddler leads the audience further astray by elaborating on the notion of a celibate warrior. The speaker laments that he is forced to remain *in hagostealde* ('in bachelorhood') (28b), and forgo children (27a), bride (27b), *hæmed* ('sexual intercourse, marriage') (28a), and *hyhtplega* ('joyous play') (28b), references that are so specific that the input 'warrior', with its various elements, takes over and redirects our attention from the solution 'sword' to the celibate warrior and his dilemma.[28] Whether the solution 'sword' can still be discerned in these lines depends once more on the recipient's ability to link the given details of the blend to elements of the input 'sword'. For example, Craig Williamson has done this with the creation of a third, counterfactual input space 'phallus' with the organising frame 'procreation', which highlights the qualities that the sword lacks. Williamson argues:

> There are certainly two weapons in the last part of the poem, and the hidden 'weapon' by implication—the 'weapon' that may 'battle' and beget children, the 'weapon' that the wife loves—is a phallus. The riddlic weapon, the *real* weapon, must battle valiantly without hope of begetting children (it begets only when it fails and is sent to the smithy); it must serve honorably in a real battle and bring death to men, and it reaps for its labors only scorn and insult from a woman.

> Not so with the other 'weapon'. One weapon murders men when it faithfully toils, and engenders 'children' only when it fails in its duty. The other 'weapon' engenders children when it faithfully toils. It can fight and engender, battle and be loved at the same time. The end of the riddle begins to make sense only when we realise that the sword describes itself as *unlike that other 'weapon'*.[29]

Rather than being involved in the act of joyful sexual relations and procreation, the sword kills, does not enjoy any sexual relations, and indeed is abused by a woman. Williamson's construal of the input 'phallus' thus links the two parts of the riddle by placing increased emphasis on the input 'sword' as the solution of the second part. In fact, any interpretation that favours one solution to the riddle—including the solution 'hawk' and John D. Niles's rendering of the two inputs as parts of a pun on the OE noun *wæpen*[30]—achieves this linkage. But the parts can also be linked in a different manner. John W. Tanke argues that the riddle 'is constructed in two parts, each of which supports one solution and disallows the other. The unifying principle … lies on the subjective level: first as a sword and then as a phallus, the speaker represents himself throughout the poem as a bachelor-warrior'.[31] In other words, it is the counterfactual input 1 ('warrior') that makes the two-part riddle coherent, while the individual parts have their own solution. Tanke's proposed structure accordingly suggests the presence of two riddles/blends that draw part of their information from the same input space but that could also exist independently of each other. Perhaps two riddles were combined at some stage of transmission, yet even a two-in-one riddle composition is certainly conceivable. In the end, although 'sword' seems to be a feasible solution for *Wæpnum Awyrged*, it is not the only one. As has been illustrated throughout this chapter, riddle-solving is an open-ended cognitive process that depends heavily on the reader's or listener's own input in terms of cultural insights, interpretative choices, and personal preferences.

In the end, both *Anhaga* and *Wæpnum Awyrged* are blends which are constructed piece-by-piece and which allow us to build, process, and evaluate inputs. It is this mental process that ultimately makes riddle-solving both pleasurable and challenging and that makes the Exeter riddles, which have come down to us without solutions, particularly intriguing. We have to process ambiguous clues, and since we can do this in different ways, we can also solve the riddles in different ways. It is important to remember that the solution is not so much in the texts but in the way we think, and once we change our way of thinking, we start anew.

Notes

1 Patrick J. Murphy, *Unriddling the Exeter Riddles* (University Park: Pennsylvania State University Press, 2011).

2 As early as the first half line, the riddler states that the speaker's name is *agof* spelled backwards, which produces *foga* and finally—assuming that a scribe had corrected the final *b* to *f*—*boga*.

3 The solution 'sun' was first proposed by Jennifer Neville at the International Medieval Congress (Leeds, 2016). Her discussion of *Þragbysig* can be found in Chapter 1 of this volume. Murphy favours 'bell': *Unriddling the Exeter Riddles*, pp. 71–7. For a humorous account of the many solutions, see Megan Cavell, 'Commentary for Riddle 4', in *The Riddle Ages: An Anglo-Saxon Riddle Blog*, ed. Megan Cavell with Matthias Ammon and Victoria Symons, 3 April 2013, https://theriddleages.wordpress.com/2013/04/03/notes-on-riddle-4/ (accessed 3 February 2019). Not surprisingly, some scholars, including Craig Williamson, deem the riddle to be unsolved. *The Old English Riddles of the Exeter Book* (Chapel Hill: University of North Carolina Press, 1977), pp. 141–3.

4 Gilles Fauconnier and Mark Turner, *The Way We Think: Conceptual Blending and the Mind's Hidden Complexities* (New York: Basic Books, 2002), p. 40.

5 Fauconnier and Turner, *The Way We Think*, p. 127.

6 Fauconnier and Turner, *The Way We Think*, p. 131.

7 See, for example, Craig Williamson, trans., *A Feast of Creatures: Anglo-Saxon Riddle Songs* (Philadelphia: University of Pennsylvania Press, 1982), pp. 25–36; Ann Harleman Stewart, 'Kenning and Riddle in Old English', *Papers in Language and Literature*, 15 (1979), 115–36; John Lindow, 'Riddles, Kennings, and the Complexity of Skaldic Poetry', *Scandinavian Studies*, 47 (1975), 311–27, esp. pp. 311–18. The kenning definition adopted in this paper is Rudolf Meissner's in *Die Kenningar der Skalden* (Bonn and Leipzig: Schroeder, 1921; repr. Zürich: Georg Olms, 1984), p. 2: 'Die einfache Kenning ist also ein zweigliedriger Ersatz für ein Substantivum der gewöhnlichen Rede' ('The simple kenning is thus a two-element substitute for a substantive of everyday speech').

8 Marie Nelson, 'The Rhetoric of the Exeter Book Riddles', *Speculum*, 49 (1974), 421–40, at p. 423.

9 R. D. Fulk, Robert E. Bjork, and John D. Niles, eds, *Klaeber's Beowulf and the Fight at Finnsburg*, 4th edn (Toronto: University of Toronto Press, 2008), p. 40.

10 No generic space is provided since the identification of elements shared by the determinant (input 1) and the kenning base (input 2) is often difficult. The problem of a frequently vague generic space in the integration model is pointed out by Vlatko Broz, 'Kennings as Blends and Prisms', *Jezikoslovlje (Linguistics)*, 12.2 (2011), 165–86, at

p. 177. Broz prefers the more elaborate prismatic model that was first described by Dirk Geeraerts. See also Weiwei Zhang, *Variation in Metonymy: Cross-linguistic, Historical and Lectal Perspectives* (Berlin: de Gruyter, 2016), pp. 56–63. However, I have chosen a modified integration model with incorporated relations between the inputs and the blend because, unlike the prismatic model, it is very useful for an illustration of the relationship between metaphorical kennings and riddles.

11 Cf. Alvin Lee, *Gold-Hall and Earth-Dragon: 'Beowulf' as Metaphor* (Toronto: University of Toronto Press, 1998), pp. 61–2. Lee sees a causal connection between the two meanings of *hildeleoma*. Beowulf's assault with his sword Nægling (though not called a battle-flame) incenses the dragon and evokes the reptile's deadly flames.

12 It should be noted, however, that many conventional two-element kennings in Old English and Old Norse poetry (e.g. 'sea-horse' for 'ship') do not require a particular context for their solution.

13 William Sayers, 'Exeter Book Riddle No. 5: Whetstone?', *Neuphilologische Mitteilungen*, 97 (1996), 387–92.

14 See also Anita R. Riedinger, 'The Formulaic Style in the Old English Riddles', *Studia Neophilologica*, 76.1 (2004), 30–43, at pp. 33–4.

15 Fauconnier and Turner, *The Way We Think*, p. 119.

16 In 'Formulaic Style', p. 34, Riedinger observes that no other extant Old English poem mentions the possibility of a physician healing a warrior 'probably because it would be unheroic'. Riedinger's interpretation thus provides another possible clue that exposes the 'warrior' solution as wrong, but it also reminds us that riddle-solving depends on our own understanding of the riddler's culture.

17 Riedinger, 'Formulaic Style', p. 34; Wim Tigges, 'Snakes and Ladders: Ambiguity and Coherence in the Exeter Book Riddles and Maxims', in *Companion to Old English Poetry*, ed. Henk Aertsen and Rolf Bremmer, Jr (Amsterdam: VU Press, 1994), pp. 95–118, at p. 100. See also Murphy, *Unriddling the Exeter Riddles*, pp. 69–70; E. G. Stanley, 'Heroic Aspects of the Exeter Book Riddles', in *Prosody and Poetics in the Early Middle Ages: Essays in Honour of C. B. Hieatt*, ed. M. J. Toswell (Toronto: University of Toronto Press, 1995), pp. 197–218, at pp. 205–6.

18 See also Murphy, *Unriddling the Exeter Riddles*, p. 70.

19 Sayers, 'Exeter Book Riddle No. 5', pp. 388–90. Note that Sayers also refers to the solution 'chopping block'.

20 Sayers, 'Exeter Book Riddle No. 5', p. 390.

21 Wolfgang Iser, 'The Reading Process: A Phenomenological Approach', in *The Implied Reader: Patterns of Communication in Prose Fiction from Bunyan to Beckett* (Baltimore: Johns Hopkins University Press, 1974), pp. 274–94. See also Wolfgang Iser, *Der Akt des Lesens*, 2nd edn (Münich: Wilhelm Fink, 1976), pp. 284–301.

22 See, for example, Williamson, *Old English Riddles*, pp. 193–9; Murphy, *Unriddling the Exeter Riddles*, pp. 206–14.
23 Marie Nelson, 'Old English Riddle 18 (20): A Description of Ambivalence', *Neophilologus*, 66 (1982), 291–300; Lawrence K. Shook, 'Old English Riddle No. 20: *Heoruswealwe*', in *Franciplegius: Medieval and Linguistic Studies in Honor of Francis Peabody Magoun, Jr*, ed. J. Bessinger, Jr and R. Creed (New York: NYU Press, 1965), pp. 194–204.
24 Shook, 'Old English Riddle No. 20', pp. 198–200 and 201–3. For a critique of Shook's interpretation, see John W. Tanke, 'The Bachelor-Warrior of Exeter Riddle 20', *PQ*, 79 (2000), 409–27, at p. 421, n.3.
25 Donald Kay, 'Riddle 20: A Revaluation', *Tennessee Studies in Literature*, 13 (1968), 133–9. Note that *Hasofag* (R.11) does not sustain both sexual and non-sexual solutions throughout the whole riddle, either.
26 Williamson, *Old English Riddles*, pp. 193–5; Nelson, 'Old English Riddle 18 (20)', pp. 291–2; Melanie Heyworth, 'Perceptions of Marriage in *Exeter Book Riddles 20* and *61*', *Studia Neophilologica*, 79 (2007), 171–84, at pp. 173–4.
27 Hilda R. E. Davidson, *The Sword in Anglo-Saxon England, its Archaeology and Literature* (Oxford: Clarendon, 1962), pp. 153–4.
28 The emphasis on the source rather than on the target has made Heyworth focus on the riddler's portrayal of marriage in the lines. According to Heyworth, marriage is presented as a 'joyful institution within which sexual intercourse may be enjoyed'. 'Perceptions of Marriage', p. 181.
29 Williamson, *Old English Riddles*, pp. 194–5 (Williamson's italics).
30 John D. Niles, *Old English Enigmatic Poems and the Play in the Texts* (Turnhout: Brepols, 2006), pp. 137–9.
31 Tanke, 'Bachelor-Warrior', p. 409.

7
Humour and the *Exeter Book* riddles: incongruity in *Feþegeorn* (R.31)

Jonathan Wilcox

Humour theory is thriving these days. In such disciplines as cognitive psychology, sociology, philosophy, political science, cultural studies, and linguistics, in the practice of stand-up, cartooning, and clowning, scholars and practitioners are attempting to define just what constitutes humour and how it is created.[1] In this chapter, I will provide a brief introduction to humour theory in order to address the question of what makes the *Exeter Book* riddles funny. I will ground my analysis in a reading of *Feþegeorn* (R.31), which has been relatively neglected of late, and yet which exemplifies many of the pleasures and complexities of the *Exeter Book* riddles.

Three distinct theories have traditionally competed for defining how humour works, although the three may be more compatible than their partisans acknowledge. Incongruity theory is the most fundamental. Incongruity appears to be the *sine qua non* for a perception of humour and incongruity-resolution may be the essential mechanism underlying its effect.[2] Incongruity involves some transgression from what is expected, an effect that Schopenhauer describes as a perception that threatens a conception; Raskin and Attardo, working within a more linguistic frame, call this a clashing of conflicting scripts; while the cognitive psychologists, Hurley, Dennett, and Adams, see the process as the displacement of a strongly-held but stealthily-arrived-at assumption in the mind which is proven to be wrong.[3] While some form of incongruity is essential for humour, it is never a sufficient explanation since some incongruities are creepy, some plain odd, and only some trigger laughter. What is needed is appropriate incongruity, as Oring suggests.[4] Unpacking incongruity and showing how it is appropriate is the essential work of humour analysis.

Superiority theory, which has a long and prominent role in the critical literature, derived from Aristotle and articulated by Hobbes and Bergson among others, suggests an appropriate domain for the incongruity, since the object of humour is seen as in some way put down by it, with a sense of relief in the viewer that there do not go I.[5] In clarifying the approach, Hobbes articulates laughter as an expression of 'sudden glory' at the realisation of superiority, suggesting how the perception of humour builds up the perceiver. Humour is in some ways close to *Schadenfreude* in laughing at the folly revealed in others, but such laughter can also be sympathetic and can be directed at one's previous self. Bergson is particularly concerned with how derisive laughter critiques the overly mechanistic. While the name makes this approach sound unpleasantly snobbish, the underlying theory is surprisingly productive for explaining how humour is a liberating and humanising force.

Release theories provide another way of thinking about the processes occurring during the resolution of incongruity.[6] They suggest that the audience lives in a constant state of constraint from which humour allows a temporary reprieve. Freud is the most famous exponent of this theory, suggesting that jokes (which for him are a limited subset of tendentious humour and are always about sex and violence) provide a momentary freeing from the repression of sexual and violent urges. Such release highlights why the breaking of taboos can be such a fruitful arena for humour. A different version of release theory suggests that humour saves mental energy as we realise that the set-up does not require serious problem solving. Play and the signals that define play prove to be a useful element in detecting humour.[7]

If incongruity is the essential mechanism for humour, much recent work has helped to give this an appropriate context. For something to be humorous, it needs to operate in an appropriate domain (lacking magnitude according to Aristotle), often depending on a move from high to low (the carnivalesque inversion of Bakhtin).[8] Humour occurs within a paradox of identification and distance: there is no humour if we are disengaged, but also none if we are too close, so we need the right distance, either of emotional tenor or of time.[9] McGraw and Warner use the term 'benign violation' to explain the way the incongruity must involve some sort of breach (of decorum or reason or epistemological level) and yet must not be so extreme as to be threatening or truly shocking.[10] Of course, the breaking point, either in the direction of dullness or of alienation, varies for different members of an audience, hinting at the challenge facing those who create humour and those trying to pinpoint it. Boundary crossing is potentially fruitful for humour, giving the necessary edginess, even as it is also particularly fraught.[11]

Such boundary crossing, shock, and distance are probably happening in literature of the past, but they can be hard to pinpoint.

More observational studies of humour suggest the significance of the framing of the humour act. The humorist or humorous text signals the presence of humour (through voice or aspect or verbal markers), and the work of humour can then follow its own rules of not sense-making.[12] Irony presents an interesting case here, because the marker of humour is masked, enabling misunderstanding, and this presents a particular challenge for engaging humour of the long past, as can be seen in scholarly disagreements on the validity of reading irony in Old English literature.[13] In a brilliant sociological study of Dutch joke tellers, Giselinde Kuipers demonstrates how much humour is about creating community and reminds us how utterly fundamental class and gender are in the perception and response, with women more marked as humour appreciators, men more marked as humour producers.[14] The community aspect is probably relevant to the performance of all Old English poetry, although fine-grained distinctions in audience response are notoriously hard to establish.

Laughter is part of the sign language of the humorous mode, and some theorists take laughter as a convenient diagnostic for humour, but the relation proves tenuous in all cases and particularly vexed in reading from the past. While laughter has to appear spontaneous to be believed, observational studies show that it is social, interactional, and complicatedly controlled.[15] Laughter can mark derision, suggest superiority, mask fear, register relief, express joy, or acknowledge a social compact as well as recognise humour. In Old English literature (as in the Bible), when laughter is mentioned the laughter of scorn or derision dominates, with occasional instances of relief or sociability.[16] This does not mean that humour is lacking or that early medieval audiences failed to laugh at the funny bits, just that accounts of laughter are a poor index for uncovering that humour.

The mechanisms for the creation of humour might be summarised as follows: humour comes from an incongruity, a doubleness of script, clashing in some appropriate way. The appropriate inappropriateness often involves some surprising ambiguity of meaning or a shift in register or a departure from an expected form. The element of surprise speaks to an issue of timing in which the processing of the humorous stimulant needs to involve a rapid (or simultaneous) comprehending of the opposing scripts. The doubleness usually involves some turn downwards in register or decorum or moral seriousness, and hence humour is often taboo-breaking, which may add to its appeal. The whole process must grab an audience's attention and not repel that audience, which requires the right balance of empathy and alienation, and the audience is often primed in some way to be receptive to a perception of humour.

Many of the elements that create humour are also fundamental to riddles. Aristotle sees the purpose of a riddle as 'to describe a fact in an impossible combination of words (which cannot be done with the real names for things, but can be with their metaphorical substitutes)', which suggests the fundamental idea of incongruity through verbal ingenuity.[17] Archer Taylor gives a more grounded definition, suggesting a riddle 'compares an object to another entirely different object', which is a recipe for incongruity.[18] He further unpacks the mechanism involved, pointing to the way that riddles often feature a positive descriptive element which is metaphorical and a negative descriptive element described literally. Riddles thus depend on both metaphor (in the analogy) and metonymy (through the literal restrictive condition), a state worked out in relation to the *Exeter Book* riddles by Ann Harleman Stewart, who stresses the centrality of paradox for understanding the riddles.[19] Paradox centres on a conceptual incongruity.

Riddles in general centre, of course, on the indeterminacy of language, often taking advantage of semantic ambiguity. The very game of the riddle encourages the audience to keep as many possibilities in mind as possible, not knowing which sense and context will resolve into a solution and which will be a blind. This delay of judgement pushes to an extreme the Just-In-Time processing that Hurley, Dennett, and Adams postulate as the underlying cognitive mechanism for semantic retrieval significant to understanding humour.[20] Riddles offer a dizzying array of possible ambiguities. Patrick J. Murphy provides a grounding for that multiplicity by pointing out how many of the *Exeter Book* riddles include a metaphorical description that points to what Murphy calls a riddle's 'focus': 'an underlying metaphor that lends coherence to the text's strategy of obfuscation.'[21] Murphy concedes that sometimes the underlying obfuscations work piecemeal, but suggests that 'the dark clues of Old English riddles often add up to something quite coherent, shaped as they are by extended implicit metaphors'. This idea is valuable for considering the creation of humour since the gap between the focus created by the dark clues and the solution is a space in which to look for the appropriately inappropriate doubleness that is humorous incongruity.

Other aspects also point to the humour of the riddles. While it is unfashionable to speculate too much about the unrecoverable oral performance of Old English poetry, records survive for a few performance contexts and others can be reasonably guessed at. Scenes of conviviality imagine the performance of poetry as part of the pleasure of communal feasting, as in the celebrations at Heorot after the apparent slaying of Grendel, and such an occasion would be a reasonable site for imagining the posing of poetic riddles.[22] When Cædmon excuses himself from the scene of workers' conviviality on the monastic estate at Whitby, it would seem reasonable to assume that some of his fellow labourers might have recited a riddle as the harp came around, creating interactive entertainment. Recent work on the *Exeter Book* riddles has convincingly shown how they are gathered from different sources with different histories of transmission, during which they could have been performed in limitless additional contexts.[23] The Leiden Riddle shows that one riddle got recorded in very different milieux, written into a ninth-century manuscript from Fleury in addition to the *Exeter Book*, and with textual differences demonstrating modification in performance.[24] While the exchanges of riddles between Solomon and Saturn or between Alcuin and Pippin suggest the posing of riddles in a learned context,[25] the sound of the celebration at Heorot or the turn-taking conviviality of the workers at Whitby suggest a more raucous context that would provide a kind of priming for humour loosely analogous to a contemporary stand-up comedy club. In such a context, any of the riddles would likely be received as humorous.

The case for humour is most straightforward in the riddles of sexual *double entendre*, where the consistently doubled solution allows for a developed incongruity, while the frisson of breaking taboos adds to the comic impact. Riddles that do not rely on sexual *double entendre* were also funny, but the mechanism requires more work of critical explanation. In the remainder of this chapter, I endeavour to provide such an explanation for the test case of *Feþegeorn*.

Is þes middangeard   missenlicum
wisum gewlitegad,   wrættum gefrætwad.
Ic seah sellic þing   singan on ræcede;
wiht wæs nower   werum on gemonge,
sio hæfde wæstum   wundorlicran.
Niþerweard [onhwyrfed]   wæs neb hyre,
fet ond folme   fugele gelice;

no hwæþre fleogan mæg   ne fela gongan,
hwæþre feþegeorn   fremman onginneð,
gecoren cræftum,   cyrreð geneahhe
oft ond gelome   eorlum on gemonge,
siteð æt symble,   sæles bideþ,
hwonne ær heo cræft hyre   cyþan mote
werum on wonge.   Ne heo þær wiht þigeð
þæs þe him æt blisse   beornas habbað.
Deor domes georn,   hio dumb wunað;
hwæþre hyre is on fote   fæger hleoþor,
wynlicu woðgiefu.   Wrætlic me þinceð,
hu seo wiht mæge   wordum lacan
þurh fot neoþan,   frætwed hyrstum.
Hafað hyre on halse,   þonne hio hord warað,
bær, beagum deall,   broþor sine,
mæg mid mægne.   Micel is to hycgenne
wisum woðboran,   hwæt sio wiht sie.[26]

[This world is made beautiful in various ways, adorned with ornaments. I saw a wondrous thing sing in the hall; there was nowhere a creature among men which had a more wonderful shape. Its (or: her) beak (or: countenance) was turned downwards, it was like a bird in foot and hand (or: feet and hands were like a bird); nevertheless it cannot fly nor walk much, yet foot-walking-eager it begins to act, choice in skills, it turns (or: goes) frequently, often and a lot among men of status, sits at a feast, awaits the opportunity, when it may make known its skill to men at that place. It does not at all partake there of that which warriors have for their joy. A brave one (or: wild beast) eager for glory, it remains dumb, yet in its foot is a beautiful voice, a lovely sound-gift. It seems wondrous to me, how that creature can sport with speech from below through the foot adorned with ornaments. It has on its neck, when it guards the hoard, naked, resplendent in rings, its brother (or: brothers), kin with strength. It is much to ponder for a wise speech-bearer (or: speech-bearers) what that creature may be.]

Prominent in this riddle is the idea of wonder. Many a *wiht* in the riddles is wondrous, of course, but there seems to be particular stress on the remarkable nature of the *sellic þing* ('wondrous thing') (3b) here, that is so very *wundorlic* in *wæstum* ('wonderful in shape') (5) and *wrætlic* ('wondrous') (18b) in its production of sound, as is emphasised in the opening two lines (even if they do recur in the very next riddle).[27] The wonder-rich nature of the object plays into the challenge of the riddling puzzle, further emphasised in the formula of the closing line and a half, where even *wisan woðboran* ('wise speech-bearers') will need much thought to figure out what this *wiht* may be. Through that implied challenge, the riddle agonistically mocks the puzzled audience and thereby enables a stance of superiority for those who come up with an answer. Such emphasis on wonder encourages a hypersensitivity in the audience, who are encouraged to be attentive to all of the multiple possibilities of semantics and syntax, and of poetic expression and accumulating imagery, to arrive at a solution. Such openness to multiplicity at every level is a significant part of the pleasure of riddles and encourages the discovery of incongruities, opening multiple avenues for humour.

In the case of *Feþegeorn*, the *wiht* has the jumbled body parts common in a riddle creature, including that downward *neb* ('beak or countenance') (6), the feet and hands (or foot and hand) like a bird (7), further prominent emphasis on a foot (17 and 20) and (possibly) a neck (21). The creature's state is also implied by the verbs that describe its actions, which suggest the ability to sing (3) turn (10), and sit (12), and clear signs of intentionality (12b–14a, 16a). The underlying image pattern here is what Barley would call a monster, an apparently animate creature with parts that do not quite add up.[28] In most riddles, this shadow monster will resolve into a straightforward recognisable object or creature, although the *Exeter Book* riddle sequence plays comically with this convention by including the occasional case that does not, like the One-Eyed Seller of Garlic of *XII Hund Heafda* (R.86).[29] The body part given most emphasis here is the foot, and the riddle is fascinated by the *wiht*'s perambulation. The creature could not fly nor walk (*gongan*) (8b) and yet is *feþegeorn* ('foot-walking eager') (9a), a *hapax legomenon*, building on the idea of *feþe*, which the *DOE* glosses as '(power of) movement or walking/going on foot'.[30] Instead, the creature turns, sits, and waits (10b, 12a, 12b).

The *georn* ('eager') of *feþegeorn* (9a) resonates with the same word in the second half of the poem, where the creature is *domes georn* ('eager for glory') (16a) and where the foot is puzzlingly associated with sound rather than with locomotion (17a, 20a). Indeed, an additional cluster of images centres on sound, presented through multiple paradoxes. In a synaesthetic start, the viewer *saw* the wondrous thing *sing* in the hall (3). From line 16b onwards, the creature remains dumb and yet has a beautiful voice, a *woðgiefu* ('comely gift of sound') (18a)—another *hapax legomenon*, suggesting a careful effect—in, of all places, its foot (15b–18a). This unlikely detail is repeated in further description in the next two lines, now explicitly marvelled at by the riddle's focalisation. The creature sports with words (*wordum lacan*, 19b), apparently participating in the human attribute of speech, but does so from below through its foot (20a), which returns to the attributes of the monstrous.

Play with the animate/inanimate and human/not human boundaries continues in the account of dress. The creature is *frætwed hyrstum* ('adorned with ornaments') (20b, as anticipated in lines 1–2), yet is *bær* ('naked') (22a)—if that is an adjective and not a verb, and if it applies to the subject without grammatical agreement of gender[31]—but nonetheless proud in rings (*beagum deall*, 22a). This is the interpretation of the major editors, although the multiplicity of possibilities extends to syntax and part of speech as well as to semantics and imagery, and an initial reading of line 22a might assume *bær* is a verb, past tense of *beran*, in which case the poetic adjective *deall*, with just seven surviving occurrences according to the *DOE* ('proud in or of; resplendent with' with dative object) might be read as an odd spelling of the significantly more common noun *dæl*, 'part, portion' (with ca. 1500 occurrences according to the *DOE*) so that the creature 'bore a portion of rings'. In any event, the trappings (or even their lack) sound strikingly human.

Another set of clues points more towards the avian than the human. The creature's hands and feet (7a)—if nominative plural, or hand and foot if dative singular: the forms are ambiguous and either structure is possible—are explicitly like a bird (*fugele gelice*, 7b), even if the ability to fly is then denied (8a). That statement of bird-ness gets an audience thinking about the avian, even if the explicitness of the simile makes it unlikely as the solution to the riddle. The *neb* that is downwards in line 6 could be the beak of a bird (B-T's first sense for the noun), even as it could also be a nose or countenance (B-T's third sense). Imagining the *wiht* as a bird fits well with the presence of adornments on a naked body in a lightly metaphorical reading of a bird's plumage, seen elsewhere in the *Exeter Book* riddles in the description of the swan (*Ferende Gæst* [R.7] 4a, 6b) or barnacle goose (*Neb wæs Min on Nearwe* [R.10] 7b–8) or chickens (*X Gebroþor ond Sweostor* [R.13] 9b, 10b). The emphasis on singing and distinctive beautiful sound also hints at the avian, as in the swan of *Ferende Gæst* or the nightingale of *Eald Æfensceop* (R.8). The distinctive attribute *feþegeorn* (9a) may pun on *feþer* ('feather').[32] *Deor*, in line 16a, establishes another ambiguity: if this is an adjective used substantively, this would be a brave one (*DOE*, *s.v. deor* adjective, mostly poetic), but, if a noun, an animal—*DOE*, *s.v. deor* noun, sense 1, 'animal, beast (usually only undomesticated quadrupeds, esp. savage beasts or game, but also fabulous animals)'—here metaphorically standing for a bird.

The creature's boldness is also hinted at in the place of the action. The *wiht* is *on rœcede* ('in the hall') (3b), an apparently martial or noble masculine context that adds a puzzle of gender. An early medieval English audience would expect pronouns to agree with the gender of nouns rather than biological gender, and since *wiht* is a feminine noun, the chiming feminine pronouns would not necessarily signal sex, and yet their super-abundance (5a, 6b, 13a, 14b, 16a, 21a, 21b) in an enigmatic context probably hints at natural gender.[33] The apparently female creature nevertheless operates in a very masculine space among male people (*werum*) (4). It sits at the feast (12a) among high-status males (*eorlum*, 11b) before it may make known its skill to those masculine individuals (*werum*, 14a). It does not participate in the joy of the martial men (*beornas*), presumably the drinking of alcohol (14b–15). The creature operates among men and yet seems separated from them and their pleasures.

The animate or human status of the *wiht* and the question of gender is particularly apparent in the penultimate sentence (21–3a), which introduces the idea of kin (*mǣg*, with a long vowel, m. 'kinsman' or f. 'kinswoman', unless this is the common modal auxiliary verb with a short vowel, *mæg*, 'can') and of a brother or brothers (*broþor*, 22b)—the form is the same for nominative or accusative singular or plural—even if the subject of the sentence is ambiguous. The most obvious candidate is the creature, naked (but the form *bær* lacks agreement with the grammatical gender of *wiht*, either tipping towards natural gender of the opposite sex or marking a mistake) and proud in rings, who has her brother(s) on her neck, when she guards or holds the hoard or treasure, a kinswoman with strength. The syntax also allows for a different subject, potentially her brother of line 22b, who, naked (now with agreement of grammatical gender), proud of rings, has her (*hyre*, 21a) on (his) neck, kinsman with strength. It is also possible that the sentence has another subject altogether, who has her, when she guards or holds the hoard or treasure, on (his) neck with some unstated connection to her brother (or brothers), kin (held) with strength. Syntax and the referents of the pronouns are puzzling, and an astute audience would keep all the possibilities in mind.

On a first hearing or reading, that audience probably absorbs the information available from the poem without settling on a single solution, accepting as many possibilities for the words as they can hold. A sustained run of images hints at what might be a solution, but an experienced audience would exercise caution, knowing that it might also be a blind. Such an audience here is probably holding the idea of the avian, of a paradoxical foot, and of special sound made in a hall, with hints of fierceness and beauty, of body parts and adornments, and of treasure and kin, pondering what is false focus, what is convincing solution.

Each of the riddle's paradoxes provides a localised incongruity and so might create humour. An audience that ponders whether *deor* is a noun or an adjective might find that very trickiness of language humorous, augmented by the conceptual play between a wild animal (the most likely referent for *deor* as noun) and a fierce person (the most likely referent for *deor* as adjective). Similarly, an audience might delight at the localised ambiguity of *mæg* in line 23a as a noun that could be masculine or feminine but is here undecidable. More radically, if vowel length was fudged in the recital or if the poem were read visually, the audience might note the possibilities of kin in a noun or permission in a verb. In most conditions, such ambiguity would likely exasperate, but in the playful world of the riddles, the audience might delight in the uncovering of such incongruity of language.

Such localised incongruities are very frequent in riddles and would likely be acknowledged but passed over rapidly, perhaps provoking a passing smile. Longer lasting, and more effective as a locus for humour, are the incongruities borne between image clusters and solution. To look at those first requires arriving at a solution. In *Feþegeorn*, the ability to generate sound through its foot is the emphatic clue given most significance in the interpretation of most scholars. The emphasis on sound suggests a musical instrument and the location of that sound's production and details of the appearance suggest … a bagpipe.

Bagpipes traditionally consist of the cured skin of a whole sheep or goat, hair side in, flesh side out, with pipes tied into the neck and fore-legs. The chanter, extending downwards, has finger stops and a reed, while one or more drones extending upwards provide fixed-pitch accompaniment. Air is supplied through a blow-pipe.[34] The foot in the riddle is probably a metaphor for the downward-angled chanter from which much of a bagpipe's sound emerges, and/or for the drone (or drones) extending upwards, but somewhat leg-like, from which the rest of the sound emerges. The naked form (if naked it be) is either the unadorned bag or the unadorned windpipe, while the brother or brothers are the drone or drones, carried on the neck of the instrument. Alternatively, the single drone could be unadorned and seen as supporting the rest of the instrument on its neck, or the whole instrument, some part unadorned, is carried on the neck of the player. Rings probably adorn the chanter and/or the drones and/or the blow-pipe, as ring structures help secure the pipes to the bag, and this functional use often leads to further ring-like decoration. The hoard or treasure of line 21b is the breath of the piper, which serves as the wind to sound the pipes, a fundamental detail of a bagpipe and one which helps to motivate the paradox of the simultaneously animate and inanimate status of a crafted object which, nevertheless, has breath, metaphorical voice, and the ability to walk when brought to life as a musical instrument. The variation in girth of the bag may be hinted at by the wondrous nature of the *wæstum* ('form' or 'growth' or 'fruit') of line 5.

Winternitz comments on the ubiquity of bagpipes in early agrarian societies,[35] and their ubiquity makes likely their presence in early medieval England, even if they are not straightforwardly represented from there. It is likely that bagpipes are subsumed under other forms of musical pipes, sometimes designated by *chorus* or *musa* in Latin, perhaps by *pipe oððe hwistle* in Old English.[36] Niles suggests **blæst-pipe* as the most likely specific term in Old English, even though the word is not attested in the surviving corpus.[37] Bagpipes are often represented in England from the later Middle Ages, including examples of an angel playing a bagpipe on the Minstrel's Gallery at Exeter Cathedral from c. 1360 and on a roof boss from Winchester Cathedral.[38] Closer to the early medieval period is a representation of a boy probably playing a bagpipe at the foot of King David playing his harp in the Hunterian Psalter from c. 1170.[39] The instrument is so common in the late Middle Ages, and so widely spread, that I think it is reasonable to assume bagpipes were a feature of early medieval England, even if the surviving record lacks specificity beyond this riddle.

If bagpipe is the solution, many of the image clusters that have built up to it are blinds, false possibilities, focuses that an audience will likely continue to hold alongside the solution. A musical instrument does not have an actual foot, of course, and yet the simultaneous activation of the idea of the foot of a living creature with the downward-extending chanter of a bagpipe and/or the upward-extending drone (or drones) creates a comic incongruity as the audience views the musical instrument as a living creature with body parts, then drops the image of the living for the manufactured. The eagerness to be foot-walking (*feþegeorn*) (9a) is a particularly memorable version of the same conceit, since bagpipes do not themselves walk, but they are traditionally played while walking, so that the bagpipe depends on such perambulation to come to metaphorical life. The idea of sporting with words works similarly, simultaneously conjuring human speech and the communicative possibilities of music. A similar incongruity is triggered by the adornments or undress which seem to be further human attributes, and by the family relations, as well as by the hints of desire and volition. Viewing a gangly-limbed musical instrument simultaneously as a human triggers an appropriately inappropriate match with a move from the potentially-serious to the flippant that makes for humour.

The further false focus of the avian creates perhaps the strongest strain of comic incongruity. Birds sing, often with much beauty, if sometimes rather anarchically to a human ear; musical instruments sing, often with much beauty, if sometimes with the hint of an anarchic out-of-control quality in the case of bagpipes to the ears of most non-pipers. Birds fit well in the uneasy humanity of the *wiht*, with their potential to mimic the human voice, and their apparent pride in beautiful adornments, through which, in view of their animal nature, they gently parody the human pride in such attributes. While a bagpipe does not obviously look like a bird, the image of *neb niðerweard* with limbs above in lines 6–7 suggests the chanter as the *neb* and the drone (or drones) and windpipe as legs, sketching the broad outline of some inverted large bird, such as a heron (or stork or crane). While playing a bird is, of course, an impossibility, it is an incongruity which was apparently appreciated by at least one other creator of the time, a late-eleventh-century Spanish illustrator of Beatus of Liebena's *Commentary on the Apocalypse*, who provided as a space-filler the image of two jugglers, both wearing grotesquely colourful garb, dancing with improbably birdlike (?) footwear, one of whom plays a musical instrument, while the other clutches a large bird by the neck while swinging a knife in an action that parallels (and faintly suggests?) the playing of an instrument.[40] There is something appropriately inappropriate in the yoking of an ungainly trapped bird to an ungainly musical instrument.[41]

A few further images worked out in the poem probably also generate comic incongruity. A sack of bare skin with jutting elements in a heavily masculine context seems redolent of male sexual anatomy, and there is a hint of humorous breach of taboo in the public display of such a determinedly strutting form. The sexual focus is minimal in this riddle, but is briefly triggered by the adjective *bær* (22). Such a lurking overtone adds a paradox to the grammatical gender of the *wiht*, which might tally with a feminine noun like *gecynd* in standing for male genitals,[42] but probably provokes comic incongruity at the distance between grammatical and anatomical gender as this possible focus is considered and then left behind by an audience.

The breath animating the musical instrument may also remind an audience of the bagpipe's reputation for the unsubtle volubility of a windbag. This is an aspect picked up in the most famous of English medieval bagpipers, the Miller of Chaucer's *Canterbury Tales*, whose choice of instrument signals a loud-mouthed attention-grabber, 'a janglere and a goliardeys', who is as happy to invert social hierarchies as he is to open doors with his head.[43] If these overtones were operative in early medieval England, they would give an added sense of paradox to the instrument's presence in the high-status hall among warriors rather than in some more unruly performance space.

While *Feþegeorn* plays with multiple appropriate incongruities through the comic irony of the false image clusters, humour may be all the more prevalent because the solution itself is an object inclining to the comic. Humour accrues to the bagpipe for its lack of subtlety as an object built on a literal windbag. Bagpipes can encode the windiness of unrestrained speech or the flatulent pouring forth of an unrestrained body. Such humour is seen in two representations in the fourteenth-century Luttrell Psalter.[44] A marginal image on fol. 176r portrays a piper playing an instrument with a single drone, with hints of the grotesque in his puffed-up cheeks, and hints of comedy in the decoration, at the entry to the chanter, of a sculpted human head, given high status through a crown, but recursively presented with puffed-up cheeks and prominent hair that echo the instrument's player. The instrument itself is faintly funny here, but is all the more so when a strikingly similar version is presented in a drollery on fol. 185v, where the drone now proceeds out of the backside of a hybrid beast, with the indecorousness stressed through the addition of another head visibly blowing with protruding cheeks, here proceeding from the beast's backside. The windiness of this particular instrument encourages comic play in a Bakhtinian inversion of the body's usual decorum and *Feþegeorn* probably benefits from such undertones in its presentation of the bagpipe as an inverted creature.

Humour abounds in *Feþegeorn* and humour theory is useful for explaining it. The humour depends on appropriate incongruity, while the puzzle presented by the riddle depends on ambiguity and multiple possibilities that create both local and extended comic incongruities. Humour may be seen as the superiority of a moment of sudden glory, and solving the riddle involves such a moment, one-upping the taunting defiance of the riddle's conclusion. Humour involves some kind of release, and answering the riddle provides release, with hints of breaking taboos, more through entertaining for a moment the jumble of mismatched body parts than through the very fleeting challenge to sexual decorum. Humour values sociability and the priming that comes from a context signalling the need for laughter, while the riddle surely operated in a social context that primed an audience to be ready for a puzzle and the enjoyment of a good laugh.

Comic laughter would probably be most fully released by *Feþegeorn* as an audience came to realise that the creature described is a bagpipe, although there remains some scope for doubting whether that is the necessary solution.[45] That very uncertainty exemplifies another pleasure of the *Exeter Book* riddles in their continuing indeterminacy. It is easy to imagine individuals in an audience vying to defend their best guess at the solution, stitching together the clues in a way that works for their case, and pointing to the weakness of alternative solutions. Such a riddle-telling session provides just the context that would encourage every utterance to be seen as potentially funny. Comic release comes from puzzling out an upside-down bird as a bagpipe—a non-threatening *bizarrerie* fleetingly inverting the normal world. In the absence of attested evidence for how audiences responded to the riddles, contemporary humour theory provides significant analytical tools for unpacking the humour in terms of play and performance context, superiority and release, and, above all, appropriate incongruity.

Notes

1 Victor Raskin, ed., *The Primer of Humor Research* (Berlin: de Gruyter, 2008), provides a useful collection of essays approaching humour theory from different disciplinary perspectives; Oliver Double, *Getting the Joke: The Inner Workings of Stand-Up Comedy*, 2nd edn (London: Methuen, 2013), provides discussion from the practitioners' point of view. Noel Carroll, *Humour: A Very Short Introduction* (Oxford: Oxford University Press, 2014), provides a convenient overview.

2 See John Morreall, *Comic Relief: A Comprehensive Philosophy of Humor* (Hoboken: Wiley, 2009), for a valuable account that builds on incongruity theory.

3 See Salvatore Attardo, 'A Primer for the Linguistics of Humor', in *Primer of Humor Research*, ed. Victor Raskin (Berlin: de Gruyter, 2008), pp. 101–55; Matthew M. Hurley, Daniel C. Dennett, and Reginald B. Adams, Jr, *Inside Jokes: Using Humor to Reverse-Engineer the Mind* (Cambridge, MA: MIT Press, 2011).

4 Elliott Oring, *Joking Asides: The Theory, Analysis, and Aesthetics of Humor* (Logan: Utah State University Press, 2016).

5 Henri Bergson, *Laughter: An Essay on the Meaning of the Comic*, trans. Cloudesely Brereton and Fred Rothwell (London/New York: Macmillan, 1911). See Barry Sanders, *Sudden Glory: Laughter as Subversive History* (Boston: Beacon, 1995), for an engaging account making good use of superiority theory.

6 See Sigmund Freud, *Jokes and their Relation to the Unconscious*, trans. James Strachey (London: Routledge, 1960); Elliott Oring, *Jokes and their Relations* (Lexington: University of Kentucky Press, 1992).

7 See further Johan Huizinga, *Homo Ludens: A Study of the Play Element in Culture* (London: Routledge, 1949).

8 Mikhail Bakhtin, *Rabelais and His World*, trans. Hélène Iswolsky (Bloomington: Indiana University Press, 1984).

9 See Todd McGowan, *Only A Joke Can Save Us: A Theory of Comedy* (Evanston, IL: Northwestern University Press, 2017).

10 Peter McGraw and Joel Warner, *The Humor Code: A Global Search for What Makes Things Funny* (New York: Simon and Schuster, 2014).

11 See Sharon Lockyer and Michael Pickering, eds, *Beyond the Joke: The Limits of Humour* (Basingstoke: Palgrave, 2005), on the risks and ethical issues involved.

12 See Michael Mulkay, *On Humour: Its Nature and Place in Modern Society* (Oxford: Polity, 1988), for an outstanding study.

13 See, for example, Elise Louviot, *Direct Speech in Beowulf and Other Old English Narrative Poems* (Cambridge: D. S. Brewer, 2016); in contrast with Tom Clark, *A Case for Irony in Beowulf, With Particular Reference to its Epithets* (Bern: Peter Lang, 2003).

14 Giselinde Kuipers, *Good Humor, Bad Taste: A Sociology of the Joke*, 2nd edn (Berlin: de Gruyter, 2015).

15 See Robert R. Provine, *Laughter: A Scientific Investigation* (New York: Viking, 2000).

16 See Hugh Magennis, 'Images of Laughter in Old English Poetry, with Particular Reference to the 'hleahtor wera' of The Seafarer', *ES*, 73 (1992), 193–204; John D. Niles, 'Byrhtnoth's Laughter and the Poetics of Gesture', in *Humour in Anglo-Saxon Literature*, ed. Jonathan Wilcox (Cambridge: D. S. Brewer, 2000), pp. 11–32.

17 Aristotle, *The Poetics*, trans. James Hutton (New York: Norton, 1982), ch. 22.
18 Archer Taylor, *English Riddles from Oral Tradition* (Berkeley: University of California Press, 1951), p. 1.
19 Ann Harleman Stewart, 'Old English Riddle 47 as Stylistic Parody', *Papers on Language and Literature*, 11 (1975), 227–41; Ann Harleman Stewart, 'Kenning and Riddle in Old English', *Papers on Language and Literature*, 15 (1979), 115–36.
20 Hurley, Dennett and Adams, *Inside Jokes*.
21 Patrick J. Murphy, *Unriddling the Exeter Riddles* (University Park: Pennsylvania State University Press, 2011), p. 18.
22 On imagined scenes of feasting, see Hugh Magennis, *Images of Community in Old English Poetry* (Cambridge: Cambridge University Press, 1996). On likely performance contexts, see Karl Reichl, ed., *Medieval Oral Literature* (Berlin: de Gruyter, 2012).
23 See Mercedes Salvador-Bello, *Isidorean Perceptions of Order: The Exeter Book Riddles and Medieval Latin Enigmata* (Morgantown: West Virginia University Press, 2015); Peter Orton, 'The Exeter Book *Riddles*: Authorship and Transmission', *ASE*, 44 (2015), 131–62.
24 See my 'Transmission of Literature and Learning: Anglo-Saxon Scribal Culture', in *A Companion to Anglo-Saxon Literature*, ed. Phillip Pulsiano and Elaine M. Treharne (Oxford: Blackwell, 2001), pp. 50–70.
25 See Daniel Anlezark, ed., *The Old English Dialogues of Solomon and Saturn* (Cambridge: Brewer, 2009); Martha Bayless, 'Alcuin's *Disputatio Pippini* and the Early Medieval Riddle Tradition', in *Humour, History and Politics in Late Antiquity and the Early Middle Ages*, ed. Guy Halsall (Cambridge: Cambridge University Press, 2002), pp. 157–78.
26 The emendation in 6a is taken from Bernard J. Muir, ed., *The Exeter Anthology of Old English Poetry*, 2nd edn, 2 vols (Exeter: University of Exeter Press, 2000), I, p. 307.
27 On wonder in the riddles, see Peter Ramey, 'The Riddle of Beauty: The Aesthetics of Wrætlic in Old English Verse', *MP*, 114 (2017), 457–81; Peter Ramey, 'Crafting Strangeness: Wonder Terminology in the Exeter Book Riddles and the Anglo-Latin Enigmata', *RES*, 69 (2018), 201–15; Patricia Dailey, 'Riddles, Wonder, and Responsiveness in Anglo-Saxon Literature', in *The Cambridge History of Early Medieval English Literature*, ed. Clare A. Lees (Cambridge: Cambridge University Press, 2013), pp. 451–72; and Rhodes' Chapter 2 in this volume. For further discussion of the production of sound, see Brooks' Chapter 4 in this volume. Lines 1–2 recur as the opening of the next riddle, *Grindan wið Greote* (R.32).
28 Nigel F. Barley, 'Structural Aspects of the Anglo-Saxon Riddle', *Semiotica*, 10 (1974), 143–75.

29 See further my 'Mock-Riddles in Old English: Exeter Riddles 86 and 19', *Studies in Philology*, 93 (1996), 180–7. See also Borysławski's discussion of the riddle in Chapter 8 of this volume.
30 Muir's full-stop at the end of line 8 slightly spoils this paradox, where Krapp and Dobbie's comma allows the contrasting *hwæþres* to play across lines 8–9.
31 Muir follows Williamson in emending to *baru*, which perhaps prematurely decides both points.
32 As suggested by Donald K. Fry, 'Exeter Riddle 31: Feather-Pen', in *De Gustibus: Essays for Alain Renoir*, ed. J. M. Foley, C. J. Womack, and W. A. Womack (New York: Garland, 1992), pp. 234–49.
33 For further discussion of grammatical gender, see Cavell, Dale, and Salvador-Bello in Chapters 3, 10, and 12 of this volume.
34 On bagpipes, see William A. Cocks, Anthony C. Baines, and Roderick D. Cannon, 'Bagpipe', in *Grove Music Online* (Oxford University Press, 2001), www.oxfordmusiconline.com (accessed 4 February 2019).
35 Emanuel Winternitz, *Musical Instruments and their Symbolism in Western Art* (New York: Norton, 1967).
36 See *DOE, s.v. hwistle, wistle*, sense a.
37 John D. Niles, *Old English Enigmatic Poems and the Play of the Texts* (Turnhout: Brepols, 2006), p. 146, n.10.
38 Image of the angel playing a bagpipe is available at: https://upload.wikimedia.org/wikipedia/commons/b/b0/Exeter_Cathedral_Minstrels%27_Gallery.jpg (accessed 3 February 2019). Thirteenth-century examples from Spain survive in illustrations in Escorial MS of *Cantigas de Sancta Maria* of Alfonso the Wise of Castile (1252–84).
39 Glasgow University, Special Collections, MS Hunter U. 3. 2 (Hunter MS 229), fol. 21v. Detail available at: http://special.lib.gla.ac.uk/images/psalter/H229_0021vdetail3.jpg (accessed 3 February 2019).
40 London, British Library, MS Add. 11695, fol. 86r. The MS was produced at Santo Domingo de Silos in northern Spain between 1091 and 1109. Images freely available on the British Library's Digitised Manuscripts website: www.bl.uk/manuscripts/FullDisplay.aspx?ref=Add_MS_11695 (accessed 3 February 2019).
41 A possible example of some version of this image in early medieval England is seen in the bird-feet and ?drones protruding behind the seated figure in the Junius Manuscript (Oxford, Bodleian Library, Junius 11), p. 57, available at http://image.ox.ac.uk/show?collection=bodleian&manuscript=msjunius11 (accessed 3 February 2019). The text here is the genealogy of Genesis 4–5; the figure is usually interpreted as Cainan enthroned, but Linden Currie, who kindly brought this image to my attention (pers. comm.), suggests association with Jubal, 'the father of them that play upon the harp and the organs' (*ipse fuit pater canentium cithara et organo*, Gen. 4:21, 'the lyre and pipe' in the Revised Standard Version).

42 *DOE*, *s.v. gecynd*, sense 6b.

43 Geoffrey Chaucer, 'General Prologue', 545–66; quotation from line 560, glossed as 'a teller of dirty stories' and 'buffoon' in Larry D. Benson, ed., *The Riverside Chaucer*, 3rd edn (Boston: Houghton Mifflin, 1987), p. 32. The Miller is illustrated playing a bagpipe with a single drone while on a horse in the Ellesmere Chaucer (Huntingdon Library, MS EL 26 C 9), fol. 34v, from the early fifteenth century: available at http://hdl.huntington.org/cdm/ref/collection/p15150coll7/id/2838 (accessed 3 February 2019). Winternitz, *Musical Instruments*, pp. 72–5, establishes the association with jugglers and beggars, even as he points to the capacious musical taste of angels, who also associate with what otherwise looks like a non-elite instrument.

44 London, British Library, MS Add. 42130. Images freely available on the British Library's Digitised Manuscripts website at www.bl.uk/manuscripts/FullDisplay.aspx?ref=Add_MS_42130 (accessed 3 February 2019).

45 Fry, 'Exeter Riddle 31', makes a good case for quill, which picks up the bird imagery, the paradox of being dumb but speaking words, the prominent downward foot, and the metaphorical family—but ultimately is unsatisfying, I think, because of the feast-hall setting and the adornments.

8

Memory and transformative fear in the *Exeter Book* riddles

Rafał Borysławski

The intention of this chapter is to view several of the Old English riddles through the prism of fear: how fear and memories of fear act in the riddles as vehicles of interpretative and moral transformations. I will argue here that, once the concepts of fear and memory are applied to the study of the riddles, a number of them reveal themselves as little short of meditative parables. This is because fear and memory are connected to ideas intrinsic to riddles: to what initially appears unknown, shadowy and uncertain, as well as to the experience of recognition and the relief stemming from it. All these are common to the form of the riddle, but also to the state of anxiety and to the act of recollection. I will argue that, because of the nature of the poetic riddle and of Old English riddles in particular, memory and fear are their intrinsic *sine qua non*. The two are mutually interdependent, because fear is conditioned by the memory of an experience one wishes to avoid, while remembering is often strengthened by the emotional extremity of fear.

This chapter considers how the types of fear operating within the Old English riddles lend them a particular capacity to corroborate the early Christian view of seemingly negative experiences that must be understood as positively transformative. Thus at least some of the Old English riddles may be read as miniature lessons and parables of Christian thinking. I begin by discussing the ways in which memory and fear are related to the riddle formula on structural, narrative and meta-textually affective levels; I then move to a broad overview of the ways in which fear was understood in medieval Christian thought; and finally I proceed to the discussion of transformative fear in three *Exeter Book* riddles: *XII Hund Heafda* (R.86), solved as 'One-Eyed Seller of Garlic'; *Gryrelic Hleahtor* (R.33), solved as 'Iceberg'; and *Nama Min is Mære* (R.26), solved as 'Bible'.

Riddles and memory

There are several dimensions in which riddles are related to memory, and these may have both narrative and mnemotechnic aspects. First is the sense of memory as the experience of remembering: if our memory of something or someone is the only presence of what is tangibly absent, then Old English riddles exemplify this process, because their very nature is constructed around the absence of their solutions. They rely on individual memories of the features and associations of their objects, and they may thus be described as linguistic memories. Naturally, riddles also rely on the dexterity of their audience's memory, and, on the narrative level, the Old English riddles frequently invoke the former states of the riddled objects, which themselves are presented in the riddles as giving accounts of their individual memories.

Secondly, riddles are related not only to the ability to remember things but also to the art of memory training. In their relation to wisdom contests, dialogues, and memory games, poetic riddles have much in common with mnemotechnic devices and with the ways in which memory—an individual's mental capacity to remember things—was schooled. The inherent playfulness of riddles predisposes them to didactic functions, as Aristotle famously asserts in his *Rhetoric*, in which he notes the connection between riddles and teaching through the means of metaphor, and the propensity of riddles to supply particularly apt metaphors: '[g]ood riddles do, in general, provide us with satisfactory metaphors: for metaphors imply riddles, and therefore a good riddle can furnish a good metaphor.'[1] Later he develops the theme further, stating that the deliberate deceitfulness of riddles makes them especially successful in evoking new associations in order to make striking and memorable points:

> Most smart sayings are derived from metaphor, and also from misleading the hearer beforehand. For it becomes more evident to him that he has learnt something, when the conclusion turns out contrary to his expectations, and the mind seems to say, 'How true it is! But I missed it.' ... And clever riddles are agreeable for the same reason; for something is learnt, and the expression is also metaphorical.[2]

The didactic element of a riddle or a cleverly constructed metaphor is therefore established on the foundation of what Aristotle called *anagnorisis* (ἀναγνώρισις), a sudden revelation effected by a sense of surprise. As will be shown later, the psychological sensation of fear may elicit similar reactions of surprise and a relief of tension through sudden recognition.

The riddle form, in conjunction with its use for the training of memory, was employed in ancient and medieval didactic dialogues composed as sets of questions and answers. Such dialogues, competitive exchanges of often enigmatic questions and answers, were widespread in the literatures of the early medieval Europe, and include the *Solomon and Saturn* dialogues,[3] the didactic disputation between Alcuin and Pippin, Charlemagne's son,[4] and the contests of wits in the *Poetic Edda*[5] and *Hervarar saga*,[6] from Old English, Latin and Old Norse traditions respectively. Old English gnomic poems expressly praise the idea of acquiring wisdom from an act of exchange between questioning and answering agents. In the *Exeter Book*, both *Maxims I* and *The Order of the World* open with invocations of such events, with the words *gydd* and *run* invoking enigmas and secrets as well as wise speech, judgement and knowledge. *Maxims I* implores its intended interlocutor to ask wise questions and stresses that the task of the sage is to exchange *gieddum*—'wise speeches', but also 'riddles':

> Frige mec frodum wordum!   Ne læt þinne ferð onhælne,
> degol þæt þu deopost cunne!   Nelle ic þe min dyrne gesecgan
> gif þu me þinne hygecræft hylest   ond þine heortan geþohtas.
> Gleawe men sceolon   gieddum wrixlan. (1–4)

> [Question me with wise words. Do not let your mind be hidden or keep the secret that you know most profoundly. I will not tell you my secrets if you hide the wise craft of your mind and your heart's thoughts. Wise men should exchange wise sayings/riddles/songs/poems.]

The Order of the World, having opened with a similar request to ask questions, states that the true understanding of the world may only be attained once the craft of speaking mysteries is remembered, practised, and appreciated as it was in the past:

> Is þara anra gehwam   orgeate tacen,
> þam þurh wisdom   woruld ealle con
> behabban on hreþre,   hycgende mon,
> þæt geara iu,   gliwes cræfte,
> mid gieddingum   guman oft wrecan,
> rincas rædfæste;   cuþon ryht sprecan,
> þæt a fricgende   fira cynnes
> ond secgende   searoruna gespon
> a gemyndge mæst   monna wiston. (8–16)

> [For each of those who knows how to hold all the world in his heart through wisdom, for a thinking man, this is a manifest sign—what long ago men, warriors firm in wisdom, often created with the craft of song, with wise sayings/riddles/songs. They knew how to speak correctly, so that [they were] always asking of the race of men and speaking the web of mysteries, always mindful of what the greatest of men knew.]

Thus, riddles were present in literary discourses of wisdom, and their relation to the discovery and perpetuation of wisdom was appreciated. *Maxims I*'s preceptive statement that *þing sceal gehegan / frod wiþ frodne—biþ hyra ferþ gelic* ('the wise must hold a meeting with the wise—their souls/minds must be alike') (18b–19) thus may be illustrative of the 'meeting' between the riddle's puzzle and those who are confronted with it. True wisdom is not located in either side individually but in the intellectual exchange and communion between the riddle and those attempting to grapple with its answer.

Three levels of fear and the Old English riddles

The second issue, that of fear, may initially appear to be more removed from the riddle genre than other emotional states, such as those related to laughter and surprise. However, in the triangle spanning riddles, memory, and the sense of the unexpected we may observe connections between riddles and fear or anxiety. Contemporary psychology understands fear to be an emotional state aroused in an individual by some external or internal stimulus or stimuli. Jeffrey Alan Gray, one of the most prominent clinical psychologists who has studied this emotional state, speaks of it as 'one form of emotional reaction to the threat of punishment, where a "punishment" may be operationally defined as any stimulus which members of the species concerned will work to terminate, escape from or avoid'.[7] Fear and anxiety are distinguished from each other in psychology and in philosophy, the first as a response to some specific stimulus, such as the fear of dishonour or the fear of death, and the second as a more general, unobjectified sensation.[8] They are manifested in riddles on three levels: structural, narrative, and affective. In all three, the desire to 'terminate, escape from or avoid' is crucial for the transformative potential of fear in the riddles.

Firstly, the sense of the unexpected, peculiar, and obscure is the basis of the riddles' process of defamiliarisation. The riddles thus share qualities with the sensations of fear and anxiety—sensations that are incited by unfamiliar, surprising, and unexpected stimuli. Secondly, on the narrative level, fear and anxiety are not only connected with the technique of defamiliarisation and disorientation common to all riddles but also present in the Old English riddles as the emotional states invoked and reminisced about by the very objects of the riddles speaking with anthropomorphised voices about their own fear-inducing experience. And finally and most importantly for the transformative power of fear in riddles, fear and anxiety are present among them on the affective—the metanarrative and metatextual—level. That is, riddles are inherently interactive by the very nature of their genre and the interaction that they require; the act of solving and guessing the riddle is essentially of a confrontational nature. Not only are the Old English riddles open about their confrontational nature in their frequent call to *saga hwæt ic hatte* ('say what I am called'), teasing their audiences into figuring out their identities, but they also metaphorically hark back to the so-called *Halsrätsel* ('neck-riddles') formula familiar, for instance, from *Vafþrúðnismál*.[9] What is at stake in the Old English riddles, of course, is not the life of those who are confronted by them, but it is the honour or disgrace merited by their intellectual abilities. Since each riddle is essentially a game of wits and a challenge posed before the members of its audience, it is also a threat to their reputation, potentially bringing shame and humiliation caused by the intellectual inability to solve the riddle. The act of grappling with a riddle is, therefore, potentially fraught with the fear of being derided, if not by one's companions who know the solution, then at least by the imagined author of the riddle. Such thinking seems to be exemplified by a dry-point runic message beside *Wynn ond Is* (R.64), ᛒᚢᚾᚹᚦ, which has been interpreted to mean *beo unreþe* ('be gentle').[10] Even if the inscription does not indicate fear proper, at the very least it displays frustration with an attempt to unravel the riddle's solution.

Understanding fear in medieval Christian thought

Not much critical material has been published exclusively on fear in the early Middle Ages, chiefly because it is an emotional state and a defensive mechanism which is a response to external circumstances. It has, therefore, always been studied in the contexts of its stimuli. One of the most extensive sociohistorical studies of fear, albeit concerning a later period, that between the so-called high Middle Ages and the late early modern era, was completed by Jean Delumeau in his *La peur en occident*, translated into English as *Sin and Fear: The Emergence of a Western Guilt Culture.*[11] In it, Delumeau distinguishes between fear and its objects, and more general anxieties, according to the philosophical distinctions of Søren Kierkegaard and Paul Tillich.[12] The study is a chronological overview and may seem a little erratic: Delumeau discusses, in the following order, the sea, otherness and alterity, magic, infertility, wolves, divination, comets, astrology and the influence of celestial bodies, the dead and spirits, ghosts and revenants, darkness, plague, famine, and social upheavals. He moves to the fears associated with the ruling classes in the second part of the book, some of which have aspects in common with anxieties, as he discusses eschatological and misogynistic fears, as well as the fear of Satan, non-Christian religions, Jews, magic, and heresies. Many of these fears could be pertinent to the Old English period, with its fear of the dangerous elements, Viking incursions, the monstrous, and the demonic. What Delumeau's work lacks, however, is an attempt to understand the ambivalent psychological reactions that fear involves. Already in antiquity, fear implied a degree of wisdom and contributed to the delineation of courage: in Plato's *Laches* dialogue, courage is described as the knowledge of 'what things to fear and what to be confident about, both in war and everything else'.[13] The Judeo-Christian tradition highlighted the fundamental significance of the *timor Dei* ('fear of God'), which marked the difference between humanity and divinity. The Book of Proverbs famously places fear at the onset of any search for wisdom: 'The fear of the Lord is the beginning of wisdom, and knowledge of the Holy One is understanding' (NIV 9:10). And early Christian patristic authors such as St Ambrose, St Hilary of Poitiers, St Augustine, and St Jerome emphasised that Christ's most human and humanising moment was his experience of fear as he was sweating blood and praying to let the cup pass him by in the Agony in the Garden of Gethsemane.[14]

Perhaps the text that most expressly discusses the significance of fear to learned early medieval audiences was Gregory the Great's commentary on the Book of Job, the *Magna Moralia*, known more popularly as the *Moralia in Iob* ('Morals in the Book of Job'). Gregory analyses the detrimental power of fear in Book II: *Nonnunquam se timor cordi insinuat, et uires nostrae fortitudinis turbat; et eo minores contra aduersa existimus, quo quaedam perdere immoderatius dilecta formidamus* ('Sometimes fear sneaks into the heart and weakens the powers of our fortitude; and we prove the less able to act against adversity, the more unable we are to restrain the fear of losing something in which we find contentment').[15] But earlier in his monumental work and more significantly for the discussion of Christian virtues, Gregory reiterates the Book of Proverbs' statement that the fear of God is the true source of wisdom and argues that such fear advances the fearful towards righteousness. In Book I's parable of the sons preparing and holding feasts which correspond to the seven Christian virtues, Gregory lists the fear of God as one of them: *Timor in die suo conuiuium facit; quia dum premit mentem, ne de praesentibus superbiat, de futuris illam spei cibo confortat* ('The fear [of God] holds a feast in its day, since as it tames the mind so that it does not pride itself in the present things, it strengthens the mind with the nourishment of hope for what is to come in future').[16] This fear is not presented as paralysing but rather as a form of sustenance and motivation, leading towards hope, and, ultimately, towards a moral transformation. Nevertheless, Gregory clarifies that the motivating capacity of fear is only possible once such fear acts in concert with other virtues; indeed, the sons in the parable are intended to dine at one another's feast. Fear on its own, Gregory explains, is useless and dangerously detrimental to any good deed: *Timor quoque ipse nisi has etiam uirtutes habuerit, ad nullum opus procul dubio bonae actionis surgit, quia dum ad cuncta trepidat, ipsa sua formidine a bonis omnibus torpens uacat* ('Also fear in itself does not rise to any good deed unless it co-operates with other virtues, for it quivers and is paralysed by anything, and as such it is unable to do anything good').[17] And thus, just as Gregory later juxtaposes vices with the virtues that counter them, he lists *timor* as a vice countered with *fortitudo* ('courage'), even as he positions it as a virtue which may be used *contra superbiam* ('against pride').[18]

The King Alfred-inspired rendering of the Boethian *Metres*, even if it does not dwell much on fear alone, follows the sense of the argument of the *Moralia*, and, as well as mentioning the *metodes ege* ('fear of the creator') (*Metre 20*, 71b), it exhorts an act of courage against fear; that is, it exhorts its reader to relinquish the destructive fear of worldly troubles: *þu scealt eac yfelne ege anforlætan, / woruld-earfoða* ('you must also abandon the wrongful fear of worldly troubles') (*Metre 5*, 28–9a).[19] Although not made explicit, fear in this work is once again presented as an encouragement to act and not as a state that is purely senseless and debilitating. In addition, the Old English *Boethius* highlights the balance that fear (and anxiety) bring into existence. Thus *Metre 12* states that, just as light does not exist without darkness, so fear is necessary for the human condition and for its sense of purpose:

Nænegum þuhte
dæg on þonce, gif sio dimme niht
ær ofer eldum egesan ne brohte. (15–17)

[The day would not seem a pleasure to anyone if the dark night did not previously bring fear among men.][20]

Fear and the Old English riddles

All the moral and psychological types of fear mentioned above are present in various configurations within the Old English riddles as well. Their sequence in the *Exeter Book* begins with a text (or texts)[21] that speaks of inciting both fear in those who witness an elemental power and respect for the divine power controlling it. It is literally the begin-with-an-earthquake-and-work-up-to-a-climax formula. Although this opening does not present a narrative in which fear may be discussed as a morally transformative and ambivalent emotion or provide a basis for a parabolic reading of a riddle, several of the *Exeter Book* riddles do, including the relatively disregarded *XII Hund Heafda* (R.86), which may serve as an epigraph to all the functions of fear in the riddles:

Wiht cwom gongan þær weras sæton
monige on mæðle, mode snottre;
hæfde an eage ond earan twa,
ond twegen fet, twelf hund heafda,
hryc ond wombe ond honda twa,
earmas ond eaxle, anne sweoran
ond sidan twa. Saga hwæt ic hatte.

[A creature came walking where many men sat in assembly in a wise mood. It had one eye and two ears and two feet, twelve hundred heads, a back and a belly and two hands, arms and shoulders, one neck and two sides. Say what I am called.]

Jonathan Wilcox discusses *XII Hund Heafda* as a mock-riddle and an example of the Old English sense of parody,[22] and Dieter Bitterli includes it among the riddles on numerical monstrosities,[23] but it is also an apt example of how the ambivalence of fear functions within this literary form. The apparent, jocular solution is well known, thanks to the similarity of this riddle to one of

Symphosius's *Enigmata*,[24] but, before it is revealed, the riddle is ominous and foreboding because of the fundamental incongruity and disruption of reality that it employs in the figure of a one-eyed but multiheaded creature. In *XII Hund Heafda*, fear is therefore present both within its narrative frame (in the form of what must be initially understood as a frighteningly monstrous polycephalic *wiht* interrupting the meeting of the wise) and also in the difficulty that the riddle poses to the uninitiated or to those ignorant of its solution—the riddle's threat to the reputation of its audience. It mirrors the confrontation in the riddle between the trespasser and the *weras* ... *snottre* ('wise men') (1b–2), to whom the riddle, as it were, 'comes' in its animate form. Just as the audience is meant to disentangle the identity of the *wiht*, so are the wise men of the riddle expected to identify the *wiht* not as a threat, but in fact as an opportunity which, given the presence of the heads of garlic, may even possess a healing function.

All this clearly represents a potential humbling of the audience, which may be linked with the Christian understanding of the role of fear. At the same time, the riddle incites the action of disarming the fear by engaging with the *wiht* and guessing the solution. Finally, on an even more remote level, the apparent one-eyed seller of garlic may have something in common with another one-eyed guest, known for confronting his interlocutors and probing their wisdom in impossible contests of wits.[25] Whether we may indeed see Odin here, whose many names may be likened to the twelve hundred heads in the riddle and whose two sides may correspond to Hugin and Munin, is impossible to corroborate, but the fear of the uncanny is palpable, up to the point when, typically for the riddles, the audience experiences the relief when tension becomes humour—when the Symphosius-inspired solution is revealed. And yet, before the humour of the riddle is made apparent, it resounds with dark tones. These tones are revisited a millennium or so later in the haiku-like riddle by Peter Reading from the 1999 collection of riddle poems honouring the *Exeter Book*: 'Soon and silently, in a dark suit ... / men at the mead-bench, meditate, name him'.[26] The answer to the modern English riddle is 'death', arriving as soon and as unexpectedly as the one-eyed creature of *XII Hund Heafda*.

This riddle is an example of the three levels of fear mentioned earlier. On the structural level, fear is present in the incongruity and the unexpectedness that are the essence of the conceit behind the riddle. On the narrative level, it is present in the audacious confrontation between a singular, yet multiheaded creature and the many *snottre weras*. Lastly, on the affective level, fear is present in the potential humiliation lurking in the confrontative call to state the identity of the riddle's protagonist. The call to *saga hwæt ic hatte* ('say what I am called') (7b) is even more curious and, perhaps, ominous here, as its first-person form is incompatible with the grammar of the main part of the riddle narrated in the third person.

Towards a conclusion: fear and transformation in the riddles

Finally, there are two other riddles in which fear appears as a constituent of the transformation: *Gryrelic Hleahtor* (R.33), solved as 'Iceberg', and *Nama Min is Mære* (R.26), solved as 'Bible'. They are both examples of riddles in which objects recount their previous experience. Altogether there are some fifteen other riddles in the Exeter collection in which the riddle-subjects' first-person recollections of their past lives and past transformations are meant to guide the audience to the solution: *Mec Deadne Ofgeafun* (R.9 'Cuckoo'), *Neb Wæs Min on Nearwe* (R.10 'Barnacle Goose'), *Wæpenwiga* (R.14 'Horn'), *Bindere ond Swingere* (R.27 'Mead'), *Hyhtlic Gewæd* (R.35 'Mailcoat'), *Be Sonde Muðlease* (R.60 'Rune Staff'), *Heafod Sticade* (R.61 'Helmet'), *Mearcpaþas Walas Træd* (R.72 'Ox'), *Brægnloca* (R.73 'Lance'), *Feaxhar Cwene* (R.74, whose solution is unclear), *Feþeleas* (R.77 'Oyster'), *Frod Wæs Min Fromcynn* (R.83 'Gold'), *Beorcade Wancode* (R.87 'Bellows'), the incomplete *Brunra Beot* (R.92 'Book or Beech'), and *Gingra Broþor Mec Adraf* (R.92 'Inkhorn').[27] While fear does not always feature prominently in these riddles, their objects often talk about being forced to suffer sudden transformations that have been imposed on them.

The 'Bible' of *Nama Min is Mære* and the 'Iceberg' of *Gryrelic Hleahtor* are especially emblematic of this narrative strategy, but they exemplify two different types of transformative fear. In the case of *Nama Min is Mære*, fear is experienced internally by its subject in its initial stage, while in *Gryrelic Hleahtor* fear is external, experienced by those who are confronted with the riddle's object. Although fear is not explicitly mentioned in the Bible riddle, it appears to be implied in the riddle's first part, in which we hear the lamentation of a creature which, surprisingly, is already dead and which nonetheless undergoes the torments of being drowned, scraped and cut—processes involved in the production of parchment. *Gryrelic Hleahtor* is structured differently. The iceberg itself seems free of fear, but it is explicitly described as inciting fear in others: it is *egesful on earde* ('fearsome on earth') (4a). In the end, it speaks of the metamorphoses it undergoes: from a terrifying, death-dealing feminine creature ravaging and immobilising boats, to the nourishment which is a blessing to people and the lands they inhabit. Both riddles speak, therefore, of the miraculous transformation of fear into hope, which takes place on the three levels in which fear operates in riddles: structurally, the fear of the unknown that each riddle creates is transformed into the peace of its solution; narratively, the riddles' objects either incite fear in others (the iceberg) or experience fear (the tortured animal); and affectively, the riddles enhance the perspectives of their audiences, who are invited to see beyond fear and understand that what initially seemed fearsome is vital and enriching.

In *Gryrelic Hleahtor* the riddle begins with an object that is portrayed as monstrously large, mocking everything and everyone with its confrontational *hleahtor ... gryrelic* ('terrible laughter') (3b); it is *hetegrim* ('malignantly cruel') (5a) and *biter beadoweorca* ('bitter in its battle-works') (6a) as it destroys ships. But then it also utters the surprisingly tender and poignant words of family relations and love in the final five lines. Their culmination comes in the *liss* ('mercy') (14b) of the life that the iceberg's water brings to people:

Wiht cwom æfter wege   wrætlicu liþan,
cymlic from ceole   cleopode to londe,
hlinsade hlude;   hleahtor wæs gryrelic,
egesful on earde,   ecge wæron scearpe.
Wæs hio hetegrim,   hilde to sæne,
biter beadoweorca;   bordweallas grof,
heardhiþende.   Heterune bond,
sægde searocræftig   ymb hyre sylfre gesceaft:
'Is min modor   mægða cynnes
þæs deorestan,   þæt is dohtor min
eacen up liden,   swa þæt is ældum cuþ,
firum on folce,   þæt seo on foldan sceal
on ealra londa gehwam   lissum stondan'.

[A creature came on the wave, wondrously sailing, splendidly shouting, crying to the land, resounding loudly; her laughter was terrible, fearsome on earth; her edges were sharp. She was malignantly cruel, slow in battle, bitter in battle-works, carving shield-walls harshly. Bound with hateful charm, she spoke with a treacherous craft about her own creation: 'My mother, a maiden of the kind that is dearest, is my daughter, swollen with growth; it is known among people, to men among folk, that she shall stand on the earth, on all the lands, with mercies.']

In *Nama Min is Mære* the narrative transformation of fear takes place in the transition between the foulness and misery of the animal's torment and the slow realisation that the cleansing of its hide ultimately leads to the production of the scriptural manuscript:

Mec feonda sum feore besnyþede,
woruldstrenga binom, wætte siþþan,
dyfde on wætre, dyde eft þonan,
sette on sunnan, þær ic swiþe beleas
herum þam þe ic hæfde. Heard mec siþþan
snað seaxses ecg, sindrum begrunden;
fingras feoldan (1–7a).

[Some enemy took my life, deprived me of the world-power, later wetted me, dipped me in water, took me out again, set me in the sun where I quickly lost the hair that I had. Later the edge of a long knife cut hard on me, cleared me of impurities; fingers folded me].

The riddle's narrative of transformation entails the clash between the mundane nature of the animal at the beginning of the riddle (if a goat were to be used in the production of the parchment, it might bear an additional devilish connotation) and the holiness of the object it is transformed into in its second part.

Narratively, these transformations of fear involve the high dramas of evocative and graphic descriptions of scenes of destruction and panic in *Gryrelic Hleahtor* and scenes of horrific agony in *Nama Min is Mære*, the latter perhaps also alluding to the agony and passion of Christ, the living Book.[28] Such powerfully expressive imagery may be particularly effective in the third, affective level of the transformation of fear in the riddles, which concerns the transformations of senses that take place within the audiences confronted with their texts. As in biblical exegesis, the senses of the riddles are transposed from their literal levels to a level that might have a tropological, or moral, dimension. It is on this level of transformation that both riddles gain the qualities of parables, offering lessons in the transformative power of suffering and fear. In *Nama Min is Mære*, the cleansing torment experienced by the nameless animal may indirectly correspond to the cleansing of the human soul which may only be truly cleansed once the Book, the outcome of the animal's agony, is not only physically produced, but also followed and adhered to by its human audience. In the parabolic understanding of this riddle, then, the animal undergoes a process similar to the redemption of the soul: from the purifying pain to the beauty of wisdom and enlightenment. Meanwhile, the fear that the iceberg of *Gryrelic Hleahtor* incites in people resembles the *timor Dei* that Gregory the Great presented in his *Moralia*: the fear that can have an edifying aspect when working with and complementing virtues. As a Christian parable, the *Gryrelic Hleahtor* teaches that, once the fearsome object is treated with the respect that results from an understanding of the mystery of its own creation and identity, the apparently loathsome being reveals its true sense of bringing life and sustenance to mankind. In all likelihood, implicit here is also the symbolism of the water of baptism. The riddle's iceberg is emblematic of what seems to be harsh, but in essence is indispensable, just as fear is understood to be indispensable in Gregory's work and in the Old English *Boethius*. The chastising fear that both riddles portray leads not only to the transformation of fear into hope; it also becomes a parabolic and multidimensional lesson in the necessity of fear for the human condition.

In conclusion, many Old English riddles invoke the experience of fear, both generally as their structural *sine qua non* and specifically as an element of their narratives. This chapter's focus on fear reveals how these riddles may serve as a form of therapy to alleviate existential ills. Indeed, in reading the riddles, audiences rediscover the experience of fear that is, eschatologically, philosophically, and psychologically, a constant reminder of human finiteness and the human condition itself. The riddles thus speak of the humanising and transformative potential of the humbling power of fear and may even serve to mitigate the fear of fear itself.

Notes

1 Aristotle, *The Art of Rhetoric*, trans. John Henry Freese (London: Heinemann, 1967), p. 357, bk 3, ch. 2.

2 Aristotle, *The Art of Rhetoric*, p. 409, bk 3, ch. 11.

3 For a recent edition see Daniel Anlezark, ed. and trans., *The Old English Dialogues of Solomon and Saturn* (Cambridge: D.S. Brewer, 2009). Elaine Tuttle Hansen offers a discussion of the enigmatic dimension of the dialogues in *The Solomon Complex: Reading Wisdom in Old English Poetry* (Toronto: University of Toronto Press, 1988), pp. 41–67.

4 The full title of Alcuin's work is *Disputatio regalis et nobilissimi iuuenis Pippini cum Albino scholastico* ('A Royal and Noble Discussion

Between the Young Pippin and Alcuin the Scholar'). See E. Ann Matter, 'Alcuin's Question-and-Answer Texts', *Rivista di Storia della Filosofia*, 45.4 (1990), 645–56.

5 See Hilda R. E. Davidson, 'Insults and Riddles in the *Edda* Poems', in *Edda: A Collection of Essays*, ed. Haraldur Bessason and Robert J. Glendinning (Winnipeg: University of Manitoba Press, 1985), pp. 25–46.

6 Christopher Tolkien, ed. and trans., *The Saga of King Heidrek the Wise* (London: Nelson, 1960). For a recent discussion of some of the saga's riddles, see Hannah Burrows, 'Enigma Variations: *Hervarar saga*'s Wave-Riddles and Supernatural Women in Old Norse Poetic Tradition', *JEGP*, 112.2 (2013), 194–216.

7 Jeffrey Alan Gray, *The Psychology of Fear and Stress* (Cambridge: Cambridge University Press, 1987), p. 3.

8 See Paul Tillich, *The Courage to Be* (New Haven: Yale University Press, 1980), pp. 36–9.

9 For a discussion of the neck-riddle formula, see Michael Elias, 'Neck-Riddles in Mimetic Theory', *Contagion*, 1.2 (1995), 189–202. For the neck-riddle in *Vafþrúðnismál*, see Ármann Jakobsson, 'A Contest of Cosmic Fathers: God and Giant in *Vafþrúðnismál*', *Neophilologus*, 92.2 (2008), 263–77.

10 For the discussion of the dry-point inscription, see Craig Williamson, ed., *The Old English Riddles of the Exeter Book* (Chapel Hill: University of North Carolina Press, 1977), p. 237; and Bernard J. Muir, ed., *The Exeter Anthology of Old English Poetry: An Edition of Exeter Dean and Chapter MS 3501*, 2nd edn, 2 vols (Exeter: University of Exeter Press, 2000), II, p. 708.

11 Jean Delumeau, *La peur en occident (XIVe–XVIIIe siècles)* (Paris: Librairie Arthème Fayard, 1978); trans. by Eric Nicholson as *Sin and Fear: The Emergence of a Western Guilt Culture* (Cambridge: Cambridge University Press, 1994).

12 Søren Kierkegaard, *Fear and Trembling*, trans. Alastair Hannay (London: Penguin Classics, 2003); Tillich, *The Courage to Be*.

13 Plato, *The Laches*, in *The Dialogues of Plato, Volume III: Ion, Hippias Minor, Laches, Protagoras*, trans. R. E. Allen (New Haven: Yale University Press, 1996), 195a, p. 78.

14 For an overview of early medieval perspectives on the Agony in the Garden of Gethsemane and on the early medieval understanding of Christ's fear, see Kevin Madigan, 'Ancient and High-Medieval Interpretations of Jesus in Gethsemane: Some Reflections on Tradition and Continuity in Christian Thought', *Harvard Theological Review*, 88.1 (1995), 157–73.

15 Gregory the Great, *Moralia in Iob*, ed. Marci Adriaen (Turnhout: Brepols, 1979), 2.49.76, p. 105.

16 *Moralia in Iob*, 1.32.44, p. 49.

17 *Moralia in Iob*, 1.32.45, p. 49.
18 *Moralia in Iob*, 2.49.77, p. 106.
19 Malcolm R. Godden and Susan Irvine, ed. and trans., *The Old English Boethius with Verse Prologues and Epilogues Associated with King Alfred*, Dumbarton Oaks Medieval Library (Cambridge, MA: Harvard University Press, 2012), pp. 208 and 30.
20 Godden and Irvine, *Old English Boethius*, pp. 132–3.
21 Michael Lapidge persuasively argues that the three initial riddles should be answered as one riddle to which the answer is *pneuma*, the cosmic breath; see 'Stoic Cosmology and the Source of the First Old English Riddle', *Anglia*, 112 (1994), 1–25. For an overview of critical considerations whether the three opening riddles should be understood to be one long text see Muir, *Exeter Anthology*, II, pp. 606–7. See also the discussion by Paz in Chapter 11 of this volume.
22 Jonathan Wilcox, 'Mock-Riddles in Old English: Exeter Riddles 86 and 19', *Studies in Philology*, 93.2 (1996), 180–7.
23 Dieter Bitterli, *Say What I am Called: The Old English Riddles of the Exeter Book and the Anglo-Latin Riddle Tradition* (Toronto: University of Toronto Press, 2009), pp. 68–71.
24 Symphosius's *Enigma 94, Luscus alium vendens* ('one-eyed garlic vendor'). See Symphosius, *The Enigmas of Symphosius*, ed. and trans. Raymond Theodore Ohl (Philadelphia: University of Pennsylvania Press, 1928), pp. 128–9. This solution is now generally accepted as the solution to *XII Hund Heafda*. See Donald K. Fry, 'Exeter Book Riddle Solutions', *Old English Newsletter*, 15 (1981), 22–33; Muir, *Exeter Anthology*, II, p. 738.
25 See Jakobsson, 'Contest of Cosmic Fathers', pp. 263–77.
26 Peter Reading, 'Riddle 69', in *The New Exeter Book of Riddles*, ed. Kevin Crossley-Holland and Lawrence Sail (London: Enitharmon Press, 1999), n.pag., no. 69.
27 For a comprehensive overview of the solutions proposed to the Exeter Book riddles by various scholars see Muir, *Exeter Anthology*, II, pp. 655–63, 693, and 735–9.
28 See Bitterli, *Say What I am Called*, pp. 177–8.

9
Monstrous healing: Aldhelm's leech riddle

Peter Buchanan

> mihi composuit nomen fortuna cruentem
> [fortune has made for me a bloody name] (2).[1]

So begins, and ends, modern critical attention to Aldhelm's enigma of the leech or *sanguisuga*, which has been classified by Nicholas Howe as a standard exemplum of Isidorian etymologising wordplay,[2] and which has generally suffered the same neglect that others of Aldhelm's *Enigmata* have endured, except in those rare instances where Anglo-Latin is relevant to the interpretation of the Old English riddles.[3] However, Aldhelm's riddle of the bloodily-named *sanguisuga* is a complex text whose murky waters conceal tangled roots of terror and desire, damnation and salvation, Satan and Christ, human and animal, echoes of texts both distant and immediately at hand. The leech unsettles settled boundaries, queering expected dichotomies through the monstrous healing offered through its bloody kiss.

Over the course of this chapter, I introduce the text of the enigma and develop a methodological framework that draws on Mel Y. Chen's analysis of animacy as a way of understanding relationships between different kinds of beings and bodies in order to analyse the abjection of 'lowly' creatures like leeches in relation to humans.[4] My readings of the enigma through the lens of Chen's work develop in tandem with an exploration of Aldhelm's lexical choices throughout the poem, with a consideration of how these choices may be viewed in light of both Aldhelm's other works and also his reading of early Christian Latin poets such as Prudentius. These lexical resonances suggest hidden depths lurking beneath the waters of the leech's swamp. Finally, I broaden my discussion of the leech in dialogue with new theoretical perspectives drawn from the fields of animal studies by scholars such as Alphonso Lingis and Karl Steel and new materialisms in the work of Jane

Bennett in order to argue for the importance of understanding the leech not simply as a poem but as an animal body acting both in concert with and against the rhetorical ornament of the poem.

While the riddle of the *sanguisuga* has been little noticed in literary analyses, it holds an important place in the history of medicine. M. L. Cameron observes that, '[a]part from a few fragments, all surviving Anglo-Saxon medical texts belong to the last two centuries of the Anglo-Saxon period'.[5] Thus, Aldhelm's *Enigmata*, written in the late seventh century, offer important early information about early medieval medical practices. Moreover, as Cameron writes, 'nowhere in Old English medicinal texts is the bloodletting use of the leech mentioned'.[6] However, in order for Aldhelm's riddle to successfully disclose *rerum enigmata clandistina* ('the hidden meaning of things') (7–8),[7] his stated aim in the preface of the collection, his audience would have to recognise the medicinal use of leeches as something familiar. In fact, Aldhelm's desire to disclose the hidden meaning of things holds especially true for animals; as Dieter Bitterli notes, Aldhelm has 'a notable fondness for the animal world', and '[m]ore than a third of [his] *Enigmata* deals with beasts, both real and mythical, indigenous and exotic'.[8]

The riddle itself reads:

> Lurida per latices cenosas lustro paludes;
> Nam mihi composuit nomen fortuna cruentum,
> Rubro dum bibulis vescor de sanguine buccis.
> Ossibus et pedibus geminisque carebo lacertis,
> Corpora vulneribus sed mordeo dira trisulcis
> Atque salutiferis sic curam praesto labellis. (1–6)[9]
>
> [Pale yellow in hue, I haunt the foul waters of swamps, for fortune has made for me a 'bloody' name, since I am nourished by thirsty mouthfuls of red blood. I am devoid of bones, arms, and paired feet, but I bite dying bodies with three-forked wounds and thus I provide a remedy from my health-bringing lips.]

The riddle bears the hallmarks of Aldhelm's style: the alliteration of *lurida* ... *latices* ... *lustro*, *cenosas* ... *composuit* ... *cruentum* and *bibulis* ... *buccis*, which might as well double as a tongue-twister; and the use of distinctive vocabulary, which, though far less recondite in his poetry than in his prose, creates lexical echoes drawn from his reading of poetic sources as well as across his own poetic corpus.

The first five lines of the poem create a grotesque figure, which is transformed by the turn in the sixth line that forces a re-evaluation of the leech. Aldhelm's linguistic strategies for rendering the leech grotesque accord well with the forms of dehumanisation described by Mel Y. Chen in *Animacies*. Chen uses the concept of animacy hierarchies, which organise different forms of matter according to their ability to act, to map a web of interactions between human, animal, and so-called inanimate matter, and categories of language, race, and queerness. Chen treats the animacy hierarchy, a creation of anthropological linguistics, 'as naturally also an ontology of *affect*: for animacy hierarchies are precisely about which things can or cannot affect—or be affected by—which other things within a specific scheme of possible action'.[10] Chen's project originates in observations about how we use language to limit the ability of abjected matter to act in the world, and to discover the fluidity of animacy and its potential to 'materialize, replenish, and trouble ideologies, sentiments, and ontologies of race, humanness, and security'.[11]

The first type of dehumanisation that Chen discusses is 'an approximation toward death'.[12] This approximation functions as a way of limiting the future horizons of the body, drawing on disability theorists who observe that 'certain living states of being … have been marked as equivalent to death'.[13] The leech approximates death in several ways. Its sucking cheeks are filled with red blood, and yet it is blood that is no longer circulating in an organism, having been transformed from sustaining force to sustenance. The bodies that the leech feeds upon are also the *dira*, those that are near-death, and the structure of the poem creates the anticipation that the leech serves to push the nearly dead over the edge. This proximity to and identification with death begins the dehumanising process, which is continued in what Chen would describe as 'transformation (or, indeed, imaginative transmogrification: the transformation into a grotesque or fantastic appearance)'.[14] This transformation is accomplished by the litany of lack that the leech recites, *Ossibus, et pedibus, geminisque … lacertis* ('bones and feet and twinned arms'). The word for arms, *lacertus*, in particular refers to 'the muscular portion of the arm',[15] and each loss of a body part renders the leech more alien and also moves it further down the animacy hierarchy from humans, who possess the qualities it has lost. The leech does not have bones to give structure to its body, feet to impel movement, or arms to provide it with the strength to act. The leech is left a seemingly inanimate lump, incapable of acting upon humans except for those who occupy a near-death state. All that the leech consists of in the poem are its cheeks sopping wet with blood, its biting mouth, and its lips. The leech is rendered all face.

What is at stake in the leech's abject place in the animacy hierarchy? As a matter of literary devices, the leech's abjection sets up the turn in the last line of the poem. But it also accords with a tendency to see creatures like lowly annelids as almost inert, as barely capable of acting upon the world like a human or some higher animal, and yet within this ferment of ideas the leech reveals itself as more capable than expected, though armed only with a sucking mouth. The leech's transformation into the fantastic represents not a settled state but a profoundly unsettled one, and as the leech speaks to the reader—a riddlic trope that appears especially appropriate for a speaker that is all mouth—we discover words and images competing for expression within a single body.

The words that Aldhelm puts in the mouth of the leech are remarkable both for the lexical choice and for Aldhelm's tendency to build up resonances with earlier works as well as across his own corpus.[16] There are a few especially distinctive items in the riddle of the *sanguisuga* that reward closer attention. The first is *trisulcus*, a word that literally means 'three-furrowed' but in practice typically meant 'three-cleft, three-forked, threepointed; threefold, triple'.[17] Here *trisulcus* refers to the medicinal leech's three-pronged bite, but as we will see below, it derives from a description of a serpent's forked tongue, in which case one of the three forks refers to the main trunk of the tongue receding into the serpent's mouth. This is in fact exactly the case in the only other instance in which Aldhelm uses the word, in his prose hagiography of virgin saints: *velut contritus coluber linguis trisulcis sibilans* ('like a snake that's been trodden on, hissing with forked tongue').[18] A possible source of *trisulcus* is the fourth-century poet Prudentius's poetic account of the origin of sin from the *Hamartigenia*, in a depiction of the serpent in the Garden of Eden: *Simplex lingua prius uaria micat arte loquendi / Et discissa dolis resonat sermone trisulco* ('His tongue, once single, flickers with the varied art of speaking and now treacherously split resounds with forked speech') (201–2).[19] This usage echoes in turn Virgil's description of a serpent's tongue in the pastoral landscape of the *Georgics*: *arduus ad solem et linguis micat ore trisulcis* ('And rearing up to the sun, [the serpent] darts from its mouth a forked tongue').[20]

In her commentary on the *Hamartigenia*, Martha Malamud notes Prudentius's adaptation of Virgil's description of the serpent:

> His tongue, which had been single, *simplex*, before, now splits. Skilled in the art of eloquence, *arte loquendi*, it utters 'fissured words', *sermone trisulco*, a phrase that echoes Vergil's description of a snake with a similarly three-forked tongue ... in a passage of great symbolic significance in the *Georgics* ... In the symbolic scheme of the *Georgics*, the snake is the physical embodiment of the plague ...; his presence threatens the whole pastoral world with destruction. Prudentius keeps the georgic symbolism here: his serpent also introduces disaster to the natural world. But this serpent delivers his venom not through his fangs but through his *lingua*, which, as was the case with the irrepressibly verbal Saint Cyprian, carries the meanings of both the physical organ, 'tongue', and that which the tongue produces, 'language'.[21]

Prudentius extends the semantic range of *trisulcus* by applying it not to the physical aspect of the snake's tongue, the *linguis* of Virgil's text, but to the speech produced by the tongue. Both *lingua* and *sermo* are divided and, as in the enigma of the *sanguisuga*, the language used to describe this state draws on the rhetoric of disability. The snake's tongue was once *simplex*, a word which suggests at once the wholeness of the body and its honest and artless nature. It is only when the body is disfigured and the tongue split that the tongue finds art and the ability to wield words to deceive and dissimulate.

The verbal and thematic resonance between this passage from the *Hamartigenia* and *Enigma 43* seems especially strong, although one should be careful about asserting direct influence in situations involving a single word rather than a collocation of multiple words. However, Andy Orchard has already noted the extensive influence of all of Prudentius's poems on Aldhelm's lexical choices, including the influence of the *Hamartigenia*.[22] Aldhelm would have been familiar with the passage, and the physical similarities between the leech and the serpent provide a powerful point of contact. The enigma shimmers with deceptive rhetoric, the forked speech of the serpent, although here the deception lies not in fair words but foul. The leech uses its skill in the *ars loquendi* to set up the reader with false expectations, namely that it is akin to the serpent in bringing about a fall, when instead, in the final line, it offers health through its kiss.

The leech's lips are described as *salutifer*, health-bringing, a word that appears five other times in Aldhelm's poetic corpus and never in his prose. Every instance of the word except for the one concerning the leech is in the *Carmen de virginitate*, and an examination of these other appearances makes it clear that there is much more at stake than simply health; it is salvation that the word offers:

Namque salutiferum mundus baptista Tonantem
Diluit aequoreis mergens in gurgite limphis (409)[23]
[Indeed the pure Baptist immersed the salvation-bringing Thunderer in the stream, drenching Him with water]

Saepe salutifero correxit dogmate pagos (687)[24]
[Often he improved the country-folk with health-giving doctrine]

Dira salutifero restaurans ulcera fotu (769)[25]
[healing hideous ulcers by means of curative care]

Atque salutiferam morbis impendere curam (1083)[26]
[And [Cosmas and Damian were able to] apply a saving cure for diseased persons]

Pace salutiferis populum stipante coronis (2094)[27]
[Peace encompassed the people with wreaths of salvation.]

In line 409, it is Christ himself, being baptised by John, who is described as the *salutiferum … Tonantem*, 'the salvation-bringing Thunderer' in Lapidge and Rosier's translation. In fact, the translations offered by Lapidge and Rosier give us a good measure of the range of meaning. In line 687, Saint Martin gives *salutifero … dogmate* ('health-giving doctrine'). In line 769, Antony provides *salutifero … fotu* ('curative care'), in 1083, Cosmas and Damian give a *salutiferam … curam* ('saving cure'), and line 2094 speaks of *salutiferis … coronis* ('wreaths of salvation'). These other instances of *salutifer* reveal a word that for Aldhelm is tied closely with concerns of the soul at least as much as, if not more than, concerns of the body. *Salutifer* is not simply salubrious but salvific,[28] and the enigma re-enacts the mystery of the resurrection, as the bodies that are *dira* are revivified through the wounds inflicted upon them by the leech. The leech speaks with the serpent's voice, but kisses with Christ's lips.

But even its lips are layered with inter- and intra-textuality. *Labellum* ('lip') is the last word whose lexical resonances I want to explore in Aldhelm's work. It serves elsewhere as a way of marking a particular kind of touch, one rooted in desire, an inner touch that symbolises the reception of both Christ's touch and of the words of earlier poets. In the *Carmen de virginitate*, Aldhelm writes:

Non, sicut cecinit sponsali carmine vatis,
Mellea tunc roseis haerescunt labra labellis,
Dulcia sed Christi lentescunt labra labellis. (1158–60)[29]

> [The 'honey-sweet lips' did not, as the poet sang in the betrothal song, 'cling to his rosy lips', but rather Christ's sweet lips lingered on his.]

Here Aldhelm quotes and then adapts a line from the *Epithalamium Laurentii*, a poem often attributed to the fourth-century poet Claudian due to its collocation with his works in manuscripts. Its anonymous author is the figure Aldhelm invokes in line 1158 as the *vatis* ('poet'), who sang a *sponsali carmine* ('wedding song'). In line 1159, Aldhelm adapts line 80 from the *Epithalamium*, which reads, *Mellea tunc roseis haerescant basia labris* ('then honeyed lips adhered to rosy lips').[30] Aldhelm directly borrows the first four feet, but the last two, the poetic cadence, are altered, *basia labris* appearing as *labra labellis*. The shift in the poetic cadence from *basia labris* to *labra labellis* emphasises the mirrored image of lips pressing against lips in a kiss and suggests a union of touching and touched. In the subsequent line, Aldhelm repeats the cadence, while changing the identity of the figure kissing Chrysanthus from Daria, his bride, to Christ, whose lips linger, *lentescunt*, upon Chrysanthus's. *Lentescunt* contrasts sharply with the verb in the previous line, which falls into the same metrical position, *haerescunt* ('adhere or attach to').

Aldhelm presses his own lips to the words of the past, and by speaking these words he allows their writing, in this remediated form, to touch new readers. While the words on the page emphasise a literal touch, the act of speaking the words forms an affective relationship between past authors and present readers—in whatever present that may be—who find their lips tarrying with and upon the lips of the untouchable past. This affective touch across time suggests what Carolyn Dinshaw has described as a queer historical impulse, in which the quotation of textual fragments 'theatricalizes our lives in turn, empties them of the impossible function of mere expressivity (of a soul, of a depth) and renders them capable of further *touching*—other lives, other texts'.[31] Dinshaw's understanding of quotation as a queer practice for creating community across time takes on added significance in the riddle of the leech, in which the kiss of the leech crosses species but also echoes across time, with the animal kiss being figured as a bridal kiss offered by Christ that also echoes the words of an earlier poet. The layered textuality of Aldhelm's writing allows multiple discourses of desire to coexist across the tissue of his poems.

Aldhelm later returns in the *Carmen* to the remixed Pseudo-Claudian in a passage that has some other interesting lexical resonances with *Enigma 43*:

> Aspidis ut morsum spernebat basia buccis,
> Dulcia sed Christi compressit labra labellis,
> Oscula dum supero defixit limpida sponso. (2136–8)[32]
>
> [She (Eustochium) spurned kisses on her cheeks as the bite of an asp, but rather pressed the sweet kisses of Christ to her lips, and gave in return pure kisses to her supreme Spouse.]

In addition to *labellis*, we also see *buccis* yet again and the participial form of *mordeo*. Reading this text alongside the leech enigma, it is amusing to note that Eustochium spurns kisses like the bite of an asp, but in the enigma the bite of the serpentine leech becomes the salvific kiss of Christ. This duality that subverts expectations is not incidental to the leech's abjected animal nature; it is integral to it. As the already inhuman leech is further dehumanised, as it is reduced to a mouth that scavenges food from the dying, as the terror of its appearance emerges from the foul waters of the swamp, it redeems those it feeds upon as well as itself through an act of desire, a sexualised hunger expressed in the touching of its lips to the skin of another's body. It is this touch that reveals the mystery at the heart of the riddle, a touch filled with animal necessity and queer desire. Even as the leech demonstrates control of elaborate rhetorical strategies to deceive, making full use of human linguistic resources, it is in the moment that the leech stops speaking and is most fully acting as an animal that it has the greatest effect.

What do we learn from our confrontation with the leech? In considering the face of animals and what humans gain from contact with them, Alphonso Lingis writes,

> In contact with the cockatoo who, though he can clutch with a vice-grip around a perch while sleeping, relaxes his claws on the arm of an infant and never bites the ear he affectionately nibbles at, and who extends his neck and spreads his wings to be caressed in all the softness of his down feathers, the infant discovers that her hands are not just retractile hooks for grabbing, but organs to give pleasure. In contact with the puppy mouthing and licking his legs and fingers and face the infant discovers his lips are not just fleshy traps to hold in the food and his tongue not just a lever to shift it into the throat, but organs that give, give pleasure, give the pleasures of being kissed. In feeling the lamb or the baby skunk extending its belly, its thighs, raising its tail for stroking the infant discovers her hands, her thighs, and her belly are organs to give pleasure.[33]

Coming into contact with a leech is a very different experience from coming into contact with a puppy, and that is at least in part because Aldhelm's riddle undertakes a recuperative task with the leech and demonstrates the fundamental instability in the discourses of abjection employed throughout the poem and echoed in other literature. We can find pleasure in Aldhelm's varied language, in his clever troubling of dichotomies, in the false expectations that he builds up and then subverts. But these pleasures are all with the poem as a discursive object. What pleasures are there for us in the leech as animal? What pleasures are there for us in being kissed by the leech? What pleasures are there in being food for others? If Lingis's infant discovers her own hands as organs capable of giving pleasure through the stroking of a lamb or baby skunk, what do we discover of ourselves in our interaction with Aldhelm's leech?

We discover ourselves as bodies that matter and bodies of matter, that not only act but are acted upon. We discover ourselves as food, as vital matter that is not cordoned off from material existence but a fundamental part of it, and as bodies in the riddle that give their substance as sustenance to the leech. In *Vibrant Matter*, Jane Bennett has written eloquently about the eating encounter, although from the perspective of the human eater rather than the human eaten: 'If the eaten is to become food, it must be digestible to the out-side it enters. Likewise, if the eater is to be nourished, it must accommodate itself to the internalised out-side. In the eating encounter, all bodies are shown to be but temporary congealments of a materiality that is a process of becoming, is hustle and flow punctuated by sedimentation and substance'.[34] In being eaten, humans discover themselves as something to be digested. In Bennett's materialism, all bodies are equally 'congealments of … materiality', but the phenomenology of inside and outside space is reversed. A leech takes the body of a human into itself, even as it injects anti-coagulants into the human body to render it digestible. As Aldhelm's leech is abjected, so too are the humans that feed it, to the point that they ultimately occupy a lower spot on the animacy hierarchy than the leech, and in that moment when the leech seems to be most animal and the human most insensate, dead matter, the bodies give reciprocally and re-animate. We find the pleasure of having our imagined superiority undone by the leech's abjection.

Part of this pleasure lies in the subversion of the horror of cannibalism. In his work exploring how discourses of animality in the medieval period construct the idea of the human, Karl Steel has written on the horror of anthropophagy:

> Any examination of the particular cultural fascination with anthropophagy among all the other -phagies should examine what humans lose as humans when they are eaten. The special horror of anthropophagy derives primarily from its violation of codes, not of polity or faith, nor even of species, but of privilege. Anthropophagy confounds the distinction between human and other animal lives, between what can be murdered and what can only be slaughtered, by digesting what the regime of the human demands be interred within a grave. The special horror of anthropophagy is therefore its impossibility: a human who has been slaughtered and eaten, who has lost the exemption from being eaten through which it defines itself as not an animal, may have ceased to be recognizable as an *anthropos*.[35]

Steel's argument focuses on loss, that what humans lose when eaten by other humans is the privilege of not being eaten, the privilege of legal recourse within a juridical system rather than the simple expedient of slaughter and consumption. The power of the leech's riddle, however, is that it subverts the narrative of anthropophagy. The leech takes on human attributes through its speaking voice and its intentional use of rhetorical skill, even as it draws on discourses of human disability to construct an alternative way of understanding its animal nature. The apparent intelligence of the leech even as it prepares to feast on the blood of the deathly human body suggests the horror not simply of being consumed by an animal, but by an animal endowed with human abilities, that is rhetorically constructed as a kind of human. In the anthropophagic encounter, the human discovers itself as not only flesh to be consumed but also the consumer of its own flesh, and the loss of privilege incurred is as much a function of one as the other. However, the abjected leech turns this narrative on its head, using its rhetorical skill to position itself higher on the animacy hierarchy than the human body which is stripped of its powers of animation by deathly illness. The leech, contrary to all expectation, occupies not a lower position or even an equal position in the animacy hierarchy, but a higher one. The loss of privilege for the human is even more profound. And yet, it is not loss that characterises the riddle, for this reversal of fortune, this loss of the privilege of superiority to the leech, leads instead to the human being reanimated, set into motion, into activity once more. The leech consumes the human body, but only partly, and rather than being slaughtered by the leech's attentions, our bodies are given life by them.

This quality of liveliness, of animation, in response to the animal touch speaks strongly to the importance of understanding the leech's riddle, and riddles generally, as something more than just a language game. The power of riddles lies not only in the clever concealing of truth but in the revelation of it, in the doubled use of language as a means of animating bodies in surprising ways. This capacity of language is captured well by Chen:

> Words more than signify; they affect and effect. Whether read or heard, they complexly pulse through bodies (live or dead), rendering their effects in feeling and active response. They are a first level of animation, one in which we deeply linguistic creatures attached to our own language are caught, but not the last. Indeed, language is but one discourse among many in a cacophony of anti-, re-, and mis-coordinations between objects, things, and beings. It sometimes only sees itself; if it sees outside of itself, it sometimes responds only with itself; and it sometimes must be left altogether, perishing in the nonlanguage the moment demands.[36]

The words of the leech must do more than signify; they pulse through its own living body and through the deathly bodies of its victims, affecting them with its healing touch and effecting the resurrection of the body. As deeply linguistic creatures, in anthropomorphising the leech, we imbue it with (some) human capacity, even as we strip it of others.[37] It is a first level of animation for the leech, but, unlike the human caught in language, the leech transforms the horror of anthropophagy into the mystery of resurrection, as the linguistic discourse gives way to other modes of coordination between beings. If we see the mystery of the leech as a function of purely linguistic ornament, as is too often the case for scholars dealing with the Anglo-Latin riddle tradition,[38] we miss out on the power that is revealed when language perishes upon the lips and gives way to a more carnal discourse between bodies that the moment of resurrection demands.

One of the leech's peculiar pleasures is its rootedness in an especially earthy milieu, the *palus*, the English fen, enacting the mystery of salvation in a physical context that is not particularly exalted. Contrast this with John Donne's 'The Canonization', which invokes a different creature as a metaphor for both salvation and a carnal act:

> The Phoenix riddle hath more wit
> By us; we two being one, are it.
> So, to one neutral thing both sexes fit,
> We die, and rise the same, and prove
> Mysterious by this love. (23–7)[39]

Donne's invocation of resurrection in the figure of the phoenix as a riddlic metaphor for the consummation of carnal desire draws on the allegorical associations of the fantastic bird, abstracting and elevating sex to the realm of divine mystery. The metaphysical conceit becomes a way of using language to cover up the truth of things. The wit of the leech's riddle lies in the opposite movement, grounding salvation in the muck, and rather than two humans becoming one, animal and human exchange places, with the human's flesh providing sustenance to the leech while the leech's bite heals the human and sets it into motion, resurrecting it from death, simultaneously giving the appearance of taking life in inhuman slaughter while in fact giving it through the mystery of salvation.

The enigma of the *sanguisuga* lies in its habit of never quite being what we expect, of confronting us with a face that seems at once terrifying and alien and also all too familiar, a silent creature imbued with a speaking voice by Aldhelm's poetic art, but that ultimately allows words to give way to a commerce between bodies grounded in physical touch. Rather than being a straightforward instance of etymological play, much deeper mysteries are revealed by Aldhelm's tendency to pile up lexical resonances that reflect both his wide reading and his habit of recycling what he reads and writes into new contexts. The leech's surprising ability to act and affect the human reveals truths about our own animal nature that both unsettle our privileged position in hierarchies of agency and come with the pleasure of an erotic touch that heals body and spirit and renders the human body as edible matter. Rather than being the figure of horror that it first reveals itself as, the leech is an animal that animates the human, provoking pleasure with its desirous touch and confronting us with the inadequacy of our understanding of our place in the world.

Notes

1 All citations of Aldhelm's work throughout this essay will be to Aldhelm, *Opera omnia*, ed. Rudolf Ehwald, MGH, Auctores Antiquissimi, 15 (Berlin: Weidmann, 1919). Poetry is cited by line parenthetically in the text. All translations of Aldhelm's work are from Aldhelm, *Aldhelm: The Poetic Works*, trans. Michael Lapidge and James L. Rosier (Cambridge: D. S. Brewer, 2009) and *Aldhelm: The Prose Works*, trans. Michael Lapidge and Michael Herren (Cambridge: D. S. Brewer, 2009). Translations are cited by page in the notes. The quotation here is Aldhelm, *Enigma 43*, in *Opera omnia*, p. 116; *Poetic*

Works, p. 78. For a modern poetic translation of Aldhelm's riddles, see A. M. Juster, trans., *Saint Aldhelm's Riddles* (Toronto: University of Toronto Press, 2015). Other texts by Aldhelm referred to in the course of this essay, with the corresponding page numbers in *Opera omnia*, include: the preface to the *Enigmata*, pp. 97–9; *Carmen de virginitate*, pp. 350–471; and *Prosa de virginitate*, pp. 226–323.

2 Nicholas Howe, 'Aldhelm's *Enigmata* and Isidorian Etymology', *ASE*, 14 (1985), 37–59.

3 See Janie Steen, *Verse and Virtuosity: The Adaptation of Latin Rhetoric in Old English Poetry* (Toronto: University of Toronto Press, 2008), especially ch. 5, pp. 89–109, which discusses the adaptation of Aldhelm's *Lorica* and *Creatura enigmata* in the riddles of the *Exeter Book*.

4 Mel Y. Chen, *Animacies: Biopolitics, Racial Mattering, and Queer Affect* (Durham, NC: Duke University Press, 2012).

5 M. L. Cameron, *Anglo-Saxon Medicine* (Cambridge: Cambridge University Press, 1993), p. 25.

6 Cameron, *Anglo-Saxon Medicine*, p. 25.

7 Aldhelm, *Poetic Works*, p. 70.

8 Dieter Bitterli, *Say What I Am Called: The Old English Riddles of the Exeter Book and the Anglo-Latin Riddle Tradition* (Toronto: University of Toronto Press, 2009), p. 22. For Aldhelm's animal riddles, see also M. L. Cameron, 'Aldhelm as Naturalist: An Examination of Some of His *Enigmata*', *Peritia*, 4 (1985), 117–33; Mercedes Salvador-Bello, 'Allegorizing and Moralizing Zoology in Aldhelm's *Enigmata*', *Revista Canaria de Estudios Ingleses*, 68 (2014), 209–18.

9 Aldhelm, *Poetic Works*, p. 78.

10 Chen, *Animacies*, p. 30.

11 Chen, *Animacies*, p. 17.

12 Chen, *Animacies*, p. 43.

13 Chen, *Animacies*, p. 43.

14 Chen, *Animacies*, p. 44.

15 See Charlton T. Lewis and Charles Short, eds, *A Latin Dictionary, Founded on Andrews' Edition of Freund's Latin Dictionary* (Oxford: Clarendon, 1879), *s.v. lacertus* (hereafter referred to as Lewis & Short).

16 See Andy Orchard, *The Poetic Art of Aldhelm* (Cambridge: Cambridge University Press, 1994), especially ch. 4, pp. 126–238, which demonstrates in substantive depth the extent of Aldhelm's echoes of both other authors and his own poetic compositions. For Aldhelm's use of classical and early medieval allusion, see also Steen, *Verse and Virtuosity*, pp. 92 and 98–9; Emily V. Thornbury, 'Aldhelm's Rejection of the Muses and the Mechanics of Poetic Inspiration in Early Anglo-Saxon England', *ASE*, 36 (2007), 71–92; Sinéad O'Sullivan, 'Aldhelm's *De virginitate*—a Patristic Pastiche or Innovative Exposition?', *Peritia*, 12 (1998), 271–95.

17 Lewis & Short, *s.v. trisulcus.*
18 Aldhelm, *Prosa de Virginitate*, ch. 50, p. 306; *Prose Works*, p. 118.
19 Prudentius, *Aurelii Prudentii Clementis carmina*, ed. M. P. Cunningham, CCSL, 126 (Turnhout: Brepols, 1966).
20 Virgil, *Georgics*, ed. Richard F. Thomas, 2 vols (Cambridge: Cambridge University Press, 1988), 3.349.
21 Prudentius, *The Origin of Sin: An English Translation of the 'Hamartigenia'*, trans. Martha Malamud (Ithaca, NY: Cornell University Press, 2011), p. 104.
22 Orchard, *Poetic Art of Aldhelm*, pp. 175–8. See especially Orchard's comments that '[t]races of all of Prudentius's works are more numerous in Aldhelm's verse than has been hitherto supposed' (p. 175), and '[o]ne might conclude that Aldhelm had access to the sort of manuscript containing the complete works of Prudentius' (p. 178). See also Sinéad O'Sullivan, 'Aldhelm's *De virginitate* and the Psychomachian Tradition', *Mediaevalia*, 20 (2001), 313–37.
23 Aldhelm, *Poetic Works*, p. 112.
24 Aldhelm, *Poetic Works*, p. 118.
25 Aldhelm, *Poetic Works*, p. 120.
26 Aldhelm, *Poetic Works*, p. 126.
27 Aldhelm, *Poetic Works*, p. 149.
28 It is interesting to note, however, that glosses from the manuscript do not pick up on this possibly doubled meaning in the riddle. In BL MS Royal 12.C.xxiii, the *curam* provided is glossed as *i. sanitatem uel medicinam.* Nancy Porter Stork, *Aldhelm's Riddles in the British Library MS Royal 12.C.xxiii* (Toronto: Pontifical Institute of Mediaeval Studies, 1990), p. 151.
29 Aldhelm, *Poetic Works*, p. 128.
30 Pseudo-Claudian, *Epithalamium dictum Laurentio*, pp. 417–19, in Claudian, *Claudii Claudiani carmina*, ed. John Barrie Hall, Bibliotheca scriptorum Graecorum et Romanorum Teubneriana 119M (Leipzig: K. G. Saur, 1985).
31 Carolyn Dinshaw, *Getting Medieval: Sexualities and Communities, Pre- and Postmodern* (Durham, NC: Duke University Press, 1999), p. 49.
32 Aldhelm, *Poetic Works*, p. 150.
33 Alphonso Lingis, 'Animal Body, Inhuman Face', in *Zoontologies: The Question of the Animal*, ed. Cary Wolfe (Minneapolis: University of Minnesota Press, 2003), pp. 165–82, at p. 170.
34 Jane Bennett, *Vibrant Matter: A Political Ecology of Things* (Durham, NC: Duke University Press, 2010), p. 49.
35 Karl Steel, *How to Make a Human: Animals and Violence in the Middle Ages* (Columbus: Ohio State University Press, 2011), p. 124.
36 Chen, *Animacies*, p. 54.
37 On the uses and perils of anthropomorphising animals, see the essays collected in Robert W. Mitchell, Nicholas S. Thompson,

and H. Lyn Miles, eds, *Anthropomorphism, Anecdotes, and Animals* (Albany: SUNY Press, 1997); Lorraine Daston and Gregg Mitman, eds, *Thinking With Animals: New Perspectives on Anthropomorphism* (New York: Columbia University Press, 2005); Walter S. Melion, Bret Rothstein, and Michel Weemans, eds, *The Anthropomorphic Lens: Anthropomorphism, Microcosmism, and Analogy in Early Modern Thought and Visual Arts* (Leiden: Brill, 2015).

38 See Howe, 'Aldhelm's *Enigmata*', p. 46, which describes the leech riddle as 'a straightforward etymon riddle'. Howe discusses only lines 2 and 3 of the poem and concludes that 'to understand the name is to understand the thing itself'.

39 John Donne, 'The Canonization', *The Songs and Sonnets of John Donne*, ed. Theodore Redpath, 2nd edn (Cambridge, MA: Harvard University Press, 2009), pp. 237–8.

10

Freolic, sellic: an ecofeminist reading of *Modor Monigra* (R.84)

Corinne Dale

Ecofeminism, loosely defined as the study of the relationship between the oppression of nature and the oppression of women, has become an increasingly popular mode of analysis in the past few years, but has only very recently been brought into the study of Old English literature. In terms of the Old English riddles, our exploration of the relationship between woman and nature is only just beginning. Here, I apply ecofeminist theory to *Modor Monigra* (R.84) to show how the gendering of the solution, 'water', is more than a simple matter of grammatical gender and comes from the biblical tradition of depicting Wisdom as a powerful female figure who 'transcends narrow female stereotypes'.[1] Where many aspects of the natural world are depicted as controlled and shaped by men in the riddle collection, water is depicted as *freolic* 'free' and, like Woman Wisdom, undercuts the 'oppressive hegemony of patriarchal systems'.[2]

The depiction of women in the Old English riddles is complex, since we are dealing with literal and metaphorical layers; when a woman is interacting with an object like an onion in *Staþol min is Steapheah* (R.25), for example, we also have to consider the implications of her interaction with a metaphorical penis. Switching an everyday natural entity (like an onion) to a phallic image, as we process the riddle in our minds, changes the way we view the woman's actions and, by extension, her nature; a woman skilfully making use of earth's produce becomes a woman boldly engaging in a sexual act. Likewise, we also encounter women who form the metaphor of a riddle-subject, such as the one in *Hasofag* (R.11), whom Craig Williamson calls both a 'lovely, dangerous lady' and a 'seductress'.[3] The subject is 'wine in a cup', but the writer also conjures up an image of a woman in beautiful garments who leads men on *unrædsiþas* ('unwise journeys') (4a). Another example of a woman as metaphor is the warrior-woman of *Gryrelic Hleahtor*

(R.33). The object is literally an iceberg, but it is disguised as a dangerous female figure who is said to perform *biter beadoweorca* ('fierce battle-work') (6a).

What also complicates the depiction of gender in the riddles, beyond the literal and figurative, is the issue of what inspired the writer(s) to employ a particular gender in the first place. Was it because of the grammatical gender of the solution, as John D. Niles has argued?[4] *Ea*, for example, is a feminine noun, so perhaps the author of *Modor Monigra* chose to depict the subject 'water' as a female figure because of this. But then, what about the Old English words *wæter* and *flod*, which are both masculine? Perhaps the writer(s) chose to employ a particular gender in a riddle's description because of deep-rooted ancient traditions that assign a gender to a particular object instead? The depiction of the iceberg as female in *Gryrelic Hleahtor*, for example, may have been influenced by the enduring popularity of the mother-as-daughter paradox.[5] Or perhaps it was early medieval cultural beliefs that influenced the writer(s), whereby certain entities were seen to bear traits traditionally associated with either a man or a woman? For example, *Feþegeorn* (R.31)—to which we shall return in a moment—draws similarities between a musical instrument and a cup-bearing woman who serves guests in the hall.

Frustratingly, no scholar of early medieval England has satisfactorily sought to investigate these many factors. Indeed, quite often gender in the riddles is ignored altogether or else relegated to a side note. In Anita R. Riedinger's discussion of the depiction of the iceberg as a warrior in *Gryrelic Hleahtor*, for example, there is no mention of gender and one can only assume Reidinger saw nothing significant in the riddle-poet's use of *hio*. Riedinger says, 'this poet, like others of the riddle tradition, misleads his audience by disguising his subject with the formulaic imagery of a warrior'.[6] Indeed, Riedinger offers a gender-neutral subject in her translation of the riddle.[7] However, studies by Heide Estes, Clare A. Lees and Gillian R. Overing have sought to turn the tide when it comes to gender in the riddles.[8] Lees' and Overing's discussion of *Gryrelic Hleahtor*'s iceberg/warrior-woman, as part of a wider investigation into the depiction of women in early medieval literature,[9] shows how far we have come from Stopford A. Brooke's 1892 discussion and translation of the same riddle, which saw Brooke referring to the subject using masculine pronouns (for, surely, the Old English writer could not have conceived of a warrior who was, in fact, female?).[10]

There are many routes into a study of gender in the riddles, and one logical step would be to apply what we know about gender from studies of other Old English texts. One particular area of research that is helpful is the study of female constriction and enclosure. Such studies have focused mainly on *Wulf and Eadwacer* and *The Wife's Lament*—texts whose female narrators have also been interpreted as male in the past. The work of Shari Horner and Stacy S. Klein, for example, can offer some interesting insights into the riddles' depiction of gender. Horner argues that the female subject in Old English literature is 'enclosed by many layers—textual, material, discursive and spatial',[11] while Klein considers the restrictive nature of the movements assigned to the female subject in the elegies. In her 2006 study of stasis and movement, Klein argues that, unlike the Wanderer and Seafarer, 'whose identities are inextricably intertwined with their valiant efforts to cross land and sea', the female narrators of *The Wife's Lament* and *Wulf and Eadwacer* are 'notably unable to negotiate space'.[12] For Klein, the experiences of the female characters 'underscore a sense of their forced confinement'; the Wife, for example, 'is restricted to an endlessly repetitive cycle of movements dictated by her environment'.[13]

Looking at *Feþegeorn*'s subject, which Lees and Overing describe as a 'fully feminized object, a mighty kinswoman anxious to prove her skills in the hall',[14] we find a female subject whose movements are similarly constricted. *Feþegeorn*'s solution is widely considered to be a musical instrument, with most critics agreeing on 'bagpipes',[15] but the riddle also describes a feminine subject that is yearning for movement. We might envisage the subject as being similar to Wealhtheow, the cup-bearing hostess in *Beowulf*, who proactively moves among the men, rather than merely waiting on them. Here is the riddle in full:

Is þes middangeard missenlicum
wisum gewlitegad, wrættum gefrætwad.
Ic seah sellic þing singan on ræcede;
wiht wæs nower werum on gemonge
sio hæfde wæstum wundorlicran.
Niþerweard onhwyrfed wæs neb hyre,
fet ond folme fugele gelice;
no hwæþre fleogan mæg ne fela gongan.
Hwæþre feþegeorn fremman onginneð,
gecoren cræftum, cyrreð geneahhe,
oft ond gelome eorlum on gemonge,
siteð æt symble, sæles bideþ

hwonne ær heo cræft hyre cyþan mote
werum on wonge. Ne heo þær wiht þigeð
þæs þe him æt blisse beornas habbað.
Deor, domes georn, hio dumb wunað;
hwæþre hyre is on fote fæger hleoþor,
wynlicu woðgiefu. Wrætlic me þinceð
hu seo wiht mæge wordum lacan
þurh fot neoþan. Frætwed hyrstum,
hafað hyre on halse þonne hio hord warað,
baru, beagum deall, broþor sine—
mæg mid mægne. Micel is to hycgenne
wisum woðboran hwæt sio wiht sie.

[This middle earth is adorned in various ways, splendidly ornamented. I saw a wonderful thing sing in the hall; there was not a creature among men that had a more wonderful shape. Her beak was downwards, [she had] feet and hands like a bird; yet she cannot fly nor walk much, but, yearning for motion, begins to perform, chosen for her skills, moves very earnestly and frequently among the men, sits at the feast, bides her time, when soon she is allowed to reveal her skill to the men in that place. She does not consume a bit of that which men have at the feast there. Precious, yearning for glory, she remains speechless; yet there is a fair voice in her foot, a beautiful gift of song. I think it strange how the creature, adorned with ornaments, can play words from below, through her foot. When she, bare, proud in rings, a woman with strength, possesses treasure, she has her her brothers on her neck. It is much for wise speakers to think what this creature might be.]

It is likely that, rather than simply being driven by grammatical gender, the writer saw something in the bagpipe that inspired this depiction of it as female, in particular the manner in which it moves about the hall.[16] Of course, we can say that, like a number of subjects in the riddles, the movements of *Feþegeorn*'s subject are dictated by its function: it does not travel far by design. Yet it is possible that movement might dictate the subject's gender.

Anfetu (R.58) is another example of a female subject whose movements are restricted. The subject is literally a well-beam but the writer also conjures up a female figure who, like the woman of *The Wife's Lament*, *eorðgræf pæþeð* ('paces an earth-grave') (9b). We are also told that she *wide ne fereð, / ne fela rideð* ('does not travel widely or ride far') (2b–3a). If women were traditionally perceived as controlled and constricted, it would follow that a writer might assign a female gender to an object that is similarly controlled and constricted.

In *Modor Monigra*, however, we find a female subject who does travel and is not restrained. In this riddle, the subject is not a manmade object but a part of nature; we may hypothesise that, when woman is used as a metaphor for something natural, such as water or an iceberg, she is granted more movement. This notion is compelling from an ecocritical perspective, since it shows both nature and woman as unrestrained and capable of great power. I have written previously of the depiction of nature as subjugated and controlled by humans in the riddles, but also about how *Modor Monigra*, with its roots in biblical wisdom literature, offers an image of nature as free; its creature, I suggested, shares similarities with the Leviathan or Behemoth in the Book of Job, which cannot be mastered by humans.[17] What was missing from my previous discussion was a recognition of the gender of the subject and the impact this might have on an overall reading of the riddle. By taking an ecofeminist approach to *Modor Monigra* we can see the dual liberation of both women and nature from the limitations imposed on them by an androcentric and anthropocentric point of view.

In order to explore the interpretative possibilities of an ecofeminist reading of *Modor Monigra*, we need to first return to the issue of grammatical gender and address its potential influence on the text in a more satisfactory way. Niles argues that the gender of a number of riddle-subjects is influenced by the grammatical gender of the solution—that is, not the concept of the solution, but the Old English word for that solution.[18] According to Niles, the gendered depiction of a subject can guide the reader to the correct answer. Niles gives the example of *Wiþ Wæge Winnan* (R.16), which has the answer 'anchor'. 'The exact answer is not the concept 'anchor'', he says, '[but] rather it is the OE word *ancor*, which is grammatically masculine, for the riddle is phrased in such a manner that only a masculine noun will provide the solution'.[19] However, if we try to apply this notion to *Modor Monigra*, we encounter the problem of deciding which word for water the writer was thinking of. There are many Old English words for water and the grammatical gender attached to them varies: *wæter* (n.), *ea* (f.), *lagu* (m.), *flod* (m.), *sæ* (f.) or *stream* (m.). If we apply Niles' principle, the word the author might have had in mind is *ea* or perhaps *sæ*, since the verb *beweorpeð* ('surrounds') (40a) is used, which might invoke the image of water surrounding an island. Interestingly, Niles gives the neutral solution *wæter* for the riddle, which goes against the idea that the feminised depiction of the subject could be driven by the grammatical gender of the solution. It could also be argued that some riddle-subjects, like that of *Modor Monigra*, are feminised because the word *wiht*, often used to help disguise the subject's identity, is a feminine noun. However, there are a number of riddles that use *wiht* and nevertheless clearly depict a male subject because they employ masculine pronouns: *Geoguðmyrþe Grædig* (R.38), for example, which depicts an ox, or *Orþoncum Geworht* (R.70), which has the solution 'pipe'.

Modor Monigra's subject, 'water', is not depicted as female simply because *ea* and *sæ* are feminine nouns, but also because it draws on a tradition that links women, nature and wisdom. The metaphor being employed by the riddle-writer is Woman Wisdom, just as the metaphor for *Hasofag* is a seductress of the kind we might find in Proverbs.[20] *Modor Monigra* begins by depicting its subject as both a mother and a powerful being:

An wiht is on eorþan wundrum acenned,
hreoh ond reþe; hafað ryne strongne,
grimme grymetað, ond be grunde fareð.
Modor is monigra mærra wihta.
Fæger ferende fundað æfre;
neol is nearograp. Nænig oþrum mæg
wlite ond wisan wordum gecyþan,
hu mislic biþ mægen þara cynna,
fyrn forðgesceaft; fæder ealle bewat,
or ond ende, swylce an sunu,
mære meotudes bearn. (1–11a)

[There is a creature on earth, born through wonders, violent and raging; she fiercely roars. She has a bold course and journeys by land. She is mother of many splendid creatures; the beautiful travelling one always hastens. Deep down is her tight grasp. No one can convey in words to another her appearance and manner, how manifold the strength of her race is, her ancient ancestry. The Father saw it all, her origin and end, likewise the only Son, the Creator's famous child.]

The words *hreoh* ('violent'), *reþe* ('raging') and *grymetað* ('roars') work together to emphasise the strength and ferocity of the creature, and the author later secures the creature's status as a supreme being by relating that strength is part of her ancestry in lines 8b–9a. The image of a powerful being is taken up again in lines 28–32:

hio biþ eadgum leof, earmum getæse,
freolic, sellic. Fromast ond swiþost,

gifrost ond grædgost grundbedd trideþ
þæs þe under lyfte aloden wurde
ond ælda bearn eagum sawe.

[She is dear to the prosperous, useful to the poor, free, strange; she walks the ground—the boldest and strongest, the greediest and most voracious of that which has grown under the sky and that the children of men's eyes have seen.]

Unfortunately, much of the second half of the riddle is damaged, but we are told that, among other things, she is *hæleþum frodra* ('older than heroes'), *wæstmum tydreð* ('increases in offspring') and *firene dwæsceð* ('extinguishes crimes') in lines 34b–9a.

In the Bible, Woman Wisdom is an ancient, powerful entity in female form who teaches *disciplinæ Dei* ('the knowledge of God') (Wisdom 8:4).[21] While it could be argued that Wisdom is depicted as a woman in both biblical wisdom texts and patristic writings purely because of the grammatical gender of *sapientia*, it has been suggested that there is more to the depiction. Writing about the portrayal of wisdom as a nurturing female figure in the *Collectanea Pseudo-Bedae*, Lees and Overing argue that 'to say that the grammatical gender of *sapientia* is the sole cause and explanation of this spectacularly feminine image of wisdom is simply inadequate', and that the image of Wisdom 'inevitably invokes the female body'.[22] Likewise, Carole Fontaine, writing chiefly about Proverbs and Wisdom, says, 'some deeper message beyond that of grammatical gender is being marked out by our texts when the authors choose to clothe intellectual pursuit and rectitude in female dress'.[23] However, for Fontaine, this 'deeper message' is not necessarily positive. 'If creation reaches out as Woman', she says, 'it is because in the patriarchal world Woman nurtures Man'.[24] Fontaine implies that, if we look for a deeper message we are likely to be disappointed. The female metaphor 'empowers men's undertakings', she says, and should not immediately suggest 'woman-friendly content'.[25]

In The Wisdom of Solomon, Wisdom is described as a *mater* ('mother') and a *thesaurus … hominibus* ('treasure to men') (7:12 and 14).[26] *Modor Monigra*'s water is also described as a mother (5a, 21a), and she, too, can be seen as a treasure to men; she is *eadgum leof* ('valuable to the prosperous') (28a) and *gimmum deorra* ('dearer than gems') (37b).[27] Indeed, the latter assertion resonates with Solomon's assertion that *omne aurum in comparatione illius arena est exigua, / et tamquam lutum æstimabitur argentum in conspectus illius* ('all gold in comparison of her is as a little sand, and silver in respect to her shall be counted as clay') (7:9). There are also similarities to be found between *Modor Monigra*'s water and the following description of Wisdom in The Wisdom of Solomon, from the nature and plenitude of adjectives to the portrayal of her movements:

> enim in illa spiritus intelligentiæ, sanctus, unicus, multiplex, subtilis, disertus, mobilis, incoinquinatus, certus, suavis, amans bonum, acutus, quem nihil vetat, benefaciens, humanus, benignus, stabilis, certus, securus, omnem habens virtutem, omnia prospiciens, et qui capiat omnes spiritus, intelligibilis, mundus, subtilis. Omnibus enim mobilibus mobilior est sapientia: attingit autem ubique propter suam munditiam. (7:22–24)
>
> [In her is the spirit of understanding: holy, one, manifold, subtile [*sic*], eloquent, active, undefiled, sure, sweet, loving that which is good, quick, which nothing hindereth, beneficent, gentle, kind, steadfast, assured, secure, having all power, overseeing all things, and containing all spirits: intelligible, pure, subtile. For wisdom is more active than all active things: and reacheth everywhere by reason of her purity.]

Just as Wisdom is described as *omnem habens virtutem* ('having all power') (7:23), so the riddle's solution is said to be *mægene eacen* ('endowed with power') (21b). Likewise, where Wisdom is *mundus* ('pure') (7:23), the *Modor Monigra* is said to be *clængeorn* ('yearning for purity') (27a). What is particularly striking, though, is the depiction of Wisdom as a woman who is *mobilis* ('active') and *acutus* ('quick') (7:22). Much emphasis is placed on her movement: she is *mobilibus mobilior* ('more active than all active things') (7:24) and nothing is able to hinder her (7:22). There is also a focus on movement in *Modor Monigra*: the creature is called a *ferende* ('travelling one') who *fundað æfre* ('always hastens') (5). She has a *ryne strongne* ('bold course') (2a) and *grundbedd trideþ* ('treads the ground') (29b)—the latter being an image we would not usually associate with flowing water.

The final similarity to note is the description of both Wisdom and water's beauty. Where water is said to be *fæger* ('beautiful') (5a), Solomon says of Wisdom:

> hæc speciosior sole, et super omnem dispositionem stellarum: luci comparata, invenitur prior. (7:29)
>
> [She is more beautiful than the sun, and above all the order of the stars: being compared with the light, she is found before it.]

Here, Wisdom is said to be more beautiful than the sun and stars. In *Modor Monigra*, the riddle-writer likens water to a beautiful gem:

wlite biþ geweorþad wuldornyttingum.
Wynsum wuldorgimm wloncum getenge. (25–6)

[(her) beauty is honoured with wonderful usefulness; (she is a) beautiful, wondrous gem, near to proud ones.]

Water is also said to be *hordum gehroden* ('adorned with treasures') (22a), which might refer to the way the water's surface gleams or sparkles like gems. Despite her beauty, water is a female figure that, like Woman Wisdom, is also frightening. She is adorned with treasures, but she is also powerful, strong and voracious (29b–30a), rather like the aforementioned biblical beasts, the Leviathan and the Behemoth, creatures that cannot be controlled by men.[28]

By making these comparisons, I am not suggesting that the solution to *Modor Monigra* is 'Wisdom', but rather that the riddle-writer drew on the depiction of Wisdom in order to bring the riddle into a dialogue with another text about a powerful feminised force. Ultimately, there are too many aspects of the subject's appearance and behaviour that ensure that the solution 'Wisdom' is not appropriate; Wisdom, after all, is not *hreoh ond reþe* ('violent and raging') (2a), nor can she be *hrif wundigen* ('wounded in her womb') (52b). The mention of *stanum* ('stones') and *stormum* ('storms') in line 44 is also more suggestive of an elemental force, and the challenging phrase *hrusan bið heardra* ('harder than the earth') (36a) will lead the more adept riddle-solvers to think of ice, not Wisdom, the intangible *vapor* ('vapour') of God's power (7:25).

In making these comparisons, it is also possible to extend the dialogue to another riddle about a powerful female creature: the ambiguous subject of *Earmost Ealra Wihta* (R.39). Like *Modor Monigra*, *Earmost Ealra Wihta* shares startling similarities with the depiction of Wisdom in biblical texts. In this riddle, the female creature—which few scholars acknowledge as being female—wanders the world with its *sundorcræft* ('special power'), seeking out individuals:

Gewritu secgað þæt seo wiht sy
mid moncynne miclum tidum
sweotol ond gesyne. Sundorcræft hafað
maran micle þonne hit men witen.
Heo wile gesecan sundor æghwylcne

feorhberendra; gewiteð eft feran on weg.
Ne bið hio næfre niht þær oþre,
ac hio sceal wideferh wreccan laste
Hamleas hweorfan; no þy heanre biþ. (1–9)

[Writings say that this creature is among mankind most of the time, manifest and visible. She has special powers, much more than men know. She will seek out each of the life-bearing ones individually, afterwards departs to travel on her way. She is not there another night, but she must widely travel the path of exile, roam homeless; she is not the poorer for that.]

The opening description of the creature echoes the depiction of Wisdom in The Wisdom of Solomon, where it is said: *Quoniam dignos se ipsa circuit quærens* ('she goeth about seeking such as are worthy of her') (6:17). Wisdom, like *Earmost Ealra Wihta*'s creature, is always moving, but she is not *heanre* ('lowly') (9b) because of it; her 'exile' is of a different nature. Like the riddle creature, Wisdom is also said to be visible; she is *facile videtur ab his qui diligunt eam* ('easily seen by them that love her') (6:13). The notion that the creature has *ne æfre foldan hran* ('never touched the earth') (10b) offers the opposite of the assertion in *Modor Monigra* that water *hrusan hrineð* ('touches earth') (47a) and strengthens the impression that there is a dialogue between the two texts.

The notion that *Earmost Ealra Wihta*'s creature is a power that does not have *fot ne folme* ('feet nor hands') (10a), *eagena* ('eyes') (11a), *sawle ne feorh* ('soul nor life') (16a) also supports the notion that this creature might be Wisdom. Though personified as a woman, Wisdom is, as quoted earlier, an intangible *vapor* ('vapour') (7:25). It is also true that Wisdom, like *Earmost Ealra Wihta*'s subject, can bring *frofre* ('comfort') (19b) to men, as Solomon relates:

Proposui ergo hanc adducere mihi ad convivendum,
sciens quoniam mecum communicabit de bonis,
et erit allocutio cogitationis et tædii mei. (8:9)

[I purposed therefore to take her to me to live with me: knowing that she will communicate to me of her good things, and will be a comfort in my cares and grief.]

Like *Modor Monigra*, however, there are some aspects of *Earmost Ealra Wihta* that may make us reluctant to declare 'Wisdom' the answer. One of the main issues lies in the description of the subject as *earmost ealra wihta* ('the poorest of all creatures') (14). There are no descriptions of Wisdom as 'poor' in the Bible; indeed, Solomon asks *quid sapientia locupletius?* ('what is richer than wisdom?') (8:5). The assertion that the creature is 'poor' has confounded a number of critics, with Williamson saying that he 'cannot find any proverbially poor creature in either Old English or Latin writings that would fit the exact description in the riddle'.[29] One wonders if Trautmann is right to emend *earmost* to *earuwost*, despite Williamson's protestation.[30] The word *earuwost*, meaning 'swiftest', would certainly fit the solution 'Wisdom', Wisdom being described as *acutus* ('quick') (7:22). Regardless, we must also contend with the riddle-writer's use of *woh* when contemplating Wisdom's fate, which, with its possible meanings of 'crooked', 'twisted' and 'perverse', would be an odd choice of adjective to use for Wisdom. Equally problematic is the notion that the creature has never *heofonum hran, ne to helle mot* ('touched heaven, nor can [go to] hell') (20). In Ecclesiastes, Wisdom herself declares: *Gyrum cæli circuivi sola / et profundum abyssi penetravi* ('I alone have compassed the circuit of heaven, and have penetrated into the bottom of the deep') (24:8). While *abyssi* might not refer specifically to hell, and while there is no other evidence in the scriptures of Wisdom visiting hell, it is clear that Wisdom can be found in heaven; indeed, Solomon describes Wisdom as sitting by God's throne (Wisdom 9:4).

Like *Modor Monigra*, *Earmost Ealra Wihta* depicts a subject that is able to move without constraint; she is said to *wideferh wreccan laste / hamleas hweorfan* ('always roam the path of the exile, homeless') (8b–9a). However, as mentioned earlier, the narrator is not critical of her travelling and says she is not *heanre* ('the more lowly' or 'despised') because of it. The attitude to this female creature's wanderings is very different to those expressed about the wandering woman in *Maxims I*:

> Fæmne æt hyre bordan geriseð;
> widgongel wif word gespringeð, oft hy mon wommum bilihð,
> hæleð hy hospe mænað, oft hyre hleor abreoþeð. (63b–5)

> [It is fitting for a woman to be at her embroidery; the wide-travelling woman cultivates gossip; a person often accuses her of sin. Men complain about her reprovingly. Her face often wastes away.]

Wandering, it is asserted here, not only causes others to gossip and reproach the woman, but also causes her beauty to fade. In *Modor Monigra*, travelling is not associated with faded beauty; in fact, the female subject is called the *fæger ferende* ('beautiful travelling one') (5a). These riddles seem to participate in the dialogue about female constraint; where the hostess of *Feþegeorn* (R.31) wishes to move but can only travel from one person to the next within the confines of the hall, the female figures of *Modor Monigra* and *Earmost Ealra Wihta* travel far and wide and are not condemned because of it. The movement of these women may be dictated by the nature of their literal counterparts (e.g. bagpipes or water), but their movement also suggests something about the relationship between women and the natural world, different from that offered by *The Wife's Lament*. When drawn into a metaphorical comparison, women and nature can experience freedom from the patriarchal limitations imposed on them. They stand in contrast to texts like *Ræpingas* (R.52) and *Bindere ond Swingere* (R.27), which draw men and nature into a shared experience of constraint and suffering.

However, even if we begin to contemplate what it means for the female figure to experience freedom in nature, we must recognise the fact that Woman Wisdom forms part of a patriarchal, androcentric tradition. Using the female to create meaning for a male audience can be problematic for a feminist reading and 'should not automatically suggest woman-friendly content'.[31] Wisdom's main prerogative is to instruct men in correct conduct and warn against the temptations of immoral women. In Proverbs, Woman Wisdom says, *O viri, ad vos clamito, / et vox mea ad filios hominum* ('Oh yea men, to you I call, and my voice is to the sons of men') (8:4). The image of Woman Wisdom, as well as her counterpart the Strange Woman, is an 'idealised' image created by men, as Kathleen O'Connor explains:

> they are images of womanhood invented by men and not by women whose reality they claim to embody. However, the real harm done to women lies in the stereotypical and dualistic nature of the figures. The images of the Wisdom Woman and the Strange Woman perpetuate the inhuman stereotypes of women as the madonna or the whore, the object of man's choice to lead him to life or to death.[32]

Fontaine agrees, arguing that the feminine acts as a 'mediator between a male god and the male students who are the sages' implied audience';[33] the feminine is, therefore, 'always viewed as ancillary and contingent within androcentric thought'.[34]

For some ecofeminists, however, Woman Wisdom can offer a way to challenge male-orientated wisdom. Kathleen O'Connor says the female figure 'transcends narrow female stereotypes' and 'takes on a life of her own'.[35] In a 2001 article, Laura Hobgood-Oster provides an ecofeminist reading of The Wisdom of Solomon and argues that Woman Wisdom is 'powerful, but in a transformative way that undercuts the oppressive hegemony of patriarchal systems'.[36] Furthermore, she also sees a connection between Wisdom and the natural world, observing how this personified abstract concept both 'laments over the destructive behaviour of humanity' and 'immerses herself in the material world'.[37] Through the description of her origins, Woman Wisdom 'recalls the joys of a world without oppressive rulers, Earth not subdued but innately knowing'.[38] In Proverbs, Woman Wisdom describes her origins in the following way:

> Dominus possedit me in initio viarum suarum antequam quidquam faceret a principio. Ab æterno ordinata sum, et ex antiquis antequam terra fieret … cum eo eram, cuncta componens. Et delectabar per singulos dies, ludens coram eo omni tempore, ludens in orbe terrarum; et deliciæ meæ esse cum filiis hominum. (8:22–31)
>
> [The Lord possessed me in the beginning of his ways, before he made anything from the beginning. I was set up from eternity, and of old before the earth was made … I was with him forming all things: and was delighted every day, playing before him at all times; Playing in the world: and my delights were ever to be with the children of men.]

Woman Wisdom is depicted as a playful figure here, who takes delight in the natural world.

These notions can be applied to *Modor Monigra*, which addresses the subject's origins. In the riddle, the narrator also describes the creature's ancient history, saying she is *hæleþum frodra* ('older than heroes') (36b). The narrator asserts that God, the *fæder* ('father'), *ealle bewat, / or ond ende* ('saw it all, [her] origin and end') (9b–10a). The riddle also situates its creature in a pre-lapsarian ideal, in an earth that *ær wæs / wlitig ond wynsum* ('was formerly beautiful and pleasant') (18–19). Though a lacuna makes it difficult to fully understand the meaning of lines 11–19, it seems likely that line 19 is describing Eden before the Fall of humanity. The riddle hints at the change that happened to the world after the Fall and, in doing so, speaks to a large number of other riddles in the collection that deal with post-lapsarian suffering and destruction in some form.[39]

The problem with this type of interpretation, with linking the feminine with the natural world, is that there is a danger of reinforcing the essentialist stereotype that links men to culture and women to nature. Men may be a destructive force in the riddles, but they are also creative in their destruction, producing a variety of manmade products, and it would be problematic (as well as erroneous) to argue that women are, like Woman Wisdom, figures on the edge of culture, who mourn the destruction or suffering of the natural world but do not participate in its shaping or subjugation. I think one of the mistakes we risk making here, however, is to assume that nature takes on a secondary status in the riddles, or indeed early medieval English beliefs as a whole. In the riddles, nature may be depicted as a resource with which humans can create beautiful artefacts or deadly weapons, but it is also depicted as having intrinsic worth in its own right.[40] Its usefulness requires appreciation, its power respect. Furthermore, there is an affinity to be found between humans and nature condemned to a life of suffering and servitude post-Fall that breaks down the boundaries between human and nature, nature and culture.

The riddle collection promotes the idea, too, that to have true knowledge one must know everything about the natural world. 'To be wise', says Hobgood-Oster, 'one must know Earth intimately and passionately', and one can do this if God gives *horum quæ sunt scientiam veram* ('true knowledge of the things that are') (Wisdom 7:17).[41] In The Wisdom of Solomon, Solomon teaches his readers the virtues of wisdom and asserts that true wisdom, which God gave him, includes knowing:

> naturas animalium, et iras bestiarum, vim ventorum, et cogitationes hominum, differentias virgultorum, et virtutes radicum. (7:20)
>
> [the natures of living creatures, and rage of wild beasts, the force of winds, and reasonings of men, the diversities of plants, and the virtues of roots.]

Indeed, Solomon says, *quæcumque sunt absconsa et improvisa didici: / omnium enim artifex docuit me sapientia* ('all such things as are hid and not foreseen, I have learned: for wisdom, which is the worker of all things, taught me') (Wisdom 7:21). A similar notion is found in the Book of Job, where God questions Job's knowledge and tells him that there are many things about the created world that men do not know or cannot understand. In the riddles, we find human knowledge questioned in Job-like fashion. *Modor Monigra*, for example, suggests humans lack the ability to say everything about the nature of water:

> Nænig oþrum mæg
> wlite ond wisan wordum gecyþan,
> hu mislic biþ mægen þara cynna,
> fyrn forðgesceaft (6b–9a).

> [No one can convey in words to another her appearance and nature, how manifold the strength of her race is, her ancestry].

Far from being ironic, these lines undermine the pretensions of culture and reassert nature's value in the order of the world.

Taking an ecofeminist approach to the riddles can illuminate hitherto unexplored aspects of the texts and further our understanding of both their depictions of women and nature. By thinking of women and nature as oppressed groups and looking for a relationship between them we can start to see how the two in combination challenge andro- and anthropocentric views of the world. I believe there is ample evidence to suggest that the depiction of *Modor Monigra*'s subject was inspired by Woman Wisdom and that, like Woman Wisdom in the Bible, it does not reinforce the negative stereotyping of women and nature. I do think, however, that we need to look at the collection as a whole to fully appreciate the depiction of nature and women and issues of oppression and andro- and anthropocentrism in this genre of early medieval writing. As we continue to employ the theories of ecocriticism and ecofeminism to these texts—and, indeed, across the Old English corpus—we will get a fuller picture of attitudes towards marginalised groups.

Notes

1 Laura Hobgood-Oster, 'Wisdom Literature and Ecofeminism', in *The Earth Story in Wisdom Traditions*, ed. Norman C. Habel and Shirley Wurst (Sheffield: Sheffield Academic Press, 2001), pp. 116–42, at p. 142. For further discussion of this riddle, see Oberman's Chapter 16 in this volume.

2 Kathleen O'Connor, *The Wisdom Literature* (Collegeville, MN: Liturgical Press, 1988), p. 63.

3 Craig Williamson, trans., *A Feast of Creatures: Anglo-Saxon Riddle Songs* (Philadelphia: University of Pennsylvania Press, 1982), p. 169.

4 John D. Niles, *Old English Enigmatic Poems and the Play of the Texts* (Turnhout: Brepols, 2006), p. 105.

5 This link has been noted by Patrick J. Murphy, *Unriddling the Exeter Riddles* (University Park: Pennsylvania University Press, 2011), p. 10. See also Frederick Tupper, Jr, ed., *The Riddles of the Exeter Book* (Boston: Ginn, 1910), p. 147.

6 Anita R. Riedinger, 'The Formulaic Style in the Old English Riddles', *Studia Neophilologica*, 76.1 (2004), 30–43, at p. 38.

7 Riedinger, 'Formulaic Style', p. 38.
8 See Heide Estes, *Anglo-Saxon Literary Landscapes: Ecotheory and the Environmental Imagination* (Amsterdam: Amsterdam University Press, 2017); Clare A. Lees and Gillian R. Overing, *Double Agents: Women and Clerical Culture in Anglo-Saxon England* (Philadelphia: University of Pennsylvania Press, 2001).
9 Lees and Overing, *Double Agents*, p. 104.
10 See Stopford A. Brooke, *The History of Early English Literature* (London: Macmillan, 1892), p. 181. Masculine pronouns are used in Brooke's translation, too.
11 Shari Horner, *The Discourse of Enclosure: Representing Women in Old English Literature* (New York: SUNY Press, 2001), p. 6.
12 Stacy S. Klein, 'Gender and the Nature of Exile in the Old English Elegies', in *A Place to Believe In: Locating Medieval Landscapes*, ed. Clare A. Lees and Gillian R. Overing (Philadelphia: Penn State University Press, 2006), pp. 113–31, at p. 116.
13 Klein, 'Gender and the Nature of Exile', p. 117.
14 Lees and Overing, *Double Agents*, p. 103.
15 Other solutions include 'cithara' and 'feather-pen'. See Elaine K. Musgrave, 'Cithara as the Solution to Riddle 31 of the Exeter Book', *Pacific Coast Philology*, 37 (2002), 69–84; Donald K. Fry, 'Exeter Riddle 31: Feather-pen', in *De Gustibus: Essays for Alain Renoir*, ed. John Miles Foley (New York: Garland, 1992), pp. 235–49.
16 For different readings of this riddle, see Brooks and Wilcox in Chapters 4 and 7 of this volume.
17 Corinne Dale, *The Natural World in the Exeter Book Riddles* (Cambridge: D. S. Brewer, 2017), p. 169.
18 See also the discussion of grammatical gender by Cavell, Wilcox, and Salvador-Bello in Chapters 3, 7, and 12 of this volume.
19 Niles, *Old English Enigmatic Poems*, p. 105.
20 'Wine is a mocker, strong drink is a brawler, and whoever is led astray by it is not wise' (Proverbs 20:1). For discussions of this personification, see Michael V. Fox, *Proverbs 10–31* (New Haven: Yale University Press, 2009), p. 663; Frederick Richard Lees and Dawson Burns, *The Temperance Bible-Commentary: Giving at One View, Version, Criticism, and Exposition, in Regard to all Passages of Holy Writ Bearing on 'Wine' and 'Strong Drink,' or Illustrating the Principles of the Temperance Reformation*, 2nd edn (London: S. W. Partridge, 1868), pp. 133–4.
21 For further discussion of the figure of Wisdom, see Salvador-Bello, Chapter 12 of this volume.
22 Lees and Overing, *Double Agents*, p. 209.
23 Carole Fontaine, *Smooth Words: Women, Proverbs and Performance in Biblical Wisdom* (London: T & T Clark, 2004), p. 95.
24 Fontaine, *Smooth Words*, p. 96.
25 Fontaine, *Smooth Words*, p. 96.

26 All references to the Bible are to the Latin Vulgate, for which I use *Biblia Sacra iuxta Vulgatam Clementinam*, ed. Alberto Colunga and Laurentio Turrado, 7th edn (Madrid: Biblioteca de Autores Christianos, 1985). All translations of the Vulgate are from *The Holy Bible: Translated from the Latin Vulgate* (New York: Douay Bible House, 1953).
27 For further discussion of the image of the mother, see Salvador-Bello, Chapter 12 of this volume.
28 Dale, *Natural World*, pp. 174–8.
29 Craig Williamson, ed., *The Old English Riddles of the Exeter Book* (Chapel Hill: University of North Carolina Press, 1977), p. 263.
30 See M. Trautmann, ed., *Die altenglischen Rätsel (Die Rätsel des Exeterbuchs)* (Heidelberg: Winter, 1915), p. 22; Williamson, *Old English Riddles*, p. 263. It has been argued that the creature might instead be 'Faith', which is typically portrayed in the Bible as poor. See Caroline Dennis, 'Exeter Book Riddle 39: Creature Faith', *Medieval Perspectives*, 10 (1995), 77–85.
31 Fontaine, *Smooth Words*, p. 96.
32 O'Connor, *Wisdom Literature*, p. 62.
33 Fontaine, *Smooth Words*, p. 98.
34 Fontaine, *Smooth Words*, p. 98.
35 O'Connor, *Wisdom Literature*, p. 63.
36 Hobgood-Oster, 'Wisdom Literature and Ecofeminism', p. 42.
37 Hobgood-Oster, 'Wisdom Literature and Ecofeminism', p. 35.
38 Hobgood-Oster, 'Wisdom Literature and Ecofeminism', p. 35.
39 See Dale, *Natural World*.
40 See Dale, *Natural World*, pp. 103–22.
41 Hobgood-Oster, 'Wisdom Literature and Ecofeminism', p. 42.

11

Mind, mood, and meteorology in *Þrymful Þeow* (R.1–3)[1]

James Paz

The riddles of early medieval England show an interest in every aspect of Creation no matter how enormous or how insignificant, from the littlest worm to the light of the sun and moon.[2] These riddles present us with entities that overwhelm us as human beings, and they direct our attention towards creatures that we might otherwise ignore. As I have argued elsewhere, riddles offer us a glimpse into phenomena that we sometimes fail to perceive with our senses, capturing the secret lives of everyday things through playful language.[3] Although medieval writers are often characterised as adhering to strict ontological hierarchies (the *scala naturae* which situates God at the summit of Creation, followed by angels, then humans and then animals and plants and stones), in the world of the riddles a rich array of entities—beasts and birds, tools and weapons, food and drink, weather, stars and planets—appear on an equal footing as lively, sentient, talkative *wihta* ('creatures'). These weird creatures challenge us to rethink the ways in which we, as humans, attempt to codify the world, expanding our ordinary modes of cognition.

It is an opportune time to be re-reading and rethinking such a set of texts. Contemporary theorists are taking fundamental questions about the nature of matter and the place of embodied humans within a material world in exciting new directions. The so-called 'new materialists' generally eschew commonsense distinctions between organic and inorganic, animate and inanimate, at the ontological level, ascribing agency to all kinds of nonhuman things and troubling the conventional idea that active agents are exclusively human.[4] Although much of this theoretical work focuses on the modern age, the early medieval *Exeter Book* riddles provide the perfect field for these kinds of discussion and can deepen our understanding of nonhuman agency and ontology.

Just as the Old English riddles range from tiny insects to astronomical bodies, recent studies in thing theory, object-oriented ontology, and other strands of new materialism have turned their attention to issues of scale. For example, Levi R. Bryant's concept of onticology proposes a horizontal or 'flat' ontology where objects of all sorts and at different scales equally exist without being reducible to other objects. Flat ontology invites us to think in terms of collectives and entanglements between a variety of actors of different types, at a variety of different temporal and spatial scales.[5] Timothy Morton has questioned whether human sensory experience allows direct access to reality at extreme scales, employing the term 'hyperobjects' to describe entities of such vast dimensions that they defeat traditional ideas about what a thing actually is. You cannot pick up and examine a so-called hyperobject as easily as you could an apple or a cup. They exceed human apprehension, but we constantly notice their local manifestations. Hyperobjects are so massively distributed across time and space that they appear to be everywhere and nowhere; they can be experienced in part yet any particular materialisation never reveals the totality of the hyperobject: for instance, you can feel a raindrop on your skin but that raindrop does not enable you to encounter climate itself. Morton argues that the anthropocentric concept of the 'world' is over because the weather—and indeed nature itself—is no longer the neutral backdrop that stays passive while we play out our human dramas in front of it. For Morton, hyperobjects challenge assumptions of human mastery and our powers of cognition. We can philosophise about the existence of ordinary things like apples or cups, but hyperobjects cannot quite be grasped—either physically or intellectually.[6]

When Morton claims that the 'world' is over, he is writing from the perspective of a literary scholar trained as a Romanticist and he is talking about the end of the modern world, a world in which human beings interact with apples or cups according to Newtonian laws and post-Enlightenment commonsense. However, this apocalypse may have taken place in the premodern past as much as in the postmodern future.

The first riddle of the *Exeter Book* attributes a first-person voice to a nebulous natural phenomenon, a meteorological event, rather than a solid, bounded material artefact. *Þrymful Þeow* begins by speaking of a series of storms and natural disasters:

> Hwylc is hæleþa þæs horsc ond þæs hygecræftig
> þæt þæt mæge asecgan, hwa mec on sið wræce,
> þonne ic astige strong, stundum reþe,
> þrymful þunie, þragum wræce

fere geond foldan, folcsalo bærne,
ræced reafige? (1–6a)

[Who of men is so sharp and so mind-skilled that they may say who drives me on my way, when I arise strong, stand fierce, roar with might, at times vengeful, and fare around the earth, when I burn houses, ravage halls?]

The text goes on to describe a windstorm creating chaos on land, a submarine earthquake, a storm at sea, and a thunderstorm back on land. The riddling challenge is to resolve what seems to be a variety of wild, devastating forces into a coherent solution. Verbal power becomes the key to not only knowing but controlling the violent moods of an inhuman nature.[7] Speaking the correct response has proved tricky, but apparently not impossible.

Previous critics have helped this process along by revealing the influence of classical and early medieval cosmology on the 'storm' riddle, quoting cosmological writings extensively as evidence that the poet has drawn on a scientific tradition stretching from Plato to Bede.[8] For example, in Book 2 of his *Natural History*, Pliny the Elder states that the mutable, sublunary sphere is the realm of the winds (*ventorum hoc regnum*) and that most storms come from this realm:

Infra lunam haec sedes, multoque inferior (ut animadverto propemodum constare), infinitum ex superiore natura aeris, infinitum et terreni halitus miscens utraque sorte confunditur. Hinc nubila, tonitrua et alia fulmina, hinc grandines, pruinae, imbres, procellae, turbines, hinc plurima mortalium mala et rerum naturae pugna secum.

[This region below the moon, and a long way below it (as I notice is almost universally agreed), blends together an unlimited quantity from the upper element of air and an unlimited quantity of terrestrial vapour, being a combination of both orders. From it come clouds, thunderclaps and also thunderbolts, hail, frost, rain, storms and whirlwinds; from it come most of mortals' misfortunes, and the warfare between the elements of nature.][9]

The weight of medieval cosmological and meteorological evidence suggests that early medieval English writers from Bede onwards considered a range of natural disturbances as part of the atmospheric power of the sublunar air. Charles W. Kennedy first argued that what were then considered to be the second and third riddle constituted a single riddle, with *wind* (an Old English, as well Modern English, word) as the solution, since medieval meteorology understood the wind as being responsible for storms, seaquakes and earthquakes.[10] Craig Williamson extended the *wind* solution to the first riddle as well; in his view, all three should be read as one continuous text.[11] I follow his practice here.

Of most interest in relation to my own theories about this riddle is Erika von Erhardt-Siebold's 1949 interpretation of it as 'the atmosphere'.[12] Her answer, she makes clear, is not 'atmosphere' in the modern sense but rather the Graeco-Roman conception of the sublunar air. In this cosmological model, the outer atmosphere communicates with the atmosphere in the interior of the earth, where the earth is thought of as highly porous body with caverns and veins in its interior and with openings leading to its surface. The corporeality of the earth is recognised by Aldhelm in his *Enigma 73, Fons*. Here, the 'spring' says, *Per cava telluris clam serpo celerrimus antra / Flexos venarum girans anfractibus orbes* ('Through the hollows of the earth I secretly creep swiftly, winding my twisted circuit along the curves of its arteries') (1–2).[13]

Aldhelm, of course, penned his own 'wind' riddle: *Enigma 2* in his collection of one hundred Latin *enigmata*. For Aldhelm, the image of the devastating wind, an invisible but mighty force, was a reminder of God's unseen power.[14] But the image of breath is also a common trope for the soul, and the Latin language encouraged associations between the wind or air and the breath, spirit or soul. Indeed, Latin *anima* embraced multiple meanings in the philosophical vocabulary of late antiquity. It could refer to the air, as one of the four elements, but also to the vital principle that animates all living beings. Authorities such as Augustine and Boethius, and early medieval English writers including Alcuin, Alfred, and Ælfric, wrestled with the problem of how the rational human soul differed from the life-spirit animating the rest of Creation.[15] Recent research by Mercedes Salvador-Bello has shown how indebted Old English poets and composers of literary riddles were to the encyclopaedic works of Isidore of Seville,[16] and Isidore is inconsistent about the relationship between the *anima* (soul) and *anemos* (wind). In the *Etymologiae*, Isidore insists that the human soul is not identical to air and therefore the Greeks were wrong to think that air inhaled through the mouth animated the body. Yet elsewhere in the *Etymologiae*, Isidore claims that the soul is called 'spirit' when it respires (*dum spirat, spiritus est*) and, in the *Differentiae*, he maintains that in the lungs there is contained air, which is dispersed by the heart through the arteries, so that gradually the air animates the entire body.[17] The latter description creates a striking parallel with the movements of the atmosphere through the caverns or 'arteries' of the earth.

For some ancient philosophers, such as the Stoics, the wind or air could even represent an aspect of consciousness. Like Williamson, Michael Lapidge takes the first three riddles to be a single, unified riddle and goes on to argue that the solution is the Stoic concept of *pneuma* (πνεῦμα). *Pneuma* was the 'cosmic breath' that pervaded and animated the body of the entire universe, which, in Stoic cosmology, was a living being whose parts were linked together in one vast cosmic sympathy. As part of his argument, Lapidge contends that the early medieval riddler had been influenced by Seneca's writings on nature, where the Stoic concept of *pneuma* is rendered into Latin as *spiritus*.[18]

Although my own reading of *Þrymful Þeow* identifies more vernacular imagery at work, I do agree that the natural force of the wind overlaps with psychological or spiritual qualities. My aim in this chapter is not to pinpoint a classical source for the text, but the examples of the Greek *pneuma* and Latin *anima* do indicate that learned early medieval poets may well have been aware of cosmological systems in which the wind was not simply an external element, separate from the human body, mind, and soul.[19] Earthquakes and thunderstorms are caused by a conflict between the 'interior' of the earthly body and its 'exterior' expulsions and movements. The sublunar air is thought to be the cause of these disturbances, but images of air or breath could also call to mind the vital principle that permeates and animates all living beings. Human beings cannot be sure whether we are inside or outside, apart from or a part of, the storm. The caverns of the earth are visceral, and the violent wind moves through us as well as around us.

In the remainder of this chapter, I aim to demonstrate that the storms of *Þrymful Þeow* overwhelm human beings to such an extent that we cannot stand outside them and observe or interpret them in a detached manner. Therefore, they can be understood as hyperobjects. In his definition of the hyperobject, Morton makes a distinction between 'mind-blowing' climate change and the easier to conceptualise and more manageable topic of the weather. However, Heide Estes contends that, while modern weather-imaging satellites are capable of seeing storm systems in their global entirety, for the 'weather-channel deprived Anglo-Saxons, storms are apprehensible only in their local effects', and therefore the storms described by these texts fit the definition of hyperobject when situated in their early medieval context.[20] The earth-shaking, sea-churning, hall-burning, ship-wrecking, body-drowning storms described by the riddle hardly constitute a neutral backdrop that stays passive while we play out our human dramas in front of it, and the power of the wind destabilises dualisms like subject–object, human–nonhuman and self–other, as well as internal–external. In *Þrymful Þeow*, the wind or sublunar air needs to be confined and restrained within the hollows of the earth, lest it break loose and wreak havoc. I argue that this situation resembles descriptions of the volatile human mind found elsewhere in Old English poetry, further breaking down the boundary between the 'internal' human self and 'external' nonhuman nature.

The opening *Exeter Book* riddle draws on cosmology and meteorology, then, to depict the volatility of the sublunary world and our own enmeshment with that unsettled, moody world beneath the moon, where the tempestuous nature of the winds holds sway. *Þrymful Þeow* claims that the wind must at times be contained within the interior of the earth:

> Hwilum mec min frea fæste genearwað,
> sendeð þonne under salwonges
> bearm þone bradan, ond on bid wriceð,
> þrafað on þystrum þrymma sumne,
> hæste on enge, þær me heord siteð
> hruse on hrycge. (31–36a)

> [Sometimes my master confines me firmly, then sends me under the earth-hall, its broad bosom, and one of the powers drives me to a halt, restrains me in the darkness, violently in the narrow space, where hard earth sits on my back.]

At this point, readers of Old English poetry may be struck by a feeling of recognition or even self-recognition. Compare these lines from *The Wanderer*:

> Ic to soþe wat
> þæt biþ in eorle indryhten þeaw,
> þæt he his ferðlocan fæste binde,
> healde his hordcofan, hycge swa he wille. (11b–14)

> [I know in truth that it is a noble virtue in a man, that he bind fast his spirit-enclosure, hold tight his treasure-coffer, think as he will.]

The link between an unruly mind and stormy weather is further implied in *Maxims I*, where the reader is advised: *Styran sceal mon strongum mode. Storm oft holm gebringeð* ('One must steer [guide? restrain?] a strong mind. The sea often brings a storm') (50). I would suggest that, in the storm riddle, the wind is described in terms akin to the workings and movements of the human mind

(OE *mod*, *sefa*, or *hyge*) within and without the human body. In his book *Unriddling the Exeter Riddles*, Patrick J. Murphy makes a compelling case that many of the Old English riddles are shaped by coherent metaphors, and that these metaphors determine how the riddling clues are presented to the solver:

> The simple idea is that an Old English riddle's proposition (the 'question' or description posed) may at times relate not only to an unnamed solution but also to what I call its 'focus', an underlying metaphor that lends coherence to the text's strategy of obfuscation.[21]

To be clear, I am not proposing that the solution to *Þrymful Þeow* is 'mind' but that images of the *mod* underlie the more overt descriptions of various storms. Traditionally, a metaphor is understood as a figure of speech which transfers meaning from one conceptual structure to another, allowing us to understand one domain of experience in terms of another. In this way, metaphors make us rethink the concepts we use to categorise and classify the world.[22]

But if metaphors can be formally defined as the transferral of a name or description from that which it properly signifies to that which it does not signify, then the implication is that they are essentially falsehoods. When we acknowledge them as figures of speech, metaphors soon weaken into similes. A storm is a mind; a storm is like a mind, but a storm is not actually a mind. Accordingly, Murphy states that a riddle's metaphorical focus is the 'expected response of an imagined solver who took the riddle much too literally'.[23] The underlying metaphor might be recognised, but to offer it as the solution is to be misled.

Conversely, new materialists might reframe the 'mistake' as an insight. As Kellie Robertson reminds us, '[w]here and how the line between human and nonhuman, subject and object, society and nature gets drawn is always an ideological process'.[24] Taking the metaphorical clues too literally and speaking the wrong the solution can, in this case, lead to a breaking down of the self–other boundary. A mind is a storm; a storm is a mind. I am it; it is me. For Jane Bennett, the disruption of this boundary is necessary, 'because the frame of subjects and objects is unfriendly to the intensified ecological awareness that we need if we are to respond intelligently to signs of the breakdown of the earth's carrying capacity for human life'.[25] In this way, these early medieval mind–storm riddles resonate strongly with twenty-first-century ecological concerns.

For Old English poets, the internal human world is not always fixed inside the body; it is able to move beyond the confines of the bone-house into the external world. An example of this may be found in *The Seafarer*:

> Forþon nu min hyge hweorfeð ofer hreþerlocan,
> min modsefa mid mereflode
> ofer hwæles eþel hweorfeð wide,
> eorþan sceatas, cymeð eft to me
> gifre ond grædig, gielleð anfloga,
> hweteð on wælweg hreþer unwearnum
> ofer holma gelagu. (58–64a)

> [And so now my spirit wanders beyond my heart-enclosure, my mind with the sea-flood, over the whale's home widely roams, over the surface of the earth, and the solitary flier comes again to me, yells, eager and greedy, urges my heart irresistibly on the whale-way, over the lengths of the sea.]

A similar instance of the mind breaking free from the chest occurs in *Beowulf*, where we are told that *ne meahte wæfre mod / forhabban in hreþre* ('the restless mind was unable to remain in the breast') (1150b–1151a). In this case, the unrestrained *mod* reignites old hostilities and renews the feud between the Danes and Frisians. Potentially a dangerous, rebellious force, the mind had to be bound and fettered and, surging within the chest, often threatened to burst out of one's breast-coffer. Malcolm R. Godden looked into what early medieval English writers had to say about the nature of the mind and found that the poets are more inclined to associate 'mind' with emotion and a kind of passionate volition and self-assertion.[26] Mind here seems to be closely associated with mood and is generally distinguished from the soul or spirit, which leaves the body in death and survives in another world. Furthermore, the Old English *mod* conveys a sort of 'intensification of the self that can be dangerous', and so authors often speak of the need to control and restrain the *mod*.[27]

In her 2011 book on *Anglo-Saxon Psychologies*, Leslie Lockett supports the idea that, unlike the *sawol*, the *mod* does not experience visions of the afterlife, but can nevertheless break free from its restraints and travel outwards from the human breast while engaged in acts of memory or imagination, visiting earthly people and places.[28] Lockett identifies a 'hydraulic' model of the mind in Old English literature, in which mental activity is usually localised in or around the chest or heart and where intense mental states coincide with cardiocentric swelling, boiling, or seething. This mechanism is analogous to the physical behaviour of a container of fluid exposed to heat.[29] Of particular interest is Lockett's interpretation of Lorsch *Enigma 2*, which she reads as an enigma about the mind-in-the-heart.[30]

The Lorsch riddles are twelve, anonymous Latin verse *enigmata* uniquely extant in Vatican City, Pal. Lat. 1753. The manuscript was probably compiled in the late eighth century at the Benedictine Abbey of St Nazarius at Lorsch. Founded in 764, this monastic house had well-known affiliations to early medieval England. Indeed, a number of scholars view the Lorsch riddles as an early medieval English literary product, possibly the work of multiple authors, composed and compiled in England.[31] It is worth quoting Lorsch *Enigma 2* in full:

> Dum domus ipsa mea dormit, uigilare suesco,
> Atque sub angusto tenear cum carcere semper,
> Liber ad aetheream transcendo frequentius aulam,
> Alta supernorum scrutans secreta polorum.
>
> Omnia quin potius perlustro creata sub orbe,
> Rura peragro salumque peto, tunc litora linquens
> Finibus inmensum fundum rimabor abyssi.
>
> Horrifera minime pertranseo claustra gehennae,
> Ignea perpetuae subeo sed tartara Ditis.
> Haec modico peragro speleo, si claudar in aruis,
> Mortifero concussa ruant ni ergastula casu.
>
> Sin uero propria dire de sede repellor,
> Mortis in occasu extimplo fio pulpa putrescens:
> Sic sunt fata mea diuersa a patre creata.[32]
>
> [When my house is itself asleep, I am accustomed to be awake, and although I may be ever kept under a narrow prison, I often freely climb through the heavenly court, examining the heights of heaven and the mysteries of the skies. // But indeed, I traverse all of creation under the sun, I pass through fields and seek the open sea; then, leaving the shores, I will swim the immense depth of the ocean to its limits. // I never penetrate the prisons of horrifying Gehenna, but I pass eternally fiery Tartarus, ruled by Dis. // If I am enclosed in my tiny cave during this earthly life, I pass through these places, unless my prison-house should collapse, struck by the occasion of death. // But if I am fearfully propelled from my proper seat, on the occasion of death I promptly become rotting flesh: thus are my different fates ordained by the Father.][33]

Like the Old English riddles of the *Exeter Book*, the Lorsch riddles have no title-solutions. Most editors and commentators solve the identity of this speaker as the human heart, mind, or soul. Patrizia Lendinara has argued that the entity depicted is the *mens vel animus* discussed by Alcuin in his treatise *De ratione animae*.[34] However, while Lorsch *Enigma 2* shares distinctive diction and imagery with Alcuin's treatise on the soul, Lockett points out that the enigmatic speaker of the former possesses characteristics that do not fit with the qualities of the *anima*.[35] Instead, Lockett prefers to solve this riddle with a vernacular Old English word, *breostsefa* 'the mind-in-the-heart'. She argues against the solution of *anima* because the speaker of the Lorsch riddle does not appear to be incorporeal or immortal. Rather, it should be seen as the organ responsible for thought, which can escape the prison of the body through memory or imagination.

The act of thinking allows the mind-in-the-heart to travel to distant places. And yet, unlike the Latin *anima* or the Old English concept of the *sawol*, the *breostsefa* must die when the body dies. Thus, the speaker closely resembles the weary *sefa* that the Wanderer must continuously send over the waves, or the *modsefa* or *hyge* that flies forth from the chest in *The Seafarer*. To my mind, it also shares affinities with the speaker of *Þrymful Þeow*. It is confined within a narrow prison, enclosed within a cave, and yet seeks to escape this restraint in order to explore the heights of the skies and the depths of the seas to their very limits. If Lorsch *Enigma 2* can be convincingly solved as the Old English concept of the *breostsefa*, then the echoes that exist between its imagery and the imagery found in the *Exeter Book* 'storm' riddle should alert us to the potential overlaps between human mental activities and nonhuman, natural phenomena.

These descriptions of the entity variously known as the *mod*, *hyge*, or *sefa* reveal that the Old English did make inner–outer distinctions, but the boundary that divided human interiority from the external nonhuman world was porous and permeable. Human beings did not always consciously decide when to reveal the thoughts and emotions of their minds to the outside world. Rather, the volatile *mod* needed controlling and restraining. It did not reside in the head, but probably in the chest, and was not controlled absolutely by the self, especially in the vernacular tradition.[36]

Just as the emotional, wilful *mod* travels over land and sea in acts of imagination, the *wind* in *Þrymful Þeow* fares across both earth and water, shaking and breaking and battering and burning. The assaults on the earth, the ravaging of the seas, are linked to violent emotion: *ic astige strong, stundum reþe, / þrymful þunie, þragum wræce* ('I arise strong, stand fierce, roar with might, at times vengeful') (3–4). Like the *mod*, there is a clear sense that, unrestrained, the force of the wind will relentlessly wreak destruction on everything it encounters. The human mind is turbulent: it can erupt or escape from the body; it is not detached or divided off from nature but partakes in the violent moods of the storm.

The wind also describes how, when let loose from its bonds, it seeks the seabed and begins churning up the waters:

> Hwilum ic gewite,   swa ne wenaþ men,
> under yþa geþræc   eorþan secan,
> garsecges grund.   Gifen biþ gewreged,
> fam gewealcen;
> hwælmere hlimmeð,   hlude grimmeð,
> streamas staþu beatað,   stundum weorpaþ
> on stealc hleoþa   stane ond sonde,
> ware ond wæge,   þonne ic winnende,
> holmmægne biþeaht,   hrusan styrge,
> side sægrundas. (16–25a)
>
> [Sometimes I depart, as people do not expect, under the force of the waves, seeking the earth, the bottom of the seabed. The ocean is stirred up, the foam flung around; the whale-mere roars, loudly rages, waves beat upon the shore, at times throw stone and sand, seaweed and water, down onto the steep cliffs, when I, struggling, concealed by the sea's might, stir up the earth, the broad ocean-base.]

Intense feelings of anxiety, or sometimes desire, are described by early medieval poets in similar terms as a welling or swelling up of the mind, a sudden surging of the heart, as the *mod* that resides within the human breast begins to *weallan*—a word frequently used to describe human emotions, but which also appears in poetic depictions of seawater.[37] A famous usage of *weallan* in a psychological context comes from *Beowulf*, where the hero experiences unaccustomed anxiety: *breost innan weoll / þeostrum geþoncum, swa him geþywe ne wæs* ('his breast surged inside him with dark thoughts, as was not his way') (2331b–2).

Þrymful Þeow reminds all would-be solvers, about to enter a series of intellectual challenges, of the limits of human cognition. Both our physical and mental efforts at structuring the world are thrown into disarray by a surging, swelling force that can be difficult to contain. In these riddles, the challenge of taming the wildness of nature is thus entangled with the challenge of controlling the inner self, and vice versa. To detach or separate the human mind from external phenomena is no simple task. 'Out there' can be 'in here', and 'in here' can be 'out there'.

In *Þrymful Þeow*, mental and cosmological extremities overlap. The imagery of these riddles draws our intellect outwards to the heights and depths of the universe, beyond ordinary human perception, into mysterious corners of God's Creation which exceed our ways of knowing.[38] The first section of the riddle ends with the challenge to:

Saga hwa mec þecce,
oþþe hu ic hatte, þe þa hlæst bere. (14b–15)

[Say what conceals me, or how I am called, who bears this burden.]

The next section of the riddle, echoing the speaker of Lorsch *Enigma 2*, begins with the statement that it departs under the waves, seeking the bottom of the seabed. These are more than simple descriptions or observations of 'nature'. They are self-reflexive images, commenting on the challenges of the riddling game itself, the difficulties of uncovering that which has been concealed from our minds. Here, Creation itself becomes a 'riddle that the human mind could not hope to solve'.[39] The game is made even harder because the speaker poses two questions: not only, 'Say what I am called' but also, 'Who shapes and controls me?'

Saga, þoncol mon,
hwa mec bregde of brimes fæþmum,
þonne streamas eft stille weorþað,
yþa geþwære, þe mec ær wrugon. (27b–30)

[Say, thoughtful one, who separates me from the sea's embrace, when the waters become still again, the waves obedient, which had concealed me before.]

Early critics, perhaps unconsciously, acknowledged the unknowable nature of this divine force by almost always naming and identifying the servile destroyer (*storm*, *wind*, *atmosphere*) rather than the master who drives the destroyer. Those critics who took the questions as markers that close one riddle and start another chose to answer only one aspect of what the riddler has asked.[40] Therefore, the one riddle is divided into two or three, into a parcel of storms, usually a variation of 'storm on land' and 'storm at sea'. This privileges one half of the riddle's question (say what I am called) over the other (who controls me?).

At the very start of *Þrymful Þeow*, we are asked to use the craft of our mind (*hyge*) to solve and resolve this dangerous natural event: *Hwylc is hæleþa þæs horsc ond þæs hygecræftig / þæt þæt mæge asecgan* ... ('Who of men is so sharp and so mind-skilled that they may say ...') (1–2). Similar statements occur towards the end of each section, where we are ordered to: *Saga, þoncol mon* ... ('Say, thoughtful one ...') (27b). But the human mental faculty, our ability to think and know, is repeatedly urged on by some other, unruly force: a surging, swelling force linked as much to emotion as to cognition. Just as we try to articulate a solution and close the game down, the riddle carries on, swept along by the storm, describing yet more destruction. The repeated use of *hwilum* to open each new section and the scribe's inconsistent use of end punctuation likewise imply a continuation of connected riddles rather than three separate texts that can be concluded with three separate solutions.[41]

The tension between cognition and emotion, knowledge and bewilderment, found within these texts resembles the Old English model of human thought, whereby our mind or mood batters against our more rational, intellectual faculty, creating a sense of split or multiple personalities. The relationship between wind and God echoes the relationship between mind and self in Old English poetry. As with the driver and destroyer, the self and mind may be understood as distinct, yet they also interact in an uneasy master–servant relationship, with the mind or mood urging a conscious 'I' while that 'I' seeks to control volatile emotion. Echoing the maxim quoted above, *The Seafarer* reminds us that it is our duty to control the mind: *Stieran mon sceal strongum mode, ond þæt on staþelum healdan* ('One must steer a strong mind, and hold it on firm foundations') (109). However, it is made clear that the mind is not solely under human control, for it is also God who stabilises a turbulent *mod* for us: *Meotod him þæt mod gestaþelað, forþon he in his meahte gelyfeð* ('The Measurer makes that mind steadfast in him, as he in his might grants it') (108). Again, this gnomic passage finds a parallel in the way in which a divine power is said to still and bind, rouse and restrain, the storm of *Þrymful Þeow*:

Stille þynceð
lyft ofer londe ond lagu swige,
oþþæt ic of enge up aþringe,
efne swa mec wisaþ se mec wræde on
æt frumsceafte furþum legde,
bende ond clomme, þæt ic onbugan ne mot
of þæs gewealde þe me wegas tæcneð. (40b–46)

> [The air seems still over the land and the water silent, until I burst out of my confinement, even as he guides me, the one who, at the beginning of Creation, laid fetters upon me, bonds and chains, so that I may not escape from his control, he who marks the paths out for me.]

These lines reinforce the nonhuman element of the *mod*, the workings of which are recognisable in the external world, and which, like the storm, seeks and obeys a divine might. The riddling combination of driver and destroyer seems both in the world (as a storm) and outside it (as divine power), both external to the human body (as elemental threat) and internal (as mind or mood).

The opening *Exeter Book* riddle, then, forces the reader not only to doubt human knowledge of the nonhuman but also to doubt how well we can know ourselves, what makes us human, who or what drives us, urges us on, restrains us, destroys us. The 'I' of the conscious human self may be able to restrain, to an extent, the wilful mind, but that is not the same as knowing it. And so, lurking alongside the more expressible solutions to this 'wind' or 'storm' riddle is the shadowy presence of unknowing. New materialists have started to unravel the ways that modern humans have imagined ourselves as critically distanced from nature. But premodern riddles serve as timely reminders that a more complex relationship between human self and nonhuman other existed long before our own ecological crisis at the end of the world.

Notes

1 In this chapter Riddles 1, 2, and 3 are viewed as one riddle and so quotations from them follow the text in Craig Williamson, ed., *The Old English Riddles of the Exeter Book* (Chapel Hill: University of North Carolina Press, 1977), pp. 67–70; for discussion of this choice, see below.

2 I would like to thank Megan Cavell and Jennifer Neville for organising the 'Anglo-Saxon Riddles and Wisdom' sessions at the International Medieval Congress (Leeds, 2016), where I presented an earlier version of this chapter as a conference paper. I am grateful to the audience members for their helpful comments and questions. The theoretical aspects of this essay were partly inspired by email correspondence with Michael Gossett, a doctoral candidate at St John's University, New York City. See his short essay, 'Riddle', in *Anthropocene Unseen: A Lexicon*, ed. Cymene Howe and Anand Pandian (New York: Punctum Books, forthcoming).

3 James Paz, *Nonhuman Voices in Anglo-Saxon Literature and Material Culture* (Manchester: Manchester University Press, 2017), p. 61.
4 Diana Coole and Samantha Frost, eds, *New Materialisms: Ontology, Agency, and Politics* (Durham, NC: Duke University Press, 2010), pp. 7–10.
5 Levi R. Bryant, *The Democracy of Objects* (Ann Arbor: Open Humanities Press, 2011), p. 32.
6 Timothy Morton, *Hyperobjects: Philosophy and Ecology after the End of the World* (Minneapolis: University of Minnesota Press, 2013).
7 For discussion of how Old English poets use writing to try to contain and control the natural world, see chapter 5 of Elaine Tuttle Hansen, *The Solomon Complex: Reading Wisdom in Old English Poetry* (Toronto: University of Toronto Press, 1988); chapter 6 of Jennifer Neville, *Representations of the Natural World in Old English Poetry* (Cambridge: Cambridge University Press, 1999).
8 Charles W. Kennedy, *The Earliest English Poetry* (London: Oxford University Press, 1943); Williamson, *Old English Riddles*, pp. 127–41; Michael Lapidge, 'Stoic Cosmology and the Source of the First Old English Riddle', *Anglia*, 112 (1994), 1–25.
9 Text and translation from Pliny the Elder, *Natural History*, Volume I: Books 1–2, trans. H. Rackham, Loeb Classical Library, 330 (Cambridge, MA: Harvard University Press, 1938), pp. 246–7. This passage is also quoted in Craig Williamson, trans., *A Feast of Creatures: Anglo-Saxon Riddle Songs* (Philadelphia: University of Pennsylvania Press, 1982), p. 159.
10 Kennedy, *Earliest English Poetry*, pp. 140–6 and 364–8.
11 Williamson, *Old English Riddles*, pp. 127–41.
12 Erika von Erhardt-Siebold, 'The Old English Storm Riddles', *PMLA*, 64.4 (1949), 884–8.
13 For text, see Aldhelm, 'Epistola ad Acircium (De Metris et Enigmatibus ac Pedum Regulis)', in *Aldhelmi Opera*, ed. Rudolf Ehwald, MGH, Auctores Antiquissimi, 15 (Berlin: Weidmann, 1919), p. 130. For translation, see Aldhelm, *Aldhelm: The Poetic Works*, trans. Michael Lapidge and James L. Rosier (Cambridge: D. S. Brewer, 2009).
14 See the commentary on this enigma by A. M. Juster, trans., *Saint Aldhelm's Riddles* (Toronto: University of Toronto Press, 2015), p. 85.
15 See further Malcolm R. Godden, 'Anglo-Saxons on the Mind', repr. in *Old English Literature: Critical Essays*, ed. R. M. Liuzza (New Haven: Yale University Press, 2002), pp. 284–314, at pp. 285–98.
16 Mercedes Salvador-Bello, *Isidorean Perceptions of Order: The Exeter Book Riddles and Medieval Latin Enigmata* (Morgantown: West Virginia University Press, 2015).
17 Leslie Lockett, *Anglo-Saxon Psychologies in the Vernacular and Latin Traditions* (Toronto: University of Toronto Press, 2011), pp. 206–13. Lockett argues (at p. 227) that it was not St Augustine whose views on

the soul were most widely read in England before AD 1000. Instead, Gregory the Great's *Dialogues* and the works of Isidore of Seville were consulted from the seventh to eleventh centuries and left their mark on many types of literature, including riddles.

18 Lapidge, 'Stoic Cosmology', pp. 1–25.
19 Cf. also the Gospel of John 3:7–8.
20 Heide Estes, *Anglo-Saxon Literary Landscapes: Ecotheory and the Environmental Imagination* (Amsterdam: Amsterdam University Press, 2017), p. 161.
21 Patrick J. Murphy, *Unriddling the Exeter Riddles* (University Park: Pennsylvania State University Press, 2011), p. 18.
22 See, for example, George Lakoff and Mark Turner, *More than Cool Reason: A Field Guide to Poetic Metaphor* (London: University of Chicago Press, 1989).
23 Murphy, *Unriddling the Exeter Riddles*, p. 47.
24 Kellie Robertson, 'Medieval Things: Materiality, Historicism, and the Premodern Object', *Literature Compass*, 5.6 (2008), 1060–80.
25 Jane Bennett, 'Systems and Things: A Response to Graham Harman and Timothy Morton', *New Literary History*, 43.2 (2012), 225–33, at p. 231.
26 Godden, 'Anglo-Saxons on the Mind', p. 308.
27 Godden, 'Anglo-Saxons on the Mind', p. 300.
28 Lockett, *Anglo-Saxon Psychologies*, p. 38.
29 Lockett, *Anglo-Saxon Psychologies*, pp. 62–4.
30 Lockett, *Anglo-Saxon Psychologies*, pp. 276–80.
31 For a detailed introduction to the Lorsch Riddles, see Salvador-Bello, *Isidorean Perceptions of Order*, pp. 264–74.
32 [Lorsch Riddles], 'Aenigmata anglica', in *Poetae Latini Aevi Carolini*, ed. Ernst Dümmler, MGH, 1 (Berlin: Weidmann, 1881), pp. 20–23.
33 Translation by Lockett, *Anglo-Saxon Psychologies*, pp. 277–8.
34 Patrizia Lendinara, 'Gli Aenigmata Laureshamensia', *PAN: Studi dell'Istituto di Filologia Latina*, 7 (1979), 73–90.
35 Lockett, *Anglo-Saxon Psychologies*, pp. 278–9.
36 Godden, 'Anglo-Saxons on the Mind', pp. 298–308; Lockett, *Anglo-Saxon Psychologies*, pp. 33–41. Eric Jager also argues that Old English poets treat the chest as the spiritual, intellectual and verbal centre of action in humans: 'Speech and the Chest in Old English Poetry: Orality or Pectorality?' *Speculum*, 65.4 (1990), 845–59.
37 Joyce Potter, '*Wylm* and *Weallan* in *Beowulf*: A Tidal Metaphor', *Medieval Perspectives*, 3 (1988), 191–9; Lockett, *Anglo-Saxon Psychologies*, p. 59.
38 Cf. Corinne Dale, *The Natural World in the Exeter Book Riddles* (Woodbridge: D. S. Brewer, 2017), pp. 181–93. Dale argues that the storm riddles expose the limits of wisdom, revealing aspects of Creation which lie beyond human mastery and therefore subverting an

anthropocentric worldview. She cites a passage from the Book of Job, in which God questions and admonishes Job about his knowledge of the created world, as a possible influence on these riddles.

39 Neville, *Representations of the Natural World*, p. 140.

40 For a list of previous solutions up to 1981, see Donald K. Fry, 'Exeter Book Riddle Solutions', *Old English Newsletter*, 15 (1981), 22–33. For an updated list of solutions, see Bernard J. Muir, ed., *The Exeter Anthology of Old English Poetry: An Edition of Exeter Dean and Chapter MS 3501*, 2nd edn, 2 vols (Exeter: University of Exeter Press, 2000), II, pp. 655–63 and 735–9. In *Isidorean Perceptions of Order*, pp. 291–8, Salvador-Bello makes a case for solving these riddles with not one but three answers relating to the natural phenomena described: the various storms, the speaker who provokes the phenomena (i.e. the wind), and, finally, the guiding and driving force behind the wind (i.e. God).

41 Williamson, *Old English Riddles*, p. 127.

Part III
Interactions

Introduction to Part III

Megan Cavell and Jennifer Neville

The riddles of early medieval England do not exist in a vacuum. They interact. Like other riddles, of course, they are the site of interaction between a riddler and a riddlee, but they also reveal points of contact with the world in which they were created and with which they still interact today. These interactions occur on many levels: between texts within one manuscript, between collections within an overall tradition, between genres/disciplines within an intellectual tradition, between material cultures separated by time and distance, and between poets during the translation process. In this context, comparative approaches are deeply rewarding. The chapters in this section thus seek to explore a small fraction of the interactions between early medieval English riddles and the wider world. Each of these chapters is unique and particular to itself, and we would not wish to reduce their multifarious approaches into a single, homogeneous one, but it is perhaps useful to consider them all as aspects of 'translation' in its most basic meaning of 'carrying across'. It is thus fitting that our collection ends with a chapter about creative translation.

Creative translation may indeed be seen as a comparative approach in its own right—one that insists on the coming together of two different cultural moments to create a new piece of art. The translation of early medieval English literature has a long legacy, and translation of the riddles in particular has played a prominent role. The past ten years have witnessed a creative renaissance, including volumes that bring multiple poets together in a communal translation project, those that focus our attention on individual collections which have been neglected for too long, and those that place creative translations alongside original compositions.[1] The act of translating is the act of interpretation, and it can spark new engagements with material that is otherwise distant in time and experience.

This phenomenon is, of course, nothing new. Even the very first scholars who engaged with the riddles of early medieval England recognised the interaction between Old English and Latin texts. The chapters here thus remind us that the riddles were a multilingual tradition that spanned global networks in the medieval world. At the same time, however, the chapters in this section also remind us that the riddles continue to interact with us now.

Note

1 See, for example, Greg Delanty, Seamus Heaney, and Michael Matto, eds, *The Word Exchange: Anglo-Saxon Poems in Translation* (New York: Norton, 2010); A. M. Juster, trans., *Saint Aldhelm's Riddles* (Toronto: University of Toronto Press, 2015); Miller Oberman, *The Unstill Ones: Poems* (Princeton: Princeton University Press, 2017).

12

The nursemaid, the mother, and the prostitute: tracing an insular riddle topos on both sides of the English Channel[1]

Mercedes Salvador-Bello

It is well known that riddling was particularly conspicuous as a literary genre in the British Isles. Indeed, riddles were much appreciated in monastic circles because their compact format conveniently favoured the teaching of Latin vocabulary, rhetoric, syntax, and metrics. Dating from about 686, Aldhelm's *Enigmata* constitute the earliest riddle collection produced in England that has come down to us. Following in Aldhelm's steps, Tatwine and Eusebius, both contemporary with Bede, took up the composition of a collection each.[2] In turn, an anonymous author produced a miscellany known as the *Collectanea Pseudo-Bedae* containing a variety of riddlic materials. Aldhelm's *Enigmata*, and probably also the collections by Tatwine and Eusebius, soon became part of the early medieval English school curriculum, which was eventually transferred to the continent through the work of missionaries such as Boniface, himself the author of a theological reflection on virtues and vices in the form of riddles.

With the disruption brought about by the Scandinavian invasion and progressive expansion in eastern England, this flowering of riddling was no doubt interrupted. Yet proof of its continuing success as a literary genre is found in the work of Alcuin and in the anthologising of the riddles of Aldhelm and other insular authors in continental manuscripts. Of uncertain origin and date, two further anonymous collections, the Bern and Lorsch *enigmata*, complete this notable corpus of riddles which circulated widely in the continent and have been related to scriptoria with insular connections.

In a nutshell, riddling has usually been assumed to be a literary genre that was exported from the British Isles to the continent. This was probably the case for Pseudo-Bede's *Collectanea*, which contains riddles of insular origin and has only survived in a printed copy from Basel.[3] This cultural transfer has thus been interpreted as a one-way phenomenon, disregarding the possibility of influence by continental riddling on insular collections. However, there are riddles of probable continental provenance, most notably the Bern *Enigmata*, which were no doubt known to early medieval English authors such as Aldhelm. This suggests we should pay attention to the exchange of riddles that took place on both sides of the English Channel, as I intend to do in this chapter. In order to illustrate how dynamic this cultural interplay was, I focus on a particular riddlic topos that seems to have been of special interest to insular authors: the personification of Wisdom as a nursemaid breastfeeding her numerous offspring.[4] Taking the *Sapientia* enigma found in Pseudo-Bede's *Collectanea* as a starting point, I analyse several versions of this motif, which probably has its roots in Hiberno-Latin literature. As this chapter aims to show, the *Sapientia* topos enjoyed popularity among insular authors who had learned it in their homeland but continued to use it after they migrated to the continent. Additionally, I wish to demonstrate that this well-known motif offers two other variants that occur in riddles dealing with subjects other than wisdom: the mother feeding her numerous children and the prostitute sharing food and wine with many men. In doing so, I can analyse these popular riddlic topoi in different versions that occur in both insular and continental manuscripts.

The *Sapientia* enigma

An early example of the nursemaid topos is offered in Pseudo-Bede's *Collectanea*.[5] In this florilegium of uncertain date,[6] Wisdom, the solution to the opening riddle, is described as follows: *Dic mihi, quaeso, quae est illa mulier, quae innumeris filiis ubera porrigit, quae quantum sucta fuerit, tantum inundat? Mulier ista est sapientia* ('Say to me, please, who is that woman who renders her breasts to [her] numerous sons, and just as much she is sucked, she abundantly flows? This woman is wisdom').[7] The clues play on the paradox that no matter how much human beings demand from Wisdom, they can always count on her extreme generosity, which will bring them plenty of intellectual and spiritual benefits. The fact that *Sapientia*, like virtues and vices, is a feminine noun in Latin could have triggered its personification as a nursemaid. As pointed out by Clare A. Lees and Gillian R. Overing, this grammatical gendering lies at the heart of the tradition of Prudentius's *Psychomachia*, in which vices and virtues are characterised as female figures.[8] After Prudentius, other authors continued to represent abstract qualities and concepts as female characters. In *De consolatione philosophiae*, Boethius, for example, refers to Philosophy as *uirtutum omnium nutrix* ('the nursemaid of all virtues').[9] In the Old English version of the same work, Wisdom, instead of Philosophy, is personified as Boethius's *fæstermodor* ('foster-mother').[10] Thus the characterisation of Wisdom as a nursemaid or a mother responds to a long-standing practice in Latin allegorical literature. The subject of the *Sapientia* enigma is therefore quite suitable for the beginning of the *Collectanea*, an assemblage providing diverse contents that can be ascribed to the wisdom-literature genre produced by monks targeting an aristocratic readership in the Carolingian period.[11]

As the *Collectanea* is only extant in a version of Bede's complete works from 1563, the loss of the medieval exemplar hypothetically used by printer Johann Herwagen has prevented scholarship from finding out information about the exact circumstances in which the contents of this florilegium were compiled.[12] Even though the varied materials of the *Collectanea* are difficult to date and trace geographically, Michael Lapidge has concluded that a good deal of them 'originated either in Ireland or England, or in an Irish foundation on the continent'.[13] The remarkable similarity between the *Sapientia* enigma and passages from Hiberno-Latin works has often been brought up by scholars to offer evidence for the insular connection of the *Collectanea*. The hyperbolic description of Wisdom breastfeeding her numberless offspring, as described in *Enigma 1* of the *Collectanea*, for example, closely resembles an excerpt found in the *Epitomae* by Virgilius Maro Grammaticus, an author of probable Irish origin who flourished around the mid-seventh century. The passage in question reads: *Quae est mulier illa, o fili, quae ubera sua innumeris filiis porregit, quae quantum suxa fuerint, tantum in ea inundant? Hoc est sapientia* ('Who, my son, is that woman who offers her breasts to countless offspring, and no matter how much they are sucked, they flow just as richly? That is wisdom').[14] As pointed out by Damian Bracken, a further excerpt from the biblical commentary written by Scottus Anonymous in the 640s suggests that this other Irish author knew about this topos, as he provided the following sentence: *Larga ubera sapientiae conspicite* ('Observe the plentiful breasts of wisdom').[15] The motif is also found in a passage from the *Collectaneum miscellaneum* by Sedulius Scottus, an Irish poet and grammarian who was active on the continent between 840 and 860. The phrasing offered by Sedulius is practically identical with that used by Virgilius in the passage quoted above: *Quae sit mulier illa quae ubera sua innumeris filiis porrigit; quae quantum suxa fuerint, tantum inundant? Mulier ista sapientia est* ('Who is that woman who offers her breasts to numberless sons, and, however much they are sucked, they overflow the same? This woman is wisdom').[16] Additionally, a gloss to an excerpt offered in *The Colloquy of the Two Sages*[17] and a parallel phrasing found in a hagiography of St Berach clearly associate the *Sapientia* topos with Irish literature.[18]

There is therefore sufficient evidence to suggest that the *Sapientia* enigma of the *Collectanea* could be of Irish stock. This idea also finds support in the fact that Aldhelm employs this metaphor in his letter to Heahfrith, celebrating his colleague's return from Hibernia after a six-year period of study there:

> Postquam vestram repedantem istuc ambrosiam ex Hiberniae brumosis circionis insulae climatibus, ubi ter bino circiter annorum circulo uber sofiae sugens metabatur, territorii marginem Britannici sospitem applicuisse.
>
> [after we learned from the reports of talebearers that your Ambrosia (i.e. your Wisdom), returning hither from the wintry regions of the north-west part of the island of Ireland—where it encamped for a course of thrice-two years sucking the teat of wisdom—embraced the shore of British territory safe and sound.][19]

This passage thus alludes to the knowledge that Heahfrith has acquired on this visit by 'sucking from the teat of wisdom' (*uber sofiae sugens*), a phrase that is undeniably reminiscent of the *Sapientia* motif.

This literary topos therefore most likely originated in Ireland and from there soon travelled to England with authors like Aldhelm. Eventually, it also made a leap across the English Channel thanks to writers such as Sedulius Scottus. Probably as part of an insular corpus of riddles, the *Sapientia* enigma might have similarly journeyed to the continent at an early stage. Evidence of this is the fact that the *Collectanea* shares numerous features with riddling dialogues such as the *Ioca monachorum*, which occurs in several continental codices, some of them with demonstrable insular links.[20] A copy of the *Ioca monachorum*, which is extant in St Gall, Stiftsbibliothek, Cod. Sang. 196 (second third of the ninth century)—a manuscript produced at that same monastery[21]—is of special interest for this study.[22] This text contains a close analogue of the *Sapientia* enigma offered in the *Collectanea*: *Quae est mulier quae multis filiis ubera porrigit, et quantum plus sugerint, tanto amplius redundabit? Sapientia* ('Who is the woman who offers her breasts to [her] many sons, and the more they suck, the more liberally she will overflow? Wisdom').[23] Even though this riddle has not been preserved in any other manuscript containing the *Ioca monachorum*, its occurrence in the St Gall codex proves that popular insular pieces such as the *Sapientia* enigma were transferred to the other side of the English Channel.[24]

The nursemaid topos can also be found in the enigma on Wisdom (*De sapientia*) introducing the series of twelve riddles known as *Bibliotheca magnifica*. This anonymous collection is uniquely preserved in Cambridge, University Library, Gg.5.35 (fols 423v–425r), a mid-eleventh-century manuscript from St Augustine's, Canterbury; some of the contents of this codex denote continental links.[25] In the opening poem of the *Bibliotheca magnifica*, Wisdom is described as follows:

> Terna mihi est species, oculi tot fronte sub una,
> ubera tot niveo pectore sacra tument.
> totque meo latices turgent de ventre manantes,
> lota sophistarum pro quib … quis … nitet. (7–10)[26]
>
> [My appearance is threefold, with as many eyes under just one forehead, with as many sacred breasts swelling on my snowy chest, with as many flowing springs coming out from my belly, bathed on behalf of those of the wise ones … anyone … shines].

Even if the last line is partially illegible in the manuscript, this excerpt evidently partakes of some of the key elements of the *Sapientia* topos. As observed in the poem, Wisdom's multiple and bountiful breasts are capable of satisfying wise men. Apart from this, the text betrays a knowledge of Aldhelm's *Enigma 97, Nox* ('night') (12–16), in which fame, a sister of night, is depicted by means of a quotation from Virgil's *Aeneid* as a monstrous creature with many feathers, tongues, mouths and eyes.[27]

The combined formula obviously fascinated the author of the *Bibliotheca magnifica*, since the *Sapientia* topos merges with Aldhelmian/Virgilian components in three other riddles of the series. As seen in Table 12.1, the basic rhetorical elements offered in the initial Wisdom enigma are thus reproduced with minor variations.

Leaving enigmatic texts aside, the *Sapientia* topos also occurs in the literary production of insular writers, who may have served as vehicles disseminating this motif on the continent. For example, a passage from Alcuin's *Carmen 32* clearly borrows from it when addressing Corydon, a truant student who has been led astray by

Table 12.1 Wisdom's breasts

De physica **(no. 2, ll. 19–20)**	***De arithmetica*** **(no. 3, ll. 25–6)**	***De musica*** **(no. 5, ll. 39–40)**
Inque meo turgent niveo tot pectore mammæ, / tot quibus æterno fonte fluenta manant. [On my snowy chest swell so many udders, of which, eternal fountain, (just) as many streams flow.]	*Bina patet species duplici sub fronte tot ora, / ubera tot niveo pectore sacra tument.* [A dual appearance (with) as many mouths show under a double forehead, with as many sacred udders on a snowy chest.]	*Sunt mini tres miræ species, sunt lumina trina, / ubera tot niveo pectore sacra tument.* [I have three wonderful forms, I have three eyes and as many sacred udders swelling on my snowy chest.]

drunkenness: *sophiae libros primis lac ore sub annis / suxisti et labris ubera sacra tuis* ('in your first years, (you) sucked with your mouth the milk of the books of Wisdom, from her sacred breasts, with your lips') (7–8).[28] By making a pleonastic reference to both the mouth (*ore*) and the lips (*labris*), Alcuin personifies Wisdom as the traditional breastfeeding figure, thus reminding Corydon of his debt to the monastery that provided his educational training through books, just as his mother provided his first food. The passage is also noteworthy because it alludes to Wisdom's 'holy breasts' (*ubera sacra*), a phrase that occurs in the *Sapientia* enigma from the *Bibliotheca magnifica* and the other two riddles of the same collection.[29]

Similarly, Sedulius Scottus, whose *Collectaneum* was mentioned above to illustrate a parallel to *Enigma 1* of Pseudo-Bede's *Collectanea*, made use of the *Sapientia* topos once more in his *Carmen 72*:

> duce grammatica vos ars cornupeta fandi
> protegat et scuto sacra Sophia suo;
> cuius suxistis teneris vos ubera labris. (3–5)[30]

> [with Grammar as your guide, may the thrusting art of speaking protect you and Wisdom (do the same) with her shield; (wisdom), from whose sacred teats you sucked with your tender lips.]

Sedulius thus urges his fellow brethren to let their lives be ruled by both Grammar and Wisdom. As in Alcuin's *Carmen 32*, the presence of *sacra ... ubera* in Sedulius's excerpt recalls one of the recurrent phrases offered in three of the riddles (nos 1, 3 and 5) of the *Bibliotheca magnifica* dealt with above. What becomes clear from this discussion is that the *Sapientia* topos was deeply rooted among insular writers who later refashioned it into multiple forms, as observed in the literary production of Alcuin and Sedulius on the continent.

The variants of the *Sapientia* enigma

The nursemaid topos as found in the *Sapientia* enigma from Pseudo-Bede's *Collectanea* evolved from its original form and merged with other motifs, as has already been illustrated with the Aldhelmian/Virgilian echoes found in some of the riddles of the *Bibliotheca magnifica*. These processes of adaptation and reformulation can be observed in further riddle collections focusing on subjects other than wisdom. An interesting example is found in Aldhelm's *Enigma 1, Terra* ('land'), in which the land is personified as a nursemaid, whose generous services are unjustly rewarded, since her breasts are badly injured by the toothed infants she feeds:

> Altrix cunctorum, quos mundus gestat, in orbe
> nuncupor (et merito, quia numquam pignora tantum
> inproba sic lacerant maternas dente papillas). (1–3)[31]

> [(I am) the nursemaid of all (the creatures), which the world sustains in this sphere; I am called so (i.e. 'nursemaid') appropriately, for disloyal children never cut their mother's nipples thus with their teeth.]

The clues metaphorically compare the painful cracks typically produced by intense breastfeeding with the furrows made in the land by human beings when ploughing.

A variant of the nursemaid motif discussed in the preceding section is that of the mother mistreated by her own children. A good illustration of this is Eusebius's *Enigma 6, Terra* ('land'):

> Quos alo nascentes, crescentes scindor ab illis,
> pascunturque bonis etsi me calce subigunt;
> unde seducam nunc multos et supprimo natos,
> nam perdent quod amant et nulli morte carebunt.[32]

> [I am torn apart by those whom I feed, as they are born and grow up, and are fed with good things, although they conquer me (literally, have put me under their feet). For this reason I now seduce (lead astray) and crush (literally, push down in the dirt) many of my newly-born, since they will lose what they love (i.e. their life) and none will dodge death.]

If compared to Aldhelm's *Enigma 1*, the clues of Eusebius's riddle offer a distant echo of the nursemaid motif, as the land is said to feed human beings generously: *alo* and *pascunturque bonis* (1, 2). *Enigma 6* by Eusebius also presents an interesting twist that is absent in Aldhelm's counterpart: the bountiful mother is transformed from a victim into a sort of murderess, who vindictively leads astray many of her own children and ends up burying them. The underlying idea is that of the reversal of roles, which is at the heart of the paradox offered in the text: the children turn powerful as they become adults, but the mother subdues them as they grow old.

The nursemaid topos is detected more clearly in one of the pieces from the Bern *Enigmata*, a collection which has only been preserved in continental codices although evidence of a possible connection to early medieval England has been often been pointed out by scholars.[33] Bern *Enigma 5, Mensa* ('table'), which is worth citing in full, offers an interesting version of this motif.

> Pulchra mater ego natos dum collego multos,
> cunctis trado libens, quicquid in pectore gesto.
> Nulli sicut mihi pro bonis mala redduntur.
> Oscula nam mihi prius qui cara dederunt,
> Vestibus exutam turpi me modo relinquunt.
> Quos lactaui, nudam me pede per angula uersant.[34]

> [While I, a beautiful mother, gather together my many children, I gladly give away everything I carry in my chest. No one is paid back good deeds with evil like me, since those who previously gave me loving kisses abandon me in a shameful way, stripping me of my clothes. Those whom I nursed turn my leg(s) upside down, (leaving) me naked in a corner].[35]

This text clearly uses the nursemaid topos as a starting point, as can be inferred from the personification of the table as a devoted mother who lovingly feeds her numerous children and provides them with all she has in her chest, thus implying the idea of breast-feeding that is later explicitly named with the word *lactaui* (6). The description therefore recalls the maternal characterisation of the earth in Aldhelm's *Enigma 1*, since Bern *Enigma 5* equally alludes to how the ungrateful children (the diners) treat the mother most unkindly—i.e. they take the cloth off, leaving the table *nudata* (6), 'naked', and then dismantle it—once they have finished having their meal. The reference to the progeny's cruel behaviour also evokes Eusebius's *Enigma 6*, which similarly characterises the earth as a victim of human beings. However, when compared to the other two earth riddles by Aldhelm and Eusebius, the nursemaid motif in Bern *Enigma 5* clearly takes a dramatic turn, since the *double-entendre* clues alluding to the removal of the cloth and the disassembling of the leg are shockingly suggestive of domestic rape and incest.[36]

A further version of the nursemaid theme is Tatwine's *Enigma 29, Mensa* ('table'), which rehearses the essential paradox found in the Bern riddle on the same subject:

> Multiferis omnes dapibus saturare solesco;
> quadripedem hinc felix ditem me sanxerat aetas
> esse, tamen pulchris fatim dum uestibus orner,
> certatim me predones spoliare solescunt,
> raptis nudata exuuiis mox membra relinquunt.[37]
>
> [I am used to satisfying all with plentiful meals; for this reason happy age ordained (that I should be) four-legged and sumptuous. However, when I am sufficiently adorned with beautiful clothes, thieves usually strip me eagerly (and), as soon as my booty has been plundered, they leave my naked limbs behind].

The table in this text is said to be able to feed many people, an idea that is typical of the nursemaid topos. As in Bern *Enigma 5*, the clues of Tatwine's riddle play on the paradox that such generous behaviour is unjustly rewarded, for the thieves, the metaphorical guests, devour everything that is found on the table and later treat the motherly figure (the table) in a shameful way by removing its cloth and disassembling it. These notable rhetorical affinities add to the striking verbal echoes observed in the two table riddles, which are worth comparing (see Table 12.2).[38]

The similarities are no doubt remarkable. But Tatwine's composition also clearly offers a significant rhetorical twist in the handling of the nursemaid topos, since the clues suggest the idea of

Table 12.2 Nursemaid as prostitute

Bern *Enigma 5*, ll. 5, 3, 6	**Tatwine's *Enigma 29*, ll. 3–5**
Vestibus exutam turpi me modo **relinquunt**;	Esse, tamen pulchris fatim dum **uestibus** orner.
Nulli sicut mihi pro bonis mala redduntur:	Certatim me predones spoliare solescunt,
Quos lactaui, **nudam** me pede per angula uersant.	Raptis **nudata exuuiis** mox membra **relinquunt**.

a richly dressed woman—*ditem* and *pulchris* … *uestibus orner* (2, 3)—whose custom is to satisfy everyone—*omnes* … *saturare solesco* (1)—with abundant meals—*Multiferis* … *dapibus* (1). That is, the generous woman becomes a prostitute rather than a nursemaid.[39] Nonetheless, the basic paradox offered by Bern *Enigma 5* is maintained: the woman who graciously shared her food with everyone is stripped of her clothes—*nudata* (5)—in a violent way by thieves. However, by characterising the table as a prostitute, whose previous services have been most unfairly repaid by her former customers,[40] Tatwine's *Enigma 29* is clearly offering a sophisticated variant of the nursemaid metaphor found in Bern *Enigma 5*, which in turn derives from the *Sapientia* topos.

Conclusions

The nursemaid metaphor and the closely related variants of the mother and the prostitute have therefore helped illustrate how intense the exchange of riddlic materials was on the two sides of the English Channel. From what we have seen so far it seems quite clear that the *Sapientia* topos travelled possibly from Ireland to England—as we can infer from Aldhelm's use of it in his letter to Heahfrith. From there the motif was carried to the continent. The initial riddle offered by the *Collectanea*, which ended up in an early modern copy from Basel, and the analogue found in the version of the *Ioca monachorum* found in the St Gall manuscript also seem to corroborate this hypothesis. Furthermore, the presence of the nursemaid metaphor in the *Carmina* by Alcuin and Sedulius Scottus suggests that this motif was well known among insular authors who had settled on the continent and who probably continued to propagate it. On the other hand, the *Sapientia* enigma occurring in the *Bibliotheca magnifica* extant in a manuscript of English origin similarly implies the knowledge of this riddle in England either through English sources or, alternatively, through continental transfer, as happened with other native works which had been lost in the aftermath of the Scandinavian invasions.[41]

The nursemaid topos eventually developed into the more complex motif of the unfairly rewarded mother, as illustrated in Aldhelm's and Eusebius's riddles on the earth, as well as in Bern *Enigma 5, Mensa* ('table'). The latter enigma no doubt inspired Tatwine's *Enigma 29, Mensa* ('table'), whose notable resemblance to the Bern riddle has served to exemplify the close ties between early medieval English and continental riddling, as well as to illuminate the transition from the nursemaid motif to the prostitute variant. Finally, the striking verbal and rhetorical parallels between these texts evince an active cultural interaction which can only be explained if we assume that there was an intense traffic of literary materials between the two sides of the English Channel.

Notes

1 An earlier version of this chapter was presented at the International Medieval Congress (Leeds, 2014). I must thank the organisers of the riddles sessions in that conference, Jennifer Neville and Megan Cavell, for having invited me to one of these panels and for providing many insightful comments for this chapter. My thanks also go to Mar Gutiérrez-Ortiz for her invaluable feedback on the Latin passages quoted in this chapter.

2 For the notable influence exerted by Aldhelm on later writers, see Christine E. Fell, 'Some Implications of the Boniface Correspondence', in *New Readings on Women in Old English Literature*, ed. Helen Damico and Alexandra Hennessey Olsen (Bloomington: Indiana University Press, 1990), pp. 29–43.

3 For example, five of Aldhelm's riddles are included in the *Collectanea*. These correspond to numbers 103, 200, 242, 243, and 244 of the latter work. See Martha Bayless and Michael Lapidge, eds and trans, *Collectanea Pseudo-Bedae* (Dublin: Institute for Advanced Studies, 1998), p. 4.

4 For further discussion of the personification of Wisdom as a woman, see Dale, Chapter 10 in this collection.

5 Entitled *Excerptiones patrum, collectanea, flores ex diversis, quaestiones et parabolae*, this work is found in Johann [the Younger] Herwagen, *Opera Bedae Venerabilis presbyteri Anglo-Saxonis*, 8 vols (Basel, 1563), III, pp. 647–74. It has been edited with an English translation in Bayless and Lapidge, *Collectanea Pseudo-Bedae.* See also Frederick Tupper, 'Riddles of the Bede Tradition: The "Flores" of Pseudo-Bede', *MP*, 2 (1904), 561–72, at pp. 561–5.

6 Lapidge concludes that 'the majority of its datable contents are most plausibly assigned to the middle decades of the eighth century'. Bayless and Lapidge, *Collectanea Pseudo-Bedae*, p. 12. See also Daniel Anlezark, ed., *The Old English Dialogues of Solomon and Saturn* (Cambridge: D. S. Brewer, 2009), p. 16.

7 Text from Bayless and Lapidge, *Collectanea Pseudo-Bedae*, p. 122.

8 Clare A. Lees and Gillian R. Overing, *Double Agents: Women and Clerical Culture in Anglo-Saxon England* (Philadelphia: University of Pennsylvania Press, 2001), pp. 154–5. See also the discussion of grammatical gender by Cavell, Wilcox, and Dale in Chapters 3, 7, and 10 of this volume.

9 Quoted from Claudio Moreschini, ed., *De consolatione philosophiae: Opuscula theologica* (Munich: Saur, 2005), bk 2, prose 4, p. 36. A Boethian echo may be perceived in Boniface's *Enigmata* when he refers to patience as *altrix virtutum* ('the nursemaid of virtues') (l. 9). From his *Enigmata: De virtutibus* (no. 7, 'De patientia'), quoted from Fr. Glorie, ed., *Collectiones Aenigmatum Merovingicae Aetatis*, CCSL, 133–133A (Turnhout: Brepols, 1968), 133, p. 295. Boniface probably borrowed the term *altrix* from Aldhelm's *Enigma 1* (see further discussion later in this chapter. Later in the same work, Boniface employs the same metaphor to characterise *ignorantia* as the antithesis of Wisdom, thus referring to the former as *nutrix errorum* ('the nursemaid of errors') (l. 1). From his *Enigmata: De vitiis* (no. 9, 'De ignorantia'), Glorie, *Collectiones Aenigmatum*, 133, p. 339.

10 For this passage, see Malcolm R. Godden and Susan Irvine, ed. and trans., *The Old English Boethius with Verse Prologues and Epilogues Associated with King Alfred*, Dumbarton Oaks Medieval Library (Cambridge, MA: Harvard University Press, 2012), bk 1, prose 2, pp. 12–13. For the keen concern with fosterage in early medieval England and its reflection in *Mec Deadne Ofgeafun* (R.9), see Jennifer Neville, 'Fostering the Cuckoo: Exeter Book Riddle 9', *RES*, 58 (2007), 431–46.

11 On this idea, see Anlezark, *Old English Dialogues*, p. 16.

12 See Bayless and Lapidge, *Collectanea Pseudo-Bedae*, pp. 77–83, for the hypothesis that Herwagen's version of the *Collectanea* possibly derives from a medieval exemplar produced in southern Germany.

13 Bayless and Lapidge, *Collectanea Pseudo-Bedae*, p. 12.

14 Quoted in Giovanni Polara and Luciano Caruso, eds, *Virgilio Marone Grammatico: Epitomi ed Epistole* (Naples: Liguori, 1979), 15.1.2, p. 162. Translation from Vivian Law, *Wisdom, Authority and Grammar in the Seventh Century: Decoding Virgilius Maro Grammaticus* (Cambridge: Cambridge University Press, 1995), p. 33.

15 Quoted in Damian Bracken, 'Virgilius Grammaticus and the Earliest Hiberno-Latin Literature', in *Ogma: Essays in Celtic Studies in Honour of Próinséas Ní Chatháin*, ed. Michael Richter and Jean-Michel Picard (Dublin: Four Courts, 2002), pp. 251–61, at p. 260.

16 Quoted in D. Simpson, ed., *Sedulius Scottus, Collectaneum miscellaneum*, Corpus Christianorum Continuatio Mediaevalis, 67 (Turnhout: Brepols, 1988), 2.1, p. 10.

17 This work is also known as *Immacallam in dá Thuarad* and is contained in the twelfth-century Book of Leinster—Dublin, Trinity College, MS H 2.18 (cat. 1339). For the text of this gloss, see Bayless and Lapidge, *Collectanea Pseudo-Bedae*, p. 199.

18 Bayless and Lapidge, *Collectanea Pseudo-Bedae*, p. 199.

19 Edition and translation from Aldhelm, *Aldhelmi opera*, ed. Rudolph Ehwald, MGH, Auctores Antiquissimi, 15 (Berlin: Weidmann, 1919),

p. 489; Aldhelm, *Aldhelm: The Prose Works*, trans. Michael Lapidge and Michael Herren (Cambridge: D. S. Brewer, 2009), p. 161, no. 5. Parenthetical reference as found in the latter text.

20 See Bayless and Lapidge, *Collectanea Pseudo-Bedae*, pp. 14–18.

21 It is well-known that St Gall was an Irish foundation that benefited from its strategic location on the customary route for pilgrims travelling from the British Isles to Rome. On this, see Bernhard Bischoff, *Manuscripts and Libraries in the Age of Charlemagne*, trans. Michael Gorman (Cambridge: Cambridge University Press, 1994), p. 13.

22 In this codex, this series of riddles occurs under the heading *Enigmata interrogatiua* (p. 388). For access to the digitised version, see https://www.e-codices.unifr.ch/en/csg/0196/388/0/Sequence-382 (accessed 6 February 2019).

23 Text from Walther Suchier, ed., *Das mittellateinische Gespräch Adrian und Epictitus und verwandten Texten (Joca Monachorum)* (Tübingen: Niemeyer, 1955), p. 123, no. 13.

24 It is worth mentioning that the St Gall manuscript (p. 389) contains three further pieces, occurring with the title *Item enigmata vulgaria*, which betray some notable common features with three other riddles from the *Collectanea* (nos 18, 197 and 198). For further information on this, see Bayless and Lapidge, *Collectanea Pseudo-Bedae*, p. 206; Mercedes Salvador-Bello, *Isidorean Perceptions of Order: The Exeter Book Riddles and Medieval Latin Enigmata* (Morgantown: West Virginia University Press, 2015), pp. 48–9 and 266.

25 This manuscript includes the famous *Cambridge Songs*, which were probably assembled in Germany, as well as some other poems of French provenance. See Jan M. Ziolkowski, ed. and trans., *The Cambridge Songs (Carmina Cantabrigensia)* (New York: Garland, 1994), pp. xxxii–xxxvii.

26 Quoted in J. A. Giles, ed., *Anecdota Bedae, Lanfranci, et aliorum: Inedited tracts, letters, poems, & c. of Venerable Bede, Lanfranc, Tatwin, and others* (London: D. Nutt, 1851), p. 50. I have changed MS *pectora*, as maintained in this edition, for *pectore* (8), since this noun should agree with adjective *niveo*, an ablative singular case. An edition of the *Bibliotheca magnifica* will soon appear in Andy Orchard, ed. and trans., *The Anglo-Saxon Riddle Tradition*, Dumbarton Oaks Medieval Library (Cambridge, MA: Harvard University Press, forthcoming).

27 For Aldhelm's *Enigma 97*, see Glorie, *Collectiones Aenigmatum*, 133A, p. 523. For Aldhelm's source, see Virgil, *Eclogues, Georgics, Aeneid: Books 1–6*, trans. H. Rushton Fairclough, rev. G. P. Goold, Loeb Classical Library, 63 (Cambridge, MA: Harvard University Press, 1916), 4.177 and 181–4.

28 Alcuin, 'Carmen 32', in *Poetae Latini Aevi Carolini*, 1, ed. Ernst Dümmler, MGH (Berlin: Weidmann, 1881), pp. 249–50.

29 Cf. numbers 1, 3 and 5 of the *Bibliotheca magnifica* (as discussed above).

30 Text from Sedulius Scottus, 'Carmen 72', in *Poetae Latini Aevi Carolini*, 3, ed. Ludwig Traube, MGH (Berlin: Weidmann, 1896), p. 224. Cf. *labris* (8) in Alcuin's 'Carmen 32' above.

31 Quoted in Glorie, *Collectiones Aenigmatum,* 133A, p. 383.

32 Quoted in Glorie, *Collectiones Aenigmatum,* 133A, p. 216. But I have preferred McDonald Willliams' *etsi* to Glorie's *et si* (2). See Mary Jane McDonald Williams, 'The Riddles of Tatwine and Eusebius' (unpublished PhD dissertation, University of Michigan, 1974), p. 163.

33 The exact date and provenance have not yet been firmly determined for this collection of riddles. For a summary of various scholarly views on this issue, see Salvador-Bello, *Isidorean Perceptions of Order*, pp. 255–6.

34 Quoted in Franz Buecheler and Alexander Riese, eds, *Anthologia latina: sive poesis latinae supplementum*, 3 vols in 5 (Leipzig: Teubner, 1894–1926), vol. I, part 1, p. 352. For Bern *Enigma 5*, I have preferred this edition to that found in Glorie, *Collectiones Aenigmatum*, 133, p. 551, because the order of the lines provided by the former editors makes better sense. Note that lines 3 and 4 in Buecheler and Riese's text correspond to lines 5 and 3 in Glorie's edition.

35 This description obviously implies a one-legged removable table, in which the leg (*pede*) (6) and board could be disassembled. Note that I have provided a translation of *pede*, ablative singular meaning 'foot', as plural 'leg[s]' for the convenience of the PDE translation and the intended sexual innuendo.

36 For a study of sexual clues in Latin riddles, see Mercedes Salvador-Bello, 'The Sexual Riddle Type in Aldhelm's *Enigmata*, the Exeter Book, and Early Medieval Latin', *PQ*, 90 (2011), 357–85.

37 Quoted in Glorie, *Collectiones Aenigmatum*, 133A, p. 196. Like McDonald Williams, 'Riddles of Tatwine and Eusebius', p. 144, I have supplied a comma after *orner* instead of a period, as in Glorie's edition.

38 Bold letters are used here to highlight major parallelisms. Some of these correspondences have already been pointed out by Glorie, *Collectiones Aenigmatum*, 133A, p. 551 and McDonald Williams, 'Riddles of Tatwine and Eusebius', p. 144.

39 The prostitute metaphor proved to be particularly successful, as can be ascertained from its occurrence in Aldhelm's *Enigma 80* (glass goblet). In this enigma, as well as in *Glæd mid Golde* (R.63), the goblet is personified as an alluring prostitute causing men's ruin due to her seductive stratagems (and alcohol). For further comments on this, see Salvador-Bello, 'Sexual Riddle Type', pp. 370–1, and *Isidorean Perceptions of Order*, pp. 210–11. In fact, almost all the riddles concerning wine—as well as associated subjects such as vine (Bern *Enigma*

13), goblet (Bern *Enigma 6*, Lorsch *Enigma 5*), and wine cask (Aldhelm *Enigma 78*)—in some way or another touch on the prostitute metaphor and display similar clues.

40 For the sexual overtones found in this riddle, see Salvador-Bello, 'Sexual Riddle Type', p. 364.

41 It is well-known that lost works by insular authors such as Aldhelm were brought back to England thanks to their having been preserved in continental monasteries. See, for example, Aldhelm, *Aldhelm: The Prose Works*, ed. Lapidge and Herren, p. 2: 'At this time [in the tenth century] many manuscripts of Aldhelm's works were imported into England from the continent'.

13

The moon and stars in the Bern and Eusebius riddles

Neville Mogford

De divisionibus temporum, a work of Irish origins from the Sirmond collection of computistica, describes a unit of time known as the atom thus:

> Quicquid minimum est in corporibus, quod secari aut dividi non potest, athomus dicitur, veluti sunt minutissimima grana arenarum, ut Capillus dixit: 'Findere me nulli possunt, praecidere multi'.[1]

> [Whatever is smallest in shape, and which cannot be cut up or divided, is called the atom, just like the smallest grains of sand, and just as *capillus* said: 'None can split me; many can cut me off'.]

The wording *findere me nulli possunt* is taken from a riddle, Symphosius' *Enigma 58*, *Capillus* ('hair'). It is possible that the author mistakenly attributed authorship of the riddle to a certain Capillus, but it seems more likely that the 'attribution' is itself playfully prosopopoeiac: 'just as the *hair* said'. If the latter is the correct interpretation, then it seems that the computist has cleverly reversed the primary and secondary senses of the riddle: rather than a hair pretending to be an atom, we have an atom pretending to be a hair. Of course, to get the joke, we must already know that it is a riddle and understand the principle of indivisible units. This use of a riddle to enliven a difficult concept from computus is not unique, although the relationship between computus and riddles has rarely been studied. In fact, several early medieval riddle collections include original *enigmata* on computistical or astronomical subjects. Why riddles were considered as an appropriate medium for communicating these subjects, and how these riddles fit into the tradition inherited from Symphosius, are the central questions of this chapter.

Three major riddle collections—or four, if we count the *Exeter Book* riddles—take great delight in describing various astronomical objects related to time-reckoning and chronometry, such as the moon, stars, and planets: the *Enigmata* of Aldhelm and Eusebius, and the Bern riddles. All three were written between the beginning of the seventh century and the first half of the eighth, a period in which Irish-authored computistica proliferated widely across early medieval England and the Frankish and Lombard kingdoms. The Bern collection includes sixty-three riddles, thirty-nine of which appear in their earliest form in a late eighth-century composite manuscript (Bern Burgerbibliothek, Cod. 611). They are usually considered to be anonymous, although a slightly later, Veronese manuscript (Berlin, Staatsbibliothek, Phillipps 1825) attributes them to a mysterious 'Tullius', about whom nothing more is known. Scholarly consensus is that they were probably composed in northern Italy during the seventh or eighth centuries.[2] The forty riddles of Eusebius were added to a collection of sixty riddles authored by Tatwine, the eighth-century archbishop and grammarian. Tatwine's collection is largely concerned with theological subjects and tools, and gives little attention to the themes of astronomy and timekeeping,[3] whereas his successor is more interested in animals, cosmology, and other aspects of natural science. Eusebius' real-world identity may well have been that of Hwætberht, the learned abbot of Monkwearmouth–Jarrow to whom Bede dedicated his masterpiece of computistic science, *De temporum ratione*.[4] For reasons of space, only Bern and Eusebius are discussed here, but it should be noted that Aldhelm's riddles also frequently refer to astral subjects; five have the fixed stars or planets as their direct subject (nos 8, 48, 53, 58, and 81), and another five refer to them (nos 37, 73, 86, 92, and 100), with an additional reference to Venus as the Morning Star in the proem.

Although the moon, stars, and planets are widely found in medieval riddling, Symphosius passes over them in near silence. References to the sun and the diurnal cycle appear very frequently in Symphosius, perhaps as a consequence of their Saturnalian context, but the fixed stars, planets and moon are absent as lemmata, and are only present in three minor, incidental references. As a result, Symphosius cannot be considered as the source for non-solar astronomical references made by his medieval successors, and so there is good reason to regard any such references as either wholly indigenous medieval creations or originating from sources other than Symphosius' work. Yet his influence on both the form and the content of these riddles should not be underestimated. For example, familial relations are a recurring trope not only in Symphosius, but also in the computistic riddles of Bern and

Eusebius. Symphosius describes parental relations in eight riddles (nos 14, 15, 29, 36, 37, 53, 79, and 81), and marital and sibling relations in two riddles apiece (nos. 38 and 53; 82 and 86). Parental relations are typically used to denote literal parentage (e.g. the mule is *dissimilis matri* ('unlike my mother') (1)),[5] marital relations are used only in negative constructions (e.g. the vine tells us that *nolo toro iungi* ('I do not want to be married') (1)),[6] and sibling relations are always used to describe the relationship between identical objects as one of siblings (e.g. the four wheels of a cart are *quattor aequales ... sorores* ('four identical sisters') (1)).[7] Although these three types of relationship are different, they all represent simple equivalence. But the same cannot always be said about their medieval descendants, as we shall see.

The Bern riddles

An example of the sibling trope, Symphosius' *Enigma 86*, *Perna* ('Ham') describes the relationship between two ham-cuts in terms of straightforward equivalence, by stating *una mihi soror est* ('I have one sister') (2).[8] This formula finds itself reworked in the opening line of Bern's *Enigma 56*, *De sole* ('On the sun') as an incestuous relationship between the sun and the moon:

> Una mihi soror est, unus et ego sorori.
> Coniux illa mihi, huius et ego maritus.
> Nam numquam uno sed multorum coniungimur ambo,
> Sed de longe meam praegnantem reddo sororem.
> Quotquot illa suo gignit ex utero partus,
> Cunctos uno reddo tectos de peplo nepotes.[9]

> [I have one sister, and my sister has one of me. She is my wife, and I am her husband; but we are never married, but rather are separated. And from afar I render my sister pregnant: no matter how many children she produces, born from her belly, I return them all, covered with a single robe.]

The borrowing seems at least partly designed as a compositional exercise, used to display the dative of possession, a grammatical form that the Bern riddler clearly favoured. But the similarities to Symphosius' riddle end here, for the original's mildly amusing, but asexual, banquet has been replaced by a risqué narrative of luni-solar incest. Most intriguing of all is the reference to moonlight as pregnancy in line 4. Expressions which describe the full moon in terms of birth, such as *luna nata est*, are frequently encountered in Latin literature of all periods and genres, and they are entirely conventional. That the moon and sun are *numquam uno ... coniungimur* ('never married') confirms that it is the full moon that is intended here, since this is the one lunar phase that is always nocturnal. But in this instance the 'pregnant moon' conceit has been extended to include the idea that the sun's light 'impregnates' the moon's illumination from a distance, culminating in the odd image of lunar midwifery in lines 5–6. Minst takes the *nepotes* ('children') of this relationship to be the night, whom the sun transforms with its 'cloak of light' into the day,[10] but this explanation is tenuous. More convincing is the idea that they are the months, which are spawned monthly from the pregnant (i.e. full) moon, only to be kept *cunctos ... tectos* ('covered together') within the *uno ... peplo* ('single robe') of the solar year. The implication is that the sun is covering up their progeny to hide their illicit sexual relationship. But why should the luni-solar calendar be described as deviant? Let us compare it to a much older classical riddle, ascribed to Cleobulus of Lindos by Diogenes Laertius, which also describes the calendar as a familial relationship.

> εἷς ὁ πατήρ, παῖδες δυοκαίδεκα. τῶν δὲ ἑκάστῳ
> παῖδες δὶς τριάκοντα διάνδιχα εἶδος ἔχουσαι·
> αἱ μὲν λευκαὶ ἔασιν ἰδεῖν, αἱ δ' αὖτε μέλαιναι·
> ἀθάνατοι δέ τ' ἐοῦσαι, ἀποφθινύθουσιν ἅπασαι.[11]

> [One sire there is, he has twelve sons, and each of these has twice thirty daughters different in feature; some of the daughters are white, the others again are black; they are immortal, and yet they all die.]

In Cleobulus' riddle, the solution, 'year', is expressed as a straightforward and ideal 360-day lunar year, in which every month is thirty days in length. Consequentially, familial relations here are equally straightforward, and are represented by the ideal of a harmonious classical *oikos* of equal days and nights. On the contrary, the author of Bern's *Enigma 56* appears to be conscious of the difficulties of integrating the two calendars—a problem which gave birth to the medieval science of computus—and thus represents the relationship of the sun and moon as a much more problematic and atypical one.

The second moon riddle, Bern's *Enigma 59*, *De lune* ('On the moon'), begins by referring to a *gressus*, an imperceptible difference between two adjacent points in time.

> Quo modo vehar gressu nullus agnoscere,
> cernere nec vultus per diem signa valebit.

Cotidie currens vias perambulo multas
et bis iterato cunctas recurro per annum.
Imber, nix, pruina, glacies nec fulgora nocent,
timeo nec ventum forti testudine tecta.

[I can be moved in such an increment that nobody notices, and nobody can discern the marks of my face during the day. Running daily, I wander many roads. And together in two repetitions, I reoccur throughout the year; rain, snow, frost, ice, and lightning do not injure me, nor do I, covered with a strong shell, fear the wind.]

The apparent paradox of the opening line is that something can move and yet not be seen moving. It seems unlikely that this refers to the difficulty in observing the difference between the lunar phases on two adjacent days, since this is not a problem for the keen-sighted observer. More likely, the sub-hourly 'movement' of the moon is intended. As the movement of the moon cannot be discerned with one glance, or even over the space of a few minutes, you could say in a sense that 'nobody notices' its movement. This idea appears to take its inspiration from two units of time-measurement mentioned in computus texts: the moment (1/40th hour) and the atom (variously described as 1/16th moment and 1/564th moment).[12] In the *Etymologiae*, Isidore explains that the former is the *minimum atque angustissimum* ('smallest and narrowest') unit which can be derived from the motion of the heavens,[13] and that the latter is the smallest unit of divisible time at all.[14] These definitions were later expanded upon and formalised in the Irish-influenced computus works that spread widely across England and continental Europe from the seventh century onwards. In such a context, the meaning of the *gressus* phrase would be that the moon moves in atomic increments, yet its movement can only be seen across much longer intervals of a minute or more. This theme of imperceptibility is continued into the second line, with a statement that is at first glance absurd, since the moon is frequently visible during the daytime. Just as in the previous riddle, the absurdity can be nullified only if the moon is assumed to be completely full. The lunar cycle also seems to be the subject of the 'two repetitions' in line 4, which likely refers to the cycle of full (30-day) and hollow (29-day) lunations so important in the medieval calendar.

The final two lines look back to an earlier riddle in the collection, Bern's *Enigma 2*, *De lucerna* ('On the lantern'), which uses its subject to convey the precariousness of human artifice in the face of the elements: *Nolo me contingat imber nec flamina venti*

('I do not wish to meet with the rain nor a blast of wind') (5–6). In this context, the similitude between the moon and lamp as illuminating objects also expresses the moon's superiority over the lamp as an entirely reliable luminary, a consequence of its protective 'shell'. The literal designation of the 'shell' is unclear, but it may allude to the celestial spheres that separate the moon from the earth according to the Ptolemaic model. But, by using the word *testudo*, which was normally reserved in classical Latin for a tortoise, and eventually came to mean all kinds of animal shell, the two riddles (nos 59 and 2) together form an extended, intertexual, metaphor that stretches across the animal-material (the shell), the artificial and errant (the lamp), and the natural and regular (the moon).

The Bern collection also contains a single sidereal riddle, *Enigma 62*, *De stellis* ('On the stars'), which uses the sibling trope to describe the fixed stars as if they are the inhabitants of an enormous nunnery:

> Milia conclusae domo sub una sorores
> Minima non crescit, maior nec aevo senescit
> et cum nulla parem conetur adloqui verbis,
> suos moderato servant in ordine cursus.
> Pulchrior turpentem vultu non dispicit ulla,
> odiuntque lucem, noctis secreta mirantur.

> [A thousand sisters contained in one house; the smaller does not grow, the bigger does not grow old, and, although none tries to speak to another in words, they keep their *cursus* in a controlled order. The more beautiful does not despise the ugly-faced; they hate the light, and marvel at the mysteries of night.]

The rhythm of the metaphor oscillates continually between the sisters and the stars throughout the riddle, erring first towards the sidereal when the stars are described as of fixed size and age, and then turning back towards the human in the line on the envies of the world. Unusually, rather than swinging back decisively and exclusively on the side of the lemma in the final line as one would expect, the careful selection of the verbs *odire* and *mirari* allows for either verb to be selected for an 'optimal' solution; the stars are the more likely to 'hate the light', whilst the nuns are the more likely to 'marvel at the mysteries of the night'. The central section is equally dual throughout. Just as the nuns maintain their own liturgical scheme (*suos cursus*) without chatter and as part of a regulated sequence (*moderato … in ordine*), so the stars maintain their own heavenly courses (*suos cursus*) in a divinely ordered pattern. A similar doubling technique is also found in Bern's *Enigma 60, De caelo* ('On the heavens'), in which the heavens describe themselves in terms of the sanctuary offered by religious houses—*et meo cum bonis malos recipio tecto* ('and I receive the bad with the good under my roof') (6)—and as a wondrous object—*pondere sub magno rerum nec gravor onustus* ('I carry innumerable things to be marvelled by all') (5). As such, the stars provide both a permanent source of spiritual wonder at an ordered cosmos and a model for the behaviour of mankind.

But why would the movements of the heavens provide a fitting model for the monastery? The answer can be found in the use of the stars as monastic timekeepers, and particularly for measuring out the mandated time for rising and praying the Night Office—for example, Benedict's stipulation that *octava hora noctis surgendum est* ('it is proper to rise at the eighth hour of the night').[15] The basic technique is not hard to master, although it does require diligent observation. One begins by noting the position of an easily recognisable circumpolar object, such as the stars Dubhe and Merak (i.e. the edge of the 'pan' section of the Plough), with respect to the North Star. Since one entire rotation (i.e. one sidereal day) is almost equal to one solar day (within four minutes), one can therefore use an imaginary clock face to measure the period between the first and successive observations. A more complicated, but potentially more accurate method, is to use the rising and setting of non-circumpolar objects. Relatively few records of sidereal timekeeping survive, but this is probably more a consequence of the prosaicness of this method than evidence for its absence. In the second half of the sixth century, Gregory of Tours produced a handbook on sidereal timekeeping, which included descriptions and rubricated diagrams of the constellations and their movements, charts on the daily hours of moonshine (*ratio lunae*) and monthly hours of sunlight (*ratio solis*), and a series of rules equating the rising of certain stars and asterisms with the number of psalms to be sung.[16] Cassian also mentions sidereal timekeeping in the *Institutes*. Although he does not explain the details, his choice of *stellarum cursus* rather than *stellarum ortus et occasus* to describe the system might suggest the circumpolar technique. But he is much more interested in the abstract consequences of such timekeeping: if the movements of the stars are ordered in accordance with divine reason, then their observation offers a solution to human impatience and laziness:

> Sed quamvis eum consuetudo diuturna, hora solita evigilare compellat, tamen sollicite, frequenterque stellarum cursu praestitutum congregationis tempus explorans, ad orationum eos invitat officium, ne in utroque inveniatur incautus, si vel oppressus somno statutam noctis transgrediatur horam; vel eamdem dormiturus, atque festinus ad somnum anticipet, et non tam officio spiritali, vel quieti omnium deservisse, quam requiei suae satisfecisse credatur.[17]

> [But, although daily custom impels him (i.e. the night watchman) to wake at the normal hour, nevertheless, by diligently and frequently checking the predetermined time of service by the course of the stars, he summons them to the office of prayer, lest he be found careless in one of two ways: either if, oppressed by sleep, he goes past the established hour of night, or, eager to sleep and impatient for bed, he anticipates the same, and thus cannot be trusted to have attended to the Divine Office and to everyone else's rest, as much as to have satisfied his own rest.]

Cassian's injunction is not merely a check against worldly laziness, but the replacement of a less reliable source of temporal authority with a more universal and reliable one. He contrasts the *hors solita* ('normal waking hour'), i.e. the body's biological cycle that we now know as the circadian rhythm, with a new kind of time, the *statua hora* ('established hour'). By obediently modelling one's movements on those of the stars, one can not only conquer the *opportunitas* ('happenstance') of the individual disposition, but also ensure liturgical uniformity with brethren from the past, present, and future. It is this idealised relationship between the movement of the sidereal and the human that Bern's *Enigma 62* plays upon. When it states that *suos moderato servant in ordine cursus* ('they keep their *cursus* in a controlled order') (4), it is informed by the monastic hope that the *cursus stellarum* ('course of the stars') can provide an ordered temporal map against which the nocturnal discipline of prayer, the *cursus psalmorum* ('the course of the psalms'), can be laid out.

The riddles of Eusebius

In his *Enigma 48*, *De die et nocte* ('On day and night'), Eusebius adopts the sibling trope found in Bern's *Enigma 56*—as well as in Aldhelm's *Enigma 79*, *Sol et luna* ('Sun and moon')—but here the relationship is between two sisters:

> Non sumus aequales quamvis ambaeque sorores,
> Tetrica nam facie et una stans altera pulchra

> Horrida sed requiem confert et grata laborem.
> Non simul et semper sumus at secernimur ipsi.[18]

> [We are not particularly alike, and we are both sisters, for one is sour of face, and the other is beautiful, but the horrid one brings rest and the pleasing one brings work. We exist always and not at the same time, and we are discernible from one another.]

In the first and last lines, Eusebius focuses on how siblings might be discerned from one another, alongside which he adds the weak paradox that an ugly sister might bring rest and a beautiful one might bring work. A similar trope is used in Eusebius' *Enigma 11*, *De lune* ('On the moon'), this time presenting the sun and moon as brothers:

> Non labor est penitus pergenti in lumine Phœbi,
> Sed mihi difficilis longas discurrere noctes.
> Umbriferis varias in noctibus intro figuras;
> Post ego deficiens, tunc offert lumina frater.

> [There is no work for me at all when the light of Phoebus marches forth, but it is a struggle for me to roam the long nights. I adopt various forms in the shady nights. After I have ended, my brother then gives out light.]

When read together, the two riddles play upon the idea that whereas the moon brings rest and the sun brings work for mankind, the sun brings rest and the night brings 'work' for the moon. As in the Bern collection, they both portray the moon and sun as siblings who do not appear at the same time. But here it is unlikely that the riddle is speaking only about the full moon; we are told that the moon adopts *varias figuras* ('various forms') (3) during the night hours, and that the sun only rises *post ego deficiens* ('after I have ended') (4). Moreover, the *difficilis … discurrere* ('it is difficult to roam') (2) line is so wrapped up in the reversal of work and rest that it ignores the fact that only the full moon can roam the full length of *longas … noctes* ('long nights'). It seems that Eusebius' understanding of the cosmos is so influenced by the binary ideas of night/day and work/rest that he completely ignores the empirical reality that the moon is often visible in the daylight hours. Thus, he presents sun and moon as siblings notable for their extreme dissimilarity, where one represents only day and the other represents only night. It is as if he is working purely from an idealised, literary description of the moon, without ever having seen it.

Two of Eusebius' riddles deal with the ostensibly dry topic of calendrical intercalation. The first, *Enigma 26*, *De die bissexti* ('On the leap-year day'), explains that intercalation is regular and predictable, as opposed to chance events: the riddle's subject declares that *sed neque perficiar nec forte creabor* ('I will not be brought about or be created by chance') (3), but *semper decursis nisi in ordine quatuor annis* ('instead always quarterly in succession with the running years') (4). When it tells us that it is created *cum proprii generis viginti quatuor horis* ('from twenty-four hours of a special kind') (1), the point is not simply that the leap-year is special because it is rare, but rather that it is of a different genus to regular days. The riddle's central idea is the simultaneous artificiality and naturalness of the leap-year, because it can be said to exist in two senses: it arises incrementally throughout the year (i.e. as the *quadrans* or 'quarter day'), and yet it also exists as a real, quadrennial day of twenty-four hours. It operates, as Bede put it, both *naturalis … rationis* ('according to natural reason') and *consuetudinis … humanae* ('according to human custom').[19] The second intercalation riddle, *Enigma 29*, *De aetate et saltu [lunae]* ('On the moon's age and leap')', takes the moon's age and the intercalated *saltus lunae* ('leap of the moon') as its subjects.

Rite vicenis cum quadragies octies una,
Quaque sororum formatur de more mearum,
Nempe momentis; tunc ego sola peracta videbor,
Cycli nondecimus cum deficit extimus annus.

[According to usage, with twenty times forty-eight, every one of my sisters are formed from the rule—from *momenta* of course! I alone will be seen to be completed when the nineteenth and last year of a cycle ends.]

The riddle does not seem to be designed to explain or clarify the meaning of the saltus to a beginner. As such, I cannot agree with Emily V. Thornbury that it is largely 'a versified definition', and that only the sibling element offers anything more.[20] Rather, the sibling element can only be properly understood if the reader has already brought a clear definition of the saltus with them, for the riddle's complexity is recognisable only to those who understand the technical discourse of computus.

The Alexandrian nineteen-year cycle is divided into 235 lunar months, the length of which alternates between 29 and 30 days (i.e. with a presumed average of 29.5 days). However, since a real lunar month is slightly longer than 29.5 days (the average is approximately 29.5306 days), this means that the computist must account for an error of just over 7 days across nineteen years. Although this error was largely corrected through intercalating on leap-year days and making all intercalated (i.e. 'embolismic') months 30 days long, it still left a discrepancy of just over a day. This was remedied by the saltus, an adjustment by +1 to the age of the moon, which was inserted in the nineteenth year, either on 1st January or 1st September (although Bede recommended the spring equinox on 21st March), depending on which day the computist preferred to calculate the new year from.[21] This meant that the discrepancies between the calculated and the observable moon would be increasingly visible as the cycle progressed. As a result, computists sought to measure the progress of this accumulation.

We find the earliest descriptions of it in several computus compilations of Irish provenance, including a section of the Sirmond collection that has come to be known as Pseudo-Alcuin's *De saltu lunae*, ten lines of a poem beginning *Annus solis continetur* in the same collection, and the *Computus Einsidlensis*.[22] The task, according to Pseudo-Alcuin, is to measure the difference between the age of the moon *secundum naturam* ('according to nature') and *secundum artem* ('according to artifice').[23] To do so, one must divide the saltus across the 235 lunar months of the nineteen-year cycle, and so the average monthly accumulation of the saltus is 1/235th of a day per lunar month. Since 1/235th of a day and 24/235th of an hour are not particularly useable units, both texts make use of three units of time: the moment, the 12th of a moment (called an *uncia* in the *Computus Einsidlensis*), and the atom. Since there are forty moments in an hour, there are 960 moments in the day. We can account for 940 of these moments (23.5 hours) in increments of four momenta per month, since $235 \times 4 = 940$. To account for the remaining twenty moments, we use the uncia and the atom. Since 235 divided by 12 is $19\frac{7}{12}$, an increment of one uncia per lunar month is equivalent to $19\frac{7}{12}$ moments over 235 months. This leaves $\frac{5}{12}$ moment remaining to be accounted for. The atom was considered to be 1/22560th of an hour (i.e. 1/46th uncia). So, across 235 lunar months, at one atom per month, this will account for $\frac{235}{46}$ unciae, or 5/12th of a moment. We have now accounted for 940 moments + $19\frac{7}{12}$ moments + $\frac{5}{12}$ moment, which gives a round total of 960 moments, i.e. one full day. One can therefore measure the discrepancy between the observable and calculated ages of the moon as an increment of four moments, one uncia and one atom per month.

Only once readers are sufficiently instructed in the saltus can they then recognise the central conceit, expressed through the sibling trope, that the entirely artificial one-day diminution of the saltus is a close, but unique, relative to the regular, 'real' lunation count in the epacts. In particular, the recognition that the sisters are formed both by *mos* ('rule') and *momenta* ('moments') is critical in understanding how the riddle works. The enjambment required to make sense of lines 2 and 3—not particularly common for the genre, but entirely appropriate for a riddle about the running-over of intercalation—places *momentis* in apposition to *more*. Each sibling is the child of the calendrical rules of the nineteen-year cycle, and it is in this sense that they are all sisters *formatur de more* ('formed from a rule'). But the saltus is unique among her siblings. Just as with the leap-year day, while the saltus grows up with her sisters, she is only *peractus* ('completed') after all the others have themselves been born at the end of the nineteenth year. At the same time, they are all *formatur de … momentis* ('formed from moments'), a phrase which recalls the calculation of the saltus accumulation. With this knowledge, we can then recognise the significance of the 'twenty times forty-eight' phrase: Eusebius is explaining that not only are there 960 momenta in the conventional twenty-four-hour day (40 × 24), but also that there is a corresponding excess of 960 momenta over nineteen years.

But why does Eusebius then adjust the multipliers from 40 (momenta) × 24 (hours) to 20 × 48? The answer is simply because numerical substitution is expected of an educated computist. The arbitrary use of one unit or multiplier for another, less obvious one, is common in the medieval presentation of dates and times. For example, when the poet Lutting of Lindisfarne wishes to give the year of a colleague's death (681 CE), he does so in the prolix form *sexagies decimus iam tunc et nouies nonus / annus ab aduentu Christi* ('six-times-ten and nine-times-nine years after the advent of Christ').[24] Likewise, when the Munich computist tells us that there are 6720 momenta in one week,[25] or when Hrabanus Maurus tells us that there are 197,760,960 atoms in the 365-day year,[26] they do so for no reason other than a schoolmaster's delight in calculation. We might even say that such descriptions are themselves akin to riddles, in that they seek to describe one thing in terms of another, less familiar thing for the sake of play. Eusebius' adjustment is therefore a kind of serious play, ensuring that, if one wishes to enjoy the riddle fully, one must not only be familiar with the sibling trope and the saltus accumulation, but also know how to recognise equivalent fractions.

Conclusion

Familial relations, typically simple and harmonious in Symphosius, are depicted as complex and problematic in the Bern and Eusebius lunar riddles. The difference is an inevitable consequence of historical calendrical change; the pagan Roman calendar was always essentially solar (albeit historically dependent upon the monthly observation of the new moon), whereas, from the fourth century onwards, the Christian calendar involved the increasingly complex reconciliation of lunar and solar cycles (as well as that of the weekday). Quite simply, whereas Symphosius looked to Saturnalia for inspiration, his medieval imitators looked instead to Easter. Only in Bern's single sidereal riddle are familial relationships depicted as harmonious, expressing the monastic ideal of a simple and direct temporal correspondence between the quotidian cursus in the heavens and on earth. All of the lunar riddles play upon the lore and terminology of computus, which provided much of the inspiration for these riddles. In several cases, most notably Eusebius' saltus riddle, a riddle's complexity is only truly appreciated by close reference to these sources. We can even speculate as to what individual sources were available to the authors. If, as Manitius argued, the Bern riddles were produced at Bobbio,[27] then the necessary material would have been available in the *Bobbio Computus* (Milano, Biblioteca Ambrosiana, MS H 150 inf.). And, since we know from its use in Bede's *De temporum ratione* that the Sirmond material was available in the Jarrow library at the time, it is quite possible that Eusebius (assuming that he and Hwætberht were one and the same) took his inspiration directly from either Pseudo-Alcuin or the *Annus solis continetur* poem.

The two riddle collections share an interest in the various, profound problems that arise from a complex luni-solar calendar. Out of the two, Eusebius has the greater tendency to imagine artificial descriptions of time as the dominant form of reality, whereas Bern is more concerned with observation and lived experience. In both cases, riddles, with their innate capacity for paradox, provided an excellent platform for the representation of incongruities between the natural and the artificial, the observable and the calculated, the incremental and the summative, and the perceptible and imperceptible. Interestingly, it would seem that the lunar riddles all contain two layers of paradox. The resolution of the first paradox, often involving unorthodox familial relations—how brother and sister can be legitimately married, for example, or how one sibling can be born outside the solar year—is overcome when we recognise that they actually stand in for computistic relations. But this then reveals a trickier and more profound paradox, about how an object can move and yet not be seen moving, or whether it is the calendar or the observed sky that gives the correct time. These are the kinds of questions that computists argued and lost sleep over. For example, in *De temporibus anni*, Ælfric mentions the *micel embspræc* ('great dispute') between *þa læwedan* ('the unlearned'), who measure the moon's age according to empirical reality, and *þa gelæredan* ('the educated'), who use its computed age.[28] Bede, however, was a little more uncomfortable with the idea that such discrepancies might be a source for confusion, and in *De ratione temporum*, immediately after his chapter on the saltus, he devoted another, much lengthier chapter to an explanation of the problems that might arise. The first rising of the moon on the evening of the fourth day of Creation must, reasoned Bede, be the first day of the first nineteen-year cycle (and, accordingly, the first day of the 532 year 'great cycle').[29] Thus, he argued that to call the moon new when it can be seen before sunset is to be avoided not only because it might cause confusion in the calculation of Easter, but also *ne primae conditionis ordo turbetur* ('lest the order of Creation be thrown into chaos').[30] Bede then imagines a man who has observed, in the presence of many witnesses, the Easter new moon of the nineteenth year of the cycle, two days before it is predicted on paper.[31] Here, the 'one evening' rule cannot be relied upon, because the moon's 'slowness' has marginally exceeded the limits of a single day. Bede's solution is to fall back upon the authority of the First Council of Nicaea, and to argue that occasional discrepancies were a reasonable price to pay for a unified Easter for the entire Church:

> Numquid credendum est quia illam quam nos IV Nonas Aprilis novam vidimus lunam, nemo viderit de illis CCCXVIII pontificibus qui in Nicaeno concilio residebant, nemo de minorum coetu graduum, qui illorum consiliis aderant et statutis, et non potius intelligendum, quia cum lunam anni illius paschalem a pridie Nonas Aprilis incipere signabant, aliud maius periculum per hoc declinaverint, ne videlicet si aliter decernerent, indissolubilis ille communium annorum et embolismorum status solveretur.[32]

> [Is it plausible that not one of the 318 bishops who attended the Council of Nicaea had seen this new moon which we saw on 2nd April, not one of the gathering of lesser ranks, who were present at their discussions and rulings? And is it not instead to be understood that when they recognised that the paschal moon of that year begins

on 4th April, they avoided another, greater difficulty by this, namely that if they had pronounced it otherwise, this indissoluble state of common and embolismic years would have been undermined?]

Here it is Bede's instinct as an ecclesiastical jurist that wins out over his famous empiricism. Given that even such as a man as Bede was so conflicted, we can better understand how such an apparently paradoxical conundrum would interest riddlers. One wonders whether, had they lived in another, more empirically-minded, millennium, the Bern riddler and Eusebius–Hwætberht might have become theoretical physicists, pure mathematicians, or computer scientists.

Notes

1 Bede, *De divisionibus temporum*, in *Venerabilis Bedae Opera Omnia*, ed. Jacques Paul Migne, PL 90 (Paris: Garnier, 1904), I, pp. 653–64, at p. 654.
2 A recent, comprehensive survey of existing scholarship can be found in Mercedes Salvador-Bello, *Isidorean Perceptions of Order* (Morgantown: West Virginia University Press, 2015), pp. 250–56.
3 There are a few exceptions, such as the series of increasingly bizarre riddles on the eyes (nos 18–20) and the riddle on winter weather (no. 15). The single 'astronomical' riddle is on sunbeams (no. 60). Tatwine, *Aenigmata Tatwini*, in Fr. Glorie, ed., *Collectiones Aenigmatum Merovingicae Aetatis*, CCSL, 133–133A (Turnhout: Brepols, 1968), 133, p. 207.
4 The connection is based on Bede's identification of Hwætberht with the cognomen of 'Eusebius' in his *Commentary on I Samuel*. Emily V. Thornbury has recently pointed out that this identification is not entirely secure and has tentatively hypothesised an anonymous Kentish author: *Becoming a Poet in Anglo-Saxon England* (Cambridge: Cambridge University Press, 2014), pp. 57–8.
5 Symphosius, *Enigma 37*, *Mula* ('Mule), in Glorie, *Collectiones Aenigmatum*, 133A, p. 658.
6 Symphosius, *Enigma 53*, *Vitis* ('Vine'), in Glorie, *Collectiones Aenigmatum*, 133A, p. 596.
7 Symphosius, *Enigma 77*, *Rotae* ('Wheel'), in Glorie, *Collectiones Aenigmatum*, 133A, p. 700.
8 Glorie does not recognise this in his list of analogues (*Collectiones Aenigmatum*, 133A, p. 603), but the parallel is obvious.
9 All references to the Bern riddles are from Glorie, *Collectiones Aenigmatum*, 133.
10 Glorie, *Collectiones Aenigmatum*, 133A, p. 603.

11 Diogenes Laertius, *Lives of Eminent Philosophers, Volume I: Books 1–5*, ed. and trans. Robert Drew Hicks, Loeb Classical Library, 184 (Cambridge, MA: Harvard University Press, 1925), pp. 92–3.
12 It was normally considered to be 1/564th moment, although a separate, older tradition can be found in the *Munich Computus* and the *Bobbio Computus*, as 1/15 moment in Munich, and 1/16 moment in Bobbio. Immo Warntjes, *The Munich Computus* (Stuttgart: Franz Steiner, 2010), p. 11.
13 Isidore of Seville, *Etymologiarum sive originum libri XX*, ed. W. M. Lindsay, 2 vols (Oxford: Oxford University Press, 1911), I, 5.29.2. The phrase is apparently borrowed from Augustine's use of it to distinguish between the brief, but discernible, interval in the birth of twins and the equivalent, indiscernible, movements of the stars. Augustine of Hippo, *De doctrina Christiana*, book 2, chapter 34, in *Sancti Aurelii Augustini opera omnia*, ed. Jacques Paul Migne, PL 34 (Paris: Garnier, 1865), volume 3, col. 52.
14 Isidore, *Etymologiae*, II, 13.2.1.
15 Benedict of Nursia, *Benedicti Regula*, ed. Rudolph Hanslik, Corpus Scriptorum Ecclesiasticorum Latinorum, 75 (Vienna: Hoelder-Pinchler-Tempsky, 1960), viii, pp. 52–3.
16 Gregory of Tours, *De cursu stellarum*, in *Gregorii Turonensis Opera, Part 2: Miracula et opera minora*, ed. Bruno Krusch and Wilhelm Levison, MGH, Scriptorum Rerum Merovingicarum, 1.2 (Berlin: Weidmann, 1969), ii, pp. 404–22.
17 John Cassian, *De coenobium institutis libri duodecim*, in *Joannis Cassiani Opera Omnia*, ed. Jacques Paul Migne, PL 49 (Paris: Garnier, 1846), I, 1.xvii, coll. 108-10. Cf. also 2.iii, coll. 79–80.
18 All references to the riddles of Eusebius are from Glorie, *Collectiones Aenigmatum*, 133A.
19 Bede, *Epistola ad Wicthedum*, in *Opera de temporibus*, ed. Charles W. Jones (Menasha: George Banta, 1943), p. 322.
20 Thornbury, *Becoming a Poet*, p. 58.
21 See Bede, *De temporum ratione*, in *Opera de temporibus*, ed. Jones, xlii, pp. 255–7, and Byrhtferth of Ramsey, *Enchiridion*, ed. and trans. Peter Baker and Michael Lapidge, EETS ss, 15 (Oxford: Oxford University Press, 2001), II.i, p. 68.
22 'Pseudo-Alcuin' appears as *De cursu et saltu lunae ac bissexto* in *Alcuini Opera Omnia*, ed. J. P. Migne, PL 101 (Paris: Garnier, 1863), II, pp. 984–92. The material from the *Computus Einsidlensis* is found on pp. 81–2, in a section beginning *Si vis scire unde saltus lunae accrescat cognoscito*: Einsiedeln, Stiftsbibliothek, Codex 321 (647), *e-codices, Virtual Manuscript Library of Switzerland*, e-codices.unifr.ch/en/list/one/sbe/0321 (accessed 29 April 2018). The section in the *Computus Einsidlensis* is shorter and more clearly explained. Pseudo-Alcuin is longer and more detailed, complicating things significantly by breaking

the accumulation down through each year, common and embolismic. The *Annus solis continetur* poem is printed as Sisebut, King of the Visigoths (?), 'De ratione temporum', ed. Karl Strecker, MGH, *Poetae Latini Aevi Carolini*, 4 (Berlin: Weidmann, 1914), pp. 682–6. Lines 40–8 are essentially a versification of the saltus calculations in Pseudo-Alcuin and the *Computus Einsidlensis*. The poem's repetition of the superfluous participle *ducto* appears to be modelled on the use of *ducti* in Pseudo-Alcuin to describe unit substitution, since the word is not used in *Computus Einsidlensis*. This, along with the use of *momenti duodena* rather than *Computus Einsidlensis*'s *unciae*, would suggest that the author is borrowing either directly from Pseudo-Alcuin or from a source very similar to it. Line 49 describes the saltus accumulation using the *punctum*, as per Bede, *De temporum ratione*, in *Opera de temporibus*, ed. Jones, lxii, p. 255.

23 Pseudo-Alcuin, *De cursu*, p. 985.

24 Lutting of Lindisfarne, *Epitaphium beati Bedani presbiteri*, in Michael Lapidge, 'The Earliest Anglo-Latin Poet: Lutting of Lindisfarne', *ASE*, 42 (2013), 1–26, at pp. 12–13.

25 Warntjes, *Munich Computus*, p. 36.

26 Hrabanus Maurus, *De computo*, ed. John McCulloch and Wesley Stevens (Turnhout: Brepols, 1979). Byrhtferth copies this in the *Enchiridion*, i.3, p. 116.

27 Max Manitius, *Geschichte der lateinischen Literatur*, 3 vols (Munich: C.H. Beck, 1911), I, p. 193.

28 Ælfric, *Ælfric's De temporibus anni*, ed. Martin Blake (Woodbridge: D. S. Brewer, 2009), p. 90.

29 Bede, *De temporum ratione*, in *Opera de temporibus*, ed. Jones, xliii, p. 230.

30 Bede, *De temporum ratione*, in *Opera de temporibus*, ed. Jones, xliii, p. 231.

31 Bede, *De temporum ratione*, in *Opera de temporibus*, ed. Jones, xliii, p. 232.

32 Bede, *De temporum ratione*, in *Opera de temporibus*, ed. Jones, xliii, p. 232.

14
Enigmatic knowing and the *Vercelli Book*

Britt Mize

It is admittedly an odd choice to focus a chapter about riddles on the *Vercelli Book*, which everyone knows contains no riddles, but the choice does have purpose. I want to explore an intellectual tendency, underlying both Old English riddles and many features of the *Vercelli Book*, that speaks to what early medieval writers and readers of English thought was required of them *as* writers and readers, and maybe also as humans. The works we recognise as riddles are the cleanest, clearest outcrop of something larger, something that has to do with the shape of the world, and of knowledge, and how it is gained.

Before coming to the *Vercelli Book*, I wish to frame the issues that I suggest bear on it through discussion of two very different heuristic journeys to the signifier that solves one riddle: the poem inscribed on the front panel of the ornately carved Franks Casket, a small box made of bone and produced in 8th-century Northumbria.

How to do things with whalebone

Odd choices were also made by Arthur S. Napier in preparing his 1900 or 1901 article on the Franks Casket's images and inscriptions.[1] For a small and entirely digressive part of his study, Napier called upon the techniques of biological science to analyse the casket. Though known by his contemporaries for conciseness,[2] Napier festooned that essay with elaborate footnotes, one of which explains:

> Being anxious, if possible, to ascertain exactly what the material is, I wrote to Professor E. Ray Lankester, who very kindly went to the Museum and examined the casket for me. He came to the conclusion that it is the bone of some species of whale, but took a small fragment of the casket bone with him for microscopical examination, the result of which I give in his own words:—

> 'A microscopical examination of the bone of the casket proves it to be the bone of a whale. So far as microscopic structure goes it might be that of a dugong or a whale. But the plates of bone are too large to have been cut from any bone of the dugong. There are certain highly refractive concentric and radial stripes in the dense matter of the bone of the casket as shown by the microscopic sections under high power, which are characteristic of whale and dugong but are *not* seen in walrus or any other mammal's bone, so far as I can ascertain. The sections of the casket bone have been compared for me by Dr. Ridewood and Prof. Charles Stewart, F.R.S., with the large collection of microscopic sections of bone which are preserved in the Museum of the Royal College of Surgeons. I therefore consider it *certain* that the bone of the casket is the bone of a whale, but cannot say of what species or what size.'[3]

Initiating an invasive microscopic inspection of the bone was unnecessary. Augustus W. Franks's naked-eye judgement of its origin, announced in a talk in 1859,[4] has never been doubted before or since Napier wrote; and, as Napier reports himself through Lankester's words, the size of the pieces leaves no real possibility other than whale. Equally strange is Napier's representation of events, which gravitates to the narrative rhetoric of discovery where it might have indicated verification of accepted knowledge. The note's detail and show of precision are out of step with the fact that it contains no new findings; and Napier's initial characterisation of the casket's material, in his main text, as 'the bone of *some kind of* whale'[5] seems designed to justify the scientific scrutiny he reports, undertaken by a method unlikely in any case (judging by Lankester's phrasing) to have been able to differentiate among whale species.[6] Napier went to some lengths, and caused others to do the same, to find an answer that was already known to a question no one was asking.

Eleven centuries earlier, the carver of the Franks Casket's front-panel inscription answered the same question, by different means and for very different reasons. Like most of the casket's textual elements, this inscription stands in relief in runic characters. The text wraps continuously around the panel, running first along the top edge, then down the right edge before turning back retrograde along the bottom edge, where the individual runes are reversed as well, and finishing by turning upward along the left edge.[7] When put into a more approachable format, the writing resolves into two lines of English verse with a short remainder:

Fisc flodu ahof   on fergenberig;
warþ gasric grorn   þær he on greut giswom.
Hronæs ban.

[The sea cast the fish onto a mountain; the *gasric* grew miserable where it swam onto sand. Whalebone.][8]

The final phrase, marked as a label for the main inscriptional unit by trailing outside its syntax and metre, states the topic of the little poem and links it to the box's material substance. The inscription parallels several *Exeter Book* riddles by starting with a living creature and following a part of its body through its transformation for a new career in the world of human interests: like those describing horn (*Wæpenwiga* (R.14), *Fyrdrinces Gefara* (R.80)) or the uses of an animal's hide (*Fotum Ic Fere* (R.12), *Nama Min is Mære* (R.26), and *Geoguðmyrþe Grædig* (R.38)), the 'Whalebone' poem plots the transition from living entity to biofact to artefact. In this case, however, the words do not fully contain the riddle as a semiotic package; the text requires holistic consideration with the box of bone on which it is realised. In that physical context, the provided solution gives a voice to a partially self-referential object whose materiality forces its way into the text written upon it and cannot be excluded from the act of interpretation.[9]

Both Napier and the designer of the series of carvings, then, isolated the casket's physical composition as a piece of information to be possessed and went out of their way to call attention to it. For each, as we will see, the question 'what is the casket made of?' was inseparable from a heuristic for producing an answer, and from presupposed structures of thought that could give it meaning beyond itself. Both used the question and its answer as a means of assuming a culturally authoritative voice and participation in a recognised discourse of truth. The relevant rhetorical complexes in both cases centre on the acquisition and sharing of knowledge, but they position these activities within two different epistemological systems, such that the knowledge itself represented by the term 'whalebone' is differently constituted.

It is everywhere apparent in the long, quarrelsome notes of Napier's essay that he was preoccupied with a trespass by the Swedish scholar Elis Wadstein, whose own 1900 monograph on the Franks Casket had just appeared.[10] Although Napier saw that the quality of Wadstein's work was poor and that many of his claims could easily be dismissed, it was a substantial publication—Wadstein's first in English, on an English cultural treasure bearing

English inscriptions—which put him up as an immediate rival for authority on that topic.[11] The timing was awkward, too, given that Wadstein's study came out when Napier's had been completed except for its notes.[12] But what really offended Napier was Wadstein's publication of a photograph of the casket's right side panel (housed in Florence, separate from the rest of the casket), which Wadstein had obtained indirectly from Napier and had not asked permission to use. It is in reference to this affront that mention of Wadstein's work first bursts into Napier's footnotes,[13] which seek to discredit as much as refute him. From that point forward, commentary on Wadstein's monograph runs continuously through Napier's notes, a sour subplot to Napier's own explication of each panel of the casket.

This animus is the context in which we must understand the superfluous report on the casket's material. There, by telling a tale of scientific rigour and expert judgement, Napier makes his superior intellectual 'grasp' of the object almost literal by asserting his access to the casket, and even his ability to bring about its physical manipulation, with the assistance of other specialists who are willing to act as his agents. Control of detailed data of the casket's construction functions for him as a token in a larger contest of intellectual control: the fullest mastery of information about the Franks Casket amounts to a quasi-proprietary claim upon it both as an object of analysis and as a validator of personal academic authority. Napier's narrative footnote quoted above creates for him a notional proximity to the artefact, as well as a sense of his accepted place among other professionals equally proximate to it, that complements a strategic distancing of Wadstein from the casket performed by an earlier note in which Napier had exposed Wadstein's complete dependence on the appropriated photograph and on information that Napier himself had unwittingly provided—without which, as he points out, Wadstein's newly published analysis would have been impossible.[14]

Napier deserves his reputation as an outstanding scholar, and like most academics most of the time, he preferred to think of our work as a cooperative enterprise, in which the accumulation of insights, reshaped as needed through debate, leads to the advancement of collective learning. But he happens to have written about the material composition of the Franks Casket in a moment of irritation and perceived threat, and the circumstances make especially visible certain features of Napier's academic landscape and their intellectual underpinnings, many of which remain fundamental to scholarly discourse today. Napier's answer to his own gratuitous inquiry into the casket's composition—along with which he implicitly communicates also the status and opportunity that allowed him as a more established professional to obtain that redundant answer—was a trophy of his authority as a scholar. The datum 'whalebone' concluded a process, the objective having been objectively reached. So great was his intellectual community's investment in arriving at such a point of unimpeachable finality, and so great was its rhetorical importance to Napier, that it could motivate an otherwise needless investigation.

A much different intellectual environment gave meaning to the phrase *hronæs ban* for the creator of the Franks Casket riddle, one informed by different constructions of knowledge, of authority centred on it, and of the relationships and communities defined by its seeking and attainment. A riddle is at its heart less a question to be answered than a cultural apparatus for thinking about the world: its processes, its paradoxes, and its relationships, both among natural elements (a whale, the sea, and land) and especially between those natural elements and the lives of humans (whale is reduced to bone, bone submits to the carver's tools to become a triumph of art and intellect). Rather than incising the character forms into the bone surface as is more usual—and as he does for the word 'magi' within one of the front-panel images—the craftsman has carved out the negative space around the runes to leave the characters in raised relief. It is as if the signifying components of this and the other panels were already part of the whalebone, and he has removed everything that is *not* writing or image, merely revealing the design rather than creating it. The animal's fate has not just been inscribed on its bones, but had always been written in them.

Poetry and wisdom are tightly entwined in Old English,[15] and in the vernacular riddles they are at their most indisseverable.[16] The *hronæs ban* paratext directs interpretation to the relationships that it activates among that solution, the two lines of poetry that define and are defined by it, and the box itself, including all parts of its programme of text and image. As a meditation on the tangible substance of a lost life, the poem on the front panel narrates the reorganisation of organic matter into forms and functions that will have cultural meaning. When approached through the discursive registers activated by a riddle in Old English verse, the sign 'whalebone' has value in the currency of understanding, not fact. If for Napier the material of the artefact was the target of forensic knowledge, for the casket's designer the material is a producer of sapiential knowledge, in its inalienable involvement with the carved words, as it fuels contemplation of interactions between the natural and human worlds. It sustains rather than concludes intellectual engagement for a reader sensitive to the forms of truth that the text and medium in combination suggest.

The paradigm of conditional revelation

Wisdom literature of the type represented by the 'Whalebone' poem and other Old English riddles begins by requiring intellectual labour from anyone who wishes to gain a toehold in a fragmentarily revealed topography of knowledge, and then encourages further steps into enhanced understanding through contemplation of the identity that the riddle has described estrangingly. I will call this two-stage process 'conditional revelation' and I will argue that its structure, whereby readers qualify themselves for understanding through effort, shapes other literature too. Both terms, 'conditional' and 'revelation', need further specification.

By 'conditional' I mean that, in this paradigm of discursive interaction, truth does not come and get you. Readers or hearers are positioned as learners who must care enough to confront a gateway challenge. A withheld solution to a riddle amounts to a barrier similar to that created by the textual presentation of the Franks Casket riddle, where the seeking must begin with the attempt simply to read this poem about whalebone carved in whalebone: laid out mostly in *scriptio continua*, and with the line along the bottom edge mirror-written, the front-panel text requires some work even to perceive that the riddle's solution is provided. Confronting the challenge demands in this case (beyond literacy and knowledge of runes) the diligence to puzzle out the reversed writing and locate lexical and syntactic boundaries in the cramped string of graphs. Part of the work done by this and other riddles is to define their readers as strivers who will dedicate time and effort. The texts actually produce their desired audiences, by first drawing them in through the 'deliberate fashioning of strangeness'—as with the perplexing intricacy of the casket, or the curiosity of a paradoxical description—and then training them to participate in the wonder with which they are presented.[17]

The language of the *Exeter Book* riddles often foregrounds the task of seeking an answer, but this is the path into the intellectual work of a riddle rather than its destination.[18] The agonistic dimension of the challenge is a ritual mystification, more invitation than defiance ('say what I am called'; 'now it can be known').[19] The text is designed to encode what is needed for the solution because its maker does want inquirers to join a community of the knowing, with some effort, even if they participate only through appreciation of the solution once it is disclosed. Assuming the experience many of us have as present-day teachers of *Exeter Book* riddles matches earlier reception—that people often need further prompting to arrive at the answer, or must eventually be told it—this does not gainsay the rhetorical function of the challenge, which has succeeded in driving shared interpretive engagement. By the time the solution becomes known by any means, the terms of the encounter have been set, the idea that there is a threshold for gaining entry to enhanced knowledge has been established, and whatever interaction has taken place over the initial puzzlement has made the wisdom text a social one.[20] Even for a private reader who sees a written answer immediately, the rhetorical shape of the text—in its dialogic provocation of the addressee to grapple with the identity that it defamiliarises—can dramatise or model the transactions of a community within which the reader is simultaneously tested and enriched.[21] Other kinds of estrangement may serve as the initial challenge: a cryptic textual presentation, as with the Franks Casket, or counterintuitive descriptions that must be reconciled with experience. Any form of difficulty, or difficulty of form, can create a disruption to normal perception, and with it the germ of reorientation to a wondrous world.

When the answer is not present it is easy to stall on the task of discovering it—a step that can hardly be bypassed—but the fact that solutions to riddles are frequently given, especially in Anglo-Latin contexts, shows that in a broader view of the genre the initial search is only part of what a riddle is for, and indeed an optional part.[22] The gateway challenge, whatever form it takes, ensures investment, but the epistemic work of reckoning with that initial estrangement continues, because the semiotic grammar of riddles in itself 'make[s] us realise that the grid we impose upon the world is far from a perfect fit and not the only one available'.[23] Within a riddle's performance of complexity are clues to its order,[24] summoning reader or hearer into a cooperative relationship with the crafters of intricacy and mystery—including the nonpareil artist and most adept of all riddlers, God. This cooperative relationship, which begins in confrontation of the gateway challenge and persists beyond it, is constitutive of revelation: which, in this context, is not a discrete moment in which a fact is acquired, but a state of notional involvement with others and with the world in a discourse environment that values seeking truth and an understanding of one's place in it. Revelation of this kind is ongoing, processual, and social, presuming continued ethical engagement.

Napier's evidential heuristic, with the power that inheres in a proved answer according to his and our modern epistemological habits, made from 'whalebone' a tool for securing his academic authority and rebuffing a rival; but the designer of the Franks Casket uses that same signifier to usher the thoughtful into discursive cycles of sapiential authority. The attainment of understanding as it is often conceptualised in the *Vercelli Book* is more like this than like Napier's once-and-done answer to the whalebone question. Indeed the Franks Casket riddle, with the larger design programme of which it is a part, participates in tendencies that can be found throughout the corpus of early medieval English creative arts (i.e., those of the era and regions where Old English was widely spoken): an attraction to intricacy; a tolerance or even celebration of ambiguity; a *penchant* for pushing readers to active, evaluative discernment of shifting perspectives, which I have argued elsewhere pervades the vernacular poetics.[25]

In considering further how the paradigm of conditional revelation manifests itself, I would like to move away from the reified riddle, riddle-as-thing, to think more inclusively about a simultaneously concealing and revealing attitude of text to world, which is also an attitude of writers to readers and an attitude of readers to texts. Consider the Ruthwell Cross crucifixion poem, which creates challenges similar to those of the Franks Casket for a reader. We would not say that the Ruthwell Cross poem in its material context is *a* riddle, but I do think we can say that it *riddles*. The same is true of *Wulf and Eadwacer* or *The Wife's Lament*—they riddle, though they may not be riddles—as well as *The Riming Poem*, *Aldhelm*, and any number of other Old English texts that seem designed to impel speculation or decipherment. At the smallest scale of diction, kennings and compound words also riddle when they describe a sword as a 'battle-light' or the 'leavings of hammers'.[26] Some concepts riddle, too, and they are among the favourites of early medieval English artists and poets: the Crucifixion, which Paul says is the foolishness of humans but the wisdom of God; the Incarnation; the persistence of evil in the midst of a good creation.

I am far from the first to attribute a riddling quality to much Old English poetry.[27] But (notwithstanding my choice of verb above) I would question the analogy whereby other literature is implied to be like a riddle, or to borrow techniques from the riddle, with the riddle being figured always as the prior phenomenon. It may be better to regard the interplay of obfuscation and revelation as an underlying attractor that both gives riddles their place in the literary landscape and finds expression in many other ways as well. The view I propose begins largely in agreement with John D. Niles, who takes his work on 'enigmatic' verse far beyond riddles to argue forcefully that the quality denoted by his term is widespread in Old English poetry. By prizing loose this type of textual behaviour from the specific genre of the riddle, Niles helpfully refocuses on what he calls the 'wish to astonish'.[28] But whereas Niles concentrates on the 'ludic' aspect of this tendency, the aesthetic satisfactions abounding to those who thoughtfully revisit complex texts and the games they play, I add that the ongoing interpretive action also may spill out in contemplative or educative directions from the recurring pleasures of the poem as intricate object. Texts that riddle present ever-new delights to appreciators of their sophistication; and also, at their best, they may point beyond themselves into half-seen systems of relation among humans, nature, and God. This is the enterprise that the model of conditional revelation endorses as a paradigmatic experience of mystery in and through words. The notional community of wisdom presumed and produced by such texts is mind- and person-making. Their verbal play rests on deep assumptions about truth, about God-created reality and how one must go about trying to grasp it; their writerly cleverness urges the kind of exercise that is necessary for those who would be wise, but is not always undertaken. If you want to understand truth, early medieval English intellectuals seem to say, you have to do the work. The strong implication is that the right kind of person will be willing and able to carry out that labour.

Both Niles and Patrick J. Murphy (who builds on a broadly similar vision of riddles) do acknowledge that mystified writing can serve as a gateway to extra-textual orientations that we could call sapiential. Niles concludes with a short afterword on the 'dance of wit and wisdom', and Murphy too is alert to 'the links [that the *Exeter Book* riddles] reveal in the fabric of creation',[29] but neither gives the continuing wisdom-work of such texts centrality, focusing on the mechanics of the challenge. Maybe these and other recent scholars have been reluctant to venture further down this path because it looks like a vague or speculative journey: as Niles begins his book by pointing out, we know little about the real, immediate social environments that would govern the pragmatics of vernacular poetry.[30] But we do know that at least some early medieval English writers and readers laboured with a strong sense of moral purpose, expressed plainly in other kinds of texts. The journey of following riddles' rhetoric of conditional revelation into the homelands to which it may lead benefits from some mapping when we track the presence of similar functions through a text like the *Vercelli Book*: a collection which—whatever its more specific organising principle or concept—we believe we know was compiled for serious purposes of devout contemplation and spiritual betterment.[31]

Conditional revelation in the *Vercelli Book*

I opened this chapter by acquiescing to the standard view that there are no riddles in the *Vercelli Book*, but there is certainly at least one. The manuscript contains two of the four poems that bear Cynewulf's famous runic 'signature' epilogues, and the one in *Fates of the Apostles* calls attention to itself as a simultaneous concealment and revelation, with a challenge/invitation to readers that is close kin to those found in many of the *Exeter Book* riddles. It states first that

> her mæg findan forepances gleaw,
> se ðe hine lysteð leoðgiddunga,
> hwa þas fitte fegde. (96–98a)
>
> [here someone wise in deliberation, one to whom poems are pleasing, can discover who joined together this song.]

Then at the end it declares, *nu ðu cunnon miht / hwa on þam wordum wæs werum oncyðig* ('now you can know who was made known to men in these words') (105b–106). The analogous passage in the *Elene* epilogue does not present itself plainly as a riddle, as the one in *Fates* does, but the runic acrostic there sets a similar task.[32] These so-called signatures are about identity, but they are not about biography, any more than the Franks Casket front-panel text is about zoology. The identifications of Cynewulf as poet are embedded within universalising meditations on mortality and the ephemerality of earthly goods, an unmistakable turn into wisdom discourse.

The *Vercelli Book* poems have several other points of contact with riddle-like rhetoric. The most conspicuous one outside the Cynewulfian epilogues is *The Dream of the Rood*, which has long been associated with riddles, both in its prosopopoeia and in the initial indirectness of its description of the Cross as that object slowly comes into focus for what it is.[33] The following lines would be at home in an *Exeter Book* riddle:

> geseah ic þæt fuse beacen
> wendan wædum ond bleom; hwilum hit wæs mid wætan bestemed,
> beswyled mid swates gange, hwilum mid since gegyrwed. (21b–23)

> [I saw that restless sign change in trappings and hues: sometimes it was soaked with liquid, drenched with the flow of blood, sometimes adorned with treasure.]

I believe that *Dream* also incorporates a prior text that may have come to hand as a riddle, the Ruthwell crucifixion poem already mentioned: it is not a riddle as it appears carved on the cross, but if divorced from that material context, it turns into one; so unless we imagine the creator of *Dream* to have worked directly from the Ruthwell Cross, the crucifixion poem carved there would have had a distinctly riddling intermediate career. There are other intersections with riddle-like rhetoric in the Vercelli poems as well. *Homiletic Fragment I* dwells on the dangers of a deceitful mismatch between word and thought, exploring this threat through an enigmatically presented analogy with bees, who bring both sweetness and a sting. The often cryptic *Soul and Body I* has a close affiliation in concept with *Giest in Geardum* (R.43), and the *Vercelli Book* poem's descriptions are defamiliarising enough that at one point the scribe appears to have been misled into expecting a riddler's 'tell me' challenge: he writes, *Sege nydde to me / ærest eallra* ('diligently declare to me, first of all') (fol. 103r/14).[34] Editors have seen the form of this statement as an error, and I agree for the purposes of textual criticism, but I am interested in how it got to be that way. It seems likely that the rhetorical model of the riddle attracted the scribe's miswriting.

As intriguing as these riddle-associated textual moments are, my argument is not that the *Vercelli Book* contains a slew of unrecognised riddles. Rather, I suggest that often it riddles, in two chief ways. First, at a conceptual level, the Vercelli collection repeatedly supposes the action of concealment or deferral and revelation to operate in the extratextual world of truth, so that in order to know and understand important realities a person must do qualifying work. Many of the homilies as well as the poems show a narrative preoccupation with revelation of truth only through the effort or virtue required to obtain privileged understanding. Take for instance *Dream*'s enigmatic vision of the Cross, which connects with Constantine's and Cynewulf's similar visionary or contemplative experiences as those are recounted in *Elene*.[35] The visionary in *Dream* and Cynewulf and Constantine in *Elene* must work for the revelations they receive: the first two through the penitential and vigilant spirit that gives them access to their encounters with the Cross, and Constantine through active inquiry into the meaning of his similar vision. Having met the conditions, their revelations initiate participation in a community of enlightened discourse to which they will continue contributing as producers of a cultic present known to readers. The speaker in *Dream* and Cynewulf in turn share their revelations with others, in the act of voicing the poems and perhaps in preaching,[36] and Constantine makes a place for Christianity and veneration of the True Cross in Rome.

Again and again in the *Vercelli Book* we see people being challenged by the apparently inscrutable, and either qualifying or failing to qualify themselves for subsequent and ongoing revelation. Sometimes the narration of conditional revelation takes the form of prophecy whose fulfilment in Christ must be actively recognised. Homily 1 centres on the many ways that Jesus has made himself the solution to earlier prophecy; homilies 5 and 6 catalogue portents of Christ's birth that few at that time were well situated to comprehend; and homily 16 describes ways that natural substances—water and stone—recognised his coming.[37] The same homily lists other signs of Epiphany, including the star of the Magi and the heavenly dove that appeared at Jesus' baptism. These are past events recounted historically, but the Vercelli homilies' scenes of conditional revelation sometimes turn to the future, too. A favourite topic is the uncanny phenomena that will signal the coming of Antichrist or the approach of Doomsday at the end of the present age. Homilies 2, 15, and 21 generously treat this material, and homily 2 includes a bleeding aerial cross reminiscent of the enigmatic description in *Dream*. While homilies 1 and 16 are focused on scriptural texts that had previously been cryptic but were made transparent by the coming of Christ, at least six homilies in the *Vercelli Book*—homily 16 and the others mentioned—reference inscrutable events in the natural or observed world that either were to be interpreted by the wise in the past, or will be so in the future.

The ideal human life that saints model in the *Vercelli Book* also includes interpretive activity, as they consider cryptic signs and play out scenes of intellectual confrontation. Guthlac's struggle with despair in 'homily' 23 is resolved when he shows the wisdom to pray despite his feeling of hopelessness, and the resulting fellowship of St Bartholomew fortifies him. Devils later test his discernment by speaking to him in a familiar, friendly way (*mid cuðlicum wordum*, 23.49), tempting him to excessive fasting by pretending to be impressed by and supportive of his virtue. Guthlac *sona forseah þa deofollican lare, for þan he hie þa ealle idle 7 unnytte ongeat* ('immediately rejected the devilish teaching, because he perceived it to be empty and useless') (23.80–81). Other contests of knowledge or spiritual wisdom with devils occur in *Andreas*, and in that poem, Andrew has an extended question-and-answer session with the unrecognised Christ, in which for over 600 lines Andrew and his divine interlocutor challenge each other, punctuated by each one's declarations that the other is wise and favoured by God. Andrew finally solves the puzzle for good—or rather, is given the solution—being brought into an understanding of whom he was talking to after he awakens in Mermedonia. Later, when Andrew looks back at the swath of blood and gore left by his broken body and sees that it has transformed into a track of blossoms, he reads, and we with him, the signs of his saintly status.

Such scenes of interpretation bring us back to the second main way the *Vercelli Book* fosters enigmatic knowing: at the level of encounter with text, where narrated situations like those we have seen link outward to the position and responsibilities of a reader. Discernment and intellectual labour are needed for access first to textual intelligibility and then to a larger truth and a community that it defines. After all, the people who are required to recognise the signs of Doomsday or the Antichrist in homilies 2, 15, and 21 are imagined potentially to be our own future selves, readers or hearers of those homilies. *Dream*'s and *Elene*'s accounts of their own origins, for example, position the texts as an invitation for a reader or hearer into a community of the knowing, and both poems promote a cultic devotion that does the same. Both *Andreas* and *Dream* allude to episodes they do not narrate, raising questions whose answers are deferred to later poems. *Andreas* recounts the adventures of two apostles, but begins with a declaration that

> We gefrunan   on fyrndagum
> twelfe under tunglum   tireadige hæleð,
> þeodnes þegnas. (1–3a)
> ...
> þæt wæron mære   men ofer eorðan,
> frome folctogan   ond fyrdhwate,
> rofe rincas. (7–9a)

[We have heard about twelve glory-blessed heroes under the stars in the old days, thegns of the Lord ... Those men were renowned throughout the earth, bold leaders and battle-ready, fierce warriors.]

As if to make up for the deficit of ten in the count of apostles whose stories have been told, *Andreas* is immediately followed in the manuscript by *Fates*. Similarly, *Dream* alludes to the *inventio crucis*, when the Cross says,

me ... dryhtnes þegnas,
freondas gefrunon,
ond gyredon me golde ond seolfre. (75b–77)

[thegns of the Lord, friends, found me and clothed me in gold and silver.]

Then a few leaves later, we come to *Elene*, whose purpose is to recount that event and its context in full.

Dream, *Elene*, and other texts bridge from narrated content to the world in which readers encounter the *Vercelli Book*, and the collection repeatedly demands intellectual work by those readers. The Cynewulfian epilogues are only the most conspicuous example. Homilies 2, 4, and 9 abound in paradox and effects of estrangement that cause a reader to look at something familiar in an unfamiliar way, as for instance in homily 4's description of the body as perceived by the soul. Homily 4 also contains direct speech by an entity who turns out to be a devil but is not identified at the beginning; the onus is on the reader to figure this out, much as St Guthlac must do in prose text 23. Dry bones call out to the living in homily 13, exhorting readers to consider the future, as do the bizarre numerical formulas offered by homily 9 to quantify the suffering and bliss of different versions of the afterlife: if seven men who each could speak 270 languages had all eternity to describe the torments of hell, for instance, homily 9 says they could not do it. The *Ubi sunt?* passage in homily 10 requires a reader to contemplate the answer to that most troubling of all rhetorical questions, and the next text, homily 11, asks a miniature riddle—what are spiritual candles?—before supplying the solution, that they are prophets and teachers. Here, as in the Franks Casket poem with its supplied answer, the discovery of information is less important to the rhetorical situation than considering what it *means* that prophets and teachers are spiritual candles. Revelations of truth in this manuscript are often embedded in rhetorical engagements with wisdom and paradox.

Many of the homilies and poems of the *Vercelli Book* posit a structuring of information or knowledge whereby signs inscrutable to many nevertheless contain what is needed to interpret them correctly, provided that their interpreters bring the proper ethical orientations and address themselves to the challenge with dedication and a spirit of responsibility. I do not know that the compiler of the *Vercelli Book* would have consciously identified a theme of conditional revelation as a factor in including specific texts. Yet it is clear that that person's tendencies of thought, and the types of narratives and situations to which he or she was attracted, resulted in a collection whose protocols of enigmatic knowing require the reader at times to undertake an active challenge, and very often to ponder the dynamics of such a challenge, in the search for true understanding. In this the book's compiler seems to join other early medieval English intellectuals in believing that wisdom is hard because it requires not just knowing things, but doing things: seeking, learning, teaching, and acting in virtuous concert with God and creation.

Notes

1 Arthur S. Napier, 'The Franks Casket', part 2 of Napier, 'Contributions to Old English Literature', in *An English Miscellany Presented to Dr. Furnivall in Honour of His Seventy-Fifth Birthday*, ed. W. P. Ker, Arthur S. Napier, and Walter W. Skeat (Oxford: Clarendon Press, 1901), pp. 362–81. This is the version from which I quote, but the essay was also printed separately, in booklet form with slightly modified text, as Arthur S. Napier, *The Franks Casket* (Oxford: Clarendon, 1900). On the uncertainty of publication date, see n.12 below.

2 Neil Ker, 'A. S. Napier, 1853–1916', in *Philological Essays: Studies in Old and Middle English Language and Literature in Honour of Herbert Dean Meritt*, ed. James L. Rosier (The Hague: Mouton, 1970), pp. 152–81, esp. p. 173.

3 Napier, 'Franks Casket', p. 365, n.1 (italics in original).

4 See 'Proceedings at Meetings of the Archaeological Institute for 2 August 1859', *Archaeological Journal*, 16 (1859), 386–93, at p. 391.

5 Napier, 'Franks Casket', p. 365 (italics mine).

6 Present-day techniques have been able to determine the species as sperm whale. Vicki Ellen Szabo, *Monstrous Fishes and the Mead-Dark Sea: Whaling in the Medieval North Atlantic* (Leiden: Brill, 2008), p. 55, n.79.

7 Images of the casket's front panel are available from many printed and digital sources, including Elliott Van Kirk Dobbie, ed., *The Anglo-Saxon Minor Poems*, ASPR, 6 (New York: Columbia University Press, 1942), plate facing p. 116.

8 I leave the mysterious word *gasric* untranslated; whatever its exact meaning, it is a nominal reference to the beached whale.

9 Thomas A. Bredehoft comments on the insistent materiality of the casket's texts and the necessity of taking it as an object whose inscriptions are seen for themselves, pre-textually, as well as read. See *The Visible Text: Textual Production and Reproduction from Beowulf to Maus* (Oxford: Oxford University Press, 2014), pp. 4–17.

10 Elis Wadstein, *The Clermont Runic Casket*, Skrifter utgifna af Kongl. Humanistiska Vetenskaps-Samfundet i Upsala 6.7 (Uppsala: Almqvist & Wiksells Boktryckeri-A.-B., 1900).

11 A few years Napier's junior, Wadstein had held an appointment at Uppsala since 1894 and in 1900 accepted a professorship at Gothenburg. For a sketch of Wadstein's life and publications, see Martha A. Muusses, 'Nils Elis Wadstein (Torshälla, 16 Juli 1861–Stockholm, 19 Juni 1942)', *Jaarboek van de Maatschappij der Nederlandse Letterkunde* (1950–51), 215–20.

12 Napier, 'Franks Casket', pp. 364–5, n.3. The freestanding print of Napier's essay, with a date of 1900, shows changes made to the text as it is found in the 1901 *festschrift*; yet the freestanding version identifies itself (verso of title page) as a reprint of that found in the book. Clearly a special effort was made to get Napier's work out in some form bearing a 1900 date, either antedated or printed quickly with minor textual changes while the full volume was still in production. I am glad finally to be able to acknowledge Beverley Hunt, *OED* archivist, for searching the files of Oxford University Press to help me with this enigmatic publication history (pers. comm., 2–4 June 2009).

13 Napier, 'Franks Casket', pp. 364–5, n.3.

14 Napier, 'Franks Casket', pp. 364–5, n.3.

15 Karl Reichl, 'Old English *Giedd*, Middle English *Yedding* as Genre Terms', in *Words, Texts, and Manuscripts: Studies in Anglo-Saxon Culture Presented to Helmut Gneuss on the Occasion of His Sixty-Fifth Birthday*, ed. Michael Korhammer, with Karl Reichl and Hans Sauer (Cambridge: D. S. Brewer, 1992), pp. 349–70; Rafał Borysławski, 'The Elements of Anglo-Saxon Wisdom Poetry in the Exeter Book Riddles', *Studia Anglica Posnaniensia*, 38 (2002), 35–47.

16 Elaine Tuttle Hansen, *The Solomon Complex: Reading Wisdom in Old English Poetry* (Toronto: University of Toronto Press, 1988), pp. 126–43, remains an outstanding analytical overview of the wisdom engagements of Old English riddles in both epistemological and social dimensions. Not all discussions of wisdom literature include riddles, but this seems often to be due to genre-based definitions. I accept the more expansive view of wisdom as a discursive mode with shared referential tendencies and social functions that is exemplified by Hansen, *Solomon Complex*, and Russell G. Poole, *Old English Wisdom Poetry*,

Annotated Bibliographies of Old and Middle English Literature, 5 (Cambridge: D. S. Brewer, 1998).

17 Peter Ramey, 'Crafting Strangeness: Wonder Terminology in the Exeter Book Riddles and the Anglo-Latin Enigmata', *RES*, 69 (2018), 201–15, shows the Exeter Book riddles' exceptionally strong endorsement of a sense of the marvellous; quotation from p. 202.

18 Niles observes that 'if a riddle were an orchestral piece, then hitting upon its solution would be more like finishing its prelude than hearing the suite itself'. John D. Niles, *Old English Enigmatic Poems and the Play of the Texts* (Turnhout: Brepols, 2006), p. 308.

19 *Pace* Davis, who finds in the riddle's methods a more seriously adversarial stance. Adam Davis, '*Agon* and *gnomon*: Forms and Functions of the Anglo-Saxon Riddles', in *De Gustibus: Essays for Alain Renoir*, ed. John Miles Foley (New York: Garland, 1992), pp. 110–50.

20 Cf. Hansen, *Solomon Complex*, p. 132.

21 Cf. Hansen, *Solomon Complex*, p. 134, and Steen's comments about Aldhelm's provided solutions as a prompt to contemplation of deeper meaning. Janie Steen, *Verse and Virtuosity: The Adaptation of Latin Rhetoric in Old English Poetry* (Toronto: University of Toronto Press, 2008), p. 91.

22 The interacting vernacular and Latin traditions have received good treatment in Andy Orchard, 'Enigma Variations: The Anglo-Saxon Riddle-Tradition', in *Latin Learning and English Lore: Studies in Anglo-Saxon Literature for Michael Lapidge*, ed. Katherine O'Brien O'Keeffe and Andy Orchard, 2 vols (Toronto: University of Toronto Press, 2005), I, pp. 284–304; Dieter Bitterli, *Say What I Am Called: The Old English Riddles of the Exeter Book and the Anglo-Latin Riddle Tradition* (Toronto: University of Toronto Press, 2009); Mercedes Salvador-Bello, *Isidorean Perceptions of Order: The Exeter Book Riddles and Medieval Latin Enigmata* (Morgantown: West Virginia University Press, 2015).

23 Nigel F. Barley, 'Structural Aspects of the Anglo-Saxon Riddle', *Semiotica*, 10 (1974), 143–75, at p. 144.

24 My wording is influenced by Neuman de Vegvar's reference to the situation of 'performed complexity' created by the Franks Casket, which her discussion connects insightfully to wisdom literature. Carol Neuman de Vegvar, 'Reading the Franks Casket: Contexts and Audiences', in *Intertexts: Studies in Anglo-Saxon Culture Presented to Paul E. Szarmach*, ed. Virginia Blanton and Helene Scheck (Tempe, AZ: ACMRS and Brepols, 2008), pp. 141–59, at p. 151.

25 Britt Mize, *Traditional Subjectivities: The Old English Poetics of Mentality* (Toronto: University of Toronto Press, 2013).

26 See also Olsen, Chapter 6 in this volume, for further discussion of these terms.

27 Niles, *Old English Enigmatic Poems*, pp. 44–8, surveys many prior analyses of other poetry as riddle-like.
28 Niles, *Old English Enigmatic Poems*; quotation from p. 44.
29 Niles, *Old English Enigmatic Poems*, pp. 307–10; Patrick J. Murphy, *Unriddling the Exeter Riddles* (University Park: Pennsylvania State University Press, 2011), p. 237.
30 Niles, *Old English Enigmatic Poems*, pp. 1–3.
31 Leneghan surveys current views of the Vercelli Book's rationale and purpose before offering his own analysis of the collection as showing a unifying interest in teaching; see Francis Leneghan, 'Teaching the Teachers: The Vercelli Book and the Mixed Life', *ES*, 94 (2013), 627–58. My perspective is compatible with Leneghan's, but with greater emphasis on the 'conditional' side of what I am calling conditional revelation.
32 Leneghan does refer to both the *Fates* and *Elene* passages as riddles. 'Teaching the Teachers', pp. 648 and 653.
33 At least since Margaret Schlauch, 'The *Dream of the Rood* as Prosopopoeia', in *Essays and Studies in Honor of Carleton Brown*, ed. P. W. Long (New York: NYU Press, 1940), pp. 23–34.
34 This quotation from the facsimile: Celia Sisam, ed., *The Vercelli Book*, Early English Manuscripts in Facsimile, 19 (Copenhagen: Rosenkilde and Bagger, 1976).
35 Martin Irvine, *The Making of Textual Culture: Grammatica and Literary Theory, 350–1100* (Cambridge: Cambridge University Press, 1994), pp. 437–49; Britt Mize, 'The Mental Container and the Cross of Christ: Revelation and Community in *The Dream of the Rood*', *Studies in Philology*, 107 (2010), 131–78, at pp. 156–63.
36 Mize, 'Mental Container and the Cross of Christ'; Leneghan, 'Teaching the Teachers', 644–5.
37 The *Vercelli Book* prose is cited from D. G. Scragg, ed., *The Vercelli Homilies and Related Texts*, EETS os, 300 (Oxford: Oxford University Press, 1992).

15

The materiality of fire in *Legbysig* and *Ligbysig* (R.30a and b) and an unexpected new solution

Pirkko A. Koppinen

Fire 'is a rapid chemical oxidative reaction that generates heat, light and produces a range of chemical products'.[1] Since early hominins harnessed fire at least 500,000 years ago and 'learned to maintain and control ignition', fire has had a profound material effect on human beings,[2] including those living in early medieval England, who depended on fire as a technology for heating, cooking, lighting, and manufacturing.[3] This chapter focuses on references to fire in the clues of the duplicate texts of *Legbysig* and *Ligbysig* (R.30a and b), and is informed by the notion that materiality—including that of fire—is a 'cultural process'.[4] I argue that concentrating on the function and sensory experience of materiality in literature can provide new insights and interpretations of texts and, in this case, lead to an unexpected new solution to one of the *Exeter Book* riddles.

Legbysig, *Ligbysig*, and the accepted solution, 'tree'

The riddle exists as two separate texts in the manuscript, *Legbysig* and *Ligbysig*. Liuzza notes that 'the variations in the two texts of *Riddle 30* are individually minor differences of lexicon, morphology, and syntax'.[5] I present *Legbysig* here in its modern, edited form:[6]

> Ic eom legbysig,   lace mid winde,
> bewunden mid wuldre,   wedre gesomnad,
> fus forðweges,   fyre gebysgad,
> bearu blowende,   byrnende gled.
> Ful oft mec gesiþas   sendað æfter hondum,
> þæt mec weras ond wif   wlonce cyssað.
> Þonne ic mec onhæbbe,   ond hi onhnigaþ to me
> monige mid miltse,   þær ic monnum sceal
> ycan upcyme eadignesse.

[I am busy with fire, fight with the wind, wound around with wonder, united with storm, eager for the journey, agitated by fire; (I am) a blooming grove, a burning ember. Very often companions send me from hand to hand so that proud men and women kiss me. When I exalt myself and they bow to me, many with humility, there I shall bring increasing happiness to men.]

The widely accepted answer to *Legbysig* is *beam* ('tree, log, ship, and cross'), first suggested by F. A. Blackburn in 1900, and now almost universally accepted by all editors.[7] More recently, John D. Niles has provided another variation to Blackburn's solution: *treow*, an Old English neuter noun that indicates 'a tree (or a grove of trees)'.[8] The difference between the two solutions, *beam* and *treow*, is not of great consequence; both solutions refer to a tree (1–4) that provides wood, the material from which the manmade objects revered by humans are made (5–9).

This accepted reading is based on understanding the materiality and material experience of a tree, first as a living being in the natural landscape, and then as a manmade object within human society. That is, the riddle opens with an envelope pattern created with references to the riddle creature's relationship with fire (1–3). The first half-line tells us that the creature is somehow busy with fire. In the second half-line, the creature is considered to be a tree swaying in the wind; after that, the tree's trunk is 'wound around with' its 'wonder', its foliage (2a), or perhaps the foliage of a clinging ivy; and then it is 'united with storm' in another reference of the tree at the mercy of natural forces (2b; the first is in line 1b).[9] Then the texts shift briefly to a description of a material object, perhaps a ship that is 'eager for the journey' (3a).[10] The third line completes the envelope pattern with a reference to the creature being busy with fire again (3b).

Line 4, at the centre of the text, gives the best match for a 'tree/wood' solution: the creature is now 'a blooming grove, a burning ember'. In these two clues, a supposedly flowering grove provides the wood that in turn becomes an ember when it is burned. Thus, *treow* is not only the commonsensical solution for *Legbysig* but also the one the riddle texts offer to the reader by seemingly giving away the answer midway: *bearu* ('a grove') (4a) is a 'small wood' or 'a group of trees', from which is extrapolated the singular 'tree'.[11] Yet, as Nelson, who in this instance is discussing the 'warrior' in *Torht Wiga* (R.50), notes: 'a genuine riddle would never be this open about the identity of its subject'.[12] I will return to this important line later in my discussion when I suggest the new solution.

Once line 4 is solved as a tree, it is just a matter of matching the rest of the lines (5–9) with something that is manufactured from wood, the material acquired from trees and revered by humans. As a cup, the riddle creature is passed from hand to hand (5) and kissed by proud men and women (6).[13] The image recalls the communal drinking rituals in *Beowulf* where the men drink from their lord's—or lady's—cup as a gesture of loyalty.[14] The cup in the riddles may be a wooden cup decorated with an interlace collar, such as that found in the Sutton Hoo boat burial, and a worthy drinking vessel of early medieval English royalty.[15]

The last lines present the real challenge for the solver: what is a thing which, when it 'exalt[s itself] and they bow to [it]' (30a: 7b), brings happiness to people? Or, in *Ligbysig*, what brings happiness when the 'high-spirited [ones] bow to [it] with humility' (30b: 7b). Lines 7–9 in the two versions—in their particular ways—explain how people show reverence to the riddle creature and have suggested to solvers that it is 'a cross' made from wood.[16] The Cross was an important symbol for the early medieval Christian, as is demonstrated in *The Dream of the Rood*, which describes how the tree first grows free in the forest before it is cut down and made into a gallows and then—washed with the Saviour's blood—transformed into a revered symbol of salvation, the wooden Cross. 'Given this abundance of information', Niles claims, 'there can be no doubt as to what is being described, at least in its general features: it is a tree (or a grove of trees), together with some firewood, a wooden cup, and a wooden cross'.[17]

I have laboured over the accepted 'tree' solution because it shows how understanding materiality—of both fire and the material at its mercy—is central to understanding the texts. However, investigation of the material phenomenon of fire in *Legbysig* and *Ligbysig*—together with my sensory experience of it—yields another interpretation of the riddle and enables me to see beyond the accepted reading. But before I discuss the new solution, I wish to explain briefly my methodology, which is based on the idea of materiality and my own personal experience.

Material culture and sensory experience

Material culture is widely represented and studied in Old English poems, often as a quarry for archaeologists want to dig deeper into the culture of early medieval England, of which—understandably, far removed from that era as we are today—only remnants exist today.[18] Such an approach, if undertaken carefully, can be useful, but often it has ignored the actual experience of materiality of the world at large, which is evident in poems such as the *Exeter Book* riddles.[19] An understanding of Old English language, early medieval culture, its texts and traditions, and its political and ideological contexts shapes and guides the reader's interpretation process. But textual knowledge is not enough. Experience of non-verbal reality is paramount for interpretation, as Harri Veivo points out: 'language is not an autonomous system, but functions *in contact with experience*. If there [were] no contact between the addressee's cognitive capacities and bodily being-in-the-world, language would not be able to convey information'.[20] Furthermore, as Chris Tilley points out, 'through things we can understand ourselves and others',[21] an idea that can be supported by an examination of the representation of material culture in the *Exeter Book* riddles. Elsewhere Tilley contends that, in material culture studies, 'the object world is absolutely central to an understanding of the identities of individual persons and societies'.[22] I would like to add natural phenomena to Tilley's definition of what he calls the 'object world', for natural phenomena such as fire are also experienced in our bodies through our senses.[23] The materiality of fire in *Legbysig* and *Ligbysig* exemplifies how everyday experience can be used to interpret material objects and phenomena depicted in Old English poetry.[24]

Furthermore, as Victor Buchli notes, materiality can be understood as a 'cultural process'.[25] Such cultural processes are also evident in *Legbysig*, especially in lines 5–9, which depict social rituals to which the manmade objects described in these lines are central. Moreover, as Anamaria Depner suggests, 'focusing on a thing's materiality is an approach capable of revealing an unexpected variety of meanings which otherwise would be ignored'.[26] The 'things' in *Legbysig* and *Ligbysig* are the phenomena and material objects described in the clues and, as such, these texts provide a prime example of 'materiality' as both 'physics' and 'cultural process'. As discussed earlier, the first four lines of the text deal with fire as a material phenomenon and the rest of the riddle texts describe a cultural process that culminates in the glorification of the cup and cross in human society. I will now return to the *Exeter Book* riddles and offer a brief discussion of fire in those texts before I suggest a new solution for *Legbysig* and *Ligbysig*.

Fire, a technology and natural phenomenon

The *Exeter Book* riddles depict two ignition sources available in early medieval England: lightning and manmade fire. The first, a 'natural ignition source',[27] is described in *Min Frea Fæste Genearwað* (R.3):

> earpan gesceafte
> fus ofer folcum fyre swætað
> blacan lige. (43b–5a)
>
> [Dusky creatures striving forward over people sweat fire, white flame.]

The riddle describes how lightning appears to the visual sense as a 'white flame' that runs down to earth like sweat from thunder clouds ('the dusky creatures'). The second ignition source mentioned in the *Exeter Book* riddles is manmade, as *Ymbhwyrft* (R.40) explains: *Flinte ic eom heardre þe þis fyr driveþ / of þissum strongan style heardan* ('I am harder than the flint that drives this fire from this strong hard steel') (78–9). Flint and steel are described as *dumbum twam* ('two dumb ones') (2b) in *Torht Wiga*, which has been solved as 'fire'.[28] There may be a reference to lightning in *Legbysig* and *Ligbysig* (1a), but the texts do not mention an ignition source *per se*, just the effect that fire has on the material it is used to transform.[29]

Torht Wiga also explains how early medieval English people understood the benefits of and danger posed by fire, which in human history 'has long been used and valued by humanity as a source of heat and light ... and recognised as a dangerous phenomenon':[30]

> he him fremum stepeð
> life on lissum leanað grimme
> þe hine wloncne weorþan læteð. (8b–10)
>
> [He (fire) exalts them in comfort for their joy in life, grimly rewards the one who lets him become proud.]

As the riddle states, fire can be useful and bring comfort when it is controlled. *Fotum Ic Fere* (R.12), on the other hand, describes fire as a pleasant source of heat that has a useful function: a servant girl *wyrmeð hwilum / fægre to fyre* ('sometimes warms [something] pleasantly by the fire') (10b–11a).[31] But when fire is out of control, it is a bad servant, as is explained in *Beowulf*: soon after Heorot is built, the poet tells us that it will be destroyed by the embrace of *laðan liges* ('hostile flames') (83a). We are reminded of the destructive force of fire by the damage visible in the leaves of the *Exeter Book* manuscript: part of *Ligbysig*, in between *Homiletic Fragment II* and *Be Sonde Muðlease* (R.60), was damaged by a hot poker, which has left some words illegible (in lines 2 and 4a). The mutilation by the fiery poker, which left a permanent mark on the vellum, is a reminder that the *Exeter Book* manuscript is a material object, subject to the elements, including fire.[32] Early medieval English people experienced fire through all their senses, not just through the visual and tactile senses demonstrated in *Min Frea Fæste Genearwað* and *Fotum Ic Fere*. It was a necessary part of their daily life, as it was for me when I was growing up in Finland in the 1960s and 1970s.[33]

Fire in my experience

Fire as a natural phenomenon played a part of my life as I grew up in a small village in south-eastern Finland, in a house that was heated by burning wood during the cold winters. Each room had its own wood-burning stove that was fired once a day from September until late spring—and twice a day when it was very cold. Our meals were prepared on a hob heated by burning wood in the baking oven, and the wood-burning oven of our sauna, including the stove that heated the hot water, was lit once a week for the Saturday cleansing ritual. But fire was not only part of wintry life. In our summer house by a lake, we used fire to make our meals on a barbeque, heat the sauna, and burn a *kokko* ('bonfire') to celebrate midsummer. As in *Torht Wiga*, fire was not only a beneficial servant in our life; we feared it as much as we enjoyed its servitude. I experienced the fierce nature of fire when as a child I witnessed our neighbour's house burn. Our house was made of wood and the flames sent sparks flying high in the hot August night. I was reminded of the materiality of fire and the effect it has on material culture when I translated *Legbysig* and *Ligbysig* into Finnish for *The Riddle Ages*.[34] The words in my native tongue created memories of these experiences and helped me to understand the everyday experience of fire in early medieval England. They also sparked an additional memory that led to a new, unexpected solution.

The last village smith

A neighbour of ours was one of the last village smiths in Finland. As children, we lingered outside the smithy, listened to the noises coming from there, and peeked through the gaps in the door to see flying sparks and hot, molten metal glowing in the dark. That memory made me rethink the clues in *Legbysig* and *Ligbysig*: if the surface reading of the texts provides 'tree/cross', a literal solution, then reading the clues (lines 1–4) metaphorically might reveal a different material that can be worked into the manmade object in lines 5–9. Such an approach is common in the *Exeter Book* riddles, which often use metaphorical disguises to conceal the riddle creature.[35] If we interpret the clues in *Legbysig* metaphorically, especially the ones that depict fire in lines 1a, 2b and 4, we can consider the text further and identify other materials that were available in early medieval England and that came into contact with fire, which transformed them. One such material is *ora* ('metal in its unreduced state').[36]

An alternative solution: *ora*

The masculine noun *ora* ('ore') stands for the raw material of any metal, whether gold, silver, iron, or lead. These metals were used by early medieval smiths to produce material artefacts—all with the aid of fire.[37] *Frod Wæs Min Fromcynn* (R.83), solved as 'ore', tells the metaphorical story 'of gold or silver ore wrenched from the earth, fashioned into treasures and guarded, as the treasure in *Beowulf* was guarded, until it was needed for a medium of exchange, for power', as Nelson explains.[38] *Legbysig* and *Ligbysig* do not expound such a trope of violence. Instead they depict fire as a material phenomenon harnessed to manufacturing processes.

In these texts, metal ore, like wood from a tree, is *legbysig* or *ligbysig* ('busy with fire') (1a) when worked by a smith, as the metal reacts to the heat of the fire in the smelting process. In its 'prosopopoetic monologue',[39] the creature as metal ore tells how it 'fight[s] the wind' (1b) when the bellows blow air into the furnace and the metal responds becoming hotter. In line 2a, the ore—perhaps that of gold in this case—may refer to the way gold wires are wound around into an interlace pattern on a golden cover of a gospel book, or as decoration on a sword or great golden buckle, like that found in the Sutton Hoo boat burial.[40] The ore can also be 'wound around with wonder' (2a), as, for example, a cross covered in a gold or silver sheet.[41] In line 2b, the ore is *wedre gesomnad* ('united with storm') when it is worked in the forge. As in line 1a, air is pushed into the fire that makes it 'busy' and makes the fire rage and grow into a fire storm. Sparks fly when, for example, heated iron is hammered by the smith—a sight that mesmerised me as a child. Then the ore is *fus forðweges* ('eager for the journey') (3a) as the raw metal is *fyre gebysgad* ('agitated by [the hot] fire') (3b); it melts and takes a liquid form. The ore—gold, silver, or lead—becomes runny in the smelting process and is 'eager' to flow into the mould in its process of transformation into a revered metal object, a cross or a portable altarpiece.[42] In that material process, the metal ore is transformed into a metaphorical *bearu blowende* ('blooming grove') (4a). The sensory experience of the flowering of the heated metal forged in the hands of the smith shines white, yellow, orange and red. Taken metaphorically, the heated ore is a *byrnende gled* ('burning ember') (4b) and visually similar to a burning ember of a log glowing in the hearth. Such scenes would have been familiar to early medieval English people, who had smiths working in their villages.[43] Thus line 4, when read literally, produces the 'tree/cross'-solution, but when read metaphorically, produces the new solution, *ora* ('ore').

Once lines 1–4 are solved as *ora* ('ore'), the rest of the clues can be solved in the same way as in the previous 'tree' solution; only the material of the manmade objects has changed. The familiar images still come from Christianity: a metal cross, made of gold and silver, can be kissed, as can a chalice in the communion, described in *Hring Gylden* (R.59).[44] The cross in *Dream of the Rood* will bring *blis mycel* ('great bliss') to those who seek it (139b); similarly, the riddle creature brings *eadignesse* ('happiness or joy') (9b) to people when they bow to it—that is, when they pray to the cross on the altar for their salvation.

Conclusion

The creature, the material in *Legbysig*, is transformed by the manufacturing process into a potentially life-changing object. Thus fire, at the heart of the riddle creature's narrative, partakes in a cultural process that has both material and spiritual effects on people's lives, as it promises eternal life for those who pray to it. The exact manufacturing methods and the effects that fire has on the material are difficult to glean from the elusive texts, but focusing on materiality in the double texts can lead to new interpretations and understanding of the early medieval world.

Notes

1 Andrew C. Scott, *et al.*, *Fire on Earth: An Introduction* (Chichester: Wiley-Blackwell, 2014), p. 3.
2 Scott, *et al.*, *Fire on Earth*, p. 195.
3 For early medieval life, see e.g. Sally Crawford, *Daily Life in Anglo-Saxon England* (Oxford: Greenwood, 2009).
4 Victor Buchli, 'Introduction', in *Material Culture Reader*, ed. Victor Buchli (Oxford: Berg, 2002), pp. 1–22, at p. 18. My emphasis.
5 R. M. Liuzza, 'The Texts of the Old English *Riddle 30*', *JEGP*, 87 (1988), 1–15, at p. 3 (list of textual variants at p. 4). See also A. N. Doane, 'Spacing, Placing and Effacing: Scribal Textuality and Exeter Riddle 30 a/b', in *New Approaches to Editing Old English Verse*, ed. Sarah Larratt Keefer and Katherine O'Brien O'Keeffe (Cambridge: D. S. Brewer, 1998), pp. 45–65; Jonathan Wilcox, 'Transmission of Literature and Learning', in *A Companion to Anglo-Saxon Literature*, ed. Phillip Pulsiano and Elaine Treharne (Oxford: Blackwell, 2001), pp. 50–70; Elena Afros, 'Syntactic Variation in Riddles 30A and 30B', *N&Q*, 52 (2005), 2–5.
6 I will discuss the damaged words in *Ligbysig* as appropriate. *Legbysig* 7b reads *on hin gað* (a nonsensical form) in the MS and is emended to *onhnigað* by using the text of *Ligbysig* 7b; see George Philip Krapp and Elliott Van Kirk Dobbie, eds, *The Exeter Book*, ASPR, 3 (New York: Columbia University Press, 1936), p. 338.
7 F. A. Blackburn, '*The Husband's Message* and the Accompanying Riddles of the *Exeter Book*', *JEGP*, 3 (1900), 1–13, at pp. 3–4. See the discussion of past solutions in Craig Williamson, ed., *The Old English Riddles of the Exeter Book* (Chapel Hill: University of North Carolina Press, 1977), pp. 230–1.
8 John D. Niles, *Old English Enigmatic Poems and the Play of the Texts* (Turnhout: Brepols, 2006), p. 130.
9 Williamson, *Old English Riddles*, p. 231.
10 Blackburn, '*Husband's Message*', p. 4.
11 *OED*, *s.v.* 'grove', n., sense 1.a.
12 Marie Nelson, 'Four Social Functions of the Exeter Book Riddles', *Neophilologus*, 75 (1991), 445–50, at p. 448.
13 Using the story of *Cædmon's Hymn* as evidence, Blackburn suggests that the object in line 5 can also be 'a harp', which is handed around in the hall; see '*Husband's Message*', p. 12.
14 See, e.g. *Beowulf* 491–5a, 615–24, 1014b–17a, 1024b–5a, 1169–1170a, 1192–3a, 1231.
15 See the discussion in, e.g. Martin G. Comey, 'The Wooden Drinking Vessels in the Sutton Hoo Assemblage: Materials, Morphology, and Usage', in *Trees and Timber in the Anglo-Saxon World*, ed. Michael D. J. Bintley and Michael G. Shapland (Oxford: Oxford University Press, 2014), pp. 107–21.

16 The role of the cross in the riddle is discussed in Arnold Talentino, 'Riddle 30: The Vehicle of the Cross', *Neophilologus*, 65 (1981), 129–36.
17 Niles, *Old English Enigmatic Poems*, p. 130.
18 A prime example is *Beowulf*; for a review of scholarship on archaeology and *Beowulf* since the nineteenth century, see, for example, Rosemary Cramp, '*Beowulf* and Archaeology', *Medieval Archaeology*, 1 (1957), 57–77, repr. in *The 'Beowulf' Poet: A Collection of Critical Essays*, ed. Donald K. Fry (Englewood Cliffs, NJ: Prentice-Hall, 1968), pp. 114–40; Roberta Frank, '*Beowulf* and Sutton Hoo: The Odd Couple', in *The Voyage to the Other World: The Legacy of Sutton Hoo*, ed. Calvin B. Kendall and Peter S. Wells (Minneapolis: University of Minnesota Press, 1992), pp. 47–64.
19 Materiality in the *Exeter Book* riddles is discussed in James Paz, *Nonhuman Voices in Anglo-Saxon Literature and Material Culture* (Manchester: Manchester University Press, 2017), especially chapters 2 and 3.
20 Harri Veivo, 'The New Literary Semiotics', *Semiotica*, 165 (2007), 41–55, at p. 43. Emphasis in the original.
21 Chris Tilley, 'Objectification', in *Handbook of Material Culture*, ed. Chris Tilley, *et al.* (London: SAGE, 2006), pp. 60–73, at p. 61.
22 Tilley, 'Objectification', p. 61. The word 'thing' has many meanings and connotations that are hard to pin down, but for the purposes of clarity, I consider things as material objects and phenomena. Cf. the '*irreducibility* of *things* to *objects*', in Bill Brown, 'Thing Theory', *Critical Inquiry*, 28.1 (2001), 1–22, at p. 3. Emphasis in the original. For a discussion of the Old English word *þing* in relation to 'thing theory', see Paz, *Nonhuman Voices*, pp. 7–13.
23 For a discussion of the materiality of phenomena in *Exeter Book* riddles, see e.g. Daniel Tiffany, 'Lyric Substance: On Riddles, Materialism, and Poetic Obscurity', *Critical Inquiry*, 28 (2001), 72–98. See also Chris Tilley, 'Metaphor, Materiality and Interpretation', in *The Material Culture Reader*, ed. Victor Buchli (Oxford: Berg, 2002), pp. 23–6, at p. 24.
24 I have discussed the role of the everyday experience in the meaning-making processes elsewhere. See Pirkko A. Koppinen, '*Swa þa stafas becnaþ*: Ciphers of the Heroic Idiom in the *Exeter Book* Riddles, *Beowulf*, *Judith*, and *Andreas*' (unpublished PhD thesis, Royal Holloway, University of London, 2009), pp. 41–4.
25 Buchli, 'Introduction', p. 18. My emphasis.
26 Anamaria Depner, 'Worthless Things? On the Difference between Devaluing and Sorting out Things', in *Mobility, Meaning and the Transformation of Things: Shifting Contexts of Material Culture through Time and Space*, ed. Hans Peter Hahn and Hadas Weiss (Oxford: Oxbow, 2013), pp. 78–90, at p. 88.

27 Scott, *et al.*, *Fire on Earth*, pp. 4–6.
28 Williamson, *Old English Riddles*, pp. 292–3.
29 Williamson, *Old English Riddles*, p. 231.
30 *OED*, *s.v.* 'fire', n., sense 1.a.
31 *Fotum Ic Fere* is often solved as an 'Ox', but I have solved it as *Wudu* ('wood') and suggested that the thing warmed pleasantly by the fire can be a domestic object made from wood; conversely, the clue in 11a may be litotic, with the wood burned as firewood. See Pirkko A. Koppinen, 'Breaking the Mould: Solving Riddle 12 as *Wudu* "Wood"', in *Trees and Timber in the Anglo-Saxon World*, ed. Michael D. J. Bintley and Michael G. Shapland (Oxford: Oxford University Press, 2014), pp. 158–76.
32 The damage to the manuscript is discussed in, e.g. Bernard J. Muir, ed., *The Exeter Anthology of Old English Poetry: An Edition of Exeter Dean and Chapter MS 3501*, 2nd edn, 2 vols (Exeter: Exeter University Press, 2000), I, pp. 13–15.
33 The same applies to all humanity; see e.g. Juli G. Pausas and Jon E. Keeley, 'A Burning Story: The Role of Fire in the History of Life', *BioScience*, 59 (2009), 593–601, at pp. 596–600; Scott, *et al.*, *Fire on Earth*, pp. 91–2, 98–101, and 195–289.
34 For my translations, see Pirkko A. Koppinen, 'Riddle 30a and b (or Riddle 28a and b)', in *The Riddle Ages: An Anglo-Saxon Riddle Blog*, ed. Megan Cavell with Matthias Ammon and Victoria Symons, 13 October 2014, https://theriddleages.wordpress.com/2014/10/13/riddle-30a-and-b-or-riddle-28a-and-b/ (accessed 31 August 2019); and for my commentary, see 'Commentary for Riddle 30 a and b', 21 October 2014, https://theriddleages.wordpress.com/2014/10/21/commentary-for-riddle-30a-and-b/ (accessed 30 November 2017).
35 For a discussion of metaphoric disguise in riddles, see e.g. Williamson, *Old English Riddles*, p. 26.
36 *Ora* is discussed in reference to *Frod Wæs Min Fromcynn* in Niles, *Old English Enigmatic Poems*, pp. 134–5.
37 B-T, *s.v. ora*. For early medieval English metalwork and manufacturing techniques, see e.g. Kevin Leahy, *Anglo-Saxon Crafts* (Stroud: Tempus, 2003), pp. 111–66; Elizabeth Coatsworth and Michael Pinder, *The Art of the Anglo-Saxon Goldsmith: Fine Metalwork in Anglo-Saxon England: Its Practice and Practitioners* (Woodbridge: Boydell, 2002), pp. 64–101. For the methods of blacksmithing in general, see Percy W. Blandford, *Practical Blacksmithing and Metalworking* (New York: TAB, 1988).
38 Marie Nelson, 'The Rhetoric of the Exeter Book Riddles', *Speculum*, 49.3 (1974), 421–40, at p. 426.
39 Liuzza, 'Old English Riddle 30', p. 1.
40 Angela C. Evans, *The Sutton Hoo Ship Burial* (London: British Museum Press, 2002), pp. 89–91.

41 See e.g. the Brussels Cross, discussed in Leslie Webster, '75. Reliquary Cross', in *The Golden Age of Anglo-Saxon Art, 966–1066*, ed. Janet Backhouse, D. H. Turner, and Leslie Webster (London: British Museum Press, 1984), pp. 90–92; for the colour image, see plate xxiii between pp. 176 and 177.

42 See e.g. Leslie Webster, '76. Portable Altar', in *Golden Age*, pp. 92–3.

43 Ironsmiths are discussed in, e.g. Allen J. Frantzen, *Food, Eating and Identity in Early Medieval England* (Woodbridge: Boydell, 2014), pp. 132–4; and Leahy, *Anglo-Saxon Crafts*, pp. 116–21. For a comprehensive discussion of ironwork in early medieval England, see Patrick Ottaway, 'Anglo-Scandinavian Ironwork from 16–22 Coppergate, York c. 850–1100 A.D.', 2 vols (unpublished PhD thesis, University of York, 1989).

44 The manufacturing techniques of fine metalwork are discussed in Coatsworth and Pinder, *Art of the Anglo-Saxon Goldsmith*, pp. 64–101.

16

Dyre cræft: new translations of Exeter riddle fragments *Modor Monigra* (R.84), *Se Wiht Wombe Hæfde* (R.89), and *Brunra Beot* (R.92), accompanied by notes on process

Miller Wolf Oberman

Modor Monigra (R.84)

The phrase *dyre cræft* sits in the middle of the first of two damaged sections of *Modor Monigra* (R.84). It struck me, glancing at the poem for the first time, because of its clarity—a small floating raft of remaining language poking up right in the middle of three heavily burned lines. This may be too much to ask of two words, but *dyre cræft*, or 'dear craft', seems to speak to fragmentary Old English poetry as a whole: worthy, glorious, dear, beloved, precious, costly, that which does not come cheap, or easily. Each of these linked senses of the word *dear* goes back to Old English. The *OED* cites *Gryrelic Hleahtor* (R.33) for the sense of dear as glorious (*Is min modor mægða cynnes þæs deorestan* ('my mother is of the most glorious of maiden-kind') (9)), Cynewulf's *Juliana* for tenderness (*ond se deora sunu* ('and the dear son') (725b)), and the *Anglo-Saxon Chronicle* for the sense of economic expense (*mycel hunger ofer eall Englaland and corn swa dyre* ('a great hunger over all the land of the English and corn so expensive') (*Anglo-Saxon Chronicle C*, *s.a.* 1044)[1]). Craft, too, has a confluence of linked definitions, virtually unchanged between the writing of the *Exeter Book* and our present day. *Craft/cræft* carries the sense of skill and art. It can mean human skill or art, but also magic, the occult, indicating, perhaps, uneasiness about where art and skill come from, or questions regarding the links between skill and artifice, human labour and spells or enchantments. These two words have been written and spoken and worn for a thousand years, though we rarely see them together this way now. Dear craft, worthy skill, expensive magic. A craft is something honed, perhaps to the extent that it appears too beautiful or well-made to come entirely from this world. And these fragments are dear, indeed—beloved, and rare, utterly finite.

While many translators attempt to smooth over missing language, I am fascinated by the ways in which Old English poetry allows me to walk through its bones, and part of my translation instinct is about paying respect to gaps in these poetic remains, rather than attempting to force a seeming wholeness onto them. Old English poems already exist as sites of multiple kinds of loss. Given that these few remaining poems are in a language no longer spoken, are often damaged, and that many of them are considered without literary merit, it seems crucial to engage them in a way that honours their losses, instead of attempting to offer them 'accessibility'. This place of loss and temporal and textual scarring is where I hope my translations will intervene and build.

My methods for translating fragments are guided by Walter Benjamin's foundational essay, 'The Task of the Translator', and Gayatri Chakravorty Spivak's response, 'The Politics of Translation'.[2] Benjamin argues that a translator's aim should be to allow a source text to shine through its translation. This is achieved, he writes, by a 'literal rendering of the syntax which proves words rather than sentences to be the primary element of the translator'.[3] Spivak believes that 'the task of the translator is to facilitate ... love between the original and its shadow', which she calls 'a love that permits fraying'.[4] These two perspectives are crucial to the work of translating riddles that in many places have 'frayed' or broken down at the sentence level. Instead of trying to find answers to the gaps in these riddles, these translations focus on an attempt to communicate their words, syntax, and questions. My focus here is the poems themselves, rather than any surrounding scholarship.

Benjamin's instruction to translate words and syntax, rather than sentence or meaning is simultaneously a burden and a relief when working on fragments. On one hand, parts of meaning are already unreachable while, on the other, using a sense of the text as a whole as a guide is even less useful when translating a fragment. In some sense, though, all riddles are fragmentary. They operate through withholding crucial and obvious information; they aim to cleverly trick, revealing themselves, and their 'meaning' through unusual description, through misdirection, through removal of the ordinary means of communication. They lend themselves particularly to poetry. This is not to claim all poems as riddles, but poems, like riddles, aim to reflect something of the world known to us through estrangement. Whether the joy or pain of love or its loss, or political rage, or the sense of wonder at the birth of a child, poems seek to make the world already known to us new, seen and felt as if for the first time. Poems operate in a kind of harmonics, aiming at recognition, memory, and identification, while simultaneously inflecting them with a riveting rawness.

The Old English riddle poems offer readers this same joy: the thrill of an object, for example, dangling by a thigh, which is both key and not-key at once. The 'real' key and not-key are both more alive as we consider new ways in which the things of our world may be alike. Of course, the fragmented riddles are among the most difficult (in many cases impossible) to solve. There is something freeing about this, because they remain poems, even if unsolvable. This insolvability, I hope, serves to highlight language itself, its presence and absence, and the places where presence and absence meet, which in these poems is literal and physical: they meet at the damage, where words turn to burns, and meaning is removed or changed.

In the past, when translating fragments, I have used brackets to indicate missing sections. Here I began including (as Krapp and Dobbie, and Muir do), just outside the brackets, the unburned word scraps which remain but are untranslatable. Fire is messy; it does not consume by the word. These places are blurred—are three letters of a word more like a word, or like none? In the past I have treated these gaps cleanly, as if these sections were sliced off, as if amputated, or blacked out, as if classified. Brackets are clean and non-porous—they offer almost nothing of the visual experience of looking at the damaged manuscript itself. I do not know if the choice to include the stray letters is better, but it is more honest, more straightforward. And then I moved the word fragments inside the brackets. In translation, what do the brackets truly signify? If they are meant to mark the boundaries of manuscript damage, as in Old English editions, the surviving letters should rightly sit outside the brackets. In contrast, if the brackets signify a hole in meaning (and often syntax, grammar, form), a break in the poem, a loss, then these word fragments should be inside, rather than out. They are outside the burn, but inside the loss. Perhaps this is one occasion where we can see the place where physical and metaphorical damage become distinct from one another. If an Old English edition of a text uses brackets to represent manuscript damage, perhaps a translation can use them to represent damage to meaning, or to language.

Se Wiht Wombe Hæfde (R.89)

Removing the possibility of an 'answer' still leaves us with the way that the language in these poems dances around and plays with meaning. In *Se Wiht Wombe Hæfde* the creature possesses a *wombe*, which probably just means it has a stomach, not a 'womb' as we would think of it now, but the sonic proximity of the word *wombe* to words like *woma* (a noise, a howling, a terror) and *wohum* (a bending, a crookedness, depravity, perversity, a mistake) suggest that perhaps there is only a small leap between the stomach and what can be felt in it—the way our stomachs seem to knot with fear, the way our intestines bend. In this sense, the contents of our stomachs, our *wambhord*, are more than food or drink; they are, as we all know, instinctive repositories for emotional freight. This poem is so gutted by holes that my original translation seemed almost worthless to me. Once I had removed all of the friction caused by the choices that had to be made, there seemed to be almost nothing left to the poem at all, and hence the third version, which, I hope, *is* a poem, though perhaps not the riddle from the *Exeter Book*.

Se Wiht Wombe Hæfde (R.89), v. 1[5]

[ ] the/that creature/person/animal
had/held/possessed a womb/stomach/crookedness/depravity/
tumult/terror/howling/noise
tne] was leather [*beg*
on] behind/in back.
greeted/great (as in size?)/grit [*wea*
] cunningly/craftily carried out/
worked/caused for a while again/at times [
] to press/stab/pierce, he pondered/
thought since [*u*
] so many banquets/dainties/foods/meals in that season/
space of time/for a while/continually.

Se Wiht Wombe Hæfde, v. 2

[ ] that creature
had a stomach [
tne] was leather [*beg*
on] in back.
greeted [*wea*
] cunningly carried out
for a while again [
] to pierce, he pondered

since [*u*
] so many meals in that season.

Se Wiht Wombe Hæfde, reconsidered

That creature, [who something, before the ms was burned]
possessed, had, or held a *wombe*,

[which is to say had a womb, so was, perhaps, a woman. Or, because Clark-Hall says *womb* = *wamb*, this person just has a regular human stomach, which can ache, as in *wambæcc*, swell, *wambablawung*, and whose contents are its *wambhord*. Bosworth-Toller defines *wambhord* differently, as 'the weapons contained in a fortified place.' Is that a metaphor, or is a stomach a battleground? Or, does the creature instead possess a *woma*: a noise, a howling, a terror, as in the noise of battle, a tumult, like a *swefnes*, a terror-dream. Or, the creature instead has a *wohum*, from the dative (so, indirectly) of *woh*: a bending, a crookedness. Depravity, perversity, a mistake. Indirectly, the error, the bentness, has been performed for this creature, and—]

Some part of it was leather, its behind, or, in back.

[This creature wore leather on its back, or had leathery skin, or had a stiff, cured quality about its hindquarters, maybe they were]

great, or gritty, or which greeted [*wea*
(a missing thing)
[beginning, possibly, with woe, or the beginning of *weacen*, the variant spelling of the present subjunctive of *wæcen*, so could mean wakefulness, or weakness, or to oppress, or to trouble]

and cunningly carried out, worked, or made—carefully, painstakingly, even, since *worhte*, or *weorc*, means both work and pain.

[As Stephen Barney reminds us in *Word-Hoard*, 'the association of the term "work" with the idea of distress … is ancient … we feel medicine "work" in a wound' (29).]

something important about time, here—*hwilum eft*, at times again, for a while again after, it happened more than once, or, it happened, then again. There was some kind of recurrence, repetition, for a long hour—the kind of hour that stretches out, that you can relax into, a supple hour—for a while, and then again.

[missing text here where potentially we would learn what that time contained, but it has to do with piercing

> and stabbing; he thought, he pondered, or else thought
> itself came so forcefully, so stabbingly, that it pressed,
> pierced, even, his—thinker, *him þoncade* his thought-
> bulb, his—head,]

since so many meals or dainties (food, here, giving credence to
reading *wombe* as stomach)
[had been somethinged]
in that time, in that season.

In conclusion: ritual recurrence, seasonal, or daily, but in any case continuing. Stomachs fill and empty, empty and fill, with banquets, with babies, with terror, with error, which sometimes is not our own, but comes to us, datively, indirectly passed on. These terrors ache our wombs just the same. This creature does something carefully, with skill, I like to think, with the strength and grace of hard practice, with the keen work-pain that takes hours and thought in succession, indicated by a series of foods through seasons, as this creature changes the condition of things in space, in time.

Brunra Beot (R.92)

I found *Brunra Beot* more straightforward to work on.

***Brunra Beot* (R.92)**

> I was the brag of the brown, a beam in the woods,
> a free life-bearer and a fruit of the field,
> the root of joy for men, and a woman's messenger,
> gold in their gardens. Now I am a warrior's
> hopeful war-weapon, ring [*ringed*
> [*e*] [ ] bears
> other one [ ].

The confident voice of this little poem really strikes me, particularly since it is so woodsy, making the speaker sound like a tree who is really full of itself. I struggled with the third line—it was difficult to represent the wonderful Old English compound word *wynnstaþol* in contemporary English. *Wynn* is joy, and *staþol* is a sort of foundation, or base—that which holds up the rest, either literally or metaphorically. This creature, whatever it is, is the foundation of man's joy—but 'joy-foundation' sounds bad, and the sound in this poem is so pleasurable that this pained me. I considered 'trunk', because, again, the poem is already using woods imagery, but joy-trunk seemed wrong, too. Trunks are not really foundations, and I wanted to avoid the image of 'trunk' as a box or crate, nor did I want to suggest a kind of phallic reading that may not be right here. One of the things I love most about Old English are the word compounds, and it takes a lot for me to abandon one, but sound and meaning seemed to diverge too much here to make it work. 'Ring [*ringed*' is a troubling spot as well—Muir offers *hringe be[*... but then notes that the letter following 'be' is 'g' or 't'.[6] However, because I initially worked from Krapp and Dobbie, who offer it unquestionably as *beg*, my sense of this is that it is a shield or handle of some kind, a weapon of wood, and hence, a circular (ring) displaying the rings of the tree. This may be a stretch.

Modor Monigra (R.84)

Modor Monigra (R.84), which I (and most others) take to be a description of water, and probably of the sea, is long enough to have two badly damaged sections. These burned places act a bit as waves do, or the way conversations attempted on the beach have pieces missing as waves crash through. These tatters, I think, only work to further the anonymous poet's point—the beauty of water is impossible to describe in words, it is astonishing and unlike anything.

***Modor Monigra* (R.84)**[7]

One creature is on the earth, born wonderfully
rough and wrathful, it remains strong
roars fiercely and runs over ground,
mother of many famous creatures
fair faring, ever striving, and
low in its near-grasp. No one may lead another
to how it looks or make known with words
how mislike anything is the might of its kin.
The father cares for all ancient creation,
the beginning with the end, same as his one son,
sublime child of the Measurer through [*ed*]
and that hope may [*es*] [*gœ*
] dear craft [ ]
[ ]
[*þ*] then he violently cast out [
þe] there, where any [
æ][*fter*] may not [
] other kind of earth [
] after that first was
winning and winsome [ ].

Our mother will be made more powerful,
sustained with wonders, freighted with feasts,
hoard-adorned, beloved by brave men.
Her might and main, strength surging,
her radiance is valued, put to glorious use,
winsome sun-glory, gold-adorned, devoted,
yearning for purity, increased artfully,
she is loved by the wealthy, useful to the wretched,
most free and strange, strong and stout,
grasping and greedy, treading the ground-bed,
of all who came to be beneath the under-lift,
and the sons of men saw with their eyes
that which glory wove, kin to children of earth,
still sage in spirit [* * * *]
one wiser than man's mind, host of wonders.
Harsher than the earth, older than humans,
swifter with gifts, dearer than gems,
it makes the world beautiful, brings forth fruit,
extinguishes wickedness [* * * *]
often casts down from one roof
wonders made beautiful, throughout peoples,
so that men look with astonishment across the earth.
that great [ ]creation
made of stones heaped up, storms [
len] [ ] wall of timbers
multitude [*ed*]
soil holds [*h*
etenge]
often those skills are [
] death not felled
Yet still [
du] to move the ulcerous belly
[*risse*]
The word-hoard unclosed, men [
wreoh,] opened/exposed words
how mislike anything its might is, those [*cy*]

A few choices pained me in this translation: *mærra wihta* in line 4, translated here as 'famous creatures', gets at the sense of the line but loses the wordplay inherent in *mærra*, which recalls the word *mere*, also sometimes spelled *mære*, meaning 'bounds', or 'boundaries', or 'the sea' (a remnant of this exists in our word mermaid). This word recurs in line 11, just before the first burned section of the poem, in the phrase *mære meotudes bearn*, in that case, given the context, clearly a reference to Christ. That said, it is fascinating to note the proximity between the definitions of this word (as per B-T) as 'a mere', and 'a night-mare, a monster oppressing men during sleep', and 'a boundary, limit, confine, border', and 'great, excellent, distinguished, illustrious, sublime, splendid, celebrated, famous, widely known'. The connection between a mere—a lake or sea, a body of water—and a boundary or border is clear, and perhaps there is no connection whatsoever between a boundary and fame (or illustriousness). However, these two seemingly unlike definitions hinge on a sense of differentness itself: illustriousness, and certainly sublimity are nothing if not boundaried, specialised conditions. Given the poem's insistence that its subject is *mislic* ('anything') (8a), I held these multiple definitions in mind.

Line 6: *nearograp* is a *hapax legomenon* and, as Muir notes in his commentary, 'the literal meaning is "confining or tight grasp"'.[8] I chose the perhaps even more literal translation of 'near-grasp' here for the purpose of sound, and to try to preserve something that *should* but somehow does not quite make sense to us.

Line 26: *wynsum wuldorgimm wloncum getenge*, is translated here as 'winsome sun-glory, gold-adorned, devoted', which does not account for *wuldorgimm* as a kenning. Literally 'glory-gem', this is a kenning for the sun, which does not quite come through here—and, all those 'w' sounds get lost as well, which is a shame, as in the Old English they carry a sense, through sound, of rushing awe, and, visually, of waves.

The last two lines of the poem, though damaged, are almost identical to lines 7 and 8. Here are lines 7 and 8 followed by 55 and 56:

7 wlite ond wisan wordum gecyþan
8 hu mislic biþ mægen þara cynna
55]*wreoh*] wordum geopena,
56 hu mislic sy mægen þara [*cy*

Gecyþan, in line 7 means to 'make known by words', to tell of, or to relate, whereas *Geopenian* the verb in line 55 means to open, to manifest, to show, to reveal, or even more specifically, to open a door or gate so as to admit passage. This is a brilliant little shift: *wordum gecyþan* is not really a surprising construction, but *wordum geopena* is striking, particularly once the lines are compared. In the first place, the poet wants to make clear that relating the majesty of the sea via words is too difficult, but something seems to dramatically change by the end of the poem, as the *hordword onhlid* ('the word-hoard opens/uncloses/appears') in line 54, and then the words themselves open. Reading this poem it appears as though the sea, which at first seems impossible to describe with language, bestows some of its bounty on the poet. The bounty of the sea becomes the bounty of the poem, raising the question of what that last *cy—* might have once become. Certainly, the word might be *cynna*, as in line 8 (and many *have* restored it to this; see Muir's notes for the details), but it also might have become *cyþan* ('to make known with words'). I like to imagine this mirroring might have occurred, that the impossible *gecyþan* of line 7 becomes the actualised one at the end, after the words have opened themselves. There is something aptly oceanic, wavelike about this motion. Although this is a poem gnawed at by fire, the lacuna in the riddle that exists for us *now* suggests waves, the way they suck at the sand on the beach, taking things, leaving things.

Returning to the imaginary island of *dyre cræft*, I am overly tempted to consider the much later sense of 'craft' as a sailing vessel, which fits perfectly with this water poem, if not with what is etymologically possible. Walter Benjamin, in fact, uses 'fragments of a vessel' as a metaphor for translation itself, which 'must lovingly and in detail incorporate the original's way of meaning, thus making both the original and the translation recognisable as fragments of a greater language, just as fragments are part of a vessel'.[9] Not until considering these fragmentary riddles, I think, did I grasp the utility of Benjamin's metaphor, his insistence that pieces 'that are to be glued together must match one another in the smallest details, although they need not be like one another'.[10] Because these riddles are fragments unto themselves, they offer us a reminder that all Old English poems, are 'fragments of a greater language'. I offer this kind of temporal incongruity, considering 'craft' as a vessel, for example, as a way of matching without likeness. As we drag this riddle into our time, there exists a give and take, and I think these riddles' makers would be as interested in this later use of 'craft' as I am in understanding *nearograp* as a way of holding something very tightly or closely.

There are few things that take more skill and art to make than vessels that carry humans over surfaces (the air, the sea) that we cannot naturally traverse—vessels which also seem essentially magical, if we think about them closely. While working on these riddle fragments, I was often reminded of William Carlos Williams' description of a poem in the Introduction to his 1944 collection, *The Wedge*. A poem, Williams writes, is 'a small (or large) machine made of words,'[11] a definition which makes sense here because it makes poems seem made up of action, of movement, of things that are not just made, but makers. We can set them off and let them make their own way, crafts that are crafts. This may be a perfect definition for riddle poems in particular, which are always attempting two kinds of action, as they make water or keys or birds or bells, while simultaneously creating themselves as poems.

Notes

1 For text see Katherine O'Brien O'Keeffe, ed, *The Anglo-Saxon Chronicle, a Collaborative Edition: Vol. 5. MS C* (Cambridge: Brewer, 2001).
2 Walter Benjamin, 'The Task of the Translator', in *Walter Benjamin: Selected Writings, 1: 1913–1926*, ed. M. Bullock and M. Jennings (Cambridge, MA: Belknap, 1996), pp. 253–63; Gayatri Chakravorty Spivak, 'The Politics of Translation', in *The Translation Studies Reader*, ed. Lawrence Venuti (London: Routledge, 2012), pp. 369–88.
3 Benjamin, 'Task of the Translator', p. 260.
4 Spivak, 'Politics of Translation', p. 370.
5 I did most of my translation work from the ASPR edition, but Muir's notes became indispensable to me: Bernard J. Muir, ed., *The Exeter Anthology of Old English Poetry: An Edition of Exeter Dean and Chapter MS 3501*, 2nd edn, 2 vols (Exeter: University of Exeter Press, 2000).
6 Muir, *Exeter Anthology*, I, p. 380.
7 Again, I used the ASPR edition here for my initial translation, but the notes from Muir, *Exeter Anthology*, were very helpful later on.
8 Muir, *Exeter Anthology*, II, p. 674.
9 Benjamin, 'Task of the Translator', p. 260.
10 Benjamin, 'Task of the Translator', p. 260.
11 William Carlos Williams, 'Introduction to *The Wedge*', in *Selected Essays of William Carlos Williams* (New York: New Directions, 1969), p. 256.

Afterword

Megan Cavell and Jennifer Neville

Let us return to the beginning. In bringing together a hundred riddles about a multitude of topics, from a variety of perspectives, and imbued with echoes of a wide range of sources, Aldhelm's verse collection presents us with a clear literary manifesto. We have a manifesto of our own. Unlike Aldhelm, we do not position ourselves as sole progenitors. Rather, we celebrate the communal practice that is riddling—whether composing, solving, interpreting, or editing. We aim to draw together the individual voices of the riddles and of the chapters of this volume into a communal unity that celebrates diverse methods and perspectives. Given the riddle tradition's fascination with simultaneous individuality and communality, we are genuinely surprised that no book has yet sought to bring this ethos to bear through a collection of essays on the riddles.

We hope this collection has revealed that there is no single—no 'right'—way to read these texts. Rather, the preceding chapters point us toward some of the many productive paths that we may take when approaching the riddles. We can read them, for example, in the context of how they function, as Olsen, Wilcox, and Borysławski have done. We can read them within their manuscript context and outside it, highlighting the intellectual work of their authors and/or our own lived experiences, as Salvador-Bello, Mize, Mogford, Oberman, and Koppinen have done. We can read them through the lens of poetic craft, and what that craft tells us about their world, as Brooks, Stanton, Buchanan, and Cavell have done. And we can read them to gain insights into the living world, the material world, the world of things, as Neville, Dale, Paz, and Rhodes have done. There are overlaps, naturally, and the categorisations above and in this book's sections—Words, Ideas, Interactions—arguably move, flow, collapse inward, and reconstitute themselves through the act of interpreting, just as the riddles themselves invite constant re-reading and re-interpretation of clues and solutions.

There is plenty of room for re-interpretation and plenty of opportunity for future work in the field of riddling, not only in relation to the more familiar *Exeter Book* riddles and the often-overlooked Latin collections, but also in conversation with the Scandinavian and Celtic riddle traditions. Some other types of conversations, however, are particularly urgent. As we write this conclusion, our field is grappling with its deeply entrenched legacy of racism and elitism, and—although there has been some work on intersections between class and ethnicity in the context of Old English[1]—the Latin riddles' global outlook makes them ideal candidates for such urgently needed, critically-informed readings. A great deal of important work is already emerging in the area of critical race theory and medieval studies, and there are many resources available on, for example, the Medievalists of Color website and within the crowd-sourced bibliography organised by Jonathan Hsy and Julie Orlemanski.[2] We acknowledge the work of those scholars seeking to reshape early medieval studies in light of this, including Eileen Joy, Dorothy Kim, Adam Miyashiro, Mary Rambaran-Olm, Erik Wade, and many others. We hope that this essential reshaping of the field will also reshape understandings of the multilingual riddle tradition. Likewise, although some of the chapters in this volume have explored aspects of gender and sexuality, and although work elsewhere has probed the riddles' representations of age and the life course,[3] we would like to see more critical engagement with these topics and especially with disability studies. We would like to suggest that the insights into daily life offered through the riddles' subversive concealments and manoeuvrings make them ideal texts for the study of identity in all its complexity.

This book is the opportunity to stop and take stock, but it is only one part of an ongoing conversation. Our manifesto, then, positions the riddles as a site of celebration of the multiplicity of voices embodied in the riddles and in acts of scholarly engagement. It is also an invitation, like that in *Heanmode Twa* (R.42):

> Hwylc þæs hordgates
> cægan cræfte þa clamne onleac? (11b–12)

> ['Who can unlock the bar of the hoard-gate with the power of the key?']

We all can.

Notes

1 See John W. Tanke, '*Wonfeax wale*: Ideology and Figuration in the Sexual Riddles of the Exeter Book', in *Class and Gender in Early English Literature: Intersections*, ed. Britton J. Harwood and Gillian R. Overing (Bloomington: Indiana University Press, 1994), pp. 21–42; Lindy Brady, 'The "Dark Welsh" as Slaves and Slave Traders in Exeter Book Riddles 52 and 72', *ES*, 95 (2014), 235–55.
2 The Medievalists of Color website, ed. Sierra Lomuto, Mariah Min, and Shokoofeh Rajabzadeh, http:// medievalistsofcolor.com (accessed 11 February 2019); Jonathan Hsy and Julie Orlemanski, 'Race and medieval studies: a partial bibliography', *postmedieval*, 8 (2017), 500–31, https://doi.org/10.1057/s41280-017-0072-0.
3 See Shu-Han Luo, 'Tender Beginnings in the Exeter Book *Riddles*', in *Childhood and Adolescence in Anglo-Saxon Literary Culture*, ed. Susan Irvine and Winfried Rudolf (Toronto: University of Toronto Press, 2018), pp. 71–94; Harriet Soper, 'Reading the *Exeter Book* Riddles as Life-Writing', *RES*, 68.287 (2017), 841–65.

Bibliography

In filing order, lower-case particles (de, von) are ignored, upper-case particles (De, O') are respected, and apostrophes precede other characters.

Primary sources

Ælfric, *Ælfric's Catholic Homilies: The First Series*, ed. Peter Clemoes, EETS ss, 17 (Oxford: Oxford University Press, 1997).

Ælfric, *Ælfric's De temporibus anni*, ed. Martin Blake (Woodbridge: D. S. Brewer, 2009).

Ælfric, *Die Hirtenbriefe Ælfrics*, ed. Bernard Fehr (Hamburg: Henri Grand, 1914; repr. Darmstadt: Wissenschaftliche Buchgesellschaft, 1966).

Alcuin, *Alcuini Opera Omnia*, ed. J. P. Migne, PL 101 (Paris: Garnier, 1863).

Alcuin, 'Carmina', in *Poetae Latini Aevi Carolini*, 1, ed. Ernst Dümmler, MGH, Poetae Latini Medii Aevi (Berlin: Weidmann, 1881), pp. 160–351.

Alcuin, 'Disputatio regalis et nobilissimi juvenis Pippini cum Albino scholastico', in *Altercatio Hadriani Augusti et Epicteti Philosophi*, ed. L. W. Daly and W. Suchier (Champaign: University of Illinois Press, 1939).

Aldhelm, *Aldhelm: The Poetic Works*, trans. Michael Lapidge and James L. Rosier (Cambridge: D. S. Brewer, 2009).

Aldhelm, *Aldhelm: The Prose Works*, trans. Michael Lapidge and Michael Herren (Cambridge: D. S. Brewer, 2009).

Aldhelm, *Aldhelmi Opera*, ed. Rudolf Ehwald, MGH, Auctores Antiquissimi, 15 (Berlin: Weidmann, 1919).

Alfred the Great, *King Alfred's Old English Prose Translation of the First Fifty Psalms*, ed. Patrick P. O'Neill (Cambridge, MA: Medieval Academy of America, 2001).

Alfred the Great, *King Alfred's West-Saxon Version of Gregory's Pastoral Care*, ed. Henry Sweet (London: Trübner, 1871).

Anlezark, Daniel, ed. and trans., *The Old English Dialogues of Solomon and Saturn* (Cambridge: D. S. Brewer, 2009).

Archibald, Elizabeth, ed., *Apollonius of Tyre: Medieval and Renaissance Themes and Variations* (Woodbridge: D. S. Brewer, 1993).

Aristotle, *The Art of Rhetoric*, trans. John Henry Freese (London: William Heinemann, 1967).

Aristotle, *Categories and De Interpretatione*, ed. and trans. J. L. Ackrill (Oxford: Oxford University Press, 1975).

Aristotle, *History of Animals, Volume II: Books 4–6*, trans. A. L. Peck, Loeb Classical Library, 438 (Cambridge, MA: Harvard University Press, 1970).

Aristotle, *The Poetics*, trans. James Hutton (New York: Norton, 1982).

Augustine of Hippo, *De doctrina Christiana*, in *Sancti Aurelii Augustini Hipponensis Episcopi opera omnia*, ed. Jacques-Paul Migne, PL 34 (Paris: Garnier, 1865).

Baum, Paull F., ed. and trans., *Anglo Saxon Riddles of the Exeter Book* (Durham, NC: Duke University Press, 1963).

Bayless, Martha, and Michael Lapidge, eds and trans, *Collectanea Pseudo-Bedae*, Scriptores Latini Hibernae, 14 (Dublin: Dublin Institute for Advanced Studies, 1998).

Beagle, Peter S., *The Last Unicorn* (London: Ballantine, 1971).

Bede, *Anecdota Bedae, Lanfranci, et aliorum: Inedited tracts, letters, poems, & c. of Venerable Bede, Lanfranc, Tatwin, and others*, ed. J. A. Giles (London: D. Nutt, 1851).

Bede, *Bedae Opera de temporibus*, ed. Charles W. Jones (Menasha: George Banta, 1943).

Bede, *De divisionibus temporum*, in *Venerabilis Bedae Opera Omnia*, ed. Jacques Paul Migne, PL 90 (Paris: Garnier, 1904), I, pp. 653–64.

Bede, *Beda Venerabilis. De temporum ratione liber*, ed. Charles W. Jones, CCSL, 123B (Turnhout: Brepols, 1977).

Bede, *Bede: The Reckoning of Time*, trans. Faith Wallis (Liverpool: Liverpool University Press, 1999).

Benedict of Nursia, *Regula Benedicti*, ed. Rudolph Hanslik, Regula Corpus Scriptorum Ecclesiasticorum Latinorum, 75 (Vienna: Hoelder-Pinchler-Tempsky, 1960).

[Bible] Colunga, Alberto and Laurentio Turrado, eds, *Biblia Sacra iuxta Vulgatam Clementinam*, 7th edn (Madrid: Biblioteca de Autores Christianos, 1985).

[Bible] Fischer, Bonifatius, *et al.*, eds, *Biblia Sacra Iuxta Vulgatam Versionem* (Stuttgart: Deutsche Bibelgesellschaft, 1994).

[Bible] *The Holy Bible: Douay-Rheims Version* (Baltimore: John Murphy, 1899), http://drbo.org (accessed 14 August 2019)

[Bible] *The Holy Bible: Translated from the Latin Vulgate* (New York: Douay Bible House, 1953).

Boethius, De consolatione philosophiae: Opuscula theologica, ed. Claudio Moreschini (Munich: Saur, 2005)

Boniface, 'Aenigmata Bonifatii', *Poetae Latini Aevi Carolini*, ed. Ernst Dümmler, MGH, Poetae Latini Medii Aevi, 1 (Berlin: Weidmann, 1881), pp. 1–15.

Boyle, Elizabeth, ed. and trans., 'Three Junior Clerics and their Kitten (from the Book of Leinster)', *Bloga (fragments)*, 6 March 2016, https://blogafragments.wordpress.com/2016/03/06/three-junior-clerics-and-their-kitten-from-the-book-of-leinster/ (accessed 14 August 2019).

Buecheler, Franz, and Alexander Riese, ed, *Anthologia latina: sive poesis latinae supplementum*, 3 vols in 5 (Leipzig: B. G. Teubner, 1894–1926).

Byrhtferth of Ramsey, *Enchiridion*, ed. and trans. Peter Baker and Michael Lapidge, EETS ss, 15 (Oxford: Oxford University Press, 2001).

Capella, Martianus, *Martianus Capella*, ed. James Willis (Leipzig: Teubner, 1983).

Capella, Martianus, *Martianus Capella and the Seven Liberal Arts, Vol II. The Marriage of Philology and Mercury*, trans. William Harris Stahl, Richard Johnson, and E. L. Burge (New York: Columbia University Press, 1977).

Cassian, John, *De coenobium institutis libri duodecim*, in *Ioannis Cassiani Opera Omnia*, ed. Jacques-Paul Migne, PL 49 (Paris: Garnier, 1846).

Chambers, Raymond W., Max Förster, and Robin Flower, eds, *The Exeter Book of Old English Poetry* (London: Percy Lund, 1933).

Chaucer, Geoffrey, *The Riverside Chaucer*, ed. Larry D. Benson, 3rd edn (Boston: Houghton Mifflin, 1987).

Claudian, *Claudii Claudiani carmina*, ed. John Barrie Hall, Bibliotheca scriptorum Graecorum et Romanorum Teubneriana, 119M (Leipzig: K. G. Saur, 1985).

Claudian, *On Stilicho's Consulship 2–3, Panegyric on the Sixth Consulship of Honorius, The Gothic War, Shorter Poems, Rape of Proserpina*, trans. M. Platnauer, Loeb Classical Library, 136 (Cambridge, MA: Harvard University Press, 1922).

Cross, James E., and Thomas D. Hill, eds, *The Prose Solomon and Saturn and Adrian and Ritheus* (Toronto: University of Toronto Press, 1982).

Crossley-Holland, Kevin, trans., *The Exeter Book Riddles*, rev. edn (London: Enitharmon, 2008).

Crossley-Holland, Kevin, and Lawrence Sail, ed., *The New Exeter Book of Riddles* (London: Enitharmon, 1999).

Delanty, Greg, Seamus Heaney and Michael Matto, eds, *The Word Exchange: Anglo-Saxon Poems in Translation* (New York: Norton, 2010).

Dobbie, Elliott Van Kirk, ed., *The Anglo-Saxon Minor Poems*, ASPR, 6 (New York: Columbia University Press, 1942).

Donatus, *Ars Grammatica*, ed. Heinrich Keil (Leipzig: Teubner, 1864).

Donne, John, 'The Canonization', in *The Songs and Sonnets of John Donne*, ed. Theodore Redpath, 2nd edn (Cambridge, MA: Harvard University Press, 2009), pp. 237–8.

Embricon de Mayence, *La vie de Mahomet*, ed. Guy Cambier, Collection Latomus, 52 (Brussels: Latomus, 1962).

Fulk, R. D., ed. and trans., *The Beowulf Manuscript: Complete Texts and*

The Fight at Finnsburg, Dumbarton Oaks Medieval Library (Cambridge, MA: Harvard University Press, 2010).

Fulk, R. D., Robert E. Bjork, and John D. Niles, eds, *Klaeber's Beowulf and the Fight at Finnsburg*, 4th edn (Toronto: University of Toronto Press, 2008).

Gellius, Aulus, *Attic Nights, Volume II: Books 6–13*, ed. and trans. J. C. Rolfe, Loeb Classical Library, 200 (Cambridge, MA: Harvard University Press, 1927).

Glorie, Fr., ed., *Collectiones Aenigmatum Merovingicae Aetatis*, CCSL, 133–133A (Turnhout: Brepols, 1968).

Godden, Malcolm R., and Susan Irvine, eds and trans, *The Old English Boethius with Verse Prologues and Epilogues Associated with King Alfred*, Dumbarton Oaks Medieval Library (Cambridge, MA: Harvard University Press, 2012).

Gregory the Great, *King Alfred's West-Saxon Version of Gregory's Pastoral Care* (London: Trübner, 1871).

Gregory the Great, *Moralia in Iob*, ed. Marci Adriaen, CCSL, 143–143A (Turnhout: Brepols, 1979).

Gregory of Tours, *De Cursu stellarum*, in *Gregorii Turonensis Opera, Vol 2: Miracula et opera minora*, ed. Bruno Krusch and Wilhelm Levison, MGH, Scriptorum Rerum Merovingicarum, 1 (Berlin: Weidmann, 1969), pp. 404–22.

Hasenfrantz, Robert, ed., *Ancrene Wisse*, TEAMS Middle English Texts (Kalamazoo: Medieval Institute Publications, 2000), http://d.lib.rochester.edu/teams/text/hasenfrantz-ancrene-wisse-part-eight (accessed 1 September 2019).

Herwagen, Johann [the Younger], *Opera Bedae Venerabilis presbyteri Anglo-Saxonis*, 8 vols (Basel, 1563).

Hrabanus Maurus, *De computo*, ed. John McCulloch and Wesley Stevens (Turnhout: Brepols, 1979).

Ioca Monachorum, in Walther Suchier, ed., *Das mittellateinische Gespräch Adrian und Epictitus und verwandten Texten (Joca Monachorum)* (Tübingen: Niemeyer, 1955)

Isidore of Seville, *De natura rerum*, ed. Gustav Becker (Berlin: Weidmann, 1872).

Isidore of Seville, *The Etymologies of Isidore of Seville*, trans. Stephen A. Barney, W. J. Lewis, J. A. Beach, and Oliver Berghof (Cambridge: Cambridge University Press, 2006).

Isidore of Seville, *Etymologiarum*, in *Sancti Isidori Hispalensis Episcopi Opera Omnia*, ed. Jacques-Paul Migne, PL 82 (Paris: Garnier, 1850), coll. 9–728.

Isidore of Seville, *Etymologiarum sive originum libri XX*, ed. W. M. Lindsay, 2 vols (Oxford, Clarendon, 1911).

Juster, A. M., trans., *Saint Aldhelm's Riddles* (Toronto: University of Toronto Press, 2015).

Koppinen, Pirkko A., trans., 'Riddle 30a and 30b (or Riddle 28a and 28b)', *The Riddle Ages: An Anglo-Saxon Riddle Blog*, ed. Megan Cavell with Matthias Ammon and Victoria Symons, 13 October 2014, https://theriddleages.wordpress.com/2014/10/13/riddle-30a-and-b-or-riddle-28a-and-b/ (accessed 31 August 2019).

Kotzor, Günter, ed., *Das Altenglische Martyrologium* (Munich: Bayerischen Akademie der Wissenschaften, 1981).

Krapp, George Philip, ed., *The Vercelli Book*, ASPR, 2 (New York: Columbia University Press, 1932).

Krapp, George Philip, and Elliott Van Kirk Dobbie, eds, *The Exeter Book*, ASPR, 3 (New York: Columbia University Press, 1936).

Laertius, Diogenes, *Lives of Eminent Philosophers, Volume I: Books 1–5*, ed. and trans. Robert Drew Hicks, Loeb Classical Library, 184 (Cambridge, MA: Harvard University Press, 1925).

[Lorsch Riddles], 'Aenigmata anglica', in *Poetae Latini Aevi Carolini*, ed. Ernst Dümmler, MGH, Poetae Latini Medii Aevi, 1 (Berlin: Weidmann, 1881), pp. 20–23.

[Lorsch Riddles], 'Lörscher Rätsel', ed. Ernst Dümmler, *Zeitschrift für deutsches Altertum*, 22 (1878), 258–63.

Lucretius, *On the Nature of Things*, ed. W. H. D. Rouse and Martin F. Smith, Loeb Classical Library, 181 (Cambridge, MA: Harvard University Press, 1924).

Macrobius, Ambrosius Theodosius, *Macrobius: Commentary on the Dream of Scipio*, trans. William Harris Stahl (New York: Columbia University Press, 1952).

Macrobius, Ambrosius Theodosius, *Opera Volume 2: Commentarii in Somnium Scipionis*, ed. Jacob Willis (Leipzig: Teubner, 1963).

Migne, J. P., ed., *Patrologia Latina* (Paris: Garnier, 1844–64).

Muir, Bernard J., ed., *The Exeter Anthology of Old English Poetry: An Edition of Exeter Dean and Chapter MS 3501*, 2nd edn, 2 vols (Exeter: University of Exeter Press, 2000).

Muir, Bernard J., ed., *The Exeter Anthology of Old English Poetry: The Exeter DVD*, with software by Nick Kennedy (Exeter: Exeter University Press, 2006).

Murphy, Gerard, ed., *Early Irish Lyrics, Eighth to Twelfth Century* (Oxford: Clarendon, 1956).

Murray, Kevin, ed. and trans., 'Catshlechta and Other Medieval Legal Material Relating to Cats', *Celtica*, 25 (2007), 143–59.

Oberman, Miller, *The Unstill Ones: Poems* (Princeton: Princeton University Press, 2017).

Orchard, Andy, ed. and trans., *The Anglo-Saxon Riddle Tradition*, Dumbarton Oaks Medieval Library (Cambridge, MA: Harvard University Press, forthcoming).

Peter Damian, *De perfectione monachorum*, in *Sancti Petri Damian Opera Omnia*, ed. Jacques-Paul Migne, PL 145 (Paris: Garnier, 1853).

Pinsker, Hans, and Waltraud Ziegler, eds, *Die altenglischen Ratsel des Exeterbuchs: Text mit deutscher Ubersetzung und Kommentar* (Heidelberg: Carl Winter, 1985).

Plato, *The Laches*, in *The Dialogues of Plato. Vol. III: Ion, Hippias Minor, Laches, Protagoras*, trans. R. E. Allen (New Haven: Yale University Press, 1996), pp. 47–85.

Pliny the Elder, *Natural History, Volume I: Books 1–2*, trans. H. Rackham, Loeb Classical Library, 330 (Cambridge, MA: Harvard University Press, 1938).

Pliny the Elder, *Natural History, Volume III: Books 8–11*, trans. H. Rackham, Loeb Classical Library, 353 (Cambridge, MA: Harvard University Press, 1940).

Porter, John trans., *Anglo-Saxon Riddles* (Hockwold-cum-Wilton: Anglo-Saxon Books, 2003).

Priscian, *Prisciani Institutiones Grammaticarum*, ed. Martin Hertz, 2 vols (Leipzig: Teubner, 1855).

Prudentius, *Aurelii Prudentii Clementis carmina*, ed. M. P. Cunningham, CCSL, 126 (Turnhout: Brepols, 1966).

Prudentius, *The Origin of Sin: An English Translation of the 'Hamartigenia'*, trans. Martha Malamud (Ithaca, NY: Cornell University Press, 2011).

Pseudo-Alcuin, *De cursu et saltu lunae ac bissexto*, in *Alcuini Opera Omnia*, ed. J. P. Migne, PL 101 (Paris: Garnier, 1863), II, pp. 984–92.

Scragg, D. G., ed., *The Vercelli Homilies and Related Texts*, EETS os, 300 (Oxford: Oxford University Press, 1992).

Sedulius Scottus, 'Carmina 72', in *Poetae Latini Aevi Carolini*, ed. Ludwig Traube, MGH, Poetae Latini Medii Aevi, 3 (Berlin: Weidmann, 1896), p. 224.

Sedulius Scottus, *Collectaneum miscellaneum*, ed. D. Simpson, Corpus Christianorum Continuatio Mediaevalis, 67 (Turnhout: Brepols, 1988).

Sisam, Celia, ed., *The Vercelli Book*, Early English Manuscripts in Facsimile, 19 (Copenhagen: Rosenkilde & Bagger, 1976).

Sisebut, King of the Visigoths (?), 'De ratione temporum [De eclipsibus solis et lunae]', ed. Karl Strecker, MGH, *Poetae Latini Aevi Carolini*, 4, Poetae Latini Medii Aevi (Berlin: Weidmann, 1914), pp. 682–6.

Stork, Nancy Porter, *Aldhelm's Riddles in the British Library MS Royal 12.C.xxiii* (Toronto: Pontifical Institute of Mediaeval Studies, 1990).

Symphosius, *The Enigmas of Symphosius*, ed. and trans. Raymond Theodore Ohl (Philadelphia: University of Pennsylvania Press, 1928).

Symphosius, *Symphosius: The Aenigmata: An Introduction, Text and Commentary*, ed. T. J. Leary (London: Bloomsbury, 2014).

Tatwine, *Aenigmata Tatwini*, in Fr. Glorie, ed., *Collectiones Aenigmatum Merovingicae Aetatis*, CCSL, 133–133A (Turnhout: Brepols, 1968)

Tatwine, *Tatuini Opera Omnia: Ars Tatuini*, ed. Maria de Marco, CCSL, 133 (Turnhout: Brepols, 1968).

Thorpe, Benjamin, ed., *Codex Exoniensis: A Collection of Anglo-Saxon Poetry, from a Manuscript in the Library of the Dean and Chapter of Exeter* (London: Society of Antiquaries of London, 1842).

Tolkien, Christopher, ed. and trans., *The Saga of King Heidrek the Wise* (London: Nelson, 1960).

Trautmann, Moritz, *Die altenglischen Rätsel (Die Rätsel des Exeterbuchs)* (Heidelberg: Carl Winter, 1915).

Tupper, Frederick, Jr, ed., 'Riddles of the Bede Tradition: the *Flores* of Pseudo-Bede', *MP*, 2 (1905), 561–72.

Tupper, Frederick, Jr, ed., *The Riddles of the Exeter Book* (Boston: Ginn and Company, 1910).

Virgil, *Eclogues, Georgics, Aeneid: Books 1–6*, trans. H. Rushton Fairclough, rev. G. P. Goold, Loeb Classical Library, 63 (Cambridge, MA: Harvard University Press, 1916).

Virgil, *Aeneid: Books 7–12, Appendix Vergiliana*, trans. H. Rushton Fairclough, rev. G. P. Goold, Loeb Classical Library, 64 (Cambridge, MA: Harvard University Press, 1918).

Virgil, *Georgics*, ed. Richard F. Thomas, 2 vols (Cambridge: Cambridge University Press, 1988).

Virgilius Maro Grammaticus, *Virgilio Marone Grammatico: Epitomi ed Epistole*, ed. Giovanni Polara and Luciano Caruso (Naples: Liguori, 1979)

Warner, George F., ed., *The Stowe Missal, MS. D II 3 in the Library of the Royal Irish Academy, Dublin*, 2 vols (London: Henry Bradshaw Society, 1906).

Warntjes, Immo, *The Munich Computus* (Stuttgart: Franz Steiner, 2010).

Williams, Mary Jane McDonald, ed. and trans., *The Riddles of Tatwine and Eusebius* (unpublished PhD thesis, University of Michigan, 1974).

Williamson, Craig, trans., *A Feast of Creatures: Anglo-Saxon Riddle Songs* (Philadelphia: University of Pennsylvania Press, 1982).

Williamson, Craig, ed., *The Old English Riddles of the Exeter Book* (Chapel Hill: University of North Carolina Press, 1977).

Ziolkowski, Jan M., ed. and trans., *The Cambridge Songs (Carmina Cantabrigensia)* (New York: Garland, 1994).

Secondary sources

Adams, James Noel, *The Latin Sexual Vocabulary* (Baltimore: Johns Hopkins University Press, 1982).

Afros, Elena, 'Linguistic Ambiguities in Some Exeter Book Riddles', *N&Q*, n.s. 52 (2005), 431–7.

Afros, Elena, 'Syntactic Variation in *Riddles 30A* and *30B*', *N&Q*, 52 (2005), 2–5.

Allen, Valerie J., 'Broken Air', *Exemplaria*, 16 (2004), 305–22.

Anderson, James E., '*Deor, Wulf and Eadwacer* and *The Soul's Address*: How and Where the Old English Exeter Book Riddles Begin', in *The Old English Elegies: New Essays in Criticism and Research*, ed. Martin Green (Rutherford: Associated University Presses, 1983), pp. 204–30.

Attardo, Salvatore, 'A Primer for the Linguistics of Humor', in *The Primer of Humor Research*, ed. Victor Raskin (Berlin: de Gruyter, 2008), pp. 101–55.

Backhouse, Janet, *The Lindisfarne Gospels* (Oxford: Phaidon, 1981).

Backhouse, Janet, *The Lindisfarne Gospels: A Masterpiece of Book Painting* (London: British Library, 1995).

Backhouse, Janet, D. H. Turner, and Leslie Webster, eds, *The Golden Age of Anglo-Saxon Art, 966–1066* (London: British Museum Press, 1984).

Bakhtin, Mikhail, *Rabelais and His World*, trans. Hélène Iswolsky (Bloomington: Indiana University Press, 1984).

Barley, Nigel F., 'Structural Aspects of the Anglo-Saxon Riddle', *Semiotica*, 10 (1974), 143–75.

Barney, Stephen A., *Word-Hoard: An Introduction to Old English Vocabulary*, 2nd edn (New Haven: Yale University Press, 1985).

Bayless, Martha, 'Alcuin's *Disputatio Pippini* and the Early Medieval Riddle Tradition', in *Humour, History and Politics in Late Antiquity and the Early Middle Ages*, ed. Guy Halsall (Cambridge: Cambridge University Press, 2002), pp. 157–78.

Benjamin, Walter, 'The Task of the Translator', in *Walter Benjamin: Selected Writings, 1: 1913–1926*, ed. M. Bullock and M. Jennings (Cambridge, MA: Belknap, 1996).

Bennett, Jane, 'Systems and Things: A Response to Graham Harman and Timothy Morton', *New Literary History*, 43.2 (2012), 225–33.

Bennett, Jane, *Vibrant Matter: A Political Ecology of Things* (Durham, NC, and London: Duke University Press, 2010).

Bergson, Henri, *Laughter: An Essay on the Meaning of the Comic*, trans. Cloudesely Brereton and Fred Rothwell (New York: Macmillan, 1911).

Bessason, Haraldur and Robert J. Glendinning, eds, *Edda: A Collection of Essays* (Winnipeg: University of Manitoba Press, 1985).

Bettini, Maurizio, *Voci: Antropologia Sonora del Mondo Antico* (Turin: Giulio Einaudi, 2008).

Bischoff, Bernhard, *Manuscripts and Libraries in the Age of Charlemagne*, trans. Michael Gorman (Cambridge: Cambridge University Press, 1994).

Bitterli, Dieter, *Say What I am Called: The Old English Riddles of the Exeter Book and the Anglo-Latin Riddle Tradition* (Toronto: University of Toronto Press, 2009).

Bjork, Robert E., 'Speech as Gift in *Beowulf*', *Speculum*, 69 (1994), 993–1022.

Blackburn, F. A., '*The Husband's Message* and the Accompanying Riddles of the *Exeter Book*', *JEGP*, 3 (1900), 1–13.
Blandford, Percy W., *Practical Blacksmithing and Metalworking* (New York: TAB Books, 1988).
Borysławski, Rafał, 'The Elements of Anglo-Saxon Wisdom Poetry in the Exeter Book Riddles', *Studia Anglica Posnaniensia*, 38 (2002), 35–47.
Bosworth, Joseph, and T. Northcote Toller, *An Anglo-Saxon Dictionary* (Oxford: Oxford University Press, 1898), *Supplement* by T. Northcote Toller (Oxford: Oxford University Press, 1921), Digital edition, *Bosworth-Toller Anglo-Saxon Dictionary* (Prague: Faculty of Arts, Charles University, 2010), http://bosworth.ff.cuni.cz/ (accessed 1 September 2019).
Bracken, Damian, 'Virgilius Grammaticus and the Earliest Hiberno-Latin Literature', in *Ogma: Essays in Celtic Studies in Honour of Próinséas Ní Chatháin*, ed. Michael Richter and Jean-Michel Picard (Dublin: Four Courts, 2002), pp. 251–61
Bradley, Henry, 'Two Riddles of the Exeter Book', *Modern Language Review*, 6 (1911), 433–40.
Bradshaw, John, *Cat Sense: The Feline Enigma Revealed* (London: Penguin, 2013).
Brady, Lindy, 'The "Dark Welsh" as Slaves and Slave Traders in Exeter Book Riddles 52 and 72', *ES*, 95 (2014), 235–55.
Bredehoft, Thomas A., 'First-Person Inscriptions and Literacy in Anglo-Saxon England', *Anglo-Saxon Studies in Archaeology and History*, 9 (1996), 103–10.
Bredehoft, Thomas A., *The Visible Text: Textual Production and Reproduction from Beowulf to Maus* (Oxford: Oxford University Press, 2014).
Breeze, Andrew, 'Exeter Book Riddles 4 and 43: City Gate and Guardian Angel', *Devon and Cornwall Notes and Queries* (forthcoming).
Brooke, Stopford A., *The History of Early English Literature* (London: Macmillan, 1892).
Brooks, Francesca, 'Sight, Sound, and the Perception of the Anglo-Saxon Liturgy in Exeter Book Riddles 48 and 59', in *Sensory Perception in the Medieval West*, ed. Simon C. Thomson and Michael D. Bintley (Turnhout: Brepols, 2016), pp. 141–58.
Brown, Bill, 'Thing Theory', *Critical Inquiry*, 28.1 (2001), 1–22.
Brown, Michelle P., *The Lindisfarne Gospels: Society, Spirituality and the Scribe* (London: British Library, 2003).
Brown, Ray, 'The Exeter Book's Riddle 2: A Better Solution', *English Language Notes*, 29 (1991), 1–4.
Broz, Vlatko, 'Kennings as Blends and Prisms', *Jezikoslovlje* (*Linguistics*), 12.2 (2011), 165–86.
Bryant, Levi R., *The Democracy of Objects* (Ann Arbor: Open Humanities Press, 2011).

Buchli, Victor, 'Introduction', in *Material Culture Reader*, ed. Victor Buchli (Oxford: Berg, 2002), pp. 1–22.

Burrows, Hannah, 'Enigma Variations: *Hervarar saga*'s Wave-Riddles and Supernatural Women in Old Norse Poetic Tradition', *JEGP*, 112.2 (2013), 194–216.

Bynum, Caroline Walker, 'Wonder', *American Historical Review* 102.1 (1997), 1–26.

Byrne, Sarah, Anne Clarke, Rodney Harrison, and Robin Torrence, 'Networks, Agents and Objects: Frameworks for Unpacking Museum Collections', in *Unpacking the Collection: Networks of Material and Social Agency in the Museum*, ed. Sarah Byrne, Anne Clarke, Rodney Harrison, and Robin Torrence (London: Springer, 2011), pp. 3–26.

Cameron, Angus, Ashley Crandell Amos, Antonette diPaolo Healey, *et al.*, eds, *Dictionary of Old English: A to I Online* (Toronto: Dictionary of Old English Project, 2018), http://www.doe.utoronto.ca (accessed 1 September 2019).

Cameron, M. L., 'Aldhelm as Naturalist: An Examination of Some of His *Enigmata*', *Peritia*, 4 (1985), 117–33

Cameron, M. L., *Anglo-Saxon Medicine* (Cambridge: Cambridge University Press, 1993).

Cameron, M. L., 'Anglo-Saxon Medicine and Magic', *ASE*, 17 (1988), 191–215.

Carroll, Noel, *Humour: A Very Short Introduction* (Oxford: Oxford University Press, 2014).

Cavell, Megan, 'Commentary for Riddle 4', in *The Riddle Ages: An Anglo-Saxon Riddle Blog*, ed. Megan Cavell with Matthias Ammon and Victoria Symons, 3 April 2013, https://theriddleages.wordpress.com/2013/04/03/notes-on-riddle-4/ (accessed 1 September 2019).

Cavell, Megan, with Matthias Ammon and Victoria Symons, *The Riddle Ages: An Anglo-Saxon Riddle Blog*, theriddleages.wordpress.com (accessed 31 August 2019).

Cavell, Megan, 'Powerful Patens in the Anglo-Saxon Medical Tradition and Exeter Book Riddle 48', *Neophilologus*, 101 (2017), 129–38.

Cavell, Megan, *Weaving Words and Binding Bodies: The Poetics of Human Experience in Old English Literature* (Toronto: University of Toronto Press, 2016).

Chen, Mel Y., *Animacies: Biopolitics, Racial Mattering, and Queer Affect* (Durham, NC: Duke University Press, 2012).

Clark, Tom, *A Case for Irony in Beowulf, With Particular Reference to Its Epithets* (Bern: Peter Lang, 2003).

Coatsworth, Elizabeth, and Michael Pinder, *The Art of the Anglo-Saxon Goldsmith: Fine Metalwork in Anglo-Saxon England: Its Practice and Practitioners* (Woodbridge: Boydell, 2002).

Cochran, Shannon Ferri, 'The Plough's the Thing: A New Solution to Old English Riddle 4 of the Exeter Book', *JEGP*, 108 (2009), 301–9.

Cocks, William A., Anthony C. Baines, and Roderick D. Cannon, 'Bagpipe', in *Grove Music Online* (Oxford: Oxford University Press, 2001), www.oxfordmusiconline.com (accessed 1 September 2019).
Comey, Martin G., 'The Wooden Drinking Vessels in the Sutton Hoo Assemblage: Materials, Morphology, and Usage', in *Trees and Timber in the Anglo-Saxon World*, ed. Michael J. Bintley and Michael G. Shapland (Oxford: Oxford University Press, 2014), pp. 107–21.
Coole, Diana, and Samantha Frost, eds, *New Materialisms: Ontology, Agency, and Politics* (Durham, NC: Duke University Press, 2010).
Cramp, Rosemary, 'Beowulf and Archaeology', in *The 'Beowulf' Poet: A Collection of Critical Essays*, ed. Donald K. Fry (Englewood Cliffs, NJ: Prentice-Hall, 1968), pp. 114–40.
Crane, Susan, *Animal Encounters: Contacts and Concepts in Medieval Britain* (Philadelphia: University of Pennsylvania Press, 2013).
Crawford, Sally, *Daily Life in Anglo-Saxon England* (Oxford: Greenwood, 2009).
Dailey, Patricia, 'Riddles, Wonder, and Responsiveness in Anglo-Saxon Literature', in *The Cambridge History of Early Medieval English Literature*, ed. Clare A. Lees (Cambridge: Cambridge University Press, 2013), pp. 451–72.
Dale, Corinne, *The Natural World in the Exeter Book Riddles* (Woodbridge: D. S. Brewer, 2017).
Dale, Corinne, 'A New Solution to Exeter Book Riddle 4', *N&Q*, 64 (2017), 1–3.
Daley, Jason, 'Cat Left a Pawprint in a 2,000-Year-Old Roman Roof Tile', Smithsonian.com, 2 June 2017, www.smithsonianmag.com/smart-news/cat-left-pawprint-2000-year-old-roman-roof-tile-180963556/ (accessed 13 December 2017).
Daston, Lorraine, and Gregg Mitman, eds, *Thinking With Animals: New Perspectives on Anthropomorphism* (New York: Columbia University Press, 2005).
Davidson, Hilda R. E., 'Insults and Riddles in the Edda poems', in *Edda: A Collection of Essays*, ed. Haraldur Bessason and Robert J. Glendinning (Winnipeg: University of Manitoba Press, 1985), pp. 25–46.
Davidson, Hilda R. E., *The Sword in Anglo-Saxon England: Its Archaeology and Literature* (Oxford: Clarendon, 1962).
Davis, Adam, '*Agon* and *Gnomon*: Forms and Functions of the Anglo-Saxon Riddles', in *De Gustibus: Essays for Alain Renoir*, ed. John Miles Foley (New York: Garland, 1992), pp. 110–50.
Delumeau, Jean, *La peur en occident (XIVe–XVIIIe siècles)* (Paris: Librairie Arthème Fayard, 1978), trans. Eric Nicholson, *Sin and Fear: The Emergence of a Western Guilt Culture* (Cambridge: Cambridge University Press, 1994).
Dennis, Caroline, 'Exeter Book Riddle 39: Creature Faith', *Medieval Perspectives*, 10 (1995), 77–85.

Denno, Jerry, 'Oppression and Voice in Anglo-Saxon Riddle Poems', *CEA Critic*, 70.1 (2007), 35–47.

Depner, Anamaria, 'Worthless Things? On the Difference between Devaluing and Sorting out Things', in *Mobility, Meaning and the Transformation of Things: Shifting Contexts of Material Culture through Time and Space*, ed. Hans Peter Hahn and Hadas Weiss (Oxford: Oxbow, 2013), pp. 78–90.

Dietrich, Franz, 'Die Räthsel des Exeterbuch: Verfasser, Weitere Losungen', *Zeitschrift für Deutsches Altertum und Deutsche Literatur*, 7 (1865), 232–52.

Dietrich, Franz, 'Die Rätsel des Exeterbuchs: Würdigung, Lösung und Herstellung', *Zeitschrift für deutsches Altertum*, 11 (1859), 448–90.

DiNapoli, Robert, 'In the Kingdom of the Blind, the One-Eyed Man is a Seller of Garlic: Depth Perception and the Poet's Perspective in the Exeter Book Riddles', *ES*, 81 (2010), 422–55.

Dinshaw, Carolyn, *Getting Medieval: Sexualities and Communities, Pre- and Postmodern* (Durham, NC: Duke University Press, 1999).

Doane, A. N., 'Spacing, Placing and Effacing: Scribal Textuality and Exeter Riddle 30 a/b', in *New Approaches to Editing Old English Verse*, ed. Sarah Larratt Keefer and Katherine O'Brien O'Keeffe (Cambridge: D. S. Brewer, 1998), pp. 45–65.

Doane, A. N., 'Three Old English Implement Riddles: Reconsiderations of Numbers 4, 49, and 73', *MP*, 84 (1987), 243–57.

Double, Oliver, *Getting the Joke: The Inner Workings of Stand-Up Comedy*, 2nd edn (London: Methuen, 2013).

Eco, U., R. Lambertini, C. Marmo, and A. Tabarroni, 'On Animal Language in the Medieval Classification of Signs', in *On the Medieval Theory of Signs*, ed. Umberto Eco and Costantino Marmo (Amsterdam: Benjamins, 1989), pp. 3–41.

Elias, Michael, 'Neck-Riddles in Mimetic Theory', *Contagion: Journal of Violence, Mimesis, and Culture*, 1.2 (1995), 189–202.

Estes, Heide, *Anglo-Saxon Literary Landscapes: Ecotheory and the Environmental Imagination* (Amsterdam: Amsterdam University Press, 2017).

Evans, Angela Care, *The Sutton Hoo Ship Burial* (London: British Museum Press, 2002).

Fauconnier, Gilles, and Mark Turner, *The Way We Think: Conceptual Blending and the Mind's Hidden Complexities* (New York: Basic Books, 2002).

Fell, Christine, 'A "Friwif Locbore" Revisited', *ASE*, 13 (1984), 157–65.

Fell, Christine, 'Some Implications of the Boniface Correspondence', in *New Readings on Women in Old English Literature*, ed. Helen Damico and Alexandra Hennessey Olsen (Bloomington: Indiana University Press, 1990).

Fell, Christine, Cecily Clark, and Elizabeth Williams, *Women in Anglo-Saxon England and the Impact of 1066* (London: British Museum Publications, 1984).
Fleming, Juliet, *Graffiti and the Writing Arts of Early Modern England* (London: Reaktion, 2001).
Foley, John Miles, *Oral Traditional Literature: A Festschrift for Albert Bates Lord* (Columbus: Slavica, 1981).
Fontaine, Carole, *Smooth Words: Women, Proverbs and Performance in Biblical Wisdom* (London: T & T Clark, 2004).
Formigari, Lia, *A History of Language Philosophies* (Amsterdam: Benjamins, 2004).
Fox, Michael V., *Proverbs 10–31: A New Translation with Introduction and Commentary* (New Haven: Yale University Press, 2009).
Foys, Martin, 'A Sensual Philology for Anglo-Saxon England', *postmedieval*, 5 (2014), 456–72.
Frank, Rosemary, '*Beowulf* and Sutton Hoo: The Odd Couple', in *The Voyage to the Other World: The Legacy of Sutton Hoo*, ed. Calvin B. Kendall and Peter S. Wells (Minneapolis: University of Minnesota Press, 1992), pp. 47–64.
Frantzen, Allen J., *Food, Eating and Identity in Early Medieval England* (Woodbridge: Boydell, 2014).
Freud, Sigmund, *Jokes and their Relation to the Unconscious*, trans. James Strachey (London: Routledge, 1960).
Fry, Donald K., 'Exeter Book Riddle Solutions', *Old English Newsletter*, 15.1 (1981), 22–33.
Fry, Donald K., 'Exeter Riddle 31: Feather-pen', in *De Gustibus: Essays for Alain Renoir*, ed. John Miles Foley, Chris J. Womack, and Whitney A. Womack (New York: Garland, 1992), pp. 234–49.
Gneuss, Helmut, and Michael Lapidge, *Anglo-Saxon Manuscripts: A Bibliographical Handlist of Manuscripts and Manuscript Fragments Written or Owned in England up to 1100* (Toronto: University of Toronto Press, 2014).
Göbel, Heidi, and Rüdiger Göbel, 'The Solution of an Old English Riddle', *Studia Neophilologica*, 50 (1978), 185–91.
Godden, Malcolm R., 'Anglo-Saxons on the Mind', repr. in *Old English Literature: Critical Essays*, ed. R. M. Liuzza (New Haven: Yale University Press, 2002), pp. 284–314.
Gossett, Michael, 'Riddle', in *Anthropocene Unseen: A Lexicon*, ed. Cymene Howe and Anand Pandian (New York: Punctum, forthcoming).
Gray, Douglas, 'Notes on Some Medieval, Mystical and Moral Cats', in *Langland, the Mystics and the Medieval English Religious Tradition*, ed. Helen Philipps (Cambridge: Brewer, 1990), pp. 185–202.
Gray, Jeffrey Alan, *The Psychology of Fear and Stress* (Cambridge: Cambridge University Press, 1987).

Greenblatt, Stephen, 'Resonance and Wonder', in *Exhibiting Cultures: The Poetics and Politics of Museum Display*, ed. Ivan Karp and Steven Lavine (Washington: Smithsonian Institution Press, 1991), pp. 42–56.

Grendon, Felix, 'The Anglo-Saxon Charms', *Journal of American Folklore* 22.84 (1909), 105–237.

Hall, J. R. Clark, and Herbert Dean Meritt, *A Concise Anglo-Saxon Dictionary*, 4th edn, with a supplement by Herbert D. Meritt (Cambridge: Cambridge University Press, 1961).

Hanscom, Elizabeth Deering, 'The Feeling for Nature in Old English Poetry', *JEGP*, 5 (1903–5), 439–63.

Hansen, Elaine Tuttle, *The Solomon Complex: Reading Wisdom in Old English Poetry* (Toronto: University of Toronto Press, 1988).

Hayes, Mary, 'The Talking Dead: Resounding Voices in Old English Riddles', *Exemplaria,* 20 (2008), 123–42.

Hayes, Mary, *Divine Ventriloquism in Medieval English Literature: Power, Anxiety, Subversion* (New York: Palgrave Macmillan, 2011).

Head, Pauline E., *Representations and Design: Tracing a Hermeneutics of Old English Poetry* (Albany: SUNY Press, 1997).

Healey, Antonette diPaolo, John Price Wilkin, and Xin Xiang, eds, *The Dictionary of Old English Corpus on the World Wide Web* (Toronto: Dictionary of Old English Project, 2009).

Henderson, George, *From Durrow to Kells: The Insular Gospel-books, 650–800* (London: Thames & Hudson, 1987).

Heyworth, Melanie, 'The Devil's in the Detail: A New Solution to Exeter Book Riddle 4', *Neophilologus*, 91 (2007), 175–96.

Heyworth, Melanie, 'Perceptions of Marriage in *Exeter Book Riddles 20* and *61*', *Studia Neophilologica*, 79 (2007), 171–84.

Hinton, David A., 'Weland's Work: Metals and Metalsmiths', in *The Material Culture of Daily Living in the Anglo-Saxon World*, ed. Maren Clegg Hyer and Gale R. Owen-Crocker (Liverpool: Liverpool University Press, 2013), pp. 185–200.

Hobgood-Oster, Laura, 'Wisdom Literature and Ecofeminism', in *The Earth Story in Wisdom Traditions*, ed. Norman C. Habel and Shirley Wurst (Sheffield: Sheffield Academic Press, 2001), pp. 116–42.

Holsinger, Bruce, *Music, Body, and Desire in Medieval Culture: Hildegard of Bingen to Chaucer* (Stanford: Stanford University Press, 2001).

Holthausen, Ferdinand, 'Zu altenglischen denkmälern', *Englische Studien*, 51 (1917), 180–88.

Holthausen, Ferdinand, 'Zu altenglischen Dichtungen', *Anglia*, 44 (1920), 345–56.

Horner, Shari, *The Discourse of Enclosure: Representing Women in Old English Literature* (New York: State University of New York Press, 2001).

Hough, Carole, 'Women and the Law in Seventh-century England', *Nottingham Medieval Studies*, 51 (2007), 207–30.

Howe, Nicholas, 'Aldhelm's *Enigmata* and Isidorian Etymology', *ASE*, 14 (1985), 37–59.

Howe, Nicholas, 'The Cultural Construction of Reading in Anglo-Saxon England', in *The Ethnography of Reading*, ed. Jonathan Boyarin (Berkeley: University of California Press, 1993), pp. 58–75.

Hsy, Jonathan, 'Between Species: Animal-Human Bilingualism and Medieval Texts', in *Booldly bot Meekly: Essays on the Theory and Practice of Translation in the Middle Ages in Honour of Roger Ellis*, ed. Catherine Batt and René Tixier (Turnhout: Brepols, 2018), pp. 563–79.

Hsy, Jonathan, and Julie Orlemanski, 'Race and medieval studies: a partial bibliography', *postmedieval*, 8 (2017), 500–31, https://doi.org/10.1057/s41280-017-0072-0.

Huizinga, Johan, *Homo Ludens: A Study of the Play Element in Culture* (London: Routledge, 1949).

Hurley, Matthew M., Daniel C. Dennett, and Reginald B. Adams, Jr, *Inside Jokes: Using Humor to Reverse-Engineer the Mind* (Cambridge, MA: MIT Press, 2011).

Ihde, Don, *Listening and Voice: Phenomenologies of Sound*, 2nd edn (New York: SUNY Press, 2007).

Irvine, Martin, *The Making of Textual Culture: Grammatica and Literary Theory, 350–1100* (Cambridge: Cambridge University Press, 1994).

Irving, Edward B., Jr., 'Heroic Experience in the Old English Riddles', in *Old English Shorter Poems: Basic Readings*, ed. Katherine O'Brien O'Keeffe (New York: Garland, 1994), pp. 199–212.

Iser, Wolfgang, 'The Reading Process: A Phenomenological Approach', in *The Implied Reader: Patterns of Communication in Prose Fiction from Bunyan to Beckett* (Baltimore: Johns Hopkins University Press, 1974)

Iser, Wolfgang, *Der Akt des Lesens*, 2nd edn (Munich: Wilhelm Fink, 1976).

Iser, Wolfgang, *The Implied Reader: Patterns of Communication in Prose Fiction from Bunyan to Beckett* (Baltimore: Johns Hopkins University Press, 1974).

Jager, Eric, 'Speech and the Chest in Old English Poetry: Orality or Pectorality?' *Speculum*, 65.4 (1990), 845–59.

Jakobsson, Ármann, 'A Contest of Cosmic Fathers: God and Giant in *Vafþrúðnismál*', *Neophilologus*, 92.2 (2008), 263–77.

Jember, Gregory K., 'An Interpretive Translation of the Exeter Riddles', unpublished PhD thesis (University of Denver, 1975).

Jolly, Karen Louise, 'A Cat's Eye View: Vermin in Anglo-Saxon England', in *The Daily Lives of the Anglo-Saxons*, ed. Carole Biggam, Carole Hough and Daria Izdebska (Tempe, AZ: ACMRS, 2017), pp. 105–28.

Jones, Chris, 'Where Now the Harp? Listening for the Sounds of Old English Verse, from *Beowulf* to the Twentieth Century', *Oral Tradition Journal*, 24 (2009), 485–502.

Kampling, Rainer, 'Vom Streicheln und Nutzen der Katze: Die Wahrnehmung der Katze bei christlichen Autoren von der Spätantike bis zum. 12. Jahrhundert', in *Eine seltsame Gefährtin: Katzen, Religion, Theologie und Theologen*, ed. Rainer Kampling (Frankfurt am Main: Peter Lang, 2007), pp. 95–119.

Kaplan, Robert B., ed., *The Oxford Handbook of Applied Linguistics* (Oxford: Oxford University Press, 2010).

Kay, Donald, 'Riddle 20: A Revaluation', *Tennessee Studies in Literature*, 13 (1968), 133–9.

Kennedy, Charles W., *The Earliest English Poetry* (London: Oxford University Press, 1943).

Ker, Neil, 'A. S. Napier, 1853–1916', in *Philological Essays: Studies in Old and Middle English Language and Literature in Honour of Herbert Dean Meritt*, ed. James L. Rosier (The Hague: Mouton, 1970), pp. 152–81.

Kierkegaard, Søren, *Fear and Trembling*, trans. Alastair Hannay (London: Penguin, 2003).

Kirby, Ian J., 'The Exeter Book, *Riddle 60*', *N&Q*, 48 (2001), 219–20.

Kiser, Lisa J., 'Resident Aliens: The Literary Ecology of Medieval Mice', in *Truth and Tales: Cultural Mobility and Medieval Media*, ed. Fiona Somerset and Nicholas Watson (Columbus: Ohio State University Press, 2015), pp. 152–67.

Kitchener, Andrew C., and Terry O'Connor, 'Wildcats, Domestic and Feral Cats', in *Extinctions and Invasions: The Social History of British Fauna*, ed. Terry O'Connor and Naomi J. Sykes (Oxford: Windgather, 2010), pp. 83–94.

Klein, Stacey S., 'Gender and the Nature of Exile in the Old English Elegies', in *A Place to Believe In: Locating Medieval Landscapes*, ed. Clare A. Lees and Gillian R. Overing (Philadelphia: Penn State University Press, 2006), pp. 113–31.

Klinck, Anne L., 'Anglo-Saxon Women and the Law', *Journal of Medieval History*, 8 (1982), 107–21.

Koppinen, Pirkko A., 'Breaking the Mould: Solving Riddle 12 as *Wudu* "Wood"', in *Trees and Timber in the Anglo-Saxon World*, ed. Michael D. J. Bintley and Michael G. Shapland (Oxford: Oxford University Press, 2014), pp. 158–76.

Koppinen, Pirkko A., 'Commentary for Riddle 30a and b', *The Riddle Ages: An Anglo-Saxon Riddle Blog*, ed. Megan Cavell with Matthias Ammon and Victoria Symons, 21 October 2014, https://theriddleages.wordpress.com/2014/10/21/commentary-for-riddle-30a-and-b/ (accessed 31 August 2019).

Koppinen, Pirkko A., '*Swa þa Stafas Becnaþ*: Ciphers of the Heroic Idiom in the *Exeter Book* Riddles, *Beowulf*, *Judith*, and *Andreas*', unpublished PhD thesis (Royal Holloway, University of London, 2009).

Kuipers, Giselinde, *Good Humor, Bad Taste: A Sociology of the Joke*, 2nd edn (Berlin: de Gruyter, 2015).

Lacey, Eric, 'Birds and Words: Aurality, Semantics, and Species in Anglo-Saxon England', in *Sensory Perception in the Medieval West*, ed.

Simon C. Thomson and Michael D. J. Bintley (Turnhout: Brepols, 2016), pp. 75–98.
Lakoff, George, and Mark Turner, *More than Cool Reason: A Field Guide to Poetic Metaphor* (London: University of Chicago Press, 1989).
Lapidge, Michael, *The Anglo-Saxon Library* (Oxford: Oxford University Press, 2006).
Lapidge, Michael, 'The Earliest Anglo-Latin Poet: Lutting of Lindisfarne', *ASE*, 42 (2013), 1–26.
Lapidge, Michael, 'The Hermeneutic Style in Tenth-Century Anglo-Latin Literature', *ASE*, 4 (1975), 67–111.
Lapidge, Michael, 'Stoic Cosmology and the Source of the First Old English Riddle', *Anglia*, 112 (1994), 1–25.
Larson, Greger, and Dorian Q. Fuller, 'The Evolution of Animal Domestication', *Annual Review of Ecology, Evolution, and Systematics*, 45 (2014), 115–36.
Law, Vivian, *Wisdom, Authority and Grammar in the Seventh Century: Decoding Virgilius Maro Grammaticus* (Cambridge: Cambridge University Press, 1995)
Leach, Elizabeth Eva, *Sung Birds: Music, Nature, and Poetry in the Later Middle Ages* (Ithaca, NY: Cornell University Press, 2007).
Leahy, Kevin, *Anglo-Saxon Crafts* (Stroud: Tempus, 2003).
Lee, Alvin, *Gold-Hall and Earth-Dragon: 'Beowulf' as Metaphor* (Toronto: University of Toronto Press, 1998).
Lees, Clare A., and Gillian R. Overing, *Double Agents: Women and Clerical Culture in Anglo-Saxon England* (Philadelphia: University of Pennsylvania Press, 2001).
Lees, Frederick Richard, and Dawson Burns, *The Temperance Bible-Commentary: Giving at One View, Version, Criticism, and Exposition, in Regard to all Passages of Holy Writ Bearing on 'Wine' and 'Strong Drink,' or Illustrating the Principles of the Temperance Reformation*, 2nd edn (London: S. W. Partridge, 1868).
Lendinara, Patrizia, 'Gli *Aenigmata Laureshamensia*', *PAN: Studi dell'Istituto di Filologia Latina*, 7 (1979), 73–90.
Leneghan, Francis, 'Teaching the Teachers: the Vercelli Book and the Mixed Life', *ES*, 94 (2013), 627–58.
Leo, Heinrich, *Commentatio quae de se ipso Cynevulfus, sive Cenewulfus, sive Coenevulfus poeta Anglo-Saxonicus tradiderit* (Halle: Hendel, 1857).
Lerer, Seth, 'The Riddle and the Book: Exeter Book Riddle 42 in its Contexts', *Papers on Language & Literature*, 25 (1989), 3–18.
Lerer, Seth, *Literacy and Power in Anglo Saxon Literature* (Lincoln, Nebraska: University of Nebraska Press, 1991).
Leslie, Roy F., 'The Integrity of Riddle 60', *JEGP*, 67 (1968), 451–7.
Lewis, Charlton T., and Charles Short, eds, *A Latin Dictionary, Founded on Andrews' Edition of Freund's Latin Dictionary* (Oxford: Clarendon, 1879).

Leyerle, 'The Interlace Structure of *Beowulf*', *University of Toronto Quarterly*, 37 (1967), 1–17.

Lindheim, Bogislav von, 'Traces of Colloquial Speech in OE', *Anglia*, 70 (1951), 22–44.

Lindner, Thomas, *Lateinische Komposita: Ein Glossar vornehmlich zum Wortschatz der Dichtersprache* (Innsbruck: Institut für Sprachwissenschaft der Universität Innsbruck, 1996).

Lindow, John, 'Riddles, Kennings, and the Complexity of Skaldic Poetry', *Scandinavian Studies*, 47 (1975), 311–27.

Lingis, Alphonso, 'Animal Body, Inhuman Face', in *Zoontologies: The Question of the Animal*, ed. Cary Wolfe (Minneapolis: University of Minnesota Press, 2003), pp. 165–82.

Liuzza, R. M., 'The Texts of the Old English *Riddle 30*', *JEGP*, 87 (1988), 1–15.

Lockett, Leslie, *Anglo-Saxon Psychologies in the Vernacular and Latin Traditions* (Toronto: University of Toronto Press, 2011).

Lockyer, Sharon, and Michael Pickering, eds, *Beyond the Joke: The Limits of Humour* (Basingstoke: Palgrave, 2005).

Lohr, C. H., 'The Medieval Interpretation of Aristotle', in *The Cambridge History of Later Medieval Philosophy: From the Rediscovery of Aristotle to the Disintegration of Scholasticism, 1100–1600*, ed. Norman Kretzmann, Anthony Kenny, Jan Pinborg and Eleonore Stump (Cambridge: Cambridge University Press, 1982), pp. 80–98.

Louviot, Elise, *Direct Speech in Beowulf and Other Old English Narrative Poems* (Cambridge: D. S. Brewer, 2016).

Luo, Shu-Han, 'Tender Beginnings in the Exeter Book Riddles', in *Childhood and Adolescence in Anglo-Saxon Literary Culture*, ed. Susan Irvine and Winfried Rudolf (Toronto: University of Toronto Press, 2018), pp. 71–94.

Madigan, Kevin, 'Ancient and High-Medieval Interpretations of Jesus in Gethsemane: Some Reflections on Tradition and Continuity in Christian Thought', *Harvard Theological Review*, 88.1 (1995), 157–73.

Magennis, Hugh, *Images of Community in Old English Poetry* (Cambridge: Cambridge University Press, 1996).

Magennis, Hugh, 'Images of Laughter in Old English Poetry, with Particular Reference to the "hleahtor wera" of *The Seafarer*', *ES*, 73 (1992), 193–204.

Manitius, Max, *Geschichte der lateinischen Literatur*, 3 vols (Munich: C.H. Beck, 1911).

Matter, E. Ann, 'Alcuin's Question-and-Answer Texts', *Rivista di Storia della Filosofia*, 45.4 (1990), 645–56.

McGowan, Todd, *Only A Joke Can Save Us: A Theory of Comedy* (Evanston, IL: Northwestern University Press, 2017).

McGraw, Peter, and Joel Warner, *The Humor Code: A Global Search for What Makes Things Funny* (New York: Simon & Schuster, 2014).

Meaney, Audrey L., *Anglo-Saxon Amulets and Curing Stones*, British Archaeological Reports, British Series, 96 (Oxford: Oxford University Press, 1981).

Medievalists of Color website, ed. Sierra Lomuto, Mariah Min and Shokoofeh Rajabzadeh, http://medievalistsofcolor.com

Meissner, Rudolf, *Die Kenningar der Skalden* (Bonn and Leipzig: Schroeder, 1921; repr. Zürich: Georg Olms, 1984).

Melion, Walter S., Bret Rothstein, and Michel Weemans, eds, *The Anthropomorphic Lens: Anthropomorphism, Microcosmism, and Analogy in Early Modern Thought and Visual Arts* (Leiden: Brill, 2015).

Metz, Christian and Georgia Gurrieri, 'Aural Objects', *Yale French Studies*, 60 (1980), 24–32.

Mitchell, Bruce, and Fred C. Robinson, eds, *A Guide to Old English*, 8th edn (Oxford: Blackwell, 2012).

Mitchell, Robert W., Nicholas S. Thompson, and H. Lyn Miles, eds, *Anthropomorphism, Anecdotes, and Animals* (Albany: SUNY Press, 1997).

Mize, Britt, 'The Mental Container and the Cross of Christ: Revelation and Community in *The Dream of the Rood*', *Studies in Philology*, 107 (2010), 131–78.

Mize, Britt, *Traditional Subjectivities: The Old English Poetics of Mentality* (Toronto: University of Toronto Press, 2013).

Morreall, John, *Comic Relief: A Comprehensive Philosophy of Humor* (Hoboken: Wiley, 2009).

Morton, Timothy, *Hyperobjects: Philosophy and Ecology after the End of the World* (Minneapolis: University of Minnesota Press, 2013).

Mulkay, Michael, *On Humour: Its Nature and Place in Modern Society* (Oxford: Polity, 1988).

Murphy, Patrick J., '*Bocstafas*: A Literal Reading of Exeter Book Riddle 57', *PQ*, 84 (2005), 139–60.

Murphy, Patrick J., *Unriddling the Exeter Riddles* (University Park: Pennsylvania State University Press, 2011).

Musgrave, Elaine K., 'Cithara as the Solution to Riddle 31 of the "Exeter Book"', *Pacific Coast Philology*, 37 (2002), 69–84.

Muusses, Martha A., 'Nils Elis Wadstein (Torshälla, 16 Juli 1861–Stockholm, 19 Juni 1942)', *Jaarboek van de Maatschappij der Nederlandse Letterkunde* (1950–51), 215–20.

Napier, Arthur S., *The Franks Casket* (Oxford: Clarendon, 1900).

Napier, Arthur S., 'The Franks Casket', part 2 of Napier, 'Contributions to Old English Literature', in *An English Miscellany Presented to Dr. Furnivall in Honour of His Seventy-Fifth Birthday*, ed. W. P. Ker, Arthur S. Napier, and Walter W. Skeat (Oxford: Clarendon Press, 1901), pp. 362–81.

Nelson, Marie, 'Four Social Functions of the *Exeter Book* Riddles', *Neophilologus*, 75 (1991), 445–50.

Nelson, Marie, 'Old English Riddle 18 (20): A Description of Ambivalence', *Neophilologus*, 66 (1982), 291–300.
Nelson, Marie, 'The Paradox of Silent Speech in the Exeter Book Riddles', *Neophilogus*, 62 (1978), 609–15.
Nelson, Marie, 'The Rhetoric of the *Exeter Book* Riddles', *Speculum*, 49.3 (1974), 421–40.
Neville, Jennifer, 'Fostering the Cuckoo: Exeter Book Riddle 9', *RES*, 58 (2007), 431–46
Neville, Jennifer, 'Joyous Play and Bitter Tears: The *Riddles* and Elegies', in *Beowulf and Other Stories: A New Introduction to Old English, Old Icelandic and Anglo-Norman Literatures*, ed. Richard North and Joe Allard (Harlow: Pearson Education, 2007), pp. 130–59.
Neville, Jennifer, 'A Modest Proposal: Titles for the *Exeter Book Riddles*', *MÆ* 88 (2019), 116–23.
Neville, Jennifer, *Representations of the Natural World in Old English Poetry* (Cambridge: Cambridge University Press, 1999).
Neville, Jennifer, 'The Unexpected Treasure of the "Implement Trope": Hierarchical Relationships in the Old English Riddles', *RES*, 62.256 (2011), 505–19.
Niles, John D., 'Byrhtnoth's Laughter and the Poetics of Gesture', in *Humour in Anglo-Saxon Literature*, ed. Jonathan Wilcox (Cambridge: D. S. Brewer, 2000), pp. 11–32.
Niles, John D., *Old English Enigmatic Poems and the Play of the Texts* (Turnhout: Brepols, 2006).
O'Connor, Kathleen, *The Wisdom Literature* (Collegeville, MN: Liturgical Press, 1988).
O'Connor, Terry, 'Making Themselves at Home: The Archaeology of Commensal Vertebrates', in *Anthropological Approaches to Zooarchaeology: Colonialism, Complexity and Animal Transformations*, ed. Douglas V. Campana, Pamela Crabtree, S. D. deFrance, Justin Lev-Tov and A. M. Choyke (Oxford: Oxbow, 2010), pp. 270–4.
O'Keeffe, Katherine O'Brien, 'Orality and the Developing Text of Caedmon's Hymn', *Speculum*, 62 (1987), 1–20.
O'Keeffe O'Brien, Katherine, *Visible Song: Transitional Literacy in Old English Verse* (Cambridge: Cambridge University Press, 1991).
O'Sullivan, Sinéad, 'Aldhelm's *De virginitate* – a Patristic Pastiche or Innovative Exposition?', *Peritia*, 12 (1998), 271–95.
O'Sullivan, Sinéad, 'Aldhelm's *De virginitate* and the Psychomachian Tradition', *Mediaevalia*, 20 (2001), 313–37.
Ohl, Raymond T., 'Symphosius and the Latin Riddle Tradition', *The Classical Weekly*, 25 (1932), 209–12.
Okasha, Elisabeth, 'Anglo-Saxon Inscribed Rings', *Leeds Studies in English*, 34 (2003), 29–45.
Okasha, Elisabeth, 'The Commissioners, Makers and Owners of Anglo-Saxon Inscriptions', *Anglo-Saxon Studies in Archaeology*, 7 (1994), 71–7.

Okasha, Elisabeth, 'Literacy in Anglo-Saxon England: The Evidence from Inscriptions', *Anglo-Saxon Studies in Archaeology and History*, 8 (1995), 69–74.

Okasha, Elisabeth, 'Old English *Hring* in Riddles 48 and 59', *MÆ*, 62 (1993), 61–9.

Orchard, Andy, 'Enigma Variations: The Anglo-Saxon Riddle-tradition', in *Latin Learning and English Lore: Studies in Anglo-Saxon Literature for Michael Lapidge*, ed. Katherine O'Brien O'Keeffe and Andy Orchard, 2 vols (Toronto: University of Toronto Press, 2005), I, pp. 284–304.

Orchard, Andy, *The Poetic Art of Aldhelm* (Cambridge: Cambridge University Press, 1994).

Oring, Elliott, *Jokes and their Relations* (Lexington: University of Kentucky Press, 1992).

Oring, Elliott, *Joking Asides: The Theory, Analysis, and Aesthetics of Humor* (Logan: Utah State University Press, 2016).

Orton, Peter, 'The Exeter Book *Riddles*: Authorship and Transmission', *ASE*, 44 (2015), 131–62.

Ottaway, Patrick, 'Anglo-Scandinavian Ironwork from 16–22 Coppergate, York c. 850–1100 A.D.', 2 vols, unpublished PhD thesis (University of York, 1989).

Owen-Crocker, Gale R., *Dress in Anglo-Saxon England* (Woodbridge: Boydell, 2010).

Oxford English Dictionary Online (Oxford: Oxford University Press, 2010).

Pasternack, Carol Braun, *The Textuality of Old English Poetry*, Cambridge Studies in Anglo-Saxon England, 15 (Cambridge: Cambridge University Press, 1995).

Pausas, Juli G., and Jon E. Keely, 'A Burning Story: The Role of Fire in the History of Life', *BioScience*, 59 (2009), 593–601.

Paz, James, *Nonhuman Voices in Anglo-Saxon Literature and Material Culture* (Manchester: Manchester University Press, 2017).

Poole, Kristopher, 'The Contextual Cat: Human-Animal Relations and Social Meaning in Anglo-Saxon England', *Journal of Archaeological Method and Theory*, 22 (2015), 857–82.

Poole, Russell G., *Old English Wisdom Poetry*, Annotated Bibliographies of Old and Middle English Literature, 5 (Cambridge: D. S. Brewer, 1998).

Potter, Joyce, '*Wylm* and *Weallan* in *Beowulf*: A Tidal Metaphor', *Medieval Perspectives*, 3 (1988), 191–9.

'Proceedings at Meetings of the Archaeological Institute for 2 August 1859', *Archaeological Journal*, 16 (1859), 386–93.

Provine, Robert R., *Laughter: A Scientific Investigation* (New York: Viking, 2000).

Quin, E. G., *et al.*, eds, *Dictionary of the Irish Language Based Mainly on Old and Middle Irish Materials* (Dublin: Royal Irish Academy, 1983), Digital edition: Gregory Toner, ed., *Electronic Dictionary of the Irish Language* (*eDIL*), available at www.dil.ie/ (accessed 4 January 2018).

Ramey, Peter, 'Crafting Strangeness: Wonder Terminology in the Exeter Book Riddles and the Anglo-Latin Enigmata', *RES*, 69 (2018), 201–15.

Ramey, Peter, 'The Riddle of Beauty: The Aesthetics of *Wrætlic* in Old English Verse', *MP*, 114 (2017), 457–81.

Ramey, Peter, 'Writing Speaks: Oral Poetics and Writing Technology in the Exeter Book Riddles', *PQ*, 92 (2013), 335–56.

Raskin, Victor, ed., *The Primer of Humor Research* (Berlin: de Gruyter, 2008).

Reichl, Karl, ed., *Medieval Oral Literature* (Berlin: de Gruyter, 2012).

Reichl, Karl, 'Old English *Giedd*, Middle English *Yedding* as Genre Terms', in *Words, Texts, and Manuscripts: Studies in Anglo-Saxon Culture Presented to Helmut Gneuss on the Occasion of His Sixty-Fifth Birthday*, ed. Michael Korhammer, with Karl Reichl and Hans Sauer (Cambridge: D. S. Brewer, 1992), pp. 349–70.

Riedinger, Anita R., 'The Formulaic Style in the Old English Riddles', *Studia Neophilologica*, 76.1 (2004), 30–43.

Rissanen, Matti, '*Nathwæt* in the Exeter Book Riddles', *American Notes and Queries*, 24.7–8 (1986), 116–20.

Roberts, Adam, *The Riddles of the Hobbit* (New York: Palgrave, 2013).

Roberts, J., 'Anglo-Saxon Vocabulary as a Reflection of Material Culture', in *The Age of Sutton Hoo: The Seventh Century in North-Western Europe*, ed. M. O. H. Carver (Woodbridge: Boydell, 1992), pp. 185–204.

Robertson, Kellie, 'Medieval Things: Materiality, Historicism, and the Premodern Object', *Literature Compass*, 5.6 (2008), 1060–80.

Robinson, Fred C., 'Artful Ambiguities in the Old English "Book-Moth" Riddle', in *Anglo-Saxon Poetry: Essays in Appreciation: for John C. McGalliard*, ed. Lewis E. Nicholson and Dolores Warwick Frese (Notre Dame: University of Notre Dame Press, 1975), pp. 355–62.

Rogers, Katharine M., *The Cat and the Human Imagination: Feline Images from Bast to Garfield* (Ann Arbor: University of Michigan Press, 1998).

Rogers, Katharine M., *Cat* (London: Reaktion, 2006).

Ruff, Carin, 'The Place of Metrics in Anglo-Saxon Latin Education: Aldhelm and Bede', *JEGP*, 104.2 (2005), 149–70.

Salvador-Bello, Mercedes, 'Allegorizing and Moralizing Zoology in Aldhelm's *Enigmata*', *Revista Canaria de Estudios Ingleses*, 68 (2014), 209–18.

Salvador-Bello, Mercedes, *Isidorean Perceptions of Order: The Exeter Book Riddles and Medieval Latin Enigmata* (Morgantown: West Virginia University Press, 2015).

Salvador-Bello, Mercedes, 'The Key to the Body: Unlocking Riddles 42–46', in *Naked Before God: Uncovering the Body in Anglo-Saxon England*, ed. Benjamin C. Withers and Jonathan Wilcox (Morgantown: West Virginia University Press, 2003), pp. 60–96.

Salvador-Bello, Mercedes, 'The Sexual Riddle Type in Aldhelm's *Enigmata*, the Exeter Book, and Early Medieval Latin', *PQ*, 90 (2011), 357–85.

Sanders, Barry, *Sudden Glory: Laughter as Subversive History* (Boston: Beacon, 1995).

Sayers, William, 'Exeter Book Riddle No. 5: Whetstone?', *Neuphilologische Mitteilungen*, 97 (1996), 387–92.

Schlauch, Margaret, '*The Dream of the Rood* as Prosopopoeia', in *Essays and Studies in Honor of Carleton Brown*, ed. P. W. Long (New York: New York University Press, 1940), pp. 23–34.

Schrock, Chad, 'Light without Heat: *Beowulf*'s Epistemological Morning', *ES*, 97.1 (2016), 1–14.

Scott, Andrew C., David M. J. S. Bowman, William J. Bond, Stephen J. Pyne, and Martin E. Alexander, *Fire on Earth: An Introduction* (Chichester: Wiley-Blackwell, 2014).

Sebo, Erin, *In Enigmate: The History of a Riddle, 450–1500* (Dublin: Four Courts, 2018).

Serpell, James A., 'Domestication and History of the Cat', in *The Domestic Cat: The Biology of its Behaviour*, ed. D. C. Turner and P. Bateson (Cambridge: Cambridge University Press, 3rd edn, 2014), pp. 83–100.

Shook, Laurence K., 'Old English Riddle No. 20: *Heoruswealwe*', in *Franciplegius: Medieval and Linguistic Studies in Honor of Francis Peabody Magoun, Jr*, ed. Jess B. Bessinger, Jr and Robert P. Creed (New York: NYU Press, 1965), pp. 194–204.

Shook, Laurence K., 'Riddles Relating to the Anglo-Saxon Scriptorium', in *Essays in Honour of Anton Charles Pegis*, ed. J. Reginald O'Donnell (Toronto: Pontifical Institute of Mediaeval Studies, 1974), pp. 215–36.

Siebold, Erika von Erhardt-, 'Old English Riddle No. 4: Handmill', *PMLA*, 61 (1946), 620–3.

Siebold, Erika von Erhardt-, 'The Old English Storm Riddles', *PMLA*, 64.4 (1949), 884–8.

Soper, Harriet, 'Reading the *Exeter Book* Riddles as Life-Writing', *RES*, 68.287 (2017), 841–65.

Spivak, Gayatri Chakravorty, 'The Politics of Translation', in *The Translation Studies Reader*, ed. Lawrence Venuti (London: Routledge, 2012), pp. 369–88.

Stanley, Eric G., 'Heroic Aspects of the Exeter Book Riddles', in *Prosody and Poetics in the Early Middle Ages: Essays in Honour of C. B. Hieatt*, ed. M. J. Toswell (Toronto: University of Toronto Press, 1995), pp. 197–218.

Stanton, Robert, 'Bark Like A Man: Performance, Identity, and Boundary in Old English Animal Voice Catalogues', in *Animal Languages in the Middle Ages: Representations of Interspecies Communication*, ed. Alison Langdon (New York: Palgrave Macmillan, 2018), pp. 91–111.

Steel, Karl, *How to Make a Human: Animals and Violence in the Middle Ages* (Columbus, OH: Ohio State University Press, 2011).

Steen, Janie, *Verse and Virtuosity: The Adaptation of Latin Rhetoric in Old English Poetry* (Toronto: University of Toronto Press, 2008).

Stewart, Ann Harleman, 'Kenning and Riddle in Old English', *Papers on Language and Literature*, 15 (1979), 115–36.

Stewart, Ann Harleman, 'Old English Riddle 47 as Stylistic Parody', *Papers on Language and Literature*, 11 (1975), 227–41.

Stewart, Ann Harleman, 'The Solution to Old English Riddle 4', *Studies in Philology*, 78 (1981), 52–61.

Szabo, Vicki Ellen, *Monstrous Fishes and the Mead-Dark Sea: Whaling in the Medieval North Atlantic* (Leiden: Brill, 2008).

Tabarroni, Andrea, 'On Articulation and Animal Language in Ancient Linguistic Theory', *Versus*, 50/51: *Signs of Antiquity and Antiquity of Signs*, ed. Giovanni Manetti (1988), 103–21.

Talentino, Arnold, 'Riddle 30: The Vehicle of the Cross', *Neophilologus*, 65 (1981), 129–36.

Tanke, John W., 'The Bachelor-Warrior of Exeter Riddle 20', *PQ*, 79 (2000), 409–27.

Tanke, John W., '*Wonfeax Wale*: Ideology and Figuration in the Sexual Riddles of the Exeter Book', in *Class and Gender in Early English Literature: Intersections*, ed. Britton J. Harwood and Gillian R. Overing (Bloomington: Indiana University Press, 1994), pp. 21–42.

Taylor, Archer, *English Riddles from Oral Tradition* (Berkeley: University of California Press, 1951).

Tiffany, Daniel, 'Lyric Substance: On Riddles, Materialism, and Poetic Obscurity', *Critical Inquiry*, 28 (2001), 72–98.

Tigges, Wim, 'Snakes and Ladders: Ambiguity and Coherence in the Exeter Book Riddles and Maxims', in *Companion to Old English Poetry*, ed. Henk Aertsen and Rolf Bremmer, Jr (Amsterdam: VU Press, 1994), pp. 95–118.

Tilghman, Benjamin C., 'On the Enigmatic Nature of Things in Anglo-Saxon Art', *Different Visions: A Journal of New Perspectives on Medieval Art*, 4 (2014), n.pag., http://differentvisions.org/on-the-enigmatic-nature-of-things-in-anglo-saxon-art (accessed 1 September 2019).

Tilley, Christopher, 'Introduction', in *Handbook of Material Culture*, ed. Christopher Tilley, Webb Keane, Susanne Kuechler-Fogden, Mike Rowlands and Patricia Spyer (London: SAGE, 2006), pp. 7–11.

Tilley, Christopher, 'Metaphor, Materiality and Interpretation', *The Material Culture Reader*, ed. Victor Buchli (Oxford: Berg, 2002), pp. 23–6.

Tilley, Christopher, 'Objectification', in *Handbook of Material Culture*, ed. Christopher Tilley, Webb Keane, Susanne Kuechler-Fogden, Mike Rowlands and Patricia Spyer (London: SAGE, 2006), pp. 60–73.

Tillich, Paul, *The Courage to Be* (New Haven: Yale University Press, 1980).

Thornbury, Emily V., 'Aldhelm's Cat', *Arcade: Literature, Humanities, and the World*, Stanford University blogs, 19 April 2010, http://arcade.stanford.edu/blogs/aldhelms-cat (accessed 1 September 2019).

Thornbury, Emily V., 'Aldhelm's Rejection of the Muses and the Mechanics of Poetic Inspiration in Early Anglo-Saxon England', *ASE*, 36 (2007), 71–92.

Thornbury, Emily V., *Becoming a Poet in Anglo-Saxon England* (Cambridge: Cambridge University Press, 2014).

Toner, Gregory, '*Messe ocus Pangur Bán*: Structure and Cosmology', *Cambrian Medieval Celtic Studies*, 57 (2009), 1–22.

Tristram, Hildegard L. C., 'Die irischen Gedichte im Reichenauer Schulheft', in *Studia Celtica et Indogermanica. Festschrift für Wolfgang Meid zum 70. Geburtstag*, ed. Peter Anreiter and Erzsébat Jerem (Budapest: Archaeolingua, 1999), pp. 503–29.

Tupper, Frederick, Jr, 'Solutions of the *Exeter Book* Riddles', *Modern Language Notes*, 21.4 (1906), 97–105.

Vegvar, Carol Neuman de, 'Reading the Franks Casket: Contexts and Audiences', in *Intertexts: Studies in Anglo-Saxon Culture Presented to Paul E. Szarmach*, ed. Virginia Blanton and Helene Scheck (Tempe, AZ: ACMRS and Brepols, 2008), pp. 141–59.

Veivo, Harri, 'The New Literary Semiotics', *Semiotica*, 165 (2007), 41–55.

Wadstein, Elis, *The Clermont Runic Casket*, Skrifter utgifna af Kongl. Humanistiska Vetenskaps-Samfundet i Upsala, 6.7 (Uppsala: Almqvist & Wiksells Boktryckeri-A.-B., 1900).

Walker-Meikle, Kathleen, *Medieval Pets* (Woodbridge: Boydell, 2012).

Webster, Leslie, 'Metalwork and Sculpture', in *The Golden Age of Anglo-Saxon Art, 966–1066*, ed. Janet Backhouse, D. H. Turner, and Leslie Webster (London: British Museum Press, 1984), p. 88.

Webster, Leslie, '75. Reliquary Cross', in *The Golden Age of Anglo-Saxon Art 966–1066*, ed. Janet Backhouse, D. H. Turner, and Leslie Webster (London: British Museum Press, 1984), pp. 90–92.

Webster, Leslie, '76. Portable Altar', in *The Golden Age of Anglo-Saxon Art 966–1066*, ed. Janet Backhouse, D. H. Turner, and Leslie Webster (London: British Museum Press, 1984), pp. 92–3.

Williams, Edith Whitehurst, 'What's So New about the Sexual Revolution?: Some Comments on Anglo-Saxon Attitudes toward Sexuality in Women Based on Four Exeter Book Riddles', *Texas Quarterly*, 18.2 (1975), 46–55.

Wilcox, Jonathan, 'Mock-Riddles in Old English: Exeter Riddles 86 and 19', *Studies in Philology*, 93.2 (1996), 180–87.

Wilcox, Jonathan, 'New Solutions to Old English Riddles: Riddles 17 and 53', *PQ*, 69 (1990), 393–408.

Wilcox, Jonathan, '"Tell Me What I Am": The Old English Riddles', in *Readings in Medieval Texts: Interpreting Old and Middle English Literature*, ed. David Johnson and Elaine Treharne (Oxford: Oxford University Press, 2005), pp. 46–59.

Wilcox, Jonathan, 'Transmission of Literature and Learning', in *Companion to Anglo-Saxon Literature*, ed. Phillip Pulsiano and Elaine Treharne (Oxford: Blackwell, 2001), pp. 50–70.

Winternitz, Emanuel, *Musical Instruments and their Symbolism in Western Art* (New York: Norton, 1967).

Zhang, Weiwei, *Variation in Metonymy: Cross-linguistic, Historical and Lectal Perspectives* (Berlin: de Gruyter, 2016).

Zweck, Jordan, 'Silence in the Exeter Book Riddles', *Exemplaria*, 28 (2016), 319–36.

Index

Printed in the USA
CPSIA information can be obtained
at www.ICGtesting.com
JSHW062048220324
59758JS00003B/52